A Record of Writing

An Annotated and Illustrated Bibliography of George Bowering

by Roy Miki

copyright © 1989 Roy Miki

Published with the assistance of the Canada Council; Canadian Studies Research
Tools, Social Sciences and Humanities Research Council; and the University
Publications Committee, Simon Fraser University

Talonbooks
201 / 1019 East Cordova
Vancouver
British Columbia V6A 1M8
Canada

Typeset in Stempel Garamond by Vancouver Desktop Publishing Centre and printed
and bound in Canada by Hignell Printing Ltd.

First printing February 1990

Canadian Cataloguing in Publication Data

Miki, Roy Akira, 1942 –
    A record of writing

        ISBN 0–88922–263–0
        1. Bowering, George, 1935 –   —Bibliography.
    I. Title.
    PS8503.0875Z991 1989   016.811'54   C89–091548–2
    Z8111.56.M54 1989

for
bpNichol

1944–1988

"purpose is a porpoise"

This writing, it is a life done in secret, that
is its charm. It's charm, the stolen (yeah, trickster)
moments, stolen E motion. Nobody but nobody can
stop you at that moment & say hey you're holding
that wrong let me show you.

["E"]

As certain as these rows of books
carry me from house to house,

arrange me to their will. I
squat for an hour, eye level

to those books, saying I will
read this, or I will read this,

& this way never succeed
in reading my self . . .

[from "The House"]

Table of Contents

By George: A Preface

It's September 1983, and we're on our way to Oliver BC to work on a film about George Bowering for a series on Canadian writers. On our drive there together, we talk casually about the books he's writing, about to write, and has written, and as Vancouver recedes and the Okanagan Valley approaches, we move back in time to his childhood—to those first moments in his boyhood when he knew he was going to be a writer, period.

In Greenwood, we visit the house where Bowering grew up. There, almost intact, is the back yard, at the bottom of the hill that little George set on fire, a momentous event recorded in print in *Autobiology*. We spend a long afternoon, the sun fading and the shadows growing longer, at the baseball diamond in Oliver where the high school George sat in the scorekeeper's box taking notes for his article in *The Oliver Chronicle*, a scene imagined in his first long poem, *Baseball*. We walk in the orchards where a somewhat older George worked and wondered about his future as a writer, a memory evoked in his favourite poem, "Desert Elm." And all around us, wherever we turn, lie the hills around Oliver, such a strong presence in many poems and stories, where Bowering roamed with his closest friend, Bill Trump. No one's young life is idyllic, of course, yet the aura of this place as both magical and mundane strikes home and makes me much more curious about the shape of GB's life in writing.

I cannot remember precisely when this bibliography first began, but it must have been during the spring and summer of 1984. GB was writing *Caprice* on his computer at home, a daily morning ritual, one chapter for each writing session with the research pamphlets and books spread out beside him. Since I was reading my way more or less systematically through his publications, he invited me to drop by whenever I wished to look through his collection of first editions, as well as anthologies and journals in which his writing appeared (all of which, later that year, would be shipped off to the National Library with many boxes of correspondence, manuscripts, and other papers).

I was soon immersed in an enormous collection of little magazines that published pieces of GB's writing from the 1950s to the present—and strangely, as I read through them, a steady stream of new magazines and anthologies would appear on the shelf. It didn't take me long to realize that for GB the writing life is a life, writing. In the course of a regular day, new writing projects are conceived, correspondence comes and goes all over the literary map, journals and editors request articles and reviews, and even radio stations telephone asking for programs and interviews. All the signs point to a biorhythm primed by words, in words. Small wonder, then, that so much of the routine of his writing circles the question of self: who am I that language inhabits me? and who is that *I* language passes through? and what is the signature of writing?

Buried in one of the many black notebooks GB uses to keep track of the bare facts of mundane life—these are not journals of intimate thoughts—is a sly note to future biographers, dated 10 December 1961: "Say he was a real sucker for his name in print." Is this a private true confession, or another trickster clue to confuse (future) readers? "Let us say that I, George, have come this far," we read in a discovery poem, *George, Vancouver*, which was reworked as a radio program, then transformed into the award-winning novel *Burning Water*. Of these two, *I* and *George*, the pronoun and the name, which constitutes an identity? The question brings us to that intersection where all lines lead outward to who knows where, or perhaps to what is here. For GB the beginning begins with oneself, but one's self is no longer centred, no longer a reliable source of centrality, so one writes and keeps the signature operative.

In the conventional genres that GB consistently undermines—and often parodies to show up their formal and perceptual limits—writing is often taken to be a search for identity, for unity, and for the assurance of order. In this (harbour) light, we can well understand GB's frustration when a publisher declared that the conclusion to *Burning Water* must not leave narrative ends unresolved and that the author-narrator-character cannot disappear without being accounted for. To this, GB replied:

> Oh this Vancouver book is going to be the distraction or death of me yet. Lackaday. After 10 years of researching and noting it, and then 3 years of planning the structure, and 2 years of writing and rewriting of it—to imagine a wholesale re-thinking, arrgh.
> . . . I would like to publish *The Dead Sailors* [the earlier title of *Burning Water*] there, and usually I go along with anything that people in the big city tell me, , , but this book is so much a question of belief, and I think, having my heroes be Gass and Barthelme and Hawkes and Bioy-Casares and Beckett and Robbe-Grillet and Borges and B. S. Johnson and Berger and so on, like esp. in this case, Ishmael Reed, that I might know more than folks think I know, and that I am not trying to cover laziness or amateurness with theory—
> [GB to McClelland and Stewart, 19 November 1979, McClelland and Stewart Papers, McMaster University]

For GB, the finite self is bound to the written self—and vice versa—so that the *I* and *George* become auto/graphic signs that take on a knotted existence on the page, later made public in the published work. Instead of a search for unity, then, the desire to write (and to be written) leads in the opposite direction, to a search for diversity. The *I* or the signature, "by George," is less the self named in print and more the sign of an indeterminate dissemination in a vast literary project where proliferation is the norm, and the norm is constantly undergoing transmutation. So not surprisingly, along the way, more signs are created to fill in an even greater range of *I*s: the short snappy life of *Helmut Franz* while GB was a student at UBC; the longer more extended life of the lyric poet *E. E. Greengrass*, who also wrote many reviews; the discrete life of the immigrant working poet *Edward Pratoverde*, an Italian Canadian poet who shortened his name to *Ed Prato* so he would be more contemporary and more Canadian; the reporter *Erich Blackhead* who wrote briefly for *The Georgia Straight*; and the *Panavision Kid*, who comes and goes, but who declares himself more as a signature in correspondence. Are there others out there? Perhaps, perhaps.

The restlessness of GB's writing drew me in. As I read through the early magazines, the whole gamut, from the most influential avant-garde ones of the 1960s and 1970s, to the fly-by-nighters, to the established journals, his connections with a whole generation of Canadian, American, and British writers became apparent. In the complex interchange of writers and journals, I was led through a maze of pathways from the 1950s to a generality we call the "contemporary," though in GB's library the actuality of the past remains intact through the seemingly unrelated details in a seemingly endless stream of publications.

During that spring or summer, to construct a chronological order that would facilitate my reading, I started making up cards for books written and edited, for contributions to books, for contributions to periodicals, and for what appeared to be significant miscellaneous publications, including broadsides. With no professional training as a bibliographer, I had a simple, straightforward objective: to compile a practical but far from exhaustive checklist of GB's publications, for my own use and perhaps for the use of other GB readers. By the time I had amassed a fat deck of cards, the prospect of writing a full-scale bibliography became intriguing. While the enormity of the task overwhelmed me, I found that one reference did lead back to another, and another, and another. At some point the checklist was abandoned, the archaeological impulse took over, and the search began in earnest to assemble the pieces, or as I thought of it, to unscramble the record.

As impressive as accumulated details may be, especially for a writer of GB's stature, the order constructed in a bibliography is, after all, only a record of the writing, not its explanation. Its value resides in the extent to which it initiates curiosity and offers readers the larger perspective which can lead to a fuller understanding of both writer and work. Like any scholarly venture, though, a bibliographic project is fraught with the spectre of error and the ghosts of those entries omitted (absences in the margins) that will someday materialize. What is frozen in place here is already obsolete—yet such a notion in no way subtracts from the brilliance of GB's record of writing so far.

Why the cut-off date of December 1988? Like all arbitrary ends, it was governed by human limits. "It had to end at some point," someone said. Already, as I look around, I see entries piling up, waiting to be recorded. So it all goes on, thankfully.

Acknowledgements

The amateur bibliographer who gets caught up in the wayward journey of bibliographic search soon comes to appreciate the assistance of those who can guide him to his imagined destination. The published record, set in type and bound between covers, is all too often perceived as merely a list of titles, useful for further research but with no intrinsic value. In the bare data that comprise an entry, there is little or no residue of the truly communal effort that went into its completion. This bibliography carries the traces of numerous people who have assisted me, in small and large ways, throughout the five years I have worked on it.

At Simon Fraser University, Wolfgang Richter from the Computing Centre and Susan Lord, former student in the English Department, deserve special credit for setting up the word-processing program used by Susan to enter the first data on the SFU system. The campus employment program, Work-Study Projects, enabled undergraduate students Lisa Goldberg, Lisa Robertson, Michael Thederan, and Debbie Webber to work part time in certain phases and sections of the bibliography. When the time came to download data from the SFU system to a microcomputer, Anita Mahoney, word-processing operator in the Dean of Arts' office, assisted in the necessary reformatting.

My appreciation to Charles Watts and Gene Bridwell in the Contemporary Literature Collection, Special Collections, SFU Library, for their on-going support and friendship—and for the countless times they came to the rescue to help me locate archival material. Percilla Groves, Librarian for Fine Arts, was also encouraging in the early stages of the work and, near the end, helped me find some troublesome entries while she was visiting Ontario.

I am very grateful to the staff at Interlibrary Loans, SFU Library, for processing an extraordinary number of interlibrary loan requests. Without this service, my research would have taken much, much longer.

A number of other libraries provided me with material related to GB, and to these I am grateful for their cooperation and their willingness to assist: the Literary Manuscripts Division, National Library of Canada (cited as NL); the Thomas Fisher Rare Book Library, University of Toronto; Queen's University Archives; and the William Ready Division of Archives and Research Collections, McMaster University Library (cited as McMaster University).

Various publishers responded to my annoying requests for information, in many cases for books published a long time ago. I thank the following for providing publishing data: McClelland and Stewart, Coach House, Black Moss,

House of Anansi, Talonbooks, Oberon, Longspoon, Red Deer College, Turn-stone, General, Penguin, Les Quinze, Véhicule, and Stoddart.

Thanks to the following individuals for providing information and assistance when requested: Nelson Ball for Weed/Flower Press; Tom Marshall for Quarry Press; Louis Dudek and Raymond Souster for Contact Press; Victor Coleman for Coach House Press; Nicky Drumbolis, Bookseller; Reginald Berry; Smaro Kamboureli; Ken Norris and Jim Mele for CrossCountry Press; Tim Hunter; Frank Davey; Fred Wah; William Hoffer, Bookseller; Peter Quartermain for Slug Press; Shirley Neuman for Longspoon Press; Michael Gnarowski for Golden Dog Press; Robert Lecker for ECW Press; Barry McKinnon for Caledonia Writing Series; Lise Beaudoin for Les Quinze; Robert Bertholf at the State University of New York, at Buffalo; George Henderson at Queen's University Archives; Carolyn Vachon at the National Archives of Canada; and photographers, LaVerne Clark, Karl Jirgens, Nathen Hohn, Michael Lawlor, and Paul Little.

A special debt of gratitude goes to the staff at the National Library, Literary Manuscripts Division, where the GB Papers are housed. They have given me invaluable assistance and advice from beginning to end, and I have appreciated their friendship and hospitality during my hasty trips to Ottawa. My thanks to Claude le Moine, Curator, for supporting this bibliography; to Linda Hoad, Librarian, for responding with generosity and enthusiasm to my numerous requests for information and material; and to Joyce Banks for her professional—and practical—advice on many bibliographic decisions, but especially for her suggestions on the format of descriptive entries.

My thanks also to Bruce Whiteman, formerly of McMaster University and now at McGill University, and to Carl Spadoni at McMaster University, for information and material from the McClelland and Stewart Papers.

The major portion of the research and compilation was done in the period January–August 1988 during a Research Leave grant from Canadian Studies Research Tools, Social Sciences and Humanities Research Council (SSHRC). Without this support, an annotated and illustrated bibliography would have been much more difficult to complete. I would here also like to acknowledge the special contribution of Susan MacFarlane, former graduate student in the English Department, who was employed as my Research Assistant during this grant. Her meticulous and thorough work in checking and rechecking entries and in collecting primary and secondary material was greatly appreciated.

Canadian Studies Research Tools, SSHRC, provided some financial assistance to prepare the manuscript for publication. The University Publications Committee, SFU, also supported this bibliography through a publication grant.

Thanks to Robert Kroetsch for supporting this bibliographic project, and to Karl Siegler for understanding its value.

Special thanks to Mary Schendlinger for taking this unwieldy bibliography through the publication process and for preparing the index. Such an awesome task was made a delight each step of the way because of her sure sense of design, her good nature, and her wonderfully capable intelligence. Thanks as well to Irene Niechoda, Jeff Derksen, and Colin Smith for assistance in proofreading.

My deep appreciation to George Bowering for permission to reproduce his manuscripts, to cite passages from his correspondence and published works, and to use photographs from his private collection. Quite simply, without George's generous sharing of material in his personal files and notebooks, without his always stimulating conversations on any imaginable literary subject, this bibliography could not have been done—or at least this bibliographer would not have been the one to do it. I would here also like to acknowledge the hospitality of George and Angela Bowering in opening their home to me. The intrusions have been many, over a long period of time, as I dropped by to read journals and books in their library—and to conduct the lengthy series of interviews on GB's publishing (and often personal) life. Thanks George, thanks Angela, for allowing the bibliography the room to discover its own shapely form.

Finally, to my wife, Slavia, and to my children, Waylen and Elisse, thank you for the love and laughter without which a bibliographer's life would be meaningless indeed.

Bibliographer's Note

Since a bibliography is usually used to seek out discrete items, abbreviations have been kept to a minimum. For convenience, though, the following seemed unavoidable:

GB = George Bowering
AB = Angela Bowering
SFU = Simon Fraser University
UBC = University of British Columbia
NL = National Library

Passages cited from a series of personal interviews with GB include the session number and date of interview. In all, fifteen sessions were completed:

Session 1, 10 April 1985
Session 2, 9 March 1988
Session 3, 9 May 1988
Session 4, 11 May 1988
Session 5, 16 May 1988
Session 6, 25 May 1988
Session 7, 29 September 1988
Session 8, 14 October 1988
Session 9, 18 March 1989
Session 10, 25 March 1989
Session 11, 8 April 1989
Session 12, 28 April 1989
Session 13, 4 May 1989
Session 14, 14 and 26 May 1989
Session 15, 8 June 1989

GB's idiosyncratic spelling has been left as he wrote it in his correspondence, except for the correction of a few obvious typographical errors. Additions necessary for clarity are enclosed in brackets.

A Writing/Life: A Chronology

1935: George Harry Bowering was born 1 December in Penticton BC. He was the first child of Ewart Harry and Pearl Patricia (nee Brinson), who lived in Peachland. The middle name Harry was traditional for first-born sons in the Bowering line. GB's sister Sally-Ann Patricia was born in 1937. After the Depression and the Second World War, two brothers were born, Roger Dennis in 1946 and Richard James in 1949.

Ewart was born in 1909 in Wetaskiwin, Alberta, the first child of Claire (nee Miller) and Harry, who was a circuit Baptist preacher for towns in the surrounding area. During Ewart's childhood, his family moved to West Summerland BC, so he was raised and educated in the Okanagan Valley. He studied education at Brandon College in Manitoba and at UBC, and eventually became a high school teacher in the town of Oliver.

Pearl was born in 1916 in Three Hills, Alberta, the daughter of Emmett and Maple (nee Brubacker) Brinson. Maple died before Pearl was a year old. Emmett then moved to the Okanagan Valley and remarried. Pearl was raised in the Peachland area, and met Ewart in high school when she was a student and he was a teacher. They were married on Boxing Day in 1934.

GB's family background is an interweaving of three strands: British, American, and Canadian. Ewart's father Harry (grandfather Jabez Harry of GB's poem "Grandfather") came from England; his mother Claire, Harry's second wife (his first wife died in Manitoba), was born and raised in Ontario. Pearl's parents were both from the United States. Her father Emmett came from the Ozark region of southern Missouri and her mother Maple, a Mennonite, came from Oregon.

GB started school after his family moved from Peachland to Greenwood BC, where his father taught at a small public school.

1943: GB moves to Oliver and and begins grade 3. His father becomes a chemistry and math teacher at the Southern Okanagan High School.

1950–1953: While in high school at the Southern Okanagan High School (now the Southern Okanagan Secondary School), GB writes sports columns for two local newspapers, *The Oliver Chronicle* and the *Penticton Herald*, and also writes poems and stories. He graduates from high school in June 1953.

1953–1954: GB moves to Victoria BC and enrolls in Victoria College (now the University of Victoria) to be with his girlfriend Wendy Amor who is in Normal School. He wants to study journalism at the University of Missouri to become a sports writer, but because of his relationship with Wendy and a lack of money, he decides against it.

After the term ends in the spring, during one of several breakups with Wendy, GB travels north to work with a government survey company, B. C. Topographical Survey, but the job fizzles out immediately. He joins the Royal Canadian Air Force (RCAF), enlisting in Vancouver on 10 July 1954.

1954–1957: After basic training at St. Jean in Quebec and trade training at Camp Borden in Ontario, GB is stationed at the Macdonald Air Force Base in Macdonald, Manitoba and works as an aerial photographer. There he begins writing seriously, and meets Red Lane. He reads Henry Miller and Kenneth Patchen, sends out articles and stories to magazines, and gets his first rejection slips. He writes regularly for the camp newspaper, the *Rocketeer*.

GB writes his first consciously saved poem in Oliver on 29 June 1955.

In July 1957, he leaves the RCAF and lives in Oliver for the summer.

1957–1958: GB studies in the English Department at UBC, and soon meets young writers Lionel Kearns and Gladys Hindmarch. He also joins an extracurricular writers' workshop where he meets David Bromige and Frank Davey. He literally discovers the poems of William Carlos Williams while reading through the PS section of the library.

1959–1960: GB writes a novel called "Delsing" (unpublished), a fictional account of his life to the present. He receives his BA in history and creative writing in the spring of 1960. With some students who would later be part of the *Tish* crowd, such as Fred and Pauline (Butling) Wah and Jamie Reid, he begins meeting at Warren Tallman's house to study Ezra Pound, William Carlos Williams, Charles Olson, and the poets in Donald Allen's anthology, *The New American Poetry*.

1961–1962: GB enrolls in the MA program in the English Department. In September, he becomes a founding member of the editorial collective for *Tish*, with Frank Davey, Fred Wah, Jamie Reid, and David Dawson. He also starts writing regularly for *The Ubyssey*, the UBC student newspaper, and works with *Raven*, a British-influenced student literary magazine run by Desmond Fitzgerald, David Bromige, Ian Dunn, and Mike Matthews.

1962–1963: GB studies for his MA. In May 1962 *Sticks & Stones*, planned as a Tishbook, is printed, but so poorly that the official edition is postponed and finally abandoned.

On 14 December 1962, he marries Angela May Luoma. They live on Yew Street in the Kitsilano district of Vancouver where many writers and artists live.

In March 1963, after publishing nineteen monthly issues beginning in September 1961, the original editorial collective stops producing *Tish* magazine.

In April GB submits his thesis, "Points on the Grid," a sequence of poems with an introductory essay on poetics. He gets a job offer from the English Department at the University of Alberta at Calgary (now the University of Calgary), beginning in the fall term.

In the summer of 1963, he stays in Vancouver for the Poetry Conference at UBC, organized by Warren Tallman. It is an intense summer of literary events, and he meets poets and writers from all over North America, including Charles Olson, Allen Ginsberg, Robert Creeley, Robert Duncan, Denise Levertov, and Margaret Avison.

1963–1965: GB begins teaching at the University of Calgary in September 1963. He is invited to read at the University of Arizona on 30 October, his first important reading outside of Vancouver. He writes book and theatre reviews regularly for *The Albertan* (Calgary). In the fall of 1963 he plans the magazine *Imago* and in 1964 he publishes the first issue. He and AB drive to Mexico for the first time in the summer of 1964, to visit Margaret Randall and Sergio Mondragón, editors of *El Corno Emplumado*. They return to Mexico for a month during the following summer. He writes poems for *Rocky Mountain Foot*.

Books: *Points on the Grid* and *The Man in Yellow Boots*.

1966: During May and June, GB takes a six-week trip to Europe with Tony Bellette. They drive from England to Turkey and back; on the road GB writes a travelogue, "Eye-Kicks in Europe," unpublished to date. While in England, he approaches Essex and Sussex universities with his plan to complete his PhD on Basil Bunting, but is refused; he also applies to Durham University but by the time his proposal is accepted, he has decided to attend the University of Western Ontario. He receives a Canada Council Doctoral Fellowship, and leaves Calgary in August 1966.

1966–1967: GB becomes a PhD student in the English Department at the University of Western Ontario in London. He becomes involved in various literary activities with Victor Coleman, David McFadden, and the painter Greg Curnoe. He establishes Beaver Kosmos, a series of events and readings and later a periodical publishing venture. In the summer of 1967, he is invited to serve as Writer-in-Residence at Sir George Williams University (now Concordia University) in the fall, and he accepts.

Book: *The Silver Wire*.

1967–1968: GB works as Writer-in-Residence in the English Department at Sir George Williams University. He meets many eastern Canadian writers, including John Glassco, Louis Dudek, Ron Everson, F. R. Scott, A. J. M. Smith, and D. G. Jones. He continues to edit and publish *Imago*.

Books: *Mirror on the Floor* and *Baseball*.

1968–1970: GB teaches at Sir George Williams University. In helping to organize the influential Poetry Series there, he meets the major poets of the time, both

Canadian and American. In the summer of 1970 he goes with AB to England and Ireland.

Books: *Rocky Mountain Foot* and *The Gangs of Kosmos*, which receive the Governor General's Award for Poetry, *Vibrations*, *Sitting in Mexico*, and *George, Vancouver*.

1971–1972: GB gets a Senior Arts Grant from the Canada Council. He leaves Montreal in the summer of 1971 and drives back to Vancouver. He and AB move into a commune on York Avenue.

On 6 October 1971, daughter Thea Claire is born.

Books: *Al Purdy*, *Genève*, *Touch*, and *The Story So Far*.

1972–1976: GB and AB move into a house on Balaclava Street. In 1972, GB gets a teaching position in the English Department at Simon Fraser University, to begin in the summer.

During this period, he gets involved in the Vancouver writing scene by working on the *Georgia Straight Writing Supplement* (which became Vancouver Community Press), with Gladys Hindmarch, Stan Persky, George Stanley, and others. He continues editorial and publishing work for *Beaver Kosmos Folio* and *Imago*.

Ewart Bowering dies on 12 March 1974.

Books: *Autobiology*, *Curious*, *At War with the U. S.*, *In the Flesh*, *Flycatcher*, *Imago 20*, *Letters from Geeksville*, *Allophanes*, *Poem and Other Baseballs*, and *The Catch*.

1977–1978: GB receives a Senior Arts Grant from the Canada Council. From November 1977 to February 1978 he travels to Italy, Costa Rica, and San Francisco, during which time he writes *Burning Water*.

Books: *The Concrete Island*, *A Short Sad Book*, *Concentric Circles*, *Protective Footwear*, and *Three Vancouver Writers*.

1979–1988: This period is a decade of writing in all forms—poems, fiction, essays—and major editing projects. GB travels to Australia, New Zealand, Germany, and Italy. In March 1985, he becomes Writer-in-Residence at the University of Rome, and teaches in Germany during that summer.

Books: *Another Mouth*, *Great Canadian Sports Stories*, *Burning Water*, which wins the Governor General's Award for Fiction, *Particular Accidents*, *Fiction of Contemporary Canada*, *West Window*, *A Way with Words*, *Ear Reach*, *Smoking Mirror*, *The Mask in Place*, *A Place to Die*, *Kerrisdale Elegies*, *The Contemporary Canadian Poem Anthology*, *Craft Slices*, *Seventy-one Poems for People*, *Sheila Watson and* The Double Hook, *Delayed Mercy*, *Caprice*, *Errata*, and *Imaginary Hand*.

1988–: GB continues to teach in the English Department at SFU. He and AB continue to live in the Kerrisdale district of Vancouver, and he continues to write.

Section A
Books and Pamphlets
by George Bowering

Section A consists of descriptions and annotations for books and pamphlets by GB published between 1962 and 1988, inclusive.

For each title in Section A and Section B, the following categories are used:

1. Entry number, short title, year of publication
2. The designation "Cloth issue" to indicate hardcover edition, where applicable
3. Transcription of title-page, with a vertical bar designating line-endings
4. Collation of sheets, with numbered pages and unnumbered pages in brackets
5. Page size in inches and centimeters, followed by a brief description of binding, cover design, and content on back cover
6. Content of book or pamphlet by page number, with unnumbered pages in brackets; epigraphs and dedications, where applicable, are transcribed with a vertical bar designating line-endings
7. Transcription of colophon, where applicable, with a vertical bar designating line-endings
8. Publication information, including number printed and retail price
9. Note on "Paper issue" or paperback edition, where applicable
10. Individual titles, where applicable
11. Annotations related to the composition and publication of the title

Locating precise publication information proved to be the most challenging aspect of each description. GB's books and pamphlets rarely have detailed colophons showing publication date, number of copies printed, and place of publication. Over time, some information tends to get lost, especially publication date and print run; some presses' records are either incomplete or gone. A variety of means has been used to establish reliable publishing information. In many cases, fortunately, the publisher could provide the data, but a few important publishers for GB (Oberon Press and Coach House Press, for example) reported that complete records were no longer available for all of his titles. Some information was uncovered in GB's correspondence in the NL, and some was taken from his own datebook of publications, also in the NL. In other cases, the memory of an individual connected with a publication (for example, Tom Marshall, Raymond Souster, and Victor Coleman) was the source. In still other cases, information was found in archival files (for example, the McClelland and Stewart Papers at McMaster University and the Coach House Press Papers at the NL), or if not found, pieced together from circumstantial evidence. In those instances when the number of copies printed could not be verified through a reliable source, the figure is estimated; when the date of publication differs significantly from the copyright date printed in the publication, the issue date is shown in brackets and the title is listed chronologically by that date. Other irregularities unique to a given title are noted in the annotations completing each entry.

A1   STICKS & STONES   1962

sticks | & | stones | poems by GEORGE BOWERING | with a preface by ROBERT CREELEY | cover and drawings by GORDON PAYNE | published by TISHBOOKS | Vancouver

Pp. [1] 2–8 [9] 10–13 [14] 15–21 [22–23] 24–30 [31] 32–35 [36] 37–44

5¹/₂ x 8¹/₂ in.; 14 x 21.5 cm. White paper wrappers, staple-bound. The title-page is used as the cover [see note below].

[1] title-page; 2 acknowledgements and dedication: This book is dedicated to | Robert Duncan— | the man who teaches | people to listen | GB; 3–4 "Preface" by Robert Creeley; 5 contents; 6–44 text [page 41 is misnumbered 40].

Printed in Vancouver, c. May 1962, estimated 30–50 copies, at no price [see note below].

Titles: Wattle)—Totems—(Benzedrine—Somnia—The Hockey Hero—The Brain—Cadence—Dark Around Light—Telephone Metaphysic—I Ask Her—Wrapped in Black—Eyes That Open—Ode on Green—Hopi Metaphysic—Locus Solus—Locus Primus—Moment: Cars—White Cat & a Fly—On a Black Painting by Tamayo—Trail—Old Umbrella Tree—Walking Poem—At Victory Square—Pacific Gray—The Sunday Poem—Back From Seattle—Metaphor 1—Metaphor 2—Radio Jazz—It Is a Kind of Pressure—Tuesday Night—I Think a Head On Collision—Lazarus—The Winter's Tale—The Bread

Front cover, *Sticks & Stones*

NOTES:

♦ The poems were written during the early months of *Tish*, from September 1961 to May 1962, with the exception of three poems: "Radio Jazz" written in August 1961, "Trail" in April 1961, and "On a Black Painting by Tamayo" in November 1960.

♦ *Sticks & Stones*, a book that GB says contained "poems written according to *Tish* principles," was conceived as part of a projected series of Tishbooks. Tishbook 1 was Frank Davey's *D-Day and After* (introduction by Warren Tallman), published in an edition of 400 copies and sold for 65¢. It was to be followed by *Sticks & Stones* and *On Walking* by Robert F. Grady. Around February 1962, GB and Davey went to GB's home town, Oliver, BC, to print *D-Day and After* at the local newsapaper, *The Oliver Chronicle*. They decided on the name

Rattlesnake Press, an appropriate name for a press connected to GB's roots in the Okanagan Valley.

Sticks & Stones, unfortunately, was never officially published. Apparently, to save money, it was done on the *Tish* printer but with such poor results that the publication process was disrupted—as it turned out, permanently. Initially, reprinting was held up for lack of funds, as Frank Davey explains in a letter (more a memo) to GB, dated 1 June 1962: "Margins on some pages—e. g. Creeley intro—end somewhere in the page crease. Unreadable & bad publicity so pages will have to be re-done. But have run out of money both personally and corporationally & can't buy more paper or cover stock." [GB Papers, Correspondence Frank Davey, NL]

The book would never get redone. GB recalled that it was "all printed up but it was never collated, except in small numbers; 10 or 20 copies went out that people just put together by hand, but it was never finished properly with a cover." [Session 1, 10 April 1985]

♦ Extant copies vary in poems missing. The description above is based on the copy in the Contemporary Literature Collection, SFU. Two poems, listed in the table of contents, are not printed: "Locus Solus" (p. 22) and "Metaphor" (p. 36).

♦ Staples have been removed by the SFU Library to preserve the paper. Some copies, however, are unbound and some—except the SFU copy—include one or two drawings by Gordon Payne.

♦ The SFU copy is inscribed to "Al" [Al Purdy] and dated 9 February 1963.

♦ The book would have contained illustrations by Gordon Payne, one of which was intended for the cover that never got printed. The drawings by Payne are located in the GB Papers at Queen's University.

♦ In a recent letter Fred Wah recalled: " . . . the press was messing up so we didn't finish the run; some of the plates were supposed to have drawings on them and I don't think we got those. I don't remember how many we actually did, not many because the printing was messy, maybe around 30 copies. I know I had one which I sold to SUNYAB [State University of New York at Buffalo] in the 60s when I needed some money. That's about it. Not very interesting, but I remember it because I was *Tish*'s printer and I can still see those inky sheets messing up because the rollers on our machine had had it. I think it was pretty close to the end of that run of *Tish* and we didn't do a lot of printing after that." [Letter to the author, 11 December 1988]

♦ Frank Davey in a recent letter also recalled: "The text was typed on an IBM variable-pitch typewriter onto paper plates, the impact depressing the plate & causing the hollow letters. The typewriter was rented & hard to obtain. The text was printed on an Addressograph-Multigraph Model 80 offset press by Fred Wah, with such poor results that he never bothered reproducing the drawings. I can't recall ever seeing more than one copy (George's) collated & bound, & that as a joke. Fred & I regarded it as incomplete (unlike Lionel's book) [*Songs of*

Circumstance, by Lionel Kearns], since the art hadn't been printed on the cover, & as merely an unhappy stack of scrap paper. My letter that you've unearthed indicates that both George & I believed reprinting was necessary. It indicates that we were deferring printing. I believe Contact Press's acceptance of his *Points on the Grid*, including most of the poems, soon caused us to give up all idea of bothering with reprinting. There were no copies 'officially' printed & bound by 'Tishbooks'. When I left Vancouver in Aug 63 the pages were still gathering dust on the *Tish* office shelves, & I still hadn't seen any collated copies except for the one assembled in jest by George. I think it was only laziness that caused us not to throw the lot into the garbage." [Letter to the author, 26 January 1989]

Probably Davey's memory is accurate: with the printing problems, the lack of funds, and the loss of the rented typewriter, publication was indefinitely suspended, and then later abandoned when *Points on the Grid* was accepted by the prestigious Contact Press in Toronto. While waiting though, unknown to Davey, GB collated and stapled some 15 copies for personal distribution.

♦ In April 1963, GB sent a copy, referred to as the "proofs" for the book, to the Ruth Stephan Poetry Center in Tucson, Arizona, in preparation for his poetry reading there 30 October 1963. [GB Papers, Correspondence LaVerne H. Clark, 14 May 1963, NL]

♦ Wah could not remember the exact printing date, but it appears to have occurred around the end of May 1962. *Sticks & Stones* is consistently dated 1963, but since it was not "officially" published, the date of printing is the more relevant date. Davey's letter to GB of 1 June 1962 (cited above) indicates that the poor quality printing has just been done and that GB's book will not soon be forthcoming, as announced in *Tish* 9 (14 May 1962), the same issue in which Davey's *D-Day and After* is advertised for sale. Finally, the dating of GB's poems in the collection also implies the end of May 1962. The last poem to be included, "Lazarus," was written on 14 May 1962. If the printing had been done much later in 1962 or in 1963, GB would certainly have included more recent poems—especially in a collection where all but two poems were composed in a period of nine months, from August 1961 to May 1962.

Printing *Tish*, No. 19; GB, standing (l.) with (l. to r.) David Dawson, Fred Wah, and Frank Davey; cover of *Tish 1-19*; see C83; photo by Raymond Hull

♦ Some unbound sheets remained with the *Tish* papers and were later retrieved by Vancouver bookseller William Hoffer from the last editor, Stan Persky.

♦ The book was dedicated to Robert Duncan because he "was the first one that was an actual teacher to us—not only a teacher in the sense that we were tremendously excited by the new direction that his work was giving us, but also by the fact that he actually spoke to us and read our stuff and gave us advice and published in our magazine and so forth. Of all the new American poets he was our first aegis into that whole scene." [Session 1, 10 April 1985]

♦ About the title GB commented: "*Sticks & Stones*, with an ampersand, suggested to me at the time, an Imagist sense primarily, a Williams and Pound interest in the image as an adequate symbol. There's the pun on 'words will never hurt me', 'sticks and stones and words', and so forth, but the main notion was that you built poems out of actual things—and some poems in there carry that image through, of poems made of actual things." [Session 1, 10 April 1985]

♦ A new edition of *Sticks & Stones*, including the drawings by Gordon Payne, was published by Talonbooks in October, 1989.

A2   POINTS ON THE GRID   1964

a. Cloth issue:
GEORGE BOWERING | [in red] Points | on | the | Grid | CONTACT PRESS | 28 Mayfield Avenue, Toronto, Canada
    Pp. [1–8] 9–67 [68–70]
    5³/₄ x 9 in.; 14.5 x 22.7 cm. Casebound with brown boards. Light grey dust jacket with black grid lines and red lettering on front, and publisher's blurb on front flap.
    Endleaf; [1] half-title; [2] blank; [3] title-page; [4] publishing information; [5] dedication: This book is for | LIONEL KEARNS; [6] acknowledgements; [7] contents; [8] blank; 9–67 text; [68–70] blank; endleaf.
    Published Spring 1964; 50 copies, at $3.00. Printed in Montreal by Three Star Printing and Publishing Company.
    Titles: Another Try at It—The Sunday Poem—The Night Before Morning—A Vigil of Sorts—The Heart of Lightness—A Redemption—Abort—Soliloquy on the Rocks—On a Black Painting by Tamayo—Vicar—White Cat & a Fly—Radio Jazz—Trail—Moment: Cars—History of Poets: Heathcliff—History of Poets: Jake Barnes—Academy—A Meta Physic in Things—Telephone Metaphysic—Dark Around Light—Wood—Metathesis—Locus Solus—Tuesday Night—

Front cover, *Points on the Grid*

Walking Poem—At Victory Square—Somnia—Steps of Love—The Hockey Hero—Benzedrine—The Bread—William Faulkner Dead—Family—The Girl at the Beach—Granville Street Bridge—Grandfather—M M—For A—Spanish B. C. —Hospital—From Your Son & Lover—The Red Hot Element—Meta Morphosis—Points on the Grid

b. Paper issue: as A2a, but perfect bound with paper wrappers in same colour and design as on dust jacket; 200 copies, at $2.00.

NOTES:

♦ The poems were composed during the period from November 1960 to January 1963, with one exception, "Soliloquy on the Rocks," which dates back to April 1958.

♦ GB's MA thesis at UBC, completed in the spring of 1963, was called "Points on the Grid"; see E4 to compare contents.

♦ In a letter dated 28 January 1963, Raymond Souster wrote to GB expressing interest in his work and the work of the *Tish* poets, and invited him to send Contact Press a manuscript for 1964 publications. [GB Papers, Correspondence Raymond Souster, NL]

Peter Miller wrote to GB, 17 April 1963, saying his manuscript had been read by him, Souster, and Louis Dudek and all were very impressed by the poems. Contact wanted to publish GB's book in the spring of 1964. [GB Papers, Correspondence Peter Miller, NL]

♦ GB wanted his "first book of poems, outside of the homemade thing, to be a Contact Press book, and lo and behold it was." [Session 1, 10 April 1985]

♦ On Souster's request, GB wrote a letter about himself, a paragraph of which was used for the publisher's blurb on the dust jacket: "What do I think about poetry? Mainly that the job is a spoken art and that what is written down is a score, poetry being closer to music than any other artform. The written thing is no more the poem than the score is the symphony. Scores are written because you can't take an orchestra or a poet to every farmhouse on the Canadian tundra. But meticulous care should be taken with notation of the poem, because you are trying to make a suggestion of the things the voice does. Rhythm, I've always been told, is my forte, natural thing, and that is chief concern of the way the thing lies on the page. In this way, I've been greatly indebted to Black Mountain, what with specially Olson, Creeley, Duncan. Also linguists, Trager, Whorfe (sp), Sapir. Also my favorite oldtime poets are W. C. Williams and Ez Pound. Also Chaucer, Dante, Jonson, Smart, Blake, further back."

♦ Many of the poems in this book reveal GB's interest in the New American Poetry movement at the time: " . . . you'll see poems that look like Olson and poems that look like McClure and a little bit of Ginsberg I think and all that stuff." [Session 1, 10 April 1985]

♦ GB recalled that he was fascinated by the concept of "margins" at the time: "I had a notion that I had to write a series—like I had to have a metaphor that continued from poem to poem, one that you had to work out as you went along, so margins was it for me." [Session 1, 10 April 1985]

♦ Souster wrote in a recent letter: "I well remember *Points on the Grid*. Both Peter Miller and I wanted to publish it as soon as we saw the manuscript." [Letter to the author, 17 July 1988]

♦ Of all the reviews, GB remembers the one by Phyllis Webb—"in my memory that's the most important review of it"; see H20.

♦ GB commented on the dedication to Lionel Kearns: "We knew each other before *Tish* started so we were closest friends, closest poetry friends, before any of that other stuff began. He dedicated his first book to me and I dedicated my first book to him." [Session 1, 10 April 1985]

A3   THE MAN IN YELLOW BOOTS   1965

the man in yellow boots el hombre de las bo | tas amarillas the man in yellow boots el homb | re de las botas amarillas the man in yellow b | oots el hombre de las botas amarillas the man | george bowering | traducción sergio mondragón | collages: roy kiyooka | ediciones el corno emplumado | [rule] méxico [space] 1965

   Pp. [1–5] 6–64 [8 leaves] 65–105 [106–108] 109–112

   $5^5/_8$ x $7^{11}/_{16}$ in.; 14.3 x 19.5 cm. Perfect bound with white paper wrappers. On front, a photo of crossed feet in boots, title in black ink with word "yellow" in yellow; on back, a photo of boots side by side, placed horizontally with the author's name. Cover design by Sylvia de Swaan.

   [Inside front wrapper] dedication: this book is for red lane | (1937–1964) | este libro es para red lane | (1937–1964); [1] el corno emplumado | [rule] | número 16 [bullet] octubre 1965 | [device] | the plumed horn | [rule] | number 16 [bullet] october 1965; [2] magazine information; [3] "Editor's note"; [4] "Nota de los Editores"; [5] title-page; 6–64 text; [8 unnumbered leaves of collages by Roy Kiyooka]; 65–91 text; 92–93 contents; 94–95 note on Roy Kiyooka; 96 article in Spanish; 97–105 letters from GB to the editors; [106]–112 advertisements; [inside back wrapper] patrons

   Published 1 October 1965; 3,000 copies, at $1.00. Printed in Mexico City.

   Titles: To Cleave—After Breakfast—The Typewriter—Poem For My Wife Angela—What Is It?—Inside the Tulip—Frost—The Measurer—Moon Shadow —Poor Man—David—The Grass—Vox Crapulous (alternate title: J. Edgar Hoover)—The Day Before the Chinese A-Bomb—Her Act Was a Bomb—For WCW—Canadian Cafe—Calgary Downtown Sunday—The Good Prospects— The Swing—Old Time Photo of the Present—The Kitchen Table—Recharge—Indian Summer—Old Cracker Barrel—Está Muy Caliente—The Crumbling

Wall—The English Teachers—The Descent—The Shifting Air—Breaking Up, Breaking Out—Letters from GB to *El Corno Emplumado*

NOTES:

♦ The poems were composed in a period of two years from January 1963 to January 1965.

♦ GB's poems are printed on the verso; Sergio Mondragón's translations are printed opposite them on the recto.

the man in yellow boots

el hombre de las botas

amarillas

Front cover, *The Man in Yellow Boots*

♦ The text was published as a single issue of *El Corno Emplumado*, edited by Margaret Randall and her husband Sergio Mondragón. Every fourth issue was devoted to the work of a single writer; GB's book was number 16.

♦ Randall edited the selection, beginning around August 1964, choosing from poems sent by GB from then on.

♦ GB to Randall: "I was wondering if it wd be okay for me to send you more poems than are publishable & let you help a lot in the selection of them, I am a poor judge in the selection of my own poems. I wd also feel good to see yous doing this, to see what you do with the poems. I want you to see what I'm doing." [Letter printed in *The Man in Yellow Boots*]

♦ GB and AB visited Randall and Mondragón in Mexico City during the summers of 1964 and 1965. "I guess it was between the two trips that I got the manuscript together." [Session 1, 10 April 1985]

♦ GB was connected with *El Corno Emplumado* right from its beginnings in the early 1960s: " . . . because it was publishing the same people that were published in *Evergreen Review* and all those other magazines that were doing the New American Poetry plus the Latins. And it was one of the first places that batch of easterners showed up, like Rochelle Owens and all those people around [Robert] Kelly." [Session 1, 10 April 1985]

♦ GB is listed as a representative for western Canada. "I did a little anthology of Canadian poetry in an issue that came out after this." [Session 1, 10 April 1985] [See D336]

♦ Four poems were included in *Rocky Mountain Foot*: "The Grass," "Calgary Downtown Sunday," "Indian Summer," and "The Crumbling Wall."

♦ From the "Editor's Note" on GB: "Like most poets of our generation Bowering has had the raft of jobs (weed picker, fruit packer, loader of boxcars, teacher, etc.), the struggle to make it in society, often on one meal a day (in his case spaghetti with a can of tomato soup), and certain 'turn-ons' which remain and come through when speaking of the work. All sports are important to him, baseball most of all. Zoos, too: in strange cities he has often gone to them first, once wanted to be an animal-feeder. The desert. Mexico. 'In Mexico I first saw strangers as individuals', he says, 'I got closer to people and that has always been a hard thing for me: to be close to people'."

AB and GB on their Mexico trip, summer 1964, with Akiko Trump and Margaret Randall

♦ GB: "This was the biggest publication run of any book of poetry I've ever had, 3,000 copies." [Session 1, 10 April 1985]
♦ GB: " . . . here's some special news I've never told anyone. When the book was publisht there were 5 copies done in Mexico bound in leather & buckram. (Three of them, or maybe only 2, are for sale, provided that I know & dig who gets them, and price to be workt out." [GB Papers, Correspondence Nelson Ball, 10 January 1973, NL]
♦ In an article by Margaret Randall when *The Man in Yellow Boots* was published, GB explains the connection of the title with his work as an aerial photographer in the Royal Canadian Air Force: "They used to issue regulation brown rubber boots, thousands of them all the same. One day I got tired of having to find mine and got ahold of a spray gun and a can of yellow paint. That's how I became the man in yellow boots!" [From "George Bowering: One of the Few of Our Generation Who Shall Be Remembered"; see H31].
♦ The publication date is 1 October 1965, but the issue arrived in mid-September, earlier than expected from the printer. In a letter dated 26 September 1965, Randall wrote to GB from Mexico City: "THE MAN IN YELLOW BOOTS is the talk of the town. everyone is crazy about it. people quote the poems." [GB Papers, Correspondence Margaret Randall, NL]
♦ This book is dedicated to GB's close friend Red Lane who died on December 1, 1964, as GB writes in "Red Lane," "morning of my 29th birthday." [*Seventy-one Poems for People*; see A45].

A4   THE SILVER WIRE   1966

a. Cloth issue:
The Silver | Wire | By | GEORGE BOWERING | [device] | THE QUARRY PRESS | *Kingston, Ontario*
    Pp. [1–8] 9–72
    6 x 9 in.; 15.2 x 22.7 cm. Casebound with pale green boards. White dust jacket with brown line drawing on front of a nude woman sitting on a bed; on back, a

THE SILVER WIRE

GEORGE BOWERING

Front cover, *The Silver Wire*

reproduction of a portrait of GB by Gordon Payne, with publisher's blurb. Cover design by David Brown.

Endleaf; [1] half-title; [2] blank; [3] title-page; [4] publishing information and acknowledgements; [5] dedication: *This Book is for Angela Bowering*; [6–7] contents; [8] blank; 9–72 text; endleaf.

Published June 1966; 100 copies, at $3.00. Printed in Kingston by Jackson Press.

Titles: Far from the Shore—Rime of Our Time—Angela Sleeping—Inside the Tulip—Each Morning—In Your Yellow Hair—Leg—The Winter's Tale—Wrapt in Black—Eyes That Open—Ode on Green—A Bedroom Sound—Matins—When You Run Naked—Husband—The Candle—Frost—A Sudden Measure—At the Intersection—The Dance Complete—History of Poets: Frederic Henry—Yew Street—Love & War Is Kind—The Youthful Mother, a Shape Upon Her Lap—A Corner Store Poem—It's the Climate—Thru My Eyes—The Sea Shore—Fluff—Open My Heart—The Sons of Freedom—News—John Kennedy's Grave, and the Others—Hideo Kobayashi—Universal & Particular—Circus Maximus—East to West—The Blue Shirt—Rodin's Thinker—The Cross of Bistolfi—The Eyes—Preserves—Lazarus—Shyly You Are—The Tree—Totems—The Brain—I Think a Head On Collision—April Weather—Anniversary Recall—Cadence—The Image—I Saw Some Wonder at Noon—Ex-is Sensual—Winter's Dregs—Locus Primus—The Snow—Hopi Metaphysic—Above Montana—Park Love Poem—The Measurer—Ed Dorn—Phyllis Webb—Object Lesson for Amy Lowell and Love for Ami Petersen—Red Lane—My Atlas Poet—Vancouver Island—Driving to Kelowna—Vancouver Etude—The Student of the Road—Vancouver–Courtenay–Calgary—Forest Fire Summer—Social Poem—When Visitors Come I Go—Printed into Time

b. Paper issue: as A4a, but perfect bound with paper wrappers in same colour and design as on dust jacket; 400 copies, at $2.00.

NOTES:

♦ Selection of poems written from January 1962 to April 1964, a two-year period that spans student days in Vancouver to teaching in Calgary. Many poems are related to GB's marriage to Angela Luoma, 15 December 1962.

♦ GB thought of these poems as "magazine verse" because in "those days I was publishing like crazy in lots of little mags." [Session 1, 10 April 1985]

♦ The manuscript was first sent to Fred Cogswell of *Fiddlehead* who, for financial reasons and other commitments, could not publish it, but in a letter of 26 February 1965 he recommended it to Macmillan. Although the manuscript was not accepted, GB was asked by editor J. M. Bacque to consider revision and resubmission the following year. This qualified decision was based on his reader's report, identified as Gwendolyn MacEwen in the Macmillan Papers; she favoured a shorter manuscript of the strongest poems. [Macmillan and Company Papers, McMaster University]

The manuscript was then sent to Tom Marshall and accepted for Quarry Press. In response GB wrote to Marshall: "Your letter was very welcome on the coldest night of the year." [Tom Marshall Papers, Correspondence GB, 3 January 1966, NL]

♦ GB to Marshall, 5 July 1966, on Gordon Payne's painting: "I am sending a different kind of photo, hoping you might find it interesting. It is from a painting by Gordon Payne, well-known West Coast painter who is very closely connected with the poetry scene there. In fact his studio is in the same building as the apartment of John Newlove, and almost next door to Jamie Reid." [Tom Marshall Papers, Correspondence GB, NL]

♦ GB: "That painting had a typescript poem of mine underneath, totally hidden; there's these little letters 'g-e-o-r-g-e' that you can see on the painting, but there's a whole poem underneath." [Session 1, 10 April 1985]

♦ The GB/Marshall correspondence shows that the official publication date may have been June 1966, but the issue date was later. When GB received paperback copies from Marshall on 1 September 1966, he was told the hardcovers would be bound in Toronto in the next few weeks. GB acknowledged receipt of these on 21 September 1966 and thanked Marshall "for making it such a nice looking book." [Tom Marshall Papers, Correspondence GB, NL]

♦ Six poems became part of *Rocky Mountain Foot*: "Angela Sleeping," "A Sudden Measure," "It's the Climate," "East to West," "The Snow," and "Above Montana."

♦ The title comes from William Blake's "To Summer" in *Poetical Sketches*: "Our bards are fam'd who strike the silver wire." For GB the image has to do with the "connection between the poet and heaven, the communication between the poet and heaven." [Session 1, 10 April 1985]

A5   MIRROR ON THE FLOOR   1967

a. Cloth issue:
Mirror on the | FLOOR | George Bowering | [on page opposite to title-page:] McClelland and Stewart Limited Toronto/Montreal | [device]
    Pp. [1–6] 7–160

5³/₈ x 8 in.; 13.2 x 20.2 cm. Casebound with black boards. Dust jacket with colour photo (out of focus) on front, of a naked woman on the floor looking at herself in a round mirror; on back, a photo of GB, taken by Bill Trump. Front flap with publisher's blurb, and back flap with brief biography of GB. Cover photo by Dennis Colwell. Book design by Frank Newfeld.

Endleaf; [1] half-title; [2] publisher; [3] title-page; [4] publishing information; [5] dedication: THIS BOOK IS DEDICATED TO BILL TRUMP; [6] blank; 7–160 text; endleaf.

Published 29 April 1967; estimated 1,500 copies, at $5.00.

b. Paper issue: as A5a, but perfect bound with paper wrappers in same colour and design as on dust jacket; estimated 2,500 copies, at $2.50.

c. Special "Preview" issue, estimated 1,000 copies [see note below].

NOTES:

♦ The last page of the novel is dated May 1965, Calgary. GB wrote this novel for about four years (probably 1961–64), and finished it in Calgary when he wrote the conclusion.

♦ Warren Tallman wanted the novel to be called "Vancouver Blues," but GB stuck with his own title.

♦ In a letter to McClelland and Stewart, 12 August 1965, GB says he is sending his novel on the suggestion of Earle Birney. It was accepted in December 1965. GB responded in writing, 17 February 1966: "Many thanks for your reassuring and friendly letter of last month. I had been beginning to think that it was a dream about the phone call from Toronto about your publishing my novel, a dream or a friend from there playing a practical joke. I have this end of the world feeling all the time, even when I'm on this prairie outpost of it." [McClelland and Stewart Papers, McMaster University]

Photograph of GB on back cover of *Mirror on the Floor*

♦ GB recalled: "I really wanted my first book of fiction to be published by McClelland and Stewart." [Session 1, 10 April 1985]

♦ The McClelland and Stewart editor was J. Bradley Cumings.

♦ The photo on the back cover, by GB's childhood friend Bill Trump, was taken at Kitsilano Beach (c. fall 1962/spring 1963). The character Bob Small is modelled on Trump, to whom the novel is dedicated.

♦ GB on the cover image: "She's a little bit out of focus because in 1967 you couldn't really have a sharp focus of a naked woman on the cover of your book, so they made it a bit artistic." GB had nothing to do with the design or the cover. [Session 1, 10 April 1985]

♦ GB wrote to Lionel Kearns, 12 February 1966: "My novel that's getting publisht is that very short one (200 pp) that took me 4 years to finish, that I finished last May, and the one you know abt because it begins on the model of you and me going to the pub on Main St in Vancouver, where we met that funny old guy remember who sd I was a college student but you obviously werent & no doubt abt it because he cd tell those things, and he kept calling you 'Lions'." [GB Papers, Correspondence Lionel Kearns, Queen's University Archives]

♦ GB: "My character Delsing was, in fact, named after that bozo you found in the PCL [Pacific Coast League]. He later played with Detroit. Check the one person who knew that—Hugh Hood." [GB Papers, Correspondence John McAuley, 9 September 1976, NL]

Front cover of "Preview" edition, *Mirror on the Floor*

♦ McClelland and Stewart produced advance copies of the novel for what was called "The Canadian Preview Book Society." This was an attempt to sell advance copies of selected titles by creating the appearance that members of the club would receive a special "proof" copy. Bookseller Nelson Ball explains the scheme: "McClelland and Stewart took the advance copy (misnamed a 'proof') beyond its usual function in 1967 when it initiated a pre-publication book club called the 'Canadian Preview Book Society' to sell by mail a selected list of its publications. For a subscription fee of $10.00, a member would receive preview 'proof' copies of six new titles per year, each in advance of official publication. These 'proofs' may be identified by their front covers which were printed to appear to be an in-house interdepartmental form with check marks and initials to indicate passage from one department to another. These 'proofs' are advance issues of first printings. It was hoped that direct advance sales of 1,000 to 1,500 preview copies would make total print runs of 2,500 copies viable. The project lasted for less than two years. The number of titles issued in this series probably doesn't exceed 12. Notices to subscribers and potential subscribers were sent out under a fictitious name— Donald Stewart, Special Projects Director." [Nelson Ball, *Catalogue No. 99*, July 1987, pp. 7–8]

♦ The note on the back flap describes GB as a "native of Penticton," and also says, "At various times he has worked as an aerial photographer, itinerant orchard worker, library assistant, tree painter, university lecturer, and packing-house labourer."

A6   BASEBALL   1967

BASEBALL | A POEM IN THE | MAGIC NUMBER 9
   Pp. [1–24]

Shaped in a triangle, point to the right: base 10 in. and height 6¹/₄ in.; 25.5 cm and 15.6 cm. Perfect bound with green felt paper wrappers resembling a pennant; text paper with a green ornamental baseball diamond. Design by Gar Smith.

[1] half-title; [2] blank; [3] title-page; [4] copyright; [5] dedication: FOR | JACK SPICER; [6–23] text; [24] colophon.

Front cover, *Baseball*

Colophon: designed by Gar Smith [space] printed at The Coach House Press | published with the assistance of the Canada Council | in an edition of 500 copies, November 1967.

Estimated 350 copies, at $1.25. Printed in Toronto.

Titles: 1–9

NOTES:

♦ GB had sent this poem to bp Nichol, to be published as a Ganglia press pamphlet. Nichol did not publish it but passed it on to Coach House Press, then a new publishing house. This was GB's "first Coach House connection," and he was completely surprised by the design, though "from Coach House in those days you could expect anything." [Session 1, 10 April 1985]

♦ When Coach House Press started, Wayne Clifford was responsible for soliciting the first titles. Victor Coleman recalled: "Wayne went around and spoke to me, Mike Ondaatje, and Barrie [Nichol] who was here, and Barrie brought in David Phillips and George." Designer Gar Smith was an artist who "frequented Coach House to work on various print-oriented things . . . we showed him the manuscript of *Baseball* and he quite liked it. He was working on a series of pieces that were basically pennants, or flags, so the green felt covers." Coleman set the type, Stan Bevington printed the text, and it was bound by volunteers. "I think there were about 300, maybe 350 that actually got bound. [The other sheets] were cut badly, or any number of things went wrong. Some bound copies were just so badly bound at the outset that they were thrown away." [Personal Interview, Victor Coleman, 4 November 1988]

♦ The shape of the book was so unique readers did not know how to put it on their bookshelves: "The felt is supposed to represent a baseball field, not just the shape,

but also the pennant. Artie Gold solved the problem by just nailing it to the wall like a pennant, so that's what he did above his bed." [Session 1, 10 April 1985]
♦ "The genesis of *Baseball*, according to the beginning of the poem, is that, in the beginning, God made baseball. The poem was written during the baseball season of 1965. It's dedicated to the great American poet Jack Spicer, who told us how to write a serial poem and who was also interested in baseball. He was a San Francisco Giants fan. Some of my critic friends like the poem because it's the first long poem in sections that I published. Jack Spicer died about halfway through that summer, or two-thirds of the way through that summer, in Berkeley, at the age of thirty-nine, and his death begins to enter into the last part of the poem as part of the subject. It's an important poem to me because it's a long poem that is not continuous in a narrative sense . . . doesn't have a set of characters, doesn't have a climax and all that business. All that holds it together is the fact that what's being written about is baseball. It's written in nine sections, i.e., nine innings, and it deals with my childhood memories of baseball being played in Oliver, and big-league baseball, and baseball as a metaphor, and baseball as something cosmic. But really, the subject of the book is poetry. It reflects on itself. It has a lot to say about how one makes poetry. So the love for baseball is a disguised way of talking about a love for poetry." [From "A Conversation with GB"; see C185; see also E80 and E83]
♦ Another account by GB: "The poem was begun in Vancouver and finished in Mexico City. Spicer had been here giving his famous lectures at Warren Tallman's house in the early summer. Then he had to go down to Berkeley for the Berkeley Poetry Festival in '65. I went down to Mexico City, and somebody from Oregon came down and told me that he had died just after the Berkeley thing.

"Willy Mays that year had his last really great season as a hitter and was going for the record of 61 home-runs and wound up with 51. Jack Spicer was a Giants fan, and the Giants were in first place, and Jack died, and they wound up in second at the end of the year. The 'old man in San Francisco' is not Jack Spicer, but Warren Tallman's uncle who is from Los Angeles. He and I were both Los Angeles fans, and so we had a lot of fun with Warren and the other people there who were San Francisco Giants fans. And he died that summer as well. The business of the whole season goes through too. It begins in April and ends in—was it October?—it says here September, oh that's right the season ended at the end of September in those days, hence the 'long shadows'. Now it ends in the middle of October." [From an unpublished talk, SFU, 4 March 1981; an excerpt was published as "Bowering on GB's *Particular Accidents*"; see D843]

A7   ROCKY MOUNTAIN FOOT   1969

rocky | mountain | foot | *a lyric, a memoir by George Bowering* [opposite title-page:] [device] | McClelland and Stewart Limited | Toronto/Montreal

Pp. [1–13] 14–123 [124] 125–127 [128]
5⁵/₈ x 9¹/₈ in.; 14.2 x 23.1 cm. Casebound with green and blue vertical bands of varying widths on boards. Green and blue dust jacket; on front, green and blue vertical bands of varying widths. Publisher's blurb on front flap; back flap with a photo of GB, taken by Bill Trump, and a biographical note. Jacket design by William Fox.

[1] Endleaf; half-title; [2] publisher's name; [3] title-page; [4] publishing information; [5–7] contents; [8] blank; [9] dedication: *no dedication is necessary,* | *but I would like to say hello to:* | Chief Walking Eagle | Bob Edwards | Sitting Bull | Jabez Harry Bowering | (*They were all there*); [10] blank; [11] epigraphs: O the mind, mind has mountains; cliffs of fall | Frightful, sheer, no-man-fathomed. Hold them cheap | May who ne'er hung there. Nor does long our small | Durance deal with that steep or deep. Here! creep, | Wretch, under a comfort serves in a whirlwind: all | Life death does end and each day dies with sleep. | —Gerard Manley Hopkins | [space] | Flutes, and the harp on the plain | Is a distance, of pain, and waving reeds | The scale of far off trees, notes not of course | Upon a real harp but chords in the thick clouds | And the wind reaching its arms toward west yellowstone. | —Edward Dorn; [12] blank; [13]–125 text; 126–127 acknowledgements; [128] publisher's device; endleaf.

Publicity drawing for *Rocky Mountain Foot*; courtesy of McMaster University Library

Published 1 March 1969, estimated 1,500 copies, at $3.95. Printed and bound in England by Hazell Watson and Viney Limited, Aylesbury, Bucks.

Titles: Still in the Sky—The Religious Lake—Tunnel Mountain—Mount Norquay—Calgary Now—Prairie—Geopolitic—Calgary Downtown Sunday—Indians in Calgary—The Oil—The Plain—The Grass—The Blue—The Frost—The Snow—The Dust—Above Calgary—The Crumbling Wall—The Cabin—How Can I Tell You—The Road Tells—A Sudden Measure—The Mark—Albertasaurus—30 Below—I Watch the Storm—Winter Tan, a Joke Poem—Forecast—Alberta—Another Epiphany or Was It Apocalypse—Old Snow in the New Year—East to West—High River, Alberta—The Name—The Calgary Eye-Opener—Calgary—Vancouver-Courtenay-Calgary—Indian Summer—History Is Us—The Simile—Odd Lost Sounds—Without Words—Typewriter Codices in

My Brain—An Old Conceit—Do I Hear Sundials Groan—Footprints, Fen-ceposts—Culling Specks of Straw—Warm February—Typewriters Clacking Down the Hall—The Blood Red Fuck—A Riot in Pages of the Bible—Prairie Music—I Would Not Govern—Once in a While You Catch Yourself—Zing—It's the Climate—Angela Sleeping—Over the Rockies—Above Montana—Spin-ning—CPR Window—The Weight—Harpo, a Living Stone—The Streets of Cal-gary—Forget—Stampede—& Proceed—Dear Person—Colonel Fleming et Jules et Jim—Layers 3—Let Me in Let Me Out—General in the Rockies—Cold Spell—Girls in the Snow—Spring Rime in Calgary—Mud Time—In the Calm Darkness of the Moonless Nights—Community—The White Station Wagon Strophes—Back in Vancouver for a Vancouver Visit—Nobody

NOTES:

♦ The poems in this book begin after GB left Vancouver in August 1963 to take up a teaching position at the University of Alberta, at Calgary (now the University of Calgary). The composition period extends to his second year in Calgary, through to the summer of 1966 when he moved to London, Ontario, to enroll as a PhD student at the University of Western Ontario. There is one exception to this dating, "Vancouver-Courtenay-Calgary," written 16 May 1963 and also included in *The Silver Wire*.

♦ In a letter to McClelland and Stewart, 18 November 1966, about the manuscript he was sending them, GB explained: "The book is not, I think, a collection of poems. It is a project I've been working on for 3 years, a long piece of verse writing I call a lyric, a memoir. I don't believe there has yet been such a thing publisht, at least in this country." [McClelland and Stewart Papers, McMaster University]

♦ The poems, written as they were in the period immediately after *Tish*, test out GB's theory of localism. He knew "psychologically in my head that I was only going to be in Alberta for a short time and I had got trained about writing about place in Vancouver from Olson, so I thought, I can start writing an Alberta book while I'm here." [Session 1, 10 April 1985]

♦ GB thinks of this book, not as a long poem and not as merely a collection of poems, but as a "suite" of poems—"a long thing made of little things, with connective tissue." [Session 3, 9 May 1988]

♦ The prose quotations inserted in the text were found by GB in the local newspaper and from *Our Alberta*, a number of flyers that came out from the Alberta Power Company. These documents are now located in the GB Papers at Queen's University.

♦ The lines by Gerard Manley Hopkins are the sestet of his sonnet ["No Worst, There Is None. Pitched Past Pitch of Grief"]; those from Edward Dorn are the opening lines of "Home on the Range, February, 1962."

♦ GB: "Oh god, I'd forgotten how exciting it was to be building that book; I thought I was only going to have two years on it but I had three—I had that extra time." [Session 1, 10 April 1985]

♦ GB received the Governor General's Award for Poetry in 1969 for this book and *The Gangs of Kosmos*.

A8   HOW I HEAR HOWL   1969

[title-page is used as a cover] HOW I HEAR | HOWL | by George Bowering | Beaver Kosmos Folio One

Pp. [1] 2–19 [20]

5¹/₄ x 8³/₈ in.; 13.3 x 21.2 cm. Stapled pamphlet printed on white paper.

[1] title-page; 2 publishing information; 3–18 text; 19 things to read; [20] ad for *Imago*.

Published June 1969; estimated 200–250 copies, at 25¢. Printed in Montreal.

NOTES:

♦ Dated at end of text: 1964, 1965, 1968.

♦ The title imitates the title of an influential essay/pamphlet of the time, Ed Dorn on Charles Olson, *What I See in* The Maximus Poems. Instead of seeing, GB was hearing Allen Ginsberg's *Howl*, so his essay responds to the recorded version, as he says in a prefatory note: "(Poetry is a vocal art. In the following impression of Allen Ginsberg's poem, I will refer not so much to the printed versions as to his spoken version on the Fantasy LP 7005, *Howl and Other Poems*.)"

♦ GB recalled that on the record "part one of the poem is live and parts two and three are done in a studio, so you hear a different voice, and I take that into account." [Session 2, 9 March 1988]

♦ "It was so thin I didn't bother to put a cover on it." [Session 2, 9 March 1988]

♦ Also published in a French version and in a collection of essays on Ginsberg; see G8 and C170.

A9   THE GANGS OF KOSMOS   1969

a. Cloth issue:

The Gangs | of Kosmos | George Bowering | Anansi [space] Toronto [space] 1969

Pp. [1–6] 7–14 [15] 16–23 [24–25] 26–39 [40] 41–51 [52–53] 54–64

6 x 9 in.; 15.2 x 22.8 cm. Casebound with blue paper on boards. Grey dust jacket with a charcoal print on the cover of a woman with trees behind her, from an original lithography, *Champêtre*, by Charles Pachter; on back is the same drawing continued with a side-to-back view of a woman looking toward the trees. On front

Front cover, *The Gangs of Kosmos*

flap, brief statements by writers on GB; on back flap, photograph of GB with Rachel Cox, by Marilyn Cox.

[1] title-page; [2] publishing information; [3] dedication: Love and gratitude to the three people | on the cover. [Margaret Atwood, Angela Bowering, and Charles Pachter] and epigraph: *not God merely in bread | but God in the other-half of the tree* | H. D.; [4] blank; [5] contents; [6] blank; 7–64 text.

Published September 1969; 224 copies, at $5.00.

Titles: A Comment on the Singular—The House—The Silence—Tight String Dreams—Delicate Deer—Now You—Thru—Harbour Beginnings & That Other Gleam—After My Rose Period—The Boat—Particulars on the Picture Cards—I Dont—Grandmother—The Egg—Sally Bowering & the Rooster—Dobbin—The Envies—Windigo—Martin Luther King—Our Triple Birth—Solid Mountain—Sabino Canyon—On Quadra Island—Words Like Our Daily Bread—The Believer—Hamatsa—George Speaking—Pharoah Sanders, in the Flesh—Giant Steps—Grass, Grass—Poems & Letters—The Flowers Are Easy to Paint, the Leaves Difficult—You Too

b. Paper issue: as A9a, but perfect bound with paper wrappers in same design as dust jacket above; 1,925 copies, at $2.50.

NOTES:

♦ The collection gathers poems written from 1963–69, with the majority from 1968–69.

♦ Nicky Drumbolis in his GB bibliography says this book was produced at Coach House Press; see C200 and H617.

♦ GB's datebook says the book was issued December 1969.

♦ Many poems were related to GB's move to eastern Canada, first to London, then to Montreal: "The poems have a lot to do with the fact that when I went to London, Ontario I couldn't write about my inner connection with the space I was living in anymore. Some of these poems were written the last year I was in Calgary, but a lot of them are family poems in which I would go back into my memory of my family and my memory of my childhood, like that poem called 'Dobbin'. That was the step that I made away from writing about place, as in *Rocky Mountain Foot*, the last Olson-type exercise vis-à-vis writing poems in an attempt to imitate the space that you were living in and define it at the same time, you know, all that stuff we did in *Tish* and Vancouver. I was still doing that all the time I was in Calgary. So this book has some travel poems and memory poems and condition poems, like being married poems and stuff like that. It's important in the sense that it's transitional—it's my first eastern book, let's say. It spans my last western poems and my first eastern poems." [Session 3, 9 May 1988]

♦ The collection was a "catching up book, catching up one's magazine verse" [Session 3, 9 May 1988], including poems not in *Rocky Mountain Foot*, and was edited by Margaret Atwood. She selected from poems sent by GB and shaped the order of the contents. Atwood recommended the title *You Too*; GB preferred *The Gangs of Kosmos*. [GB Papers, Correspondence Margaret Atwood, NL)

♦ The title was taken from Walt Whitman's "Democratic Vistas": "I was all caught up in Whitman and Shelley, the two poets I was reading like nuts. I was getting into prophecy, and it wasn't long after that I started doing books like *Genève*, the tarot book. In 1967 in London, Ontario I was a student instead of a teacher, so I was studying those guys a lot more than otherwise, and you didn't feel guilty about losing all that time because it was useful, right? I was taking a course on Whitman and a course on Shelley." [Session 3, 9 May 1988]

♦ The artist Charles Pachter was a friend of Dennis Lee and Margaret Atwood, founding members of House of Anansi Press, a new press at the time. GB and AB met him through Atwood.

♦ The dedication? "The three people on the cover: there's Charlie in the very middle crucified on a tree (you can barely see it because it's right on the spine of the book), and there's also the editor and my wife." GB owns the print, signed in 1968, and done in a place north of Toronto. [Session 3, 9 May 1988]

♦ GB: "The photo of Rachel Cox by Marilyn Cox was taken on the Île d'Orléans in Quebec. We were using somebody's house for a week there." [Session 3, 9 May 1988]

♦ The lines by H. D. used as an epigraph are from *Tribute to the Angels*, the second book of *Trilogy*.

♦ The book was awarded the Governor General's Award for Poetry for 1969, with *Rocky Mountain Foot*.

A10   TWO POLICE POEMS   1969

[no title-page; on cover:] [in red lettering] TWO I POLICE I POEMS I by George
I Bowering
   Pp. [1–24]
   4⁵/₈ x 6 in.; 11.9 x 15.2 cm. Staple bound with white paper wrappers. Cover front
and back with blue photo collage of police with demonstrators.
   [1] section title; [2] blank; [3–14] text; [15] section title; [16] blank; [17–23] text;
[24] blank.

Front cover, *Two Police Poems*

Published by Talonbooks, November 1969; 500
copies, at 95¢. Printed in Vancouver by Talonbooks.
   Titles: Support Your Local Police—American
Cops

NOTES:
♦ "Support Your Local Police" was composed in
August 1966; "American Cops" in June 1964.
♦ In an undated letter, Jim Brown from Talonbooks wrote to GB: "We'd like to publish two
police poems. If you have any ideas on art work or
any repulsive photos of policy [sic] men send them
along. This would probably appear sometime
around Oct. 68." [GB Papers, Correspondence Jim
Brown, NL]
♦ GB: "Talonbooks asked me for a book. I was politicized at the time, like the
police business, and I had these two police poems that I didn't want to publish in a
regular book with other poems." [Session 3, 9 May 1988]
♦ GB recalled writing "American Cops": "I was travelling through the United
States and seeing cops, so it goes from crossing the Canadian/American border
down to crossing into Mexico and saying, no more American cops." [Session 3, 9
May 1988]

A11   SITTING IN MEXICO   1970

Sitting I in I Mexico I George Bowering I *IMAGO* 12
   Pp. [1] 2–43 [44] 45 [46] 47–48
   5³/₈ x 8³/₈ in.; 13.7 x 21.2 cm. Staple bound with white paper wrappers. Black
line drawing on front cover, printed vertically of (from left to right) a bird, a figure
on a bull-like creature facing the bird, and a sunflower.
   [1] title-page; 2 publishing information and dedication: for Sergio Mondragón

& Margaret | Randall, who were largely res- | ponsible for the chances.; 3 author's note; 4–43 text; [44] blank; 45 acknowledgements; [46] blank; 47–48 *Imago* and *Beaver Kosmos Folio* titles.

Published January 1970 [copyright 1969], estimated 200–250 copies, at 75¢. Printed in Montreal.

Titles: Chihuahua—45 Mex—Las Lomas De Mexico—Mexican Dog—Early Afternoon in the Rainy Season—Teotihuacan—On Calzada Tlalpan—Mexico City Face—Dolores Street Music—Veracruz Visit—Tlalpan Scene—Plaza Mexico—Mexico—Cuernavaca—Mexico Walk—The Beach at Veracruz—The Cuernavaca Market—Mexico Quake—To Margaret Randall de Mondragón—The Artisans—Hace Mucho Calor [alternate title, Está Muy Caliente]—This Happened at a Market in the State of Puebla—Written at Margaret's Desk—Calle Triangulo—Puebla, City of the Angels—Oaxaca—Mexico, D. F.

NOTES:

♦ The poems were written during two periods: the majority in 1964, from June to November, based on GB's first trip to Mexico City; the others in 1965, from August to October, based on his second visit.

♦ The cover drawing is by a Mexican folk artist and was sent to GB by Margaret Randall.

Cover drawing, *Sitting in Mexico*

♦ GB's Mexico poems were never collected other than in this pamphlet: "I guess eventually I thought all these Mexican poems were going to go together. I don't think I ever made them up as a book to offer a professional publisher. I think that by the time the time went by, I thought all these poems are so old and so ephemeral, I'll just do them myself. I wasn't proud of them as poems; at that time I was thinking of them as poems about my time there, so they were a kind of record but I didn't think they were really good poems." [Session 12, 28 April 1989]

♦ The following note appears on the copyright page: "*Sitting in Mexico* constitutes the whole of IMAGO 12. IMAGO is the magazine of long poems & poem sequences. Address: George Bowering; English Dept.; Sir George Williams University; Montreal 107; Canada."

♦ A version of the sequence was produced as a play for voices and aired on "Anthology" (CBC), 8 December 1973; see E41.

A12   GEORGE, VANCOUVER   1970

GEORGE, VANCOUVER | a discovery poem | by George Bowering | Weed/
Flower Press | Toronto [space] 1970
   Pp. [i–ii] [1–4] 5–39 [40–42]
   4³/₄ x 8¹/₂ in.; 12 x 21.5 cm. Staple bound in cream paper wrappers with front and
back flaps. Cover has a map of Cook's Inlet with "GEORGE, | VANCOUVER"
superimposed; author's name appears on back cover.

Endleaf; [i–ii] blank; [1] title-page; [2] publishing information; [3] dedication: dedicated to Warren Tallman; [4] blank; 5–39 text; [40–41] blank;
[42] colophon; endleaf.

Colophon: Published in a limited edition | of
300 copies. | Forty copies are numbered and |
signed by the author. | This is number __. |
Weed/Flower Press, | 756A Bathurst St., | Toronto
179, Ontario, Canada.

Published 1970 [issued January 1971], at $2.00
for regular edition; $6.00 for signed edition.

NOTES:
♦ GB began this poem while in London, Ontario,
probably during the spring of 1967, and worked
on it for some six months; dated as completed in
August 1967.

Front cover, *George, Vancouver*

♦ Publisher Nelson Ball accepted the manuscript
for publication, 2 December 1969. Of the 40
signed copies sold at a higher price to help fund Weed/Flower Press, GB wrote to
Ball, 21 July 1970: "I'll be able to sign the highprice copies for sure, nice idea,
something I've never done before, believe it or not, with most of my books done
by the small presses." [GB Papers, Correspondence Nelson Ball, NL]
♦ The move to eastern Canada triggered a shift in perspective: " . . . when I went
to London, Ontario, I found out that I was either out of place or, to put it the way
I felt at the time, I couldn't get my fingers on 'place'. There didn't seem to be any
'place' there. Whether that was because it was foreign to me (although I'd lived
there when I was younger) or whether it was somebody else's place, the way I put
it was that there wasn't any 'place', all that was there was *names*. That is to say, you
couldn't get lost in the woods because there weren't any woods. There were wood
lots, and the wood lots had somebody's name attached to them, and had had for
two hundred years. So what I said was, 'what am I going to write?' During that
time I was writing poems, and I said 'okay, I'll go somewhere else', and I went into
memory, into dreams. One day in the library, for some reason or other—I don't

know why—I found the diaries of Menzies, the botanist on the last voyage of Captain George Vancouver. They had been reprinted by the British Columbia government in the early 1930s. I found that and was really fascinated. It told me a whole pile of things about the Vancouver area that I hadn't known about before. So that coincided with the fact that I had newly found myself devoted to the idea of writing, or found myself able at last to write, a book-length poem. It's a fairly short book (39 pp.), but it's still a book-length poem. So it became a poem. Later on it became a poem-for-voices-cum-play on the radio [see E36], and then it became a novel [see A35], and I had friends who were half-seriously contemplating turning it into an operetta (laughs)." [From "GB: The Fact of Place on the Canadian West Coast"; see D851]

♦ GB recommended the use of a map for the cover and Ball found reproductions of Captain Vancouver's sounding charts. "Everybody was putting maps on their books in those days." [Session 3, 9 May 1988]

♦ GB on the cover: "It makes an attractive cover because it shows how Vancouver worked, how they moved around and dropped the fathom lines up Cook's Inlet, which is in Alaska. The idea had been there for a long long time, this kind of metaphor that we all operated on one way or the other; for instance, in David Dawson's work, in which mapping around especially where water is, the edge of the water and the land, has a natural relationship with discovering how you measure poetry. And it's literally measure that we're seeing in the map, the measure of how deep the water is all the way up and down the coast, the laboriousness, but the hands-on-necessary-being-thereness of it.

"So while I was away from the place I was interested in walking around in, like the west coast and even Alberta to a certain extent, I was still writing a poem about somebody doing that, and the theme of this, what I pick up from Menzies mainly, was that Captain Cook, when he couldn't quite get it right, would fudge it. This Cook's Inlet, Captain Cook called Cook's River. He said that was the Northwest Passage. He didn't bother going to the end of it—and he was always doing that sort of thing in Australia and New Zealand, up here, and so forth. Captain Vancouver said, no you can't fudge it, you've got to go and measure it exactly. That was part of our poetic: you can't fake it by sliding in a metaphor and forgetting the measure; measure is breath, because breath is not just inspiration but it's how you live—if you don't have breath you die. So that image of measure was perfect and I was really glad that Nelson found that. It's not just a map of Cook's Inlet; it's an actual drawing of the sounding." [Session 3, 9 May 1988]

♦ GB: "I just got a thin one together from our friend Weed/Flower press, calld *George/Vancouver*. A clever puttin together of Charles Olson & Percy B. Shelley, very philosophical and space-time oriented. I tried reading the poem to an art-school crowd a couple of years ago and it fell thud." [GB Papers, Correspondence Carol Bergé, 1 January 1971, NL]

♦ This book "is the first instance where the name George gets tied in with the larger history of the coast—George comma Vancouver. It bothered me when people would just write George Vancouver; you don't get the George and you don't get the Vancouver. With the comma, you get George Bowering and Vancouver the city, very clearly. It could be the beginning of a series, or it could be an introduction: George? Vancouver. So it's a four-way cross: it's George, Vancouver—here's Vancouver the city; or George Bowering—here's Vancouver the sailor." [Session 3, 9 May 1988]

A13	AL PURDY	1971

STUDIES IN CANADIAN LITERATURE | General Editors: Hugo McPherson, Gary Geddes | AL PURDY | George Bowering | The Copp Clark Publishing Company
  Pp. [i–v] vi–vii [viii] 1–17 [18] 19–97 [98] 99–113 [114] 115–117 [118–120]
  4³/₈ x 7 in.; 11.2 x 17.7 cm. Perfect bound with orange paper wrappers. Cover with brown drawing of Purdy at a typewriter. Cover design by Alan K. Daniel.
  [i] half-title; [ii] blank; [iii] title-page; [iv] publishing information; [v] contents; vi acknowledgements; vii abbreviations of titles; [viii] blank; 1–112 text; 113 notes; [114] blank; 115–117 bibliography; [118–120] blank.
  Published in March 1971 [copyright 1970]; 2,236 copies, at $2.50. Printed in Toronto.

NOTES:
◆ The typescript is dated Montreal, September 1969. [GB Papers, NL]
◆ GB's book was number 6 in the Studies in Canadian Literature series.
◆ How did this study come about? "Copp Clark wrote me and asked if I would do one on Mordecai Richler because my article on Richler's first novel was in *Canadian Literature* [see D325]. I'm always very clever about writing articles on books that other people don't normally write articles on, so when it comes to having a collection on an author they've got to have your article! That's why I wrote the piece on Richler first, but they thought it meant that I was going to write a chapter on each of his books, so they wrote me a letter and asked if I would do a book on Richler. The series had already started. I wrote back and said, no I didn't want to do one on Richler, but I would be interested in writing on Purdy. They hadn't planned on doing one on Purdy at that time, and they wrote back and said, yes that's fine." [Session 3, 9 May 1988]
◆ This book was GB's first and last book on a single author.

A14   GENÈVE   1971

a. Cloth issue:
Genève | George Bowering | The Coach House Press 1971
    Pp. [1–48]
    5³/4 x 8³/4 in.; 14.7 x 22.2 cm. Casebound with orange boards. Brown dust jacket with floral design on front and back; rust coloured pages. On front flap, publisher's blurb with photo; on back flap, publisher's information and books in print. The dust jacket folds out to reveal the tarot cards used in *Genève* arranged circularly, from the centre out, in the order turned up by GB while composing the poem.
    Endleaf; [1–2] blank; [3] title-page; [4] publishing information; [5–6] blank; [7–44] text; [45] text dated; [46] blank; [47] colophon; [48] blank; endleaf.
    Colophon: Printed in May 1971 at The Coach House Press | in an edition of 1000 copies, 250 clothbound | and 750 in wrappers.
    Sold at $6.00. Printed in Toronto.
b. Paper issue: as A14a, but perfect bound with paper wrappers having the same design; 750 copies, at $3.00.

NOTES:
♦ Text is dated: *Montreal* | July 5, 1969–Feb 8, 1970
♦ In a letter to GB, 13 April 1970, Victor Coleman says that Coach House Press wants to publish his manuscript. [GB Papers, Correspondence Victor Coleman, NL]
♦ Coleman, house editor at the time, typeset the text and wrote the jacket copy. For the cover photo, taken by printer Stan Bevington, the tarot cards GB used (from AB's deck) were placed on an old floral carpet at Coach House Press. [Personal Interview, Victor Coleman, 4 November 1988]
♦ Composing this book was "the beginning of a ten-year sequence of writing longer book-length poems. It was made from the Geneva-Marseilles tarot pack. It was an exercise in dictation, enforced dictation, to find an outside regulator to the poem so that you could not express yourself." First, GB removed the minor arcana cards and shuffled the major arcana cards once. Every once in a while he would take out the major arcana cards left in his deck and "just turn one over—it usually happened once a week—and just write immediately on what I saw. There was something triggered me to say it's time to do it. As it turned out there was a narrative that ran all the way through. It has to do with a triangular love hassle, and sure enough, about five cards from the end, I knew the death card was coming right at the very end, and it did. It's amazing the way they wound up at the end. That's why everybody thought, aw come on you stacked the deck . . . ." [From "Bowering on GB's *Particular Accidents*"; see D843]
♦ "I was going through very strange things emotionally and in my head at the

time, so I would just use those pictures and let them spring off whatever was going on in my head." [From an interview by Don Cameron; see C57 and D590]

♦ GB to Coleman, 5 April 1970: "—by the way, the 'death' in the poem, it must be there, because it was purely by chance that it came as the last card. ooh, I suddenly twigd nearing the end that it hadnt fallen yet & might come last. & it did. cripes. that auto-psychology-biography." [GB Papers, Correspondence Victor Coleman, NL]

♦ GB to Coleman, 9 July 1970: "I'm really glad that yr doing Geneve, because yr my favrite publisher, & theres something awry in the fact that I been doing books with other people. I shd do all my books with you, but then you cdnt really handle 4 more mss a year could you? I shd get my novel ms back from M&S, whove had it for 2 and a half years, and get you to look at it. other things in the zipper case too.

"If you do do some tarot illustrations for the book (slight concern that the pictures might give away too much of the secrets) keep in mind that the pack used is the Geneva pack, as the title suggests. It is much like the Marseilles deck but not exactly. I cdnt Wait to get it." [Coach House Press Papers, Victor Coleman Correspondence, NL]

| A15 | TOUCH | 1971 |

[Boxed line on title-page] Touch | selected poems 1960-1970 | McClelland and Stewart Limited | Toronto/Montreal [opposite title-page:] George Bowering | [device]

Pp. [1–10] 11–128

5$^1/_2$ x 9 in.; 14 x 22.8 cm. Casebound with blue boards. Blue dust jacket, with "Touch selected poems 1960-1970 by George Bowering" repeated in an interweaving, circular pattern in orange calligraphic letters on front and back. Back of cover with small photo of GB at top left corner. Front and back flaps with publisher's statements. Book design by David Shaw. Photo of GB by Marilyn Spink (Cox).

Endleaf; [1] half-title; [2] half-title; [3] half-title; [4] publishing information; [5] dedication: for CO, RD, & RC [Charles Olson, Robert Duncan, and Robert Creeley]; and epigraph: *the flowers | from the shore, | | awakened | the sea*; [6] acknowledgements; [7] preface; [8–9] contents; [10] blank; 11–127 text; 128 titles by GB; endleaf.

Published 11 September 1971; estimated 1,500 copies, at $4.95.

Titles: In True Diction [Preface to *Touch*]—As Introduction—Locus Solus—Walking Poem—Family—Grandfather—The Descent—For WCW—Steps of Love—Rime of Our Time—For A—Inside the Tulip—The Snow—The Grass—Moon Shadow—Far from the Shore—The Oil—Breaking Up, Breaking Out —The Crumbling Wall—Indian Summer—The Cabin—The Frost—Early

Afternoon in the Rainy Season—Está Muy Caliente—Mexico City Face—
Dolores Street Music—The Beach at Veracruz—Baseball, a poem in the magic
number 9—The House—The Silence—The Boat—Windigo—Hamatsa—The
Egg—Dobbin—Grass, Grass—I Said I Said—Poem Written For George (1)—
Poem Written For George (2)—Round Head—Talent—No Time Left—Play
among the Stars—Pharoah Sanders, in the Flesh—Single World West—Ike &
Others—The Owl's Eye—Mars—Touch

NOTES:
♦ The idea for a "selected poems" came from McClelland and Stewart. GB agreed,
thinking at the time that he would have a "selected" approximately every ten years.
Selections were taken from *Points on the Grid*, *The Man in Yellow Boots*, *The
Silver Wire*, *Rocky Mountain Foot*, *Sitting in Mexico*, *The Gangs of Kosmos*, the
whole of *Baseball*, and some uncollected poems, written in the period from 1962 to
1970. The opening poem, "As Introduction," was written for the selection.
♦ The collection includes many longer or extended poems, such as "Ike &
Others," "Mars," "Windigo," and *Baseball*. GB "wanted to show people poems
that reached for length." [Session 3, 9 May 1988] There is also a biographical shape,
with poems from Vancouver and the *Tish* days, to Calgary, a section of Mexico
poems, and poems written in London, Ontario.
♦ The epigraph is taken from Charles Olson's "Maximus, To Gloucester, Sunday,
July 19."
♦ "This was when I started writing introductions. I loved writing little prefaces
because Creeley did, and I thought, how neat to write little introductions."
[Session 3, 9 May 1988]
♦ From GB's preface, "In True Diction," dated Montreal, February 1971: "The
question rose: how do I pick out a minority of my verses? You can choose the best
or you can choose the ones you like best or you can choose the ones that best
exhibit what you believe about poetry. But what is the first, how can you do the
second, & why should the third not be everything. I abandoned the plan of any set
guideline & fell to typing out my strophes & let's see, what will happen on the way
to a book full. It happened that most of the poems are from the early sixties because
it takes time for poems to get publisht. Okay. It also happened that quite a few are
anthology pieces—I can be influenced by critics & editors. & it happened that
more than half of my list of titles could be found in the list of titles Angela made up.
Good.
    "So the poems you have. I would like you to read them aloud, hearing that
punctuation, including the line-ending, is part of the composition. A woman in
Barrie told me that she didnt like my poetry before she came to my reading & then
she liked it—that was because she hadnt really read it, not all of what she had. If
you read aloud you can hear the rime, & rime well used is punctuation too. Please
use it well & we will work to gather, & we will play together."

29

A16   ROBERT DUNCAN: AN INTERVIEW   1971

ROBERT DUNCAN | an interview by | George Bowering & Robert Hogg | April
19, 1969 | A Beaver Kosmos Folio
  Pp. [1–32]
  5³/₈ x 8¹/₈ in.; 13.6 x 20.6 cm. Staple bound with grey-green paper wrappers.
Front cover with photo of Duncan, title in purple ink; back cover, in bottom right
corner, photo of Duncan reduced in size and reversed with a beaver, looking up at
his face, superimposed on his hand; light green pages with green type.
  [1] title-page; [2] photos of Duncan; [3] note; [4] blank; [5–31] text; [32] publishing information.
  Published November 1971; 500 copies, at 75¢. Co-published by Coach House
Press and Beaver Kosmos. Printed in Toronto at Coach House Press.

Photo of Robert Duncan, printed
in *The Montreal Star*, 1969;
courtesy Warren Tallman

NOTES:
♦ This title is Number 4 in the *Beaver Kosmos
Folio* series, edited by GB, at this time out of
Montreal; see note on this series in B2.
♦ From the note on page 3: "The interview took
place in Duncan's room at the Ritz-Carleton
Hotel in Montreal, the morning after his reading at
Sir George Williams University on April 19, 1969.
In the transcription we have tried to find some
realizable ground between the language the poet
might write & the cellular way he makes phrases
when he talks."
♦ GB recalled that Robert Duncan lost a notebook during his visit: "We had him read in quite a
large theatre room with plush seats, and he was
sitting in the theatre with his scarf on his neck and
his bag before we went up on the stage. He called me from New York and said that
he lost a notebook with all the notes for the poems he was working on. So on
Sunday I went up to the university and found some guy to let me in by proving
who I was (I had really long hair at the time). I remembered where he was sitting so
I went down the bottom right hand part of the theatre and opened up the seat, and
there was Duncan's notebook. And not once did it pass through my mind to call
him back and say, sorry Robert I couldn't find it." [Session 3, 9 May 1988]
♦ GB edited the tape for publication, leaving out some personal things. The tape is
in the GB Papers, NL; see F2.

A17   AUTOBIOLOGY   1972

AUTOBIOLOGY | GEORGE BOWERING | [rule] | [boxed outline of cover photo, Bowering as a child with his mother] | [rule] | Georgia Straight Writing Supplement | Vancouver Series | #7
Pp. [1–6] 7–103 [104]
5¼ x 7⅝ in.; 13.4 x 20.2 cm. Perfect bound in white paper wrappers with black and white photos on front and back. On front, photo of GB as a child sitting on his mother's lap; on back, photo by Jone Payne of GB with his daughter Thea, aged two months.

Unbound press sheet of cover for
Autobiology; GB Papers, NL

[1] half-title; [2] blank; [3] title-page; [4] publishing information and acknowledgements; [5] dedication: Here you are, Gladys. | You too, Ange.; [6] blank; 7–103 text; [104] colophon.

Colophon: Five hundred copies printed | at the York Street Commune | with assistance from the | Canada Council.

Published February 1972, at $1.00.

Titles: The Raspberries—The Teeter Totter—The Pollywogs—The Flying Dream—The Brush Fire—The Verandah—The Dear Path—The Breaks—Some Deaths—The Substance—The Front Yard—The Door—The Gun—Composition—Growing—Place of Birth—The Code—The Trees—Working & Wearing—The Breaks—Come—The Back Yard—It Happened—The Fruit Ranch—Roger Falling—The Childhood—St. Louis—The Lake—The First Two Towns—The Third Town—The Fourth Town—The First City—The Extractions—The Acts—The Next Place—The Pool—Fainting—The Cloves—The Fingers—The Joints—The Clamps—The Dogs—The Flesh—The Spiders—The Operations—It—The Scars—The Body

NOTES:
♦ The text is dated: London, June 12, 1970 | —Vancouver, June 12, 1971.
♦ The series of 48 sections began 12 June 1970: "It was my first book written by hand. Until then I always composed on a typewriter. I was in London, England. A friend of Angela's was married to an Irish guy that she had met in Calgary, and they were living in a section of the northern part of London, an Irish section. We were at their place—we'd been in London for a few days—and I wanted to write something. I was kind of bored sitting around while they were talking, so I thought, I'm wasting all this time, why don't I write something. I sat down and I wrote 'The Raspberries' by pen." [Session 2, 9 March 1988]
    GB continued writing the series after he got back to Montreal, through 1970

Manuscript pages, "The Raspberries," from *Autobiology*; GB Papers, NL

after that day in our front yard
when I was over three years old,
even tho the rasberries always
look't so good with all their round
pieces in a cone or bunch. But there
is a hole inside the rasberry & it
could always have a bug in it.

and 1971, completing it with "The Body" on 12 June 1971, a month after he moved back to Vancouver.

♦ "This was my way back into writing fiction, this book, which really got going again in *A Short Sad Book*." [Session 2, 9 March 1988]

♦ "There's two chapters called 'The Breaks', and when I wrote the second one I didn't know that I had written the first one. Isn't that weird? I'd totally forgotten, because I had a rule that said you're not allowed to read the book until you've finished it." [Session 2, 9 March 1988]

♦ In a letter, 21 November 1973, to the Canada Council reporting on his Arts Award for 1971–72, GB explains that *Autobiology* is "a complete change around in my writing methodology, an important one that is still producing a direction I find most important to me as I had experienced, from 1966 till 1972 a kind of rootlessness, a knowledge that I had made myself proficient in the lyrics I'd written till then, but that there was no impelling need to go on there, no invention." [GB Papers, Correspondence Canada Council, NL]

♦ GB wrote to Dennis Lee, 16 June 1971, only days after the series was completed: "Now I realize just when I'm seeing it off my desk, that it is the first book in a (at least) 3 book work. The next starts almost immediately, soon as I get these few other items out of the way. The second book [i.e. *Curious*] will likely take a year too, and it is going to be about my education as a writer, ahem." [GB Papers, Correspondence Dennis Lee, NL]

♦ GB describes the Vancouver Community Press books, edited by Stan Persky, which began as *Georgia Straight Writing Supplement* books: "Persky's idea for the book series is that the local scene be made clear, here and elsewhere. The books cost a little more than a dollar each and there will be one from each poet who has contributed nonacademically to the city's verse in the past decade. The idea of the city has been of prime importance to the Vancouver poets all that time—maybe because it's the only one we have, maybe because it is so visually definable, and because its shape defines us as it designs our poems, and maybe because without it we would all still be living between the mines and packinghouses in the rest of the province, a few thousand miles from the nearest bookstores and universities." [From "The Art of the Webfoot"; see D623]

♦ GB edited David Cull's Vancouver Community Press book; see B5.

♦ Gladys and Ange in the dedication are Gladys Hindmarch and AB.

♦ When the first edition quickly sold out, a second edition was typeset but never got done because the sheets were lost.

A18   THE SENSIBLE   1972

THE SENSIBLE | George Bowering | Massasauga Editions | 1972
Pp. [1–28]
4¹/₄ x 7 in.; 10.8 x 17.8 cm. Green paper wrappers glued to stapled sheets, with front and back flaps. Back of cover with publisher's device and image of a snake.
[1–2] blank; [3] title-page; [4] copyright; [5] dedication: *for Angela*; [6] blank; [7–23] text; [24] blank; [25] colophon; [26–28] blank.
Colophon: Published in Toronto | in a limited edition | of 200 copies | This is number __.
Published January 1972 [issued September 1972]; at $1.00.

NOTES:
♦ Composed in the fall of 1966 while GB was in London, Ontario; dated as completed 12 December 1966.
♦ Massasauga Editions, conceived and edited by Frank Davey, was a name pointing back to Rattlesnake Press, as implied in a recent letter from Davey [to the author, 26 January 1989]: "No direct connection to 'Rattlesnake Press' except that the Massasauga is a rattlesnake. Just an allusion tossed out for smart guys like you! I may still use the imprimatur again as my personal one. Almost used it for *Postcard Translation*" [by Davey, published by Underwhich Editions, 1988]. For more on Rattlesnake Press, see A1.
♦ Davey's *Griffon* [1972] and bp Nichol's *Scraptures: Basic Sequences* [1973] were also published.

A19   CURIOUS   1973

Curious | George Bowering | [photo of GB and Margaret Atwood] | The Coach House Press 1973
Pp. [1–80]
4⁷/₈ x 8³/₄ in.; 12.3 x 22.2 cm. Perfect bound with light brown paper wrappers covered by grey paper designed to appear as a dust jacket. On front cover, the same photo as on title-page, taken by AB [c. 1970] in front of the house of Margaret Atwood's parents. On front flap, a faint photo of a younger GB, cropped from a photo with Earle Birney; on back flap, a faint current photo of GB, cropped from a photo with Robin Blaser; both photos are reversed in image, but appear in normal perspective in *Curious*.
[1–2] blank; [3] half-title; [4] blank; [5] title-page; [6] publishing information; [7] dedication: This book is for Ewart Bowering & Pearl Bowering, | whose Curiosity got me going in the first place.; [8] epigraph: "Men who love wisdom |

should acquaint themselves | with a great many | particulars." | Heraclitus; [9–56] text; [57] text dated; [58–60] blank; [61–74] photos of writers; [75–80] blank.

Published c. Fall 1973; estimated 750 copies, at $4.00. Printed in Toronto.

Titles: Charles Olson—Ed Dorn—William Carlos Williams—Marianne Moore—Margaret Atwood—Jack Spicer—George Stanley—Gerry Gilbert—Robin Blaser—bpNichol—Stephen Spender—Gladys Hindmarch—John Newlove—Lionel Kearns—Margaret Randall—David McFadden—Robert Creeley—Earle Birney—Raymond Souster—Brian Fawcett—Robert Duncan—Victor Coleman—Denise Levertov—Irving Layton—Stan Persky—Alden Nowlan—Fred Wah—Frank Davey—Lew Welch—George Oppen—Daphne Marlatt—Jamie Reid—Leroi Jones—Allen Ginsberg—Phil Whalen—Al Purdy—Charles Reznikoff—Lawrence Ferlinghetti—James Reaney—D.G. Jones—Phyllis Webb—Margaret Avison—Anselm Hollo—Louis Dudek—Robert Hogg—David Bromige—Michael McClure—Bill Bissett

Curious

George Bowering

The Coach House Press 1973

Title-page, *Curious*

NOTES:

♦ The text begins with "Charles Olson," composed 25 July 1971, and continues through 1971 and 1972, ending with "Bill Bissett," composed 31 October 1972.

♦ GB: "There are 48 pieces, the same number as in *Autobiology*, one of my favourite numbers . . . When I was writing *Curious* I was very aware that this was volume two of *Autobiology*. It came right after, and I was exploring the method. *Autobiology* tends to be the same form of prose in every place, whereas this one plays around. It goes into what could be verse, other times it's straight prose, and other times a mixture, but it takes certain key phrases that were still running through my head when I was writing *Autobiology* and they show up somewhere in *Curious*." [Session 4, 11 May 1988]

♦ Often GB did not choose the writers who became subjects: "Some poets I wanted to get in I never got in, Roy Kiyooka for instance, and there are other poets I didn't particularly want but here they were, like W. H. Auden [in 'Stephen Spender']." [Session 4, 11 May 1988]

♦ To respect the serial mode of composition, the pieces were published in the order written.

♦ The title "'Curious' means careful, like the 'curious peach'—from Marvell's 'Garden'—which means very careful work. It's about poetry, so I used that word, but it also works in that other sense of 'curious', as 'What's going on here?' " GB worked back through his own life in *Autobiology*, so now he could look out at the autobiologies of other writers. [Session 4, 11 May 1988]

GB with Earle Birney in Dinosaur Park, Calgary, 1964; from *Curious*

♦ GB had met or seen every writer in the series, except William Carlos Williams, though he did once receive a letter from Flossie Williams.

♦ The same method of composition was used as for *Autobiology*: the manuscript was written by hand, then typed up with the line length determined by the size of the page.

♦ GB took photos of Ed Dorn, Margaret Atwood ("in our bedroom on Balaclava Street" in Vancouver), George Stanley (in their communal house on York Avenue in Vancouver), bp Nichol and Warren Tallman (at an art gallery in Vancouver), Gladys Hindmarch (on York Avenue), John Newlove (in his house "in the east end out by the race track in Toronto"), Robin Blaser (in his garden in West Vancouver), Lionel Kearns with AB (in Michael Macklem's kitchen in Ottawa), David McFadden (at Lake Erie), Margaret Randall (in her yard in Mexico), Earle Birney with Robert Hogg's head (in Macklem's kitchen), Brian Fawcett with son Jesse (on York Avenue), Robert Duncan (at Frank Davey's house in Toronto), Victor Coleman (at Davey's house), Stan Persky (on York Avenue), Fred and Pauline Wah (in front of the York Avenue house), Daphne Marlatt with Stan Hoffman (at GB's apartment in Montreal), Jamie Reid with his wife Carol (in Calgary "down at the museum in the park"), Al Purdy by his outhouse (at his place in Ameliasburg, Ontario), James Reaney ("during the Nihilist Party of Canada picnic in London, Ontario"), D. G. Jones (at Macklem's place), Anselm Hollo (at the State University of NY, at Buffalo), Robert Hogg, and David Bromige.

GB with Gerry Gilbert on the ferry to Sechelt, 1968, from *Curious*

AB took the photo of Gerry Gilbert with GB ("on the ferry to Sechelt") and GB with Earle Birney ("under the dinosaur in Dinosaur Park in Calgary"). [Session 4, 11 May 1988]

♦ When Margaret Atwood wrote to GB about the book, GB replied, 12 June 1974: "Now what makes ya say *Cur.* was wickid and evil and funny? Tch, tch. I just see it as a series of results of meditations, and I cant be responsible for them, can I? I mean there I am, a honed medium and they visit me, & if some angry poet bashes me, it's not fair, because I'd be but a victim of the other World and its Voices." [GB Papers, Correspondence Margaret Atwood, NL]

♦ Ewart and Pearl Bowering are GB's parents.

♦ The following appears on the acknowledgements page: "The characters in this book are all creations of the author's imagination. Any resemblances to actual people, living or dead, are coincidental."

♦ This book, with *Autobiology*, "completes a trilogy consciously begun in Montreal in 1970, with the volume, *Geneve*. I believe that the form I learned to come into in that trilogy had re-formed me and my career, and that now I have cleared the way to return to 'fiction'—a mode I had despaired of (publicly) since the reading of Beckett's *The Unnameable*." [GB Papers, Correspondence Canada Council, 21 November 1973, NL]

A20   AT WAR WITH THE U. S.   1974

AT WAR WITH THE U. S. | George Bowering
 Pp. [1–48]
 6 x 5¹⁵/₁₆ in.; 15.2 x 15.1 cm. Perfect bound with white paper wrappers. Cover by Greg Curnoe with black line drawing of a Canadian plane (red maple leaves on its wings) firing on and hitting the rear of an American plane.
 [1–2] blank; [3] half-title; [4] blank; [5] title-page; [6] publishing information; [7] dedication: *for Frank Davey*; [8] blank; [9–43] text; [46] text dated; [47–48] blank.
 Published by Talonbooks, January 1974; 500 copies, at $3.00. Printed in Vancouver.
 Titles: 1–13—Letter to Richard Nixon—14–34

NOTES:
♦ Text is dated: Jan 11/73–Aug 15/73.
♦ August 15 was the day the U. S. bombing of Cambodia stopped: "So the war was over but the reason the poem ends there is because the booklet that I was writing it in ended there." GB wrote the sequence in a notebook brought back from Japan by his artist friend Roy Kiyooka, one section per page, "except for that letter to Nixon which was on a bigger piece of paper, that I jammed in [the sequence], and that's why it doesn't have a number." August 15 was also the day GB and AB moved from Balaclava Street in Vancouver to a house in Kerrisdale on 37th Avenue (where they continue to live). "All those three things came together at once." [Session 4, 11 May 1988]

Front cover, *At War with the U. S.*

♦ The Greg Curnoe drawing, taken from David McFadden's *The Great Canadian Sonnet* (1970), reflected the anti-American climate of the times: "The things that the Americans were doing were getting more and more outrageous, but the bombing of Cambodia was just awful. The Cambodian civil war was hardly even going; there were a few Khmer Rouge in the top right corner of Cambodia, but they weren't getting anywhere, until the Americans bombed the place. Everybody

hated the American invasion of Vietnam but the bombing of Cambodia was even worse; it was somehow even more atrocious. And I liked the idea that I was writing the book in a notebook that came from Asia; it had been carried from Asia across the ocean to here and then I could write on it." [Session 4, 11 May 1988]
♦ "This is the first daybook kind of poem I'd ever written, and it might have to do with the fact that I was writing it sitting in a second floor room looking out the window from which I could see Broadway, Balaclava, and 10th Avenue. I could see a lot going on from that window, and so a lot of the time the stuff I can see gets in." [Session 4, 11 May 1988]

A21   IN THE FLESH   1974

IN THE FLESH | George Bowering | McClelland and Stewart Limited
     Pp. [1–7] 8–9 [10] 11–112
     5¹³/₁₆ x 8¹⁵/₁₆ in.; 14.7 x 22.7 cm. Perfect bound with white paper wrappers. Cover with title in bold blue letters, with GEORGE above the title and BOWERING below in turquoise letters, separated by magenta lines. On back, photo of GB and his daughter Thea, with a publisher's blurb and statements on GB. Photo by AB.
     [1] half-title; [2] blank; [3] title-page; [4] publishing information; [5] dedication: dedicated to Thea Claire, who arrived just then; and epigraph: "For the mind in time | Is a perishing bird, | It sings and is still."; [6–7] contents; 8–9 preface; [10] blank; 11–111 text; 112 acknowledgements.
     Published 28 January 1974; 2,500 copies, at $2.95.
     Titles: I Never Felt Such Love [Preface to *In the Flesh*]—Mountain I Burn—That Way, in Words—Barber Chair—Midnight Lunch—Motel Age Thoughts—Brown Globe—More Dust—The Bars—The Bigamist—The Window—Open Mind—Nine Holes—Among Friends—Apollo Eleven—The Cup—Coltrane & Che—Health—Weight—That Old Testament—Gun Man—Little Treatise on Time—Already Markt—Making a Virtue of Necessity—Arrival Time—I Cant Concentrate—Losing & Getting, to Be Getting—The Horse—Apparent—Frame—Sit Down—Building—Strangers & Friends—Prizren—Under—Feet, Not Eyes—The Ground of Lincoln County—Even the Public Conveyances Sing—North Shore, PEI—Thoughts off the Concrete Isle—Sea Way—First Night of Fall, Grosvenor Ave—Fall, Again—Place Names in the Global Village—Branches for Ron Loewinsohn—Smoking Drugs with Strangers—When I—Stab—Lines from Hollo—Fast—Not Salesmen—Out—Indulgence—Take Me, She Said, Smiling Inwardly—Chap ter—Play's a Thing—Ascension—Careering—The Breath, Release—The Mysteries—The Beginning of—While—A Man Is No Boat—Mouths—Sekhemab & Perabsen—The Sensible—To You & You

"...undeniable merit."
Al Purdy, *Canadian Literature*

"...powerful and polished."
Doug Fetherling, *Globe and Mail*

"...a poet firmly in possession of his individual voice."
Stephen Scobie, *Edmonton Journal*

Master of lyric verse, of fresh and startling imagery, Governor-General's Award winner George Bowering writes with poise and assurance, lifting language out of the ordinary, transforming speech into a delicate, sonorous music.

$2.95
0-7710-1598-4

McClelland and Stewart Limited
The Canadian Publishers

Back cover, *In the Flesh*

NOTES:

♦ The poems were composed from December 1964 to June 1971, with the majority during 1968–70. "To You & You" was written as a "l'envoi" for this collection.

♦ John Newlove was the house editor for McClelland and Stewart.

♦ From GB's Preface, "I Never Felt Such Love," dated March 1972: "The following collection is made of magazine verse written after I turned thirty. It seems to me to be not of a piece necessarily, but of a period that was entered upon & is done with. For already in my early thirties I was no longer writing magazine verse, or occasional verse. Nearly all the poems I have written in the past few years have been a book long. When I'm kidding around I refer to this present as my symphonic period. But not really kidding—you know that."

♦ GB recalled the unusual mode of composing one poem, "When I": "Nobody ever reads it, or knows about it. I took Milton's sonnet on blindness, xeroxed a whole pile of copies, and just started seeing what I could make by crossing out words." [Session 4, 11 May 1988]

♦ "The Sensible" was published as a pamphlet; see A18.

♦ GB recalled that McClelland and Stewart had a publishing hierarchy for their poets: those who could publish a book every year (e. g. Irving Layton, Earle Birney, and Al Purdy); those who could publish every two years (e. g. GB and John Newlove); and those who could publish every three years (e. g. David McFadden).

♦ The epigraph was drawn from D. G. Jones' poem "The Perishing Bird."

A22   LAYERS 1–13   1974

LAYERS 1–13 | George Bowering | Weed Flower Press | Toronto 1973
    Pp. [1–6] 7–19 [20]
    5 x 8¹/₂ in.; 12.7 x 21.5 cm. Staple bound with light grey paper wrappers. Cover with vertical layers of thick black lines. Cover drawing and design by Barbara Caruso.
    [1] half-title; [2] blank; [3] title-page; [4] acknowledgements and copyright; [5] dedication: for Greg Curnoe; [6] blank; 7–19 text; [20] blank.
    Published 31 May 1974 [copyright 1973]; 450 copies, at $1.50.
    Titles: 1–13

LAYERS 1·13

GEORGE   BOWERING

NOTES:
♦ The poems were composed over a period of years: numbers 1 to 4 during January and February 1966 in Calgary; number 5 in January 1967 in London, Ontario; numbers 6 to 12 in January and February 1968 and number 13 in February 1971, all in Montreal.
♦ GB sent Nelson Ball the manuscript on 17 April 1971. [GB Papers, Correspondence Nelson Ball, NL]
♦ GB: "I was at that time figuring out various ways to make a sequence of poems, so there was *Rocky Mountain Foot*, a suite of poems, and there was this. These poems are side glances cast on various people." [Session 6, 25 May 1988]

Front cover, *Layers 1–13*

A23   FLYCATCHER AND OTHER STORIES   1974

a. Cloth issue:
[black and white photos of people with their hands wrapped around their heads clutching various parts of their faces] FLYCATCHER | & Other Stories | George Bowering
    Pp. [1–4] 5–114 [115–116]
    5 x 7¹⁵/₁₆ in.; 12.7 x 20.2 cm. Casebound with brown boards. Dust jacket cover and spine with same image as on title-page, but centre figure is in colour and the surrounding photos are purple. On back, photo of GB as a teenager, with publisher's blurb. Design by Michael Macklem. Cover by General Idea, Courtesy of the Department of External Affairs travelling print collection.
    [1–2] blank; [3] title-page; [4] dedication: For Margaret Laurence, because she knows how is what; and epigraph: each of us like you | has died once, | each of us like you | stands apart, like you | fit to be worshipped.; 5–114 text; [115] publishing information, acknowledgements, and author's

FLYCATCHER
& Other Stories

George Bowering

Front cover, *Flycatcher and Other Stories*

note: no, Delsing hasn't yet found Ebbe, but he is still look- I ing & why not?; [116] blank.

Published by Oberon Press, September 1974; 550 copies, at $6.95. Printed in Canada by Hunter Rose Company.

Titles: The Elevator—Looking for Ebbe—Flycatcher—Ricardo and the Flower—Time and Again—Ebbe & Hattie—Wild Grapes & Chlorine—Constantinople Boots—How Delsing Met Frances & Started to Write a Novel—The Xalapa Handkerchief—Apples

b. Paper issue: as A23a, but perfect bound with paper wrappers having same design; 850 copies, at $3.50.

NOTES:

♦ Oberon accepted GB's manuscript in March 1973. Gail Low was editor for the press. [Oberon Papers, Queen's University Archives]

♦ The cover photo by General Idea is a reproduction of a lithograph, "Manipulating the Scene," published by Galerie B (Montreal) in 1973. [Oberon Papers, Queen's University Archives]

♦ The photo on back, of GB as a teenager reading *How to Win Friends and Influence People,* was probably taken by his sister Sally.

♦ GB dedicated this book to Margaret Laurence because, unlike most other Canadian fiction writers, she paid attention to language form: "I found this very unCanadian. That was part of the old fight with *Tish.*" [Session 15, 8 June 1989]

♦ The epigraph comes from H. D.'s poem "Adonis."

♦ Three stories were taken from an unfinished novel about Jamie Reid, a friend from the *Tish* days in Vancouver, called "Looking for Ebbe": "Looking for Ebbe," "Ebbe and Hattie," and "Wild Grapes & Chlorine." The note on the back, "no, Delsing hasn't yet found Ebbe, but he is still looking & why not?" implies that GB intended to finish the novel. "How Delsing Met Frances & Started to Write a Novel" was taken from GB's unpublished first novel, "Delsing," written c. 1959–61 while he was a student at UBC. "Constantinople Boots" is a revision of material taken from an unpublished travelogue, "Eye-Kicks in Europe," written in May and June 1966 during GB's first trip to Europe.

♦ Many stories belong to GB's "Lawrence" stories, the fictional name for Oliver, the small town in BC where he grew up. "Nobody else has written fiction about the Okanagan Valley, so I keep coming back to it." Along with "How Delsing Met Frances & Started to Write a Novel," other Lawrence stories include "Flycatcher," "Time and Again," and "Apples."

Why the name Lawrence? "I called it Lawrence because in those days you always took the names of places and changed them, but you changed them in such a way that they'll be recognizable. So Oliver is a man's first name or last name, and Lawrence is a man's first name or last name." [Session 14, 14 May 1989]

♦ "A lot of people thought, before they read this, that 'flycatcher' is a baseball title, but that's stupid. You don't call anybody a flycatcher in baseball. The term is never used." [Session 14, 14 May 1989]

A24   ALLOPHANES   1976

Αλλοphαηες | George Bowering | The Coach House Press Toronto
Pp. [1–56]
4¹/4 x 7¹⁵/16 in.; 10.8 x 20.2 cm. Perfect bound with light blue paper wrappers folded as a dust jacket with flaps; title, in Greek type, and author's name in dark blue; showing through a triangular opening cut in the front wrapper are lines of hieroglyphic-like script symbols on the back side of the folded-in front flap. On front flap, a photo of GB with a publisher's blurb on the composition of the text.
[1] half-title; [2] blank; [3] title-page; [4] publishing information; [5] dedication: for Robin Blaser; [6] blank; [7–55] text; [56] blank.
Published 1976; 1,000 copies, at $3.50.
Titles: I—II—III—IV—V—VI—VII (labor, life, literature) (the gods)—VIII—IX—X—XI (the egg-ziled gods)—XII—XIII—XIV—XV—XVI—XVII—XVIII The fruitful void. Athanor.—XIX *factum*—XX—XXI *Simon Magus*—XXII—XXIII—XXIV Diaspora—XXV—XXVI Dispersoid

NOTES:
♦ GB's datebook indicates that he received this book in March 1977, so the date of issue is probably early 1977.
♦ Text is dated at end: 1974–75.
♦ The 26 sections of the text were composed in handwritten form between 15 September and 8 December 1974, during an undergraduate course given by Robin Blaser at SFU in the fall semester—13 weeks, 2 lectures per week, that is, 26 lectures.
♦ GB: "It began with a sentence heard in the author's head: The snowball appears in Hell every morning at seven. It was said in the voice of Jack Spicer.
"The author knew something was up, & went deliberately to hear some more voices as best he could, & hurried to write down what they were saying. Astute readers will recognize some of them.
"Allo means all. Phanes means appearances. The poem tries not to get one without the other. The scientific usage of the term attends the shifting colours of mineral formations, such as stalactites, lights in a cave.
"The word could also be translated as those things which are other than what they at first appear to be, all taken together." [From "Look into Your Ear & Write: Allophanes"; see C128]
♦ "I happened to hear [Spicer's] voice when I was going to a series of lectures that Robin Blaser was giving on Yeats and Joyce, but mainly Yeats. And I heard it while

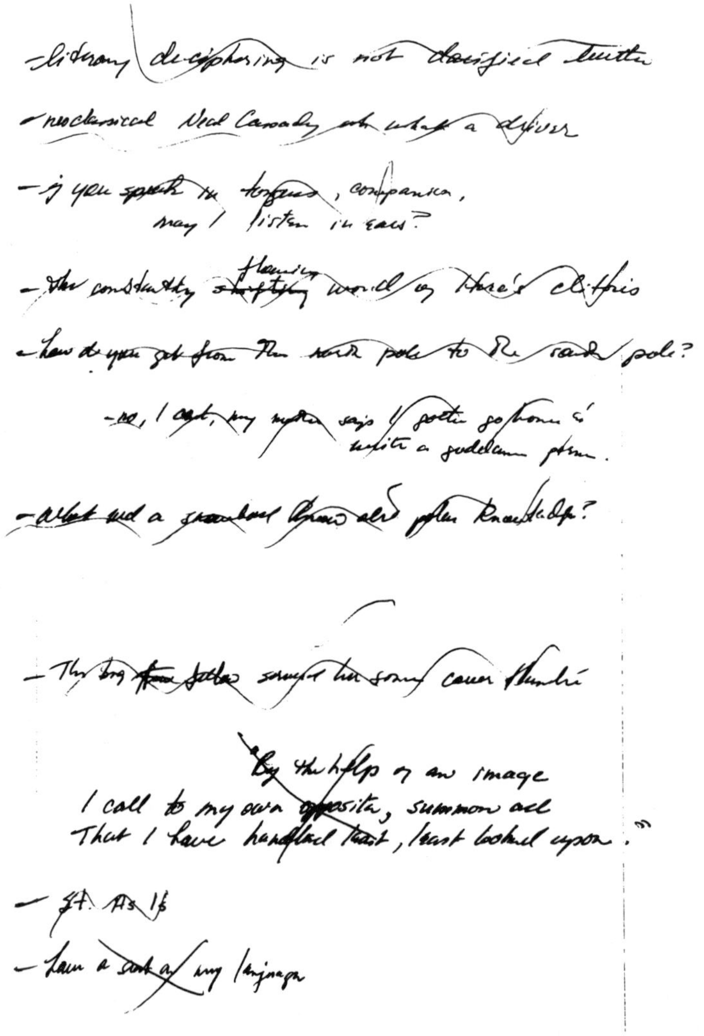
– literary deciphering is not classified truth

– neoclassical Neal Cassady oh what a driver

– if you speak in tongues, companero,
may I listen in ears?

– the constantly flaming world of Heraclitus

– how do you get from the north pole to the south pole?

– no, I can't, my mother says I gotta go home & write a goddamn poem.

– [illegible]

– [illegible]

"By the help of an image
I call to my own opposite, summon all
That I have handled least, least looked upon."

– [illegible]

– [illegible]

Manuscript page, *Allophanes*: notes for section IV; GB Papers, NL

Manuscript page, *Allophanes*: draft of section IV; GB Papers, NL

IV

Literary deciphering is not clarified butter.

By the help of an image
I call to my own opposite, summon all
that I have handled least, least lookt upon.

Have a seat on my language,
& here we go,

lecherously, thru the flowing world
of Hera's clitoris.

With a neo classical
Neal Cassady, what a driver!

How do we get from the north pole
to the south pole?

& what would a snowball
know about polar knowledge?

Drive right past that lady, that's
St. As Is.   No, lady, sorry, my mother
says I gotta come home write a god damn poem.

Look, the big fellow just served her
some *coeur flambé*.

Printed text, *Allophanes*: IV

I was sitting there so I started writing. I guess everyone thought I was just taking notes from the lecture. The pages were funny because the writing was just all over, the poem was not declaring itself in lines. The voice would come and then another voice, the poem's full of voices. And clearly some of the things Robin was saying as he was going along sparked something that went into the poem. I wasn't writing quotations from what he was saying at all, but things he said were triggering off something that I'd been reading. So that whole poem, which is 26 sections long, was all written during the lectures that I attended for his course that fall, the whole poem. I mean, *there* was a dictated poem from the guy who talked about dictation. Spicer dictated it. Then it took me about a month to twig to the fact that Spicer's *After Lorca*, a serial poem, was made up of letters that the dead poet Lorca had been writing to Spicer." [From "Bowering on GB's *Particular Accidents*"; see D843]

♦ GB, 30 October 1974, to Victor Coleman: "Here's ample warning; after a year of nopoem writing, I seem to have started on a verrry obscure what you'sd call a serial poem. It is so obscure that I already cant remember what some of the stuff comes from, and some I never did know. It goes all over the large page, and I think it might be shorter than it started off to be, like it might be just around 25 installments instead of the 40 I once feared. They are installments, in fact that was at one time what I thought the title might be. Now I dont know what it might be. The subject seems to be the history of western thought." [GB Papers, Correspondence Victor Coleman, NL]

A25   POEM AND OTHER BASEBALLS   1976

Poem and Other Baseballs | [drawing, on right side, of a sad-faced boy with a catcher's mitt on his left hand, a swollen thumb on his right hand, and a bandage on a toe] | George Bowering | Black Moss Press

Pp. [1–6] 7–44 [45–48]

$5^5/_{16}$ x $7^{15}/_{16}$ in.; 13.5 x 20.2 cm. Perfect bound with white paper wrappers. Cover with same drawing as on title-page, except that the bandage on the toe is orange.

[1] half-title; [2] blank; [3] title-page; [4] publishing information, and dedication: This expanded, second edition, is still dedicated to Jack Spicer. Also | Fielding Dawson, Joel Oppenheimer, Paul Blackburn, Raymond Souster, | Hanford Woods, and Tom Clark. Also Bobby Wine; [5] epigraph: "And as long as the old game lasts you'll hear | Of the midnight slide of P. Revere." | —*Grantland Rice*; [6] blank; 7–44 text; [45–46] blank; [47] acknowledgements; [48] blank.

Published September 1976; 700 copies, at $3.95. Printed in Erin, Ontario by Porcupine's Quill.

Titles: A Meta Physic in Things [excerpt]—Pennant Drive—The Day Before the Chinese A-Bomb—AB: The Pope—Elementary School, Oak Lake, Mani-

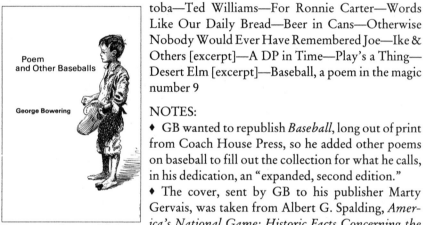

toba—Ted Williams—For Ronnie Carter—Words Like Our Daily Bread—Beer in Cans—Otherwise Nobody Would Ever Have Remembered Joe—Ike & Others [excerpt]—A DP in Time—Play's a Thing—Desert Elm [excerpt]—Baseball, a poem in the magic number 9

NOTES:

♦ GB wanted to republish *Baseball*, long out of print from Coach House Press, so he added other poems on baseball to fill out the collection for what he calls, in his dedication, an "expanded, second edition."

♦ The cover, sent by GB to his publisher Marty Gervais, was taken from Albert G. Spalding, *Amer-ica's National Game: Historic Facts Concerning the Beginning, Evolution, Development and Popularity of Base Ball With Personal Reminiscences of Its Vicis-situdes, Its Victories and Its Votaries*; cartoons by Homer C. Davenport (NY: American Sports Publishing Company, 1911). The book was given to GB by Artie Gold. Another drawing from it was used on the title-page of *Imago 20*; see B6.

Front cover, *Poem and Other Baseballs*

A26   THE CATCH   1976

THE CATCH | George Bowering | McClelland and Stewart
Pp. [1–8] 9 [10–12] 13–42 [43–44] 45–92 [93–94] 95–126 [127] 128
5⁷/₈ x 9 in.; 14.9 x 22.9 cm. Perfect bound with mustard paper wrappers. Cover with photo of orange and white fishing boat; on back, photo of GB and publisher's blurb. Cover design by Michael van Elsen.
[1] half-title; [2] blank; [3] title-page; [4] publishing information; [5] dedication: For Margaret Avison; [6] titles by GB; [7–8] contents; 9 preface; [10] blank; [11]–126 text; [127] blank; 128 acknowledgements.

Published 6 November 1976; 2,400 copies, at $4.95.

Titles: Preface [to *The Catch*]—*George, Vancouver*—*Autobiology*—CE-REALS FOR ROUGHAGE: Summer Solstice—Desert Elm—Reconsiderations—AW 1, Oct 5, 1973—AW 2, Oct 10, 1973—AW 3, Jan 5, 1974—AW 4, Mar 5, 1974—AW 5, May 5, 1974—AW 6, May 25, 1974—AW 7, Aug 4, 1974—AW 8, Aug 17, 1974—AW 9, Sep 4, 1974 Thea

NOTES:

♦ Anna Porter of McClelland and Stewart informed GB, 3 April 1975, that *The Catch* was accepted for publication, in part based on a strong recommendation by Paul Dutton, but the middle section of the manuscript, "Sousterre" [see A40], should be replaced with something else. On 16 June 1975, GB suggested that *Autobiology* be included instead, and explained: "It has never been read much by Eastern and more general readers, being done here in mimeo three years ago. I am also very high on it, and consider that I will stand on it in years to come." Porter was hesitant because for her the work was prose, not poetry, so would create a mixed book that might be hard to market. GB responded, 31 July 1975: "Recognize yr hestitation re *Autobiology*, but wd Instruct that the distinction is not really between prose and poetry but between prose and verse. Poetry can be in both prose or verse. Verse has to do with the making of lines, i.e. coming back to the margin at times, etc, while poetry has essentially to do with how one treats or is treated by the language regarding what he wants his reader to do. That is, prose directs one toward the world he presumably [is] already in, and poetry invites him into a world, a new one. Or as Hulme had it, prose is a train that tries to get you to a destination, and poetry is a pedestrian, who steps and sees every bit of the way. Well. In any case *Autobiology* is poetry, the kind of poetry I workt out that leads directly to another of my favorite poems, 'Desert Elm'." [McClelland and Stewart Papers, McMaster University]

♦ Denise Avery was the house editor for this book.

♦ The title was GB's, but then "they decided to do a boat on the front, that sense of catch. Well, it has a lot of different meanings. The preface talks about fishing though, so it makes some kind of sense, I guess, but I hadn't thought of it only that way." [Session 5, 16 May 1988]

GB wrote to Denise Avery, 22 August 1976, about the cover: "I was a little trepidatious of the scenic-ness as described, but think the design is swell." [McClelland and Stewart Papers, McMaster University]

♦ "Desert Elm" remains one of GB's most important poems: "The whole poem deals with H. D., my favourite poet. I've dedicated lots of my books to her and I think she is the best model of how to make verses, how to make language. And it's about my father. This was before he died but after he had a heart attack." [From "Bowering on GB's *Particular Accidents*"; see D843] Its 10 sections were composed during September and October 1973, a month after GB's father had a heart attack.

A27   IN ANSWER   1977

[no title-page; on cover] George Bowering | IN ANSWER [space] (to a question from the gathering
Pp. [1–4]
8¹/₂ x 11 in.; 21.5 x 28 cm. Hand stitched in green paper wrappers with the cover used as the title-page.
[1–3] text; [4] colophon.
Colophon: Published by William Hoffer and the author | for their friends | New Year 1977 | 60 copies printed
Published in Vancouver, no price.

NOTES:
♦ Text is dated: 1967, 1976.
♦ 15 copies were numbered and signed by GB.
♦ Published in *Smoking Mirror*; see A40.

A28   THE CONCRETE ISLAND   1977

THE CONCRETE ISLAND | Montreal Poems 1967–71 | George Bowering | [device] Véhicule Press | Montréal, Canada
Pp. [1–64]
4³/₄ x 6⁵/₈ in.;12.1 x 16.8 cm. Perfect bound with white paper wrappers. Cover with cartoon drawing of Montreal set up on a block of concrete on a blue sea with grey land and background. Cover design by Rick Fischer.
[1–2] blank; [3] half-title; [4] publishing information; [5] title-page; [6] dedication: for Artie Gold & Dwight Gardiner | found, around, there.; [7–8] preface; [9] blank; [10–58] text; [59] blank; [60] acknowledgements and titles by GB; [61] colophon; [62–64] blank.
Colophon: Printed & published in an edition of 500 | March 1977 by Véhicule Press, P.O. Box 125, | Station 'G', Montreal, Canada.
Sold at $3.00.
Titles: Preface [to *The Concrete Island*]—Knocking—The Imperial West—Summer Snow—White, Unseen—The Plains of Abraham—No Solitudes—Under the Spreading Chestnut Legs—Time Capsule—Revenge Against Lou the Dud—City Stones (for Charles Reznikoff)—Man with Broom—Ranchero—This Time—The Rites of Passage, Book of the Real—Classic Poetry & Its Laws—It's

There, You Can't Deny It—Where I Am—Steak & Gravy—School Girl Crush—
Three Days on the River Island—Beardsley—Montreal Poets, 1968—The Other
Poet's—Silver & Gold, the Trees—How to Be—Daniel Johnson Lying in State—
Aloha—In the Elevator—Hands & Nets—Riding the 24 Bus East—Driving
Upper Westmount—Getting Off the 24 Bus—Derelicts in the Metro Station—
Mandatory Spring Poem—Late Spring, New Week—In the Heart of Jewish
Montreal (for Curnoe etc)—Flesh Cushion—Otherwise Nobody Would Ever

Have Remembered Joe—First New England Jag—
A DP in Time—Okay, Layton Etc., Women Like
Poems—Safe in Westmount—I Take—Montreal,
Oct 1970—Bus Step—Coming to Montreal from
Vancouver

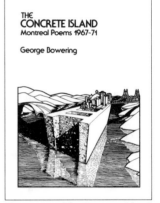

NOTES:
♦ The poems were composed during the period
from September 1968 to January 1971, with the vast
majority (21 of the 25 poems) written in 1968–69.
♦ "Véhicule Press was carrying on, in the early 70s,
the tradition of small presses of the kind that we all
love and admire. When they asked me for a book, I
said, well what can I gather together to give them a
book of? What I did was take the poems set and

Front cover, *The Concrete Island*

written in Montreal that had never been published in my other books." [Session 5,
16 May 1988]
♦ From the Preface, dated November 1975: "As I read the poems now I hear that
I wasnt really there when I was writing. Simply, many of them compare the Coast
to that concrete. Many of the others reflect rather than absorbing, detailing a daily
life bereft of muthos. It's a true story, in other words.
   "I love Montreal but it is so slight, so young, so much younger than the bearded
West Coast. So it's fitting, perhaps, that these desperate poems, seeking the lost
assurances of a young poet's method, should take Montreal as their neighbor-
hood."

A29   A SHORT SAD BOOK   1977

A | SHORT | SAD | BOOK | a novel by George Bowering | Talonbooks,
Vancouver, 1977
   Pp. [1–14] 15–39 [40–42] 43–68 [69–70] 71–103 [104–106] 107–136 [137–138]
139–168 [169–170] 171–185 [186] 187–191 [192]
   5⁹/₁₆ x 8³/₈ in.; 14 x 21.3 cm. Perfect bound with white paper wrappers, title in
blue, and GB's name in red. Cover with drawing by Greg Curnoe of former

A SHORT SAD BOOK
George Bowering

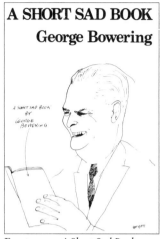

Front cover, *A Short Sad Book*

Premier of British Columbia, W. A. C. Bennett, laughing while reading *A Short Sad Book*, dated 6 September 1977. On back, photo of GB by Roger D. Bowering and publisher's blurb. Book design by David Robinson.

[1] half-title; [2] blank; [3] title-page; [4] publishing information; [5] epigraph: "Under our gaze, the simple gesture of holding out I our hand becomes bizarre, clumsy; the words we I hear ourselves speaking suddenly sound false; the I time of our minds is no longer that of the clocks; & I the style of a novel, in its turn, can no longer be I innocent." I Alain Robbe-Grillet (1954); [6] blank; [7] author's note: Dear Reader Reading: I 1. Please take your time. I 2. Also there is one dream in the following pages. I You should be able to find it.; [8] blank; [9] acknowledgements and dedication: This book is dedicated to Old Port Tipped Cigar- I illos & Murchie's coffee, without whose help it I would not have been written.; [10] blank; [11] half-title; [12] blank; [13]–185 text; [186] blank; 187–191 index; [192] publisher's titles.

Published September 1977; 2,000 copies, at $5.95. Printed in Vancouver by Hemlock Printers.

NOTES:

♦ The text was composed in Vancouver during one year, beginning 8 July 1975 and ending 28 July 1976.

♦ GB first offered the manuscript to McClelland and Stewart but was not surprised by their negative response to its form. He replied to their rejection letter: "Don't worry about saying no to *A Short Sad Book*. I didn't really expect M&S to be interested; but thought I had better send it in to be lookt at because of that little clause in the contract for the last book etc. I recognize that it is really a small press book, & I expect Talonbooks to do a little run of it in the Fall. It is appropriate that a Vancouver press do it, I suppose, and David Robinson had been asking to do a book." [GB Papers, Correspondence McClelland and Stewart, 29 March 1977, NL]

♦ The novel was handwritten in two three-ring notebooks, one chapter per writing session; each chapter was written on two pages.

♦ After completing chapter XXIII (February 1976), GB went on his spring tour, using the manuscript as his material for readings in eastern Canada. In Montreal, after reading what he had written so far, he was challenged by someone in the audience and the interchange was literally incorporated into the next chapter. The idea of bringing things into the text while writing was part of his mode of

Excerpt from manuscript page, *A Short Sad Book*, Chapter XXIV; GB Papers, NL

composition: "Everything keeps coming in, like Gertrude Stein, that famous one when her dog walked in and she dropped the word 'basket', her dog's name, into what she was writing. There's all kinds of instances when I hear something at the door and it comes in, or something goes by the window and it goes in. There's all kinds of secret stuff. In the section 'The Pretty Good Canadian Novel', there are paragraphs taken straight out of so-called great Canadian novels and just fired into the text, because they're so silly. I just picked them at random. Nobody has ever said anything about the fact that I plagiarized a paragraph out of Hugh MacLennan, a paragraph out of Mazo De la Roche, a paragraph out of Morley Callaghan, a paragraph out of Ernest Buckler, etc." [Session 14, 14 May 1989]
♦ While on his reading tour, GB was interviewed (4 March 1976) by Caroline Bayard and Jack David for *Out-Posts*; the novel-in-progress was very much on his mind as he talked about its "Canadian" content:
  "CB: What are the figure heads in Canadian history that interest you?"
  "GB: Who seems to be taking over a lot is Evangeline, from Longfellow's poem, and John A. MacDonald. Right now they're having a kind of a curious love affair on the West Coast . . . ."
  "JD: Do they get along together?"
  "GB: Yeah, they make it at one point. It's very strange. The novel itself seems to be the main character. But I don't know what's going to happen. They come up and they go away." [See C113]
♦ GB on the Gertrude Stein connection: ". . . only one person in a review ever mentioned that *A Short Sad Book* is a title that takes from *A Long Gay Book* in which Gertrude Stein . . . was writing a book that involved her sexuality. But what that would suggest immediately was that whereas 'gay' means homosexual, then 'sad' must mean heterosexual. And I sort of half believe that half don't . . . . In *A*

Short Sad Book there are female characters and male characters, and male characters and male characters, and most of the relationships between men and women in it are political relationships." [From "14 Plums"; see D748]

♦ Designer David Robinson suggested a ragged right margin, but GB felt this design could create a confusion of genre, as he explained in a letter, 19 January 1976: "I really have thought of this book as having justified right margin. I dont want readers to think of it as a KIND OF poetry any more than necessary, i. e. my constant insistence that it is a novel has to be a reinforced item, it is so important to the argument or philosophy or whatever big words I'm searching for re the text. Actually, here's my other thought: the bigger the type the better, up to a point (get it?)." [Talonbooks Papers, SFU]

♦ GB in a letter to Margaret Randall, 19 January 1976: "I am currently engaged on a book about me and Canada, a kind of love story. It is dictated writing again. I believe that only dictated writing can be in any way revolutionary, and they can argue about the source of the dictation. Nothing to do with dictator. I believe that the social realists are wrong when they abjure dictated writing and are in favor of fully controlled poetry using the approved vocabulary. The approved vocabulary will always be the only place where the protectors of the old way can be sure of control. A faith in poetry that springs from what the bourgeois call the subconscious but is really the frontiers of the creative mind, is what I want. That is the same as a trust and faith in the positive possibilities of man." [GB Papers, Correspondence Margaret Randall, NL]

♦ Dedicated to Murchie's coffee and Old Port Tipped Cigarillos, one cigarillo for each session, both of which were necessary companions for each writing session (that is, for each chapter).

A30   CONCENTRIC CIRCLES   1977

a. Cloth issue:
CONCENTRIC | CIRCLES | GEORGE BOWERING | Black Moss Press
   Pp. [1–8] 9–66 [67–72]
$4^1/4$ x $6^7/8$ in.; 10.7 x 17.5 cm. Casebound with green boards. White dust jacket with black and white photo of GB, taken by Marty Gervais; publisher's blurb on back cover.
   [1–2] blank; [3] half-title; [4] blank; [5] title-page; [6] publishing information; [7] half-title; [8] blank; 9–66 text; [67–72] blank.
   Published in Coatsworth, Ontario in September 1977; 200 copies, at $8.00. Printed in Erin, Ontario by Porcupine's Quill.

b. Paper issue: as A30a, but perfect bound with paper wrappers having same design as on dust jacket; 800 copies, at $2.40.

NOTES:

♦ Composed first as a play at UBC, c. 1960–61, and reworked as a novella in the late 1960s.

♦ GB recalled the absurdist content of the novella: "I really like the idea of a guy named Brown who wants to paint everything in the world brown—he paints the entire room brown—whereas this other guy Mel is carrying a bomb. And there are newspapers all over the floor—piled up about 3 feet deep." [Session 5, 16 May 1988]

Front cover, *Concentric Circles*

A31   PROTECTIVE FOOTWEAR   1978

PROTECTIVE | FOOTWEAR | [subtitle and names in lined box] stories and fables by | George Bowering | McCLELLAND AND STEWART
    Pp. [1–8] 9–175 [176]
    5¼ x 8 in.; 13.3 x 20.3 cm. Perfect bound with black paper wrappers. Title in outline type, designed in red, orange, yellow and white; on back, a publisher's statement, and in bottom left corner, two orange footprints enclosed in broken red lines in the shape of shoes. Cover design by David Perry.
    [1] half-title; [2] blank; [3] title-page; [4] publishing information; [5] contents; [6] blank; [7] acknowledgements; [8] blank; 9–175 text; [176] blank.
    Published in Toronto, 18 March 1978; 3,317 copies, at $6.95. Printed in Canada.
    Titles: Re Union [1974;1976]—The House on Tenth [1964;1966]—The Big Leagues [1973;1974]—Spans [1965;1976]—The Lawnmower [1963;1964]—The White Coffin [1966;1967]—Wings [1970;1972]—Have You Seen Jesus? [1964; 1968]—A Short Hagiography of Old Quebec [1973;1976]—The Hayfield [1963;1965]—Owning Up [1965;1976]—Highway Three [1962;1975;1976]—A Tale Which Holdeth Children from Play [1977;1977]—Ebbe's Roman Holiday [1973;1974]—The Creator Has a Master Plan [1976;1977]—No No No No No [1965;1966]—The Wallet: An Exercise in Sixties West Coast Bourgeois Realism [1965; 1976;1977]—Protective Footwear [1976;1976]

NOTES:

♦ Dates of composition, in brackets after the titles listed, are provided by GB in the published text.

♦ Charis Wahl was house editor for McClelland and Stewart.

♦ GB had originally called the manuscript "Owning Up" but changed his mind in a letter to Anna Porter, 14 June 1977: "Oh, if it is all right with you, I have changed my mind back about the title of the book of stories. To *Protective Footwear*, mainly because the other title is okay as a three-tiered meaning as with my last M&S book, but it is a formula for titles used 5 years ago, and I dont want to echo that; just as now I cdnt do a title such as The Forbash Project or The Keltner Decision or The Stratford Dilemma. See?" [McClelland and Stewart Papers, McMaster University]

♦ "Isn't that a boring title for a book of short stories? Think how many places in libraries where this has been catalogued behind northern parkas." [Session 14, 14 May 1989]

♦ Some stories were taken from unfinished or unpublished novels. "A Short Hagiography of Old Quebec" was drawn from a novel begun in Montreal but never finished. Three stories come from a novel only half completed, "Looking for Ebbe," with the central character Ebbe modeled on *Tish* poet Jamie Reid: "The House on Tenth," "Have You Seen Jesus?" and "Ebbe's Roman Holiday." Three stories, all rewritten, were taken from an unpublished novel, "What Does Eddie Williams Want?": "Spans," "Owning Up," and "The Wallet: An Exercise in Sixties West Coast Bourgeois Realism."

♦ "Highway Three" is a story constructed using the William Burroughs cut-up method: "I wrote the story and cut the pile of manuscript into four. Then I threw it up in the air and put it back together sort of in the order the pieces of paper came down in." [Session 14, 14 May 1989]

♦ From the publisher's blurb on the back cover: "George Bowering's tales take you out of your head and into the minds of the most engaging, offbeat assortment of everyday extraordinaries ever to trace their tracks across the pages of Canadian fiction."

A32   THREE VANCOUVER WRITERS   1979

Three Vancouver Writers: | interviews by George Bowering | 5 Preface | 7 Songs and Wisdom: an interview with Audrey Thomas | 32 Given This Body: an interview with Daphne Marlatt | 89 Starting at our Skins: an interview with Frank Davey
    Pp. [1–4] 5–52 [53] 54–180 [181–184]
    5⁵/₈ x 8⁵/₈ in.; 14.2 x 22 cm. Perfect bound with blue and orange paper wrappers. Cover with journal name *Open Letter*, title, and an old photo of six men in a car, posing in front of the Hollow Tree at Stanley Park, Vancouver BC; on back, a detail from the cover photo.
    [1] masthead of *Open Letter*; [2] acknowledgement; [3] title-page and contents;

[4] blank; 5–6 preface; 7–[181] text; [182–183] ad for *Open Letter* and back issues; [184] blank.

Published as an entire issue of *Open Letter*, Fourth Series, Number 3, Spring 1979; 800 copies, at $2.50. Printed by Coach House Press in Toronto.

Titles: Preface [to *Three Vancouver Writers*]—Songs & Wisdom: An Interview with Audrey Thomas—Given This Body: An Interview with Daphne Marlatt—Starting at Our Skins: An Interview with Frank Davey

NOTES:

♦ The cover photograph was taken from the old family album of Linda McCartney (Davey).

♦ GB had planned to interview about 10 writers, but it took him three to four months to do Daphne Marlatt alone. "When I started off, there was 700 pages of Daphne. It was amazing . . . The Audrey one is really short because I think I did it in only about two sittings or something like that, and she was off to Europe. The one with Frank I did while he was visiting here for a month, so that turns out to be the second longest one. And for the Daphne one, I went to her place once a week for three months and taped for a couple of hours." [Session 5, 16 May 1988]

♦ GB received a short-term Canada Council grant to do these interviews. He explained his strategy in a grant report, 27 July 1974: "I am literally asking them [the three Vancouver writers] everything they know about writing, and covering everything, every page they have ever done. I have enough detailed notes to write several dozen essays. In fact I am thinking, as I prepare for these things, of them as essays in which the subject gets to speak, wow. It is a 100,000-hour job! But worth it. Needless to say, I haven't been writing poetry for nearly a year." [GB Papers, Correspondence Canada Council, NL]

♦ From GB's Preface: "I think of these three inter-views as essays spoken by the co-respondents. In preparation for them, I re-read & notated all the authors' works, filling notebooks as I would for three critical articles of unusual length. Then, in the Spring & Summer of 1975 I sat down for hours, days, & weeks with the three writers, & we discussed their writings methodically & chronologically, from first publications to most recent. We recorded tape after tape, & provided an immense task for Sharon Fawcett [Thesen], who made the first transcriptions. Then I edited, cut, & typed transcriptions two more times. I managed to reduce 850 pages of typescript to 350 pages. I was glad when that part of the job was over . . .

"I do not maintain that this book will give a full sense of the thought & practice pertaining to Vancouver literature of our time. But I do believe that Canadian letters have been poorly served by the facile comments made about certain West Coast writers by people in eastern parts who have cookt up such unexamined notions as a Black Mountain 'school' & a BC-California invasion of the 'Canadian Tradition'. I wish here to give these three or four writers some space to make their actual feelings & ideas known."

A33   ANOTHER MOUTH   1979

George | Bowering | Another | Mouth | McClelland and Stewart
Pp. [1–12] 13 [14] 15–33 [34] 35–60 [61] 62–77 [78] 79–96

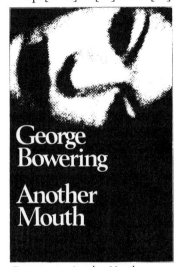

5^{13}/$_{16}$ x 9 in.; 14.8 x 22.8 cm. Perfect bound with maroon paper wrappers. Top half of cover with an image of a face placed horizontally; on back, photo of GB and a publisher's blurb. Cover design by Michael van Elsen.

[1] half-title; [2] books by GB; [3] title-page; [4] publishing information; [5] dedication: *This collection is dedicated to three artists | who have graced my life, illuminated my imagination, | & talkt my ear off: | Greg Curnoe, Roy Kiyooka, & Brian Fisher.*; [6] blank; [7] epigraph: "composed in time the rimes exist beyond the text" | bp Nichol | *The Martyrology*, Bk. 4; [8] blank; [9–10] contents; [11] half-title; [12] blank; 13 preface; 14 blank; 15–94 text; 95 acknowledgements; 96 about the author.

Front cover, *Another Mouth*

Published in Toronto, 1 August 1979; 1,100 copies, at $7.95. Printed in Canada.

Titles: A Preface [to *Another Mouth*]—Did—Last Lyrics: Across 37th Avenue —For Angela, Sheila, Marian, Sarah, Aviva, Magdelein, etc.—New Love—There's Something Wrong—Thea's Poem—April 25, 1972—In the Forest—Last Lyrics: From the Mystery—In Side—Unhappy Month—Johnny—The Old Roué & the Old Hot Number—Beyond—Last Lyrics: She's Going—The Middle-Aged Poet Dumpt at Last into the Iambic—Last Lyrics: She Pulled My Skin—Mais le rien perce—Last Lyrics: Sitting—Old Standards—River Rhine—Düsseldorf—Nearing Britain—Passport Doves—Northern Ont CP Air—Orpheus, Ears Open— Bright Land—God's Creature in Calgary—Coming to Toronto from Montreal—What Prophet—Coming to London from Toronto—Growing Older Than Your Brother in Your Autobiographical Dreams—Poundmaker—P. D.— My Real True Canadian Prophecy Poem—Amiri the Bird—Just A—The Priest— After Reading Contact & Combustion Again—Standing Under—Advice, As If—E—e. k.—The Mask of—Poet Laureate—A Poem for High School Anthologies—LII: 1—LII: 2—Losing Sight of the Terminator—Altered Poem to Willy Trump—More Like Mark Trail—Dancing—A TransCanada Poetry Quiz with No Questions about Snow—Correct Answers

NOTES:

♦ Denise Bukowski was house editor for McClelland and Stewart.

♦ GB got his title from David McFadden's poem "Another Mouth," written on the birth of his second daughter, of which GB received a handprinted copy; published in *Letters from the Earth to the Earth*.

♦ The biographical note at the end says GB was born in 1939.

♦ GB defended the inclusion of the Preface in a letter to Bukowski, 31 March 1979: "The preface. I dont think it sounds at all defensive. I think it sounds aggressive. I think that what with the debate that has sounded in the past few years, and with the horseshit that has not been properly sifted on the roses, I [sic; it] should be said. I read it at all of my readings during the tour, and no one seemed to think that I was being defensive. Those who had the ears to hear really liked it, great reactions; others who were stung by it remained there, stung. Good. I see it as an essential part of my recent and old poetic-politics.

"Or are we to fear Nationalist repercusions. Cusions?" [McClelland and Stewart Papers, McMaster University]

♦ Considered by GB his "anti-poetics book" since it contains poems using various anti-poetic devices: a preface in the form of an interview between Canadian Tradition and GB, elements of concrete and sound poems, chants, jokes and other trickster techniques, including "LII: 1" and "LII: 2," which are poems made from words taken from page 52 of two classical novels. The selection ends with a multiple choice literary quiz (with answers provided), for example:

> In E. J. Pratt's *Towards the Last Spike*, what did the railroad builders have in their blood?
>
> a.   Granite
> b.   Whiskey
> c.   Porridge
> d.   Ham & eggs
>
> CORRECT ANSWER: c. Pratt doesn't say whether they injected it or took it orally.

A34   UNCLE LOUIS   1980

UNCLE LOUIS | a poem by George Bowering | First Draft Jan 1980 | Coach House Press MS. Editions

Pp. [1–34]

7⁵/₁₆ x 11 in.; 18.6 x 28 cm. Staple bound with grey paper wrappers. Cover with the logo of Coach House Press and a section cut out revealing the title-page. Computer printout with text on recto of leaves, with the verso blank.

[1] title-page; [2–4] blank; [5–27] text; [28–30] blank; [31] colophon and list of Manuscript Editions available; [32–34] blank.

Colophon: Coach House Press Manuscript Editions are computer line-printer

copies of works-in-progress, run off and bound up 'on demand' as orders are received at the Press.
   Published January 1980; at $1.50. Printed in Toronto.
   Titles: 1–12

NOTES:
♦ Composed c. October, during the year, 1979, when GB vowed not to write poems.
♦ Probably only a handful of copies were ordered.
♦ GB: "You were supposed to just have poems in progress, and that you would have new versions of them, as you revised them. Some people did that but most didn't; usually the poems were finished and never touched again, such as this one. I think it cost you 10¢ a page. You would ask for such and such a book and they would print them off, slap this cardboard cover on them and mail them back." [Session 6, 25 May 1988]
♦ Publisher's note on colophon page: "We hope that these editions will allow readers and writers more access to each other during the compositional process. As the work is revised by the author, revisions are typed into the computer and the compositional date and draft number altered accordingly." GB did not recall ever submitting a second draft.
♦ When this poem appeared in the American magazine *Epoch*, an excerpt of GB's accompanying letter was printed at the end: "The poem . . . involves an old and well-known hobby-horse of mine, the idea of growing up in the far west and not feeling integrated in the Central Canadian experience; consequently I get a lot of flak for being un-Canadian in my sentiments and subjects, for in fact being partly to blame for the dread American influence on our writing. This from literary nationalists, most of whom live in Toronto. Thus the two voices in the poem, the second being the snotty Toronto reviewer. I get a lot of them . . . ." [See D778]

A35   BURNING WATER   1980

a. Cloth issue:
Burning Water | a novel by | George Bowering | Musson Book Company | a division of General Publishing Co. Limited | Don Mills, Ontario
   Pp. [i–ii] [1–13] 14–18 [19] 20–23 [24] 25 [26] 27–29 [30] 31–32 [33] 34–37 [38] 39–40 [41] 42–43 [44] 45–46 [47] 48–50 [51] 52–54 [55] 56–57 [58] 59–61 [62] 63–65 [66] 67–70 [71] 72–74 [75] 76–79 [80] 81–83 [84] 85–87 [88–91] 92–94 [95] 96–98 [99] 100–102 [103] 104–105 [106] 107–108 [109] 110–113 [114] 115–117 [118] 119–122 [123] 124–126 [127] 128–131 [132] 133–135 [136] 137–139 [140] 141–144 [145] 146–148 [149] 150–152 [153] 154–157 [158] 159–161 [162] 163–165 [166] 167–170 [171–173] 174–176 [177] 178–180 [181] 182–184 [185] 186–187 [188]

189–191 [192] 193–197 [198] 199–202 [203] 204–205 [206] 207–211 [212] 213–215 [216] 217–220 [221] 222–224 [225] 226–228 [229] 230–232 [233] 234–236 [237] 238–240 [241] 242–244 [245] 246–249 [250] 251–253 [254] 255–258 [259–270]

5³/₈ x 8¹/₂ in.; 13.7 x 21.5 cm. Casebound with black boards. Black and gold dust jacket with image in gold of a sailing ship on the cover; title and author's name in gold lettering; on back, a publisher's blurb. Publisher's blurb on front flap; on back flap a photo of GB with a biographic blurb. Cover design by Maureen Heel-Henderson.

Endleaf; [i] half-title; [ii] blank; [1] title-page; [2] publishing information; [3] acknowledgements; [4] blank; [5] dedication: I would like to dedicate this book, I if he does not mind, to George Whalley; [6] blank; [7]–258 text; [259–260] blank; [261] biographical note; [262–270] blank; endleaf.

Published 1 September 1980; 3,718 copies, at $14.95.

b. Paper issue:

[enclosed in a rectangular box] NEW PRESS CANADIAN CLASSICS I George Bowering I [rule] Burning Water I General Publishing Co. Limited I Toronto, Canada

Collation as above, but without [259–270]

4¹/₈ x 7 in.; 10.5 x 17.7 cm. Perfect bound with wine paper wrappers. Cover with reproduction of a detail from the painting, *Lake Donaldson* (1977), by Jane Martin; on back, a miniature of the cover painting and quotations from reviews praising *Burning Water*.

[i–ii] pages missing; [3] biographic note on GB and artist Jane Martin; [4] titles in New Press Canadian Classics series; [5] title-page; [6] publishing information; [7] acknowledgements; [8] dedication: I would like to dedicate this book, I if he does not mind, to George Whalley; [9–10] Prologue; [10]–258 text.

Published 15 February 1983; 7,599 copies, at $3.95.

c. Cloth issue [American edition]: same as A35a, except for imprint and addition of subtitle on cover, "A novel about George Vancouver, Pacific explorer." Published by Beaufort Books [the American subsidiary of General Publishing], New York, 1980; 3,000 copies, at $14.95.

d. Translation into French:

george bowering I en eaux troublés I Vancouver découvre la côte ouest, l'amour, la mort I traduit de l'anglais I par L.-Philippe Hébert I Quinze/prose étrangère

Pp. [1–8] 9–11 [12–14] 15–84 [85–86] 87–163 [164–166] 167–245 [246–256]

5¹⁵/₁₆ x 8¹³/₁₆ in.; 15 x 22.3 cm. Perfect bound in royal blue wrappers; cover with horizontal khaki bars framing an illustration, by Gilles Thibeault, of a ship tossed on a stormy sea; publisher's blurb on back. Book design by Gaéton Forcillo.

[1–2] blank; [3] half-title; [4] blank; [5] title-page; [6] publishing information; [7] dedication: *Je voudrais dédier ce livre I à George Whalley, I si ça ne l'embête pas trop.*; [8] blank; 9–245 text; [246] blank; [247] list of series titles; [248] blank; [249–250] more series titles; [251] blank; [252] printer: Achevé d'imprimer sur les

N

presses de | L'IMPRIMERIE ELECTRA* | Division de l'A. D. P. Inc. | Imprimé au Canada/Printed in Canada; [253–256] blank.
   Published 1 March 1982; 2,124 copies, at $12.95.

NOTES:
♦ GB received a Senior Arts grant from the Canada Council for the period September 1977–August 1978, during which time he wrote this novel.
♦ The subject for the novel had been in GB's mind for many years, as far back as research for *George, Vancouver* [see A12]. Over the years he kept notes on

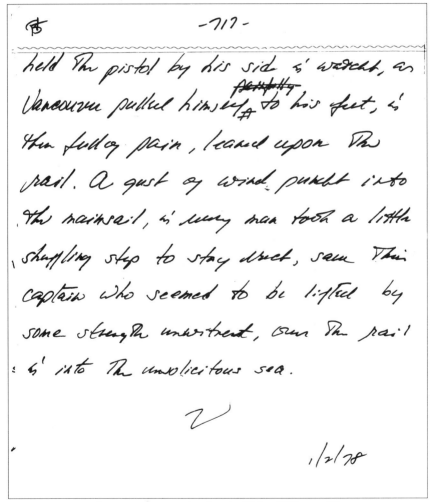

Last page of manuscript, *Burning Water*; GB Papers, NL

numerous index cards, now among his papers [NL], and these were used to write the novel.

♦ The novel was written in three hardcover notebooks bought in Vancouver's Chinatown. The writing occurred in three phases during the period 1 November 1977–1 February 1978. GB's objective was to write 1,000 words per day for each writing session. The first third was written in Italy in three weeks, in Trieste, Florence, and Padua. Back in Vancouver in late November, he wrote the second third in six weeks, but since he only got as much as he had completed during three weeks in Italy, he decided to go to Central America to continue. In early January he travelled to Guatemala, then to Costa Rica, and back to Guatemala, writing every day. After three weeks he flew back via San Francisco and stayed in Chinatown for a few days to write some more, and then at the end of January he returned to Vancouver where he wrote the last two chapters, finishing 1 February 1978.

♦ "It was wonderful feeling the pressure build up. There I was in Trieste and the thing was to fill time, and I took these long walks—miles along the waterfront—thinking the book. And I would come home and I would write for two hours [to write 1,000 words] and that would be my day's writing done. Then at the end, there I am in Costa Rica—I can still remember the hotel, it had a lovely parquet floor and it had a university radio station that played jazz all day long—and I would have to write for hours and hours to get the day's writing done, so I didn't get to explore as much. Then in San Francisco, I stayed at the Sam Wong Hotel in Chinatown. That's what Kerouac did—he stayed in hotels in Chinatown, so I thought, maybe that was his hotel." [Session 14, 26 May 1989]

♦ The earlier title was "The Dead Sailors," changed on the request of GB's publishers who were concerned with the negative effect of the word "dead" in the title of a novel.

♦ The manuscript was sent to McClelland and Stewart in April 1979, and readers' reports called for considerable revision, especially in characterization and time scheme. GB was disappointed by the assessment and replied in detail, 19 November 1979, defending the integrity of the manuscript as written and questioning the ability of the readers to understand the form of his novel: "After 10 years of researching and noting it, and then 3 years of planning the structure, and 2 years of writing and rewriting of it—to imagine a wholesale re-thinking, arrgh . . . . usually I go along with anything that people in the big city tell me , , , but this book is so much a question of belief, and I think, having my heroes be Gass and Barthelme and Hawkes and Bioy-Casares and Beckett and Robbe-Grillet and Borges and B. S. Johnson and Berger and so on, like esp. in this case, Ishmael Reed, that I might know more than folks think I know, and that I am not trying to cover laziness or amateurness with theory—" [McClelland and Stewart Papers, McMaster University]

♦ GB gave the manuscript to General Publishing where it was accepted with only

one change required: a complete rewrite of chapter 1, to
which he agreed. The original chapter 1 was published in
Open Letter; see D737.

♦ In his report to the Canada Council for his grant, 16 May
1978, GB explained the geographical shifts that accompanied the composition of the novel, beginning with the
decision to start in Trieste: "It was the way I expected it to
be. I was in a place I liked, but I was out of reach of English,
there were no winter tourists, and there was nothing in the
way of art or architecture to look at. I had a boring routine,
and I wrote a chapter each day. Then I knew I had to come
home to write the middle part. I wrote that in Vancouver.

Figure of the Chinese
boat in the notebooks
used by GB to write
Burning Water;
reproduced in the book

Then I wrote the third third in San Jose, Costa Rica, another completely boring
city, where the sound of Spanish helpt me with the important Vancouver-Quadra
part of the book. I wrote the last 2 chapters in Vancouver, after actually holing up
in a Chinese hotel in San Francisco (again without looking around) and writing
three chapters there. Now I will, as always, let the draught cool for 9 months or so,
and then re-re-rewrite . . . I am so happy to see this book, which I have been
planning, literally, since Dec 1966, sitting in three thick notebooks on my desk."
[GB Papers, Correspondence Canada Council, NL]
♦ The figure of the Chinese boat on the inside cover of the notebook was
reproduced and used on the divisions in the novel.
♦ For the title, GB was thinking of "Burning Water" as the Aztec term for the
imagination.
♦ "[Robert] Kroetsch pointed out about *Burning Water* that it was a signal that
our story did not have to be the story of people coming from Europe over to the
east coast of the United States or Canada. The Pacific is also a story, and probably
a story that we are going to see more of in the future. So Kroetsch talks about it as
a Pacific Rim kind of book, which I didn't think about at the time, but it certainly
makes sense to me." [From "Extra Basis"; see D882]

A36   PARTICULAR ACCIDENTS   1980

SELECTED POEMS | Particular Accidents | [rule] George Bowering | Edited
with an Introduction by Robin Blaser
      Pp. [1-4] 5-7 [8] 9-155 [156-160]
      5¼ x 8¼ in.; 13.2 x 20.9 cm. Perfect bound with white paper wrappers. Grey
cover with image of male figure mowing with a gas lawnmower; on back, a photo
of GB by Robert Keziere with a publisher's blurb and a statement by Xavier West.
The cover is a detail from a drawing by Jack Chambers, "Grass Box No. 2,"

graphite on paper and plexiglass, 37 x 49 in., 1968–70. Book design by David Robinson.

[1] half-title; [2] blank; [3] title-page; [4] publishing information; 5–7 contents; [8] blank; 9–28 "George Bowering's Plain Song," by Robin Blaser; 29–153 text; 154 "Editor's Note"; 155 bibliography of GB; [156–160] blank.

Published October 1980; 3,000 copies, at $3.95. Printed in Manitoba by Friesen.

Titles: Radio Jazz—Wattle)—Grandfather—Matins—Husband—Thru My Eyes—The Descent—Calgary Downtown Sunday—Grandmother—The Day Before the Chinese A-Bomb—Moon Shadow—Windigo—Baseball, a poem in the magic number 9—The House—The White Station Wagon Strophes—Brown Globe—The Sensible—Ted Williams—Talent—*George, Vancouver* [excerpt]—Among Friends—Martin Luther King—Harbour Beginnings & That Other Gleam—The Believer—Thru—*Genève* [excerpt]—Mars—The Flying Dream—The Brush Fire—The Dear Path—The Substance—The Front Yard—Place of Birth—The Code—The Acts—The Next Place—The Pool—The Scars—The Body—That Way, in Words—Margaret Atwood—bpNichol—Raymond Souster—Irving Layton—Fred Wah—Frank Davey—Daphne Marlatt—Al Purdy—Margaret Avison—Louis Dudek—Desert Elm [I, VIII]—*Allophanes*: III–V, XI (the egg-ziled gods)–XIII, XVII, XXII, XXV–XXVI Dispersoid—*A Short Sad Book*: III, VII–X, XIII, XVI–XX, XXIII, XXVII–XXVIII, XXXI, XXXVII, XXXIX, LI, LIII—Old Standards [1, 2, 8]

NOTES:

♦ Part of Talonbooks' series of "selected poems" conceived and edited by Karl Siegler. Five other books were published as a group at the same time: bp Nichol's *As Elected*, edited by Jack David; bill bissett's *Beyond Even Faithful Legends*, edited by Len Early; Daphne Marlatt's *Net Work*, edited by Fred Wah; Frank Davey's *The Arches*, edited by bp Nichol; and Fred Wah's *Loki Is Buried at Smoky Creek*, edited by GB; see B10.

♦ Each poet in the series chose a painting for the cover. GB chose a section of a painting by Jack Chambers that he saw and immediately fell for in London, Ontario in 1966: "Actually the painting is quite misrepresented on the cover. Most of it is silver grey, and then there's this efflorescence of brilliant coloured flowers that want to jump out of the painting up in the corner, but that isn't on, partly because the painting has almost been destroyed now—Jack Chambers' wife Olga kept it where some water drizzled on it, and the part with the flowers is apparently all wrecked. But I've always wanted to have some kind of a connection with that painting, so I asked to have a section of it for the cover." [Session 6, 25 May 1988]

♦ GB did not assist Blaser in making any of the choices: "Whenever anyone else is editing my stuff, I always just leave it entirely up to them." [Session 6, 25 May 1988]

♦ From the "Editor's Note": "The sub-title chosen by George Bowering is from *The Tempest*, near the end of Act V, Prospero speaking:
Sir, I invite your Highness and your train
To my poor cell, where you shall take your rest
For this one night; which, part of it, I'll waste
With such discourse as, I not doubt, shall make it
Go quick away: the story of my life,
And the particular accidents gone by
Since I came to this Isle."
♦ Xavier West, quoted on the back cover, and quoting GB in *A Short Sad Book*, is a pseudonym for the editor who could not get this said in any other way: "George Bowering has suffered more foolishness from his readers—that is, foolishness when it is not downright stupidity—than has any other Canadian writer whose work I know.
Dear Reader Reading:
1. Please take your time."

A37   WEST WINDOW   1982

[title-page in lined box] WEST | WINDOW | *The Selected Poetry of* | GEORGE | BOWERING | General Publishing Co. Limited | Toronto, Canada
    Pp. [1–10] 11 [12] 13–61 [62] 63–81 [82] 83–117 [118] 119–133 [134] 135–144
    5¹/₄ x 9 in.; 13.3 x 22.8 cm. Perfect bound with grey paper wrappers on which are magenta letters. Cover with "Spectrum Poetry Series" at top left, device at top right, and a pane of windows in the middle with metallic letters scrambled in each window, which can be used to spell title and author's name; on back, publisher's blurb. Cover by Shelagh Taylor. Design by E. J. Carson.
    [1] half-title; [2] blank; [3] title-page; [4] publishing information; [5] contents; [6] acknowledgements; [7–9] "Preface" by Sheila Watson; [10] blank; 11–144 text.
    Published 15 February 1982; 2,258 copies, at $9.95.
    Titles: *Curious* [see A 19]—*At War With the U. S.* [see A20]—*Allophanes* [see A24]—*Uncle Louis* [see A34]—BETWEEN THE SHEETS: Against Description—West Window—Which Poesy—Four Jobs—Between the Sheets

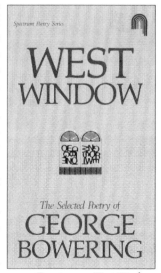

Front cover, *West Window*

NOTES:

♦ This collection was part of General Publishing's Spectrum Series of poetry titles, at the time organized by Ed Carson. Other poets in the series included Robert Kroetsch, Eli Mandel, D. G. Jones, and Gwendolyn MacEwen. Theirs were called "selected poems," but GB wanted his called "selected poetry." He wanted to gather together long poems that were published by small presses and were generally unavailable.

♦ GB recommended that Sheila Watson be asked to do an introduction. "In *Particular Accidents* Robin Blaser is working like crazy to make me a Canadian, but here Sheila Watson is working like crazy to make me an internationalist." [Session 6, 25 May 1988]

♦ "Neat title, eh? Very Shelleyan. Actually it's the window to my study, but it's also a statement to those eastern publishers that Canada needs one of these. In Shelley, it's the west wind, and the west wind destroys and creates." [Session 6, 25 May 1988]

♦ " 'Which Poesy' is a collaboration with Shelley, his 'Mont Blanc', my favourite poem . . . In an unpublished book, "Eye-Kicks in Europe," you can read that I was in Chamonix exactly 150 years after he was. I was on a six-week voyage [during May and June 1966], and I came home to Calgary and found his book *A Six-Week Voyage*. In 1816 he went on a six-week voyage to Europe and Mont Blanc was in the middle of that. I had started reading Shelley, but I didn't know about that book." [Session 6, 25 May 1988]

A38   A WAY WITH WORDS   1982

a. Cloth issue:
A WAY | WITH | WORDS | GEOR | GE BOW | ERING
    Pp. [1–4] 5–199 [200]
$5^{1}/_{2}$ x $8^{1}/_{2}$ in.; 14 x 21.5 cm. Casebound with brown boards. Light brown dust jacket. Cover design with letters arranged as on title-page; on back, publisher's blurb. Book design by Michael Macklem.
    Endleaf; [1–2] blank; [3] title-page; [4] publishing information and dedication: For Frank Davey, fellow logogriphist; 5–199 text; [200] blank; endleaf.
    Published by Oberon Press in Ottawa, 31 March 1982; 300 copies, at $19.95. Printed in Toronto by Coach House Press.
    Titles: Avison's Imitation of Christ the Artist—Why James Reaney Is a Better Poet: 1 than a Northrop Frye poet, 2 than he used to be—Reaney's Region—Roy Kiyooka's Poetry: An Appreciation—Coming Home to the World: The Poems of D. G. Jones—The Memory of Red Lane—Metaphysic in Time: The Poetry of Lionel Kearns—The Poetry of John Newlove—The Poems of Fred Wah—

Margaret Atwood's Hands—The Early Poetry of Frank Davey—Proofing the World: The Poems of David McFadden

b. Paper issue: as A38a, but perfect bound with paper wrappers having same design, and without an endleaf; 550 copies, at $9.95.

NOTES:

♦ Oberon received GB's manuscript, 23 June 1981, and sent him a publishing contract, 7 November 1981. [GB Papers, Correspondence Oberon Press, NL]

♦ The absence of a table of contents and an introduction was not GB's idea: "Michael Macklem [at Oberon] does not like table of contents and he does not like introductions." [Session 5, 28 May 1988]

♦ GB's introduction was published separately in *Brick* [see D822] and also under the title "Tradition" in *Craft Slices* [see A44]. In it he explains his objective in writing critical essays and his sense of tradition: "I am not here trying to rile the scholastic tradesmen of that important nation bounded by Toronto, Montreal and Ottawa. I am just explaining the reason behind the structure of my organized writing, including the essays I have written on Canadian poets. If I had been schooled within the snowy triangle, it is possible that I would have drafted articles on the Confederation Poets, then perhaps the thirties poets with the initials before their surnames and finally the best representative contemporaries.

"But my writing on poetry, literary rather than scholarly for the most part, reflects my education in the subject of Canadian verse. It is therefore a track of a kind of Canadian tradition. It is the evidence of what I, a Canadian poet, have found interesting in the reading I have been led to pursue. Most of my essays are stories about my companions in poetry. Others tell of predecessors whose books have come my way and made it clear to me. Some perhaps illuminate the difficulty I faced in finding for myself a Canadian tradition on a nearly trackless frontier. We have all been, since Pound and Eliot, in a position from which we must find, not simply inherit, a tradition."

♦ An essay on Michael Ondaatje was taken out by the publisher because the book would have been too long; it was included in *Imaginary Hand* as "Ondaatje Learning to Do"; see A50.

A39   EAR REACH   1982

[device] | EAR REACH: POEMS | [device] | GEORGE BOWERING | [device] | The ALCUIN SOCIETY | [device] | VANCOUVER [device] 1982 | [device]

Pp. [1–40]

6 x 4³/₄ in.; 15.1 x 12.1 cm. Staple bound with cream paper wrappers. Cover with red device.

[1] half-title; [2] blank; [3] title-page; [4] publishing information; [5] dedication:

```
                    I
                I  
            I
          I                    i i
          I
        I
         iiiiiiiiiiiiiiiiiiiiiiiiiiiiiiiiiiiiii
        iiiIiiiiiiiiiiiiiiiiiiiiiiiiiiiiiiiiiiii
        iiiiiIiiiiiiiiiiiiiiiiiiiiiiiiiiiiiiiiii
        iiiiiiiiIii              iiiiiiiiii
        iiiiiiiiiiiI             iiiiiiiiii
        iIiiiiiiiii              iiiiriiii
        iiiiiIiiiii              iiiiiiiii
        iiiiiiiiiiiiiiiiiiiiiiiiiiiii Iiiiiiii
        iiiiiiiiiiiiiiiiiiiiiiiiiiiiiiiiiIiii
        iiiiiiiiiiiiiiiiiiiIiiiiiiiiiiiiiiiii
```

MIRRORS SHOW

Mirrors show up empty, windows turn black,
and mannequins stand in couples back to back;
ripples rise in ponds unbidden by the wind,
giving old misgivings to a maiden who has sinned
against a godlike apparition dressed in green and
red and acting unimagined where mannequins stand
each meaning something to this watcher but nought
to one another, only to their fiction wrought.

Always they will gesture in the attitudes arrested
totally dependent on the climate of her heart,
wholly in the power of a dreamer interested
only in the reasons they are fixedly apart;
only when they're naked and their plastic torsos nested
does the watcher think their fiction has its start.

Facing pages of *Ear Reach*, printed by Peter Quartermain; acrostic poem,
Margaret Atwood

Manuscript of acrostic poem, Margaret Atwood; GB Papers, NL [see also A47]

with thanks to Audrey Thomas, who gave me the | little notebook this was written in.; [6] device; [7–37] text; [38] device; [39] colophon; [40] device.

Colophon: EAR REACH: POEMS BY GEORGE BOWERING | is the third in a series of chapbooks published | by The Alcuin Society. It has been printed by | Peter Quartermain at Slug Press on a 12 x 8 | Westman & Baker jobbing press on Carlyle Japan | paper, in an edition of 126 signed copies, of | which 26, lettered, are reserved for the author, | and 100, numbered, are for sale, [sic] The text and | headings are in Kennerley Old Style, other matter | largely in Caslon Old Face. Published July 1982. | *First Edition.* | This is copy __.

Sold at $10.00. Printed in Vancouver.

Titles: Mirrors Show—Cool Streets—Valour Calls—Falling Thru—Man or Beast—Brain That Vanishes—Just As We Lose—Phones Ring Out—Taking Ink—Grace Requires Age—Ready to Snap—Detachment from Self—Relief Occurs—Cool Streets—Tearing Off the Shrouds—Bones Along Her Body

NOTES:

♦ GB's poems are accompanied by typographic designs by the printer Peter Quartermain who, in a letter, 31 August 1986, explains the text to printer Glenn Goluska: "EAR REACH is the first half of a collection of acrostics called IRRi-table REACHing—a title I spell out with the 'typographical ornamentation' . . . I had originally planned to number each of the poems, too, on its facing page, but overall did not have time (save number 8, I think) [3, 7, 12, and 16 are also numbered] since the Alcuin Society kept bugging me and bugging me and bugging me. It is indeed true that the most impatient and importunate, not to say rude, patrons and clients are those for whom you do the work for free." [Letter courtesy of Peter Quartermain]

♦ "Irritable Reaching" was published in *Delayed Mercy*; see A47 for further notes on these poems.

A40   SMOKING MIRROR   1982

SMOKING MIRROR | George Bowering | Longspoon Press | [design of faint waving lines at bottom]
    Pp. [1–7] 8–17 [18–19] 20–38 [39] 40–53 [54–55] 56–62 [63–64]
    4⁷/₈ x 7⁷/₈ in.; 12.5 x 20.1 cm. Perfect bound with white paper wrappers and grey-brown pages. Cover with title in silver at top with a reversed mirror image at bottom; on back, an old photo of GB, with a publisher's blurb. Book design by Jorge Frascara.
    [1–2] blank; [3] title-page; [4] publishing information; [5–6] contents; [7–63] text; [64] blank.
    Published in Edmonton, August 1982; 500 copies, $7.50. Printed in Edmonton by Co-op Press.
    Titles: SMOKING MIRROR: Smoking Mirror—The Footprint—The Four Corners—Before the Revolution—The Water Flame—Open Mind—Diem's Machine—Fredericton Houses—Smoking Mirror in Fredericton—Smoking Mirror in Alberta—FROM A FAKE JOURNAL: In Answer (to a question from the gathering)—A Typewritten Poem—Impaucester—I Dream of Pepsi—Stuck Wasps—Onion Skins—Ice in Italy—Scraping in Italy—The Second Runner—Adonai—A Clean Park—In a Bower—Tongue on Pollen—A Poem for Once I'd Rather Type Than Speak—This Is One of Those Days—The Eucharist—Kayo—A Prayer—SOUSTERRE: Calm After—Friday Afternoon—A Poem—She Has—The Smooth Loper—My 6-Pound Dog—Poem for Monica—Not Quarreling—Spelling/Rule—Aram Saroyan—Essaying Wah—At Fairview, Burnt to the Earth, 1902—The McFadden Shopping Bag—Prose & Cons (with Frank Davey and Apple II)—Lou—The Route Out—Anvil Poem—Poetry's Witch—So—Another Week in the East

NOTES:
♦ Edited for the press by Douglas Barbour, Shirley Neuman, and Stephen Scobie.
♦ The sequence "Smoking Mirror" was composed in January and February 1968; "From a Fake Journal" includes poems written over a long period of time, December 1966–December 1982; "Sousterre" includes poems written December 1967–May 1971; "Another Week in the East" was composed in March 1977.
♦ GB worked with Scobie and Barbour in the selection of poems, many of which belong to a group of "minimalist poems" GB had been saving up for a book.
♦ On the title: " 'Smoking Mirror' is the name of the Aztec god of imagination who is also scary. The title also has do with with 'Burning Water', the Aztec word

for the imagination. 'Smoking Mirror' is a creature who sometimes talks to you in your dreams. He helps you create things, but he is also dangerous. He wears you down, and he is bad for you too; sometimes you wake up from a dream with a little footprint on your face and that's his footprint. So I think that's why Longspoon made the cover silver: it looks like smoke and it looks like a mirror too, depending on how you turn the book. It's grey when it's smoke and silver when it's a mirror."
[Session 5, 16 May 1988]
♦ The photo of GB on the back evokes the alchemic vision of bill bissett's words on his album cover, "awake in th red desert"—"I was trying to give a kind of smoking mirror image . . . The book is supposed to slip out of your fingers. If anything important happens, it's supposed to happen when you're not noticing."
[Session 5, 16 May 1988]
♦ The biographic note on the back cover contains two minor errors: GB was not born in 1936, and he won the Governor General's Award for Fiction in 1980, not 1981.

A41   THE MASK IN PLACE   1982

THE MASK | IN PLACE | Essays on Fiction in | North America | George Bowering | Turnstone Press
   Pp. [i–x] [1] 2 [3] 4–17 [18–19] 20–31 [32–33] 34–44 [45] 46–62 [63] 64–76 [77] 78–83 [84–85] 86–96 [97] 98–111 [112–113] 114–127 [128–129] 130–145 [146–147] 148–154 [155] 156–160 [161] 162–164 [165–166]
   5⁵/₁₆ x 8¹/₂; 13.8 x 21.5 cm. Perfect bound with white paper wrappers. Grey cover with red ribbons (such as would frame a theatrical tragic or comic mask) on either side of the title, boxed; on back, a statement from GB's preface and a publisher's blurb. Cover by Marsha Whiddon.
   [i] half-title; [ii] titles by GB; [iii] title-page; [iv] publishing information; [v] acknowledgements; [vi] blank; [vii] dedication: for Sheila Watson and Robert Kroetsch; [viii] epigraph: *This is what writing does in the novel.* | *Its task is to put the mask in place* | *and at the same time to point it out.* | —Roland Barthes; [ix] contents; [x] blank; [1]–2 preface; [3]–164 text; [165–166] blank.
   Published in Winnipeg, October 1982; 1,200 copies, at $9.95. Printed by Hignell Printing.
   Titles: True North Home and Fiction [Preface to *The Mask in Place*]—Hawthorne's Perilous Artifacts—The Three-Sided Room: Notes on the Limitations of Modernist Realism—And the Sun Goes Down: Richler's First Novel —That Fool of a Fear: Notes on *A Jest of God*—Snow Red: The Short Stories of Audrey Thomas—Modernism Could Not Last Forever—That Was Ida Said Miss Stein—Sheila Watson, Trickster—The Painted Window: Notes on Post-Realist Fiction—

On the Road: & the Indians at the End—Douglas Woolf's "Bank Day"—Genre-flect: A Discussion of *Agent Provocateur*—Nichol's Prose

NOTES:

♦ A companion volume to GB's essays on poetry, *A Way with Words* [see A38], gathering together his essays on fiction.

♦ From the preface, "True North Home and Fiction": " . . . one does not often find a book of essays in which criticism of Canadian texts is seen in a context broader than our 'native land'. A fine exception is *Figures in a Ground*, edited by Diane Bessai and David Jackel as a tribute to Sheila Watson's faith in a Canada that is part of the world. I also have that faith, so the arrangement of the following essays assumes that Canadian fiction is as good, though not as plentiful, as U. S. fiction, and does not suffer by being seen in a North American context.

" . . . The books discussed on these pages are not a canon . . . and they do not form a large enough library to prove anything about the course of North American fiction. I have arranged the essays so that there might be a thread leading from pre-realism through realism to post-realism, but that thread will not hold any minotaur from escape or havoc. In fact it will not even lead to daylight. But it will tell a reader where this en-mazed captive has been."

♦ The title comes from a passage from Roland Barthes' *Writing Degree Zero*, used as an epigraph to the collection.

A42   A PLACE TO DIE   1983

a. Cloth issue:

George Bowering | [photo of a male figure behind bars] | A Place to Die

Pp. [1–4] 5–127 [128]

5¹/₂ x 8¹/₂ in.; 14 x 21.5 cm. Casebound with black boards. Black dust jacket with same photo as on title-page but in red; photo continues on back, with a publisher's blurb. Cover by Pierre Gaudard. Book design by Michael Macklem.

Endleaf; [1–2] blank; [3] title-page; [4] publishing information, acknowledgements and dedication: This book is dedicated to Robert Kroetsch, | who celebrates life unstintingly.; [5 has epigraph on the same page as text begins: "I wish I were off that turning meat-wheel and safe in Heaven | dead" —Jack Kerouac] 5–127 text; [128] blank; endleaf.

Published in Ottawa by Oberon Press, 15 March 1983; 300 copies, at $19.95.

Titles: Carter Fell—A Short Story—Match-Boxes—Comparative Public Deaths—Old Bottles—Student, Petty Thief, TV Star—Arbre de Décision—The Clam-Digger—Four California Deaths

b. Paper issue: as A42a, but perfect bound with paper wrappers in same design as on dust jacket, and without an endleaf; 550 copies, at $9.95.

NOTES:

♦ The manuscript title "The World As a Place to Die" was shortened by his publisher, but for GB the longer title "is a lot more interesting idea." [Session 14, 14 May 1989]

♦ Three stories are revised sections of an unpublished novel, "What Does Eddie Williams Want?": "Match-Boxes," "Comparative Public Deaths," and "Student, Petty Thief, TV Star."

♦ "A Short Story" was written for *Fiction of Contemporary Canada*; see B9.

♦ "The Clam-Digger," originally called "The Clam-Digger and the Turtle," is a re-writing of an ancient Japanese fairy tale; according to GB's datebook, it was written in 1963.

♦ The epigraph is a variation of the closing lines of "211th Chorus," from *Mexico City Blues*, which GB heard on a tape of Kerouac reading.

A43   KERRISDALE ELEGIES   1984

KERRISDALE ELEGIES | George Bowering | The Coach House Press, Toronto
    Pp. [1–10] 11 [12] 13 [14] 15 [16] 17 [18] 19 [20–24] 25 [26] 27 [28] 29 [30] 31 [32] 33 [34–38] 39 [40] 41 [42] 43 [44] 45 [46] 47 [48–52] 53 [54] 55 [56] 57 [58] 59 [60] 61 [62–66] 67 [68] 69 [70] 71 [72] 73 [74] 75 [76–80] 81 [82] 83 [84] 85 [86] 87 [88] 89 [90–94] 95 [96] 97 [98] 99 [100] 101 [102] 103 [104–108] 109 [110] 111 [112] 113 [114] 115 [116–120] 121 [122] 123 [124] 125 [126] 127 [128–132] 133 [134] 135 [136] 137 [138] 139 [140] 141 [142] 143 [144] 145 [146] 147 [148–152]
    5^7/16 x 8^1/2 in.; 13.8 x 21.5 cm. Perfect bound with green paper wrappers. Cover with photo of GB by Michael Lawlor; on back, same photo, with publisher's blurb and a statement by Robert Kroetsch. Cover design by Gordon Robertson.
    [1] half-title; [2] blank; [3] title-page; [4] publishing information; [5] epigraph: Here a star, and there a star, | Some Lose their way. | Here a mist, and there a mist: | Afterwards—day! | EMILY DICKINSON; [6] blank; [7]–147 text; [148–151] blank; [152] colophon.
    Published 3 January 1984; 522 copies, at $8.50. Second printing, 19 November 1984; 546 copies. Third printing, 21 July 1988; 504 copies.
    Titles: Elegy One—Elegy Two—Elegy Three—Elegy Four—Elegy Five— Elegy Six—Elegy Seven—Elegy Eight—Elegy Nine—Elegy Ten

NOTES:

♦ Edited for the press by Linda Davey.

♦ Composed in handwritten form in ten sections, 15 June–1 September 1982, in lined examination booklets used at SFU.

Manuscript of opening lines from "Elegy One," *Kerrisdale Elegies*; GB Papers, NL

Dead poets' voices I have heard in my head
are not terrifying.
                    They tell me like lovers
we are worth speaking to,
                        I am a branch
a singing bird will stand on for a moment.

Like a singing branch I call out in return. How
do otherwise?
                Rather that than couple
with a swan on 41st Avenue.
                            When Hilda
appeared in my dream, she did not visit, she
walked by, into the other room,
                                and I didnt fall
in fear, but in love.

Inside.

Printed text of opening lines from "Elegy One," *Kerrisdale Elegies*

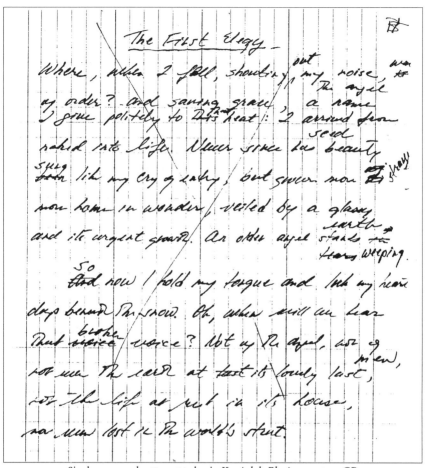

Single-page, early attempt to begin *Kerrisdale Elegies*; courtesy GB

♦ In the manuscript GB wrote in long lines, not divided as they are in the text. "I came to realize that it was written in these long lines that weren't the way the poem goes. It's a meditation and the long lines are more like something rehearsed so I couldn't use them. I had to break them up, to get it more meditative. It gets more content in a way too, because you can get more ambiguity, and you give the reader more time to supply his own ambiguity if you stop for a second and let him think about it. And if you're going to be a reader of Rilke, you'll certainly want a reader to do with you what you're doing with Rilke to begin with, so you call it 'Kerrisdale'. Everybody's got this built-in feeling about Kerrisdale—I mean that's a joke, right?—a poem set in Kerrisdale. A lot of people have picked up on that . . . saying yeah, what an interesting thing to do, to write a poem about Kerrisdale, to prove that you could even write a poem about Kerrisdale." [Session 2, 9 March 1988]

Front cover, *Kerrisdale Elegies*

♦ "I spent a long time trying to figure out how to write that poem. I was going to do what Ted Berrigan did in his *Sonnets*. He wrote the sonnets by translating from a language he didn't understand that well, and that's what I was going to do with the German, without knowing German. It didn't work. Then I thought okay, I can take parts of it and scramble it up and put holes in it and so forth, but that didn't work. I kept trying different things. One time [March 1982] I sat in a hotel room in Dallas, Texas and wrote the first page of the elegy, and I thought tomorrow I'm flying to Albuquerque so on the flight I'll cross out the parts that I don't like and see what kind of poem you get. I crossed out half of it, and then I crossed out half of what was left, and I crossed out half of what was left, and then finally I just crossed out the whole thing. I got to Santa Fe, for a reading I had to do there, and I was sitting in this cafe and I've got the copy of *Duino Elegies*, so I'm sitting at the table eating some kind of deli sandwich and reading the *Duino Elegies* and trying to figure out how else I can write this goddamn thing, and I look up at the next table and there's a young guy reading *Sonnets to Orpheus*. I thought, oh, Santa Fe is a place where Rilke happens, and I thought maybe Vancouver is a place where Rilke happens too, so a few months after I came home, I started writing." [Session 2, 9 March 1988]

A44   CRAFT SLICES   1985

a. Cloth issue:

[Reproduction in grey of cover image] | *Craft Slices by George Bowering*

Pp. [1–4] 5–152 [153–154]

5⁷/₁₆ x 8³/₄ in.; 13.8 x 21.2 cm. Casebound with black boards. Slate grey dust jacket. On the cover a painting by Wayne Davis of crockery still life in triplicate; on back, a publisher's blurb. Book design by Michael Macklem.

Endleaf; [1–2] blank; [3] title-page; [4] publishing information; dedication: Dedicated to, educated by and edited for bp Nichol; and epigraph: "Any George is gentle not particularly successful not a failure | and not in advantage and not partly" —Gertrude Stein, *Lucy | Church Amiably.*; 5–152 text; [153–154] blank; endleaf.

Published by Oberon Press, October 1985; estimated 300 copies, at $23.95. Printed in Toronto by Coach House Press.

Titles: ABC—Adding [see C102]—Anthology Poems [see C119]—Birney's Advent [see D553]—Birney's Rage [see D651]—bp's Returns [see D379]—Brown Mountain [see D758]—Brown Tish [see D758]—Canadian Modernists—Canadian Tradition [see "A Preface" to *Another Mouth*; A33]—Canadian Writers—Creative Writhing [see D785]—Creative Writing [see D785]—Creeley's Holiday [see D568]—Delivering Fiction [see C33]—Delsing and Me [see C33]—Duncan in Canada [see D685]—Duncan in Vancouver [see D685]—Duncan's War [see D354]—Eliot [see D673]—Eliot's Politics [see D673]—Fielding [see D655]—Flash Cards [see "Unexpected Objects" in *The Contemporary Canadian Poem Anthology*; B12]—Frank—Frank and George—Gerry Gilbert—Ginsberg's VW [see D401]—Gold [see C66]—Hawkes [see D673]—How to Write [see D509 and D518]—I Ching [see D715]—Important Writers—Introduction—Joe's Head [see D683]—Kingdomia—Kiyooka's Sculpture [see D433]—Kootenai Wah [see D649]—The League [see D369]—Like Siebrasse [see D511]—Long Poem [see C128]—MacEwen's Music [see D188]—Mandel's Shift [see D447]—Marlatt's Vancouver [see D649]—McFadding [see D683]—Montreal [see Preface to *The Concrete Island*; A28]—Nature [see C43]—Nature Studies [see C43]—A Nicholodeon [see D595]—Notebook—Orders Filled [see D458]—Orders Served [see D458]—Pat [see D754]—Poetry and Calendars [see D580]—Posthumous Fiction [see D684]—Post Lyric [see D647]—Purdy [see D651]—Purdy's North [see D379]—Purdy's Process [see D651]—Quebec—Quebec Anglos [see D332]—Remember Newman [see D358]—Rexroth [see D189]—Romantic Carpenter [see D473]—Say Live [see D379]—School English [see D656]—Serial Gardiner [see D603]—Seymour's Similes [see D683]—Social Cantos [see D471]—Souster's Elephants [see D304]—Sports Fiction [see C127 and Preface to *Great Canadian Sports Stories*; B8]—Stained Glass [see D725]—State Input—Still Waiting [see D646]—Stories [see C44 and Preface to *The Story So Far*; B4]—Thorny [see D358]—Three Vancouvers [see Preface to *Three Vancouver Writers*; A32]—Tradition [see D822]—Trumpet [see D638]—Ubyssey [see D743]—Ugly Winner [see D358]—Undone Tradition [see D684]—Unexpected Objects [see "Unexpected Objects" in *The Contemporary Canadian Poem Anthology*; B12]—Unwritten Essay—Uprooting [see D684]—Vanity [see D399]—Writing Dreams —W. W. E. Ross [see D437]—X [see C144]—Xenogenesis [see C144]

b. Paper issue: as A44a, but perfect bound with paper wrappers in same design as on dust jacket, and without an endleaf; estimated 550 copies, at $12.95.

NOTES:

♦ GB sent the manuscript to Oberon in March 1984, a much longer work than what was eventually published. After Michael Macklem asked for a shorter book for economic reasons, GB wrote back, 4 August 1984, that he had "removed just over 20% of the entries." Twenty-three sections were removed. [GB Papers, Correspondence Oberon Press, NL]

♦ The collection was constructed out of selections from numerous articles, re-views, and introductions written over the years, as well as unpublished material, either from notebooks or from "talk" pieces done for special occasions. GB just went through his list of publications, manuscripts, books, and magazines he had been published in "and picked out the ones I was interested in keeping as a kind of record of what I had been thinking about Canadian and American literature over the years." [Session 10, 25 March 1989]

Each piece was sliced into roughly the same length: GB thought of each section as two printed pages, or one sheet, starting uniformly on the right hand side. Though the idea was not enacted by Oberon because of the extra cost, the concept of "slice" was maintained.

After choosing a piece GB would revise it, in most cases, to make it more current. In many instances, the alterations were slight, but in some instances they were extensive.

♦ "Oberon refuses to do a contents page and an index, so I thought, I know what, I'll make an alphabetical book. You don't need a title-page and you don't need an index because you know where to find things in an alphabet. But I'm also interested in the alphabet as an organizer of things because it has sequence but no logic. I think I made a quotation from Barthes to that effect. The alphabet is a perfect way to do some list of things up because you aren't imposing any kind of step, any sense of hierarchy on your ideas." [Session 10, 25 March 1989]

♦ Why the dedication to bp Nichol? "I felt that I had stolen the title from bp [i. e. his *Craft Dinner*]. I thought for a long time about a different title, and finally I couldn't do it. It was just so good I couldn't do it." [Session 10, 25 March 1989]

♦ The sections that have been identified are cross-referenced (in the list of titles above), to direct the reader to the source in this bibliography. A few sections could not be located, even by GB. Special thanks to Susan MacFarlane for tracking down the majority of those found, and to GB for filling in some details through his memory.

♦ Some titles were previously unpublished: "ABC" was written as a preface; "Gerry Gilbert" was written as a bio-critical essay for *The Contemporary Canadian Poem Anthology* [see B12], but Gilbert decided not to be in the anthology; "Introduction" was taken from GB's introduction to a reading by Frank Davey, Robert Creeley, and Robert Duncan at the Italian Cultural Centre (1979); "Kingdomia" was written for an anthology that never got published; "Notebook" and "Unwritten Essay" were taken from notebooks; "Writing Dreams" was taken from a letter. A handful were written for an interview by Michael Mundhenk on a German radio program: "Canadian Modernists," "Canadian Writers," "Important Writers," "Quebec," and "State Input."

♦ GB on *Craft Slices*, in a letter to General Publishing, 13 November 1983: "It is part autobiography, part criticism, part literary theory, part joke, I guess; but in all it is a book of my thoughts, observations, feelings, and prejudices about my years

Section C
Books with Contributions
by George Bowering

Section C lists titles in chronological order by year; within the year, entries are arranged alphabetically.

As a writer GB works in numerous genres, and often he works in that "border-blur" area where conventional formal divisions are either undermined or abandoned. With this qualification, the genre of a title is given at the beginning of each entry. The following genres are used in this bibliography: Poem; Story; Essay; Review; Novel; Play; Prose; Translation; Interview; Interview by; Statement; Letter; Talk. An excerpt is identified as Excerpt from; for example, Excerpt from a novel.

"Essay" refers loosely to both conventional essays and to newspaper articles and columns. "Translation" refers to a translation by GB. Translations of GB's work are indicated as "Translations of." "Statement" refers to a brief statement of opinion on a subject. "Prose" refers to non-discursive writing that is not a story or a novel or a poem.

1960

C1   [Poem] *Anthology: Winter 1960*. Los Angeles: American College Poetry
Society, 1960. P. 81.
"Men Stood Up and Plundered"

1962

C2   [Poems] *Love Where the Nights Are Long: An Anthology of Canadian
Love Poems*. Selected by Irving Layton; drawings by Harold Town.
Toronto: McClelland and Stewart, 1962. Pp. 42, 49–50.
"Steps of Love"—"Dark Around Light" [Note: for GB "the first time
I had been asked by a Canadian editor to be published, so it meant that I
was somehow or another on the poetry scene" (Session 9, 18 March
1989)]

1963

C3   [Poems] *Poesie/Poetry '64*. Ed. Jacques Godbout and John Robert
Colombo. Montreal/Toronto: *Les Editions du Jour*/The Ryerson Press,
1963. Pp. 79–87.
"Eyes That Open"—"Love & War Is Kind"—"Ed Dorn"—"Family"
—"Yew Street"—"On a Black Painting by Tamayo"—"Academy"—
"The Student of the Road"—"Cadence"—"Vancouver Etude" [Note:
biographical statement on p. 79]

1964

C4   [Poem] *An Anthology for High Schools: Poetry*. By K. Phyllis Dover.
[Toronto]: Holt, Rinehart and Winston, 1964. Pp. 148–149.
"The Student of the Road"

". . . Got wd today that I am going to be in a highschool textbook called INTRO-
DUCING POETRY [sic; see C4]. First time. Terrible thing. it feeds the ego to
know kids is [sic; in] school are going to read me poem, but it is also awful to
think there the editors will put after my name: (1935–) what a thing! I hope the
editors dont say something stupid abt the poem, anyway."
[Letter from GB to Margaret Randall, 16 November 1964, published in *The Man
in Yellow Boots*; see A3]

1965

C5   [Translation] *yo soy el otro/i am the other*. By Sergio Mondragón. *Ediciones el corno emplumado colecci n acuario*, 5. Mexico: El Corno Emplumado, 1965. P. 17.
      "Tiny Sarah Dhyana" ["La Diminuta Sarah Dhyana," by Sergio Mondragón]

1966

C6   [Poems] *London Magazine Poems 1961–66*. Selected by Hugo Williams. London, England: Alan Ross, 1966. Pp. 168–172.
      "The Blue Shirt"—"To My Betrothed on the First Day of WWIII (being writ during the Cuban Crisis of 1962)"—"30 Below"—"The Boat"—"Sabino Canyon"
C7   [Story] *Modern Canadian Stories*. Ed. Giose Rimanelli and Roberto Ruberto; foreword by Earle Birney. Toronto: The Ryerson Press, 1966. Pp. 393–402.
      "Time and Again"

". . . I do remember a nice evening in Toronto in 1966. I had finally landed a short story in a big deal anthology [*Modern Canadian Stories*] from one of the big deal Toronto publishers. Ryerson Press was actually giving a wet reception for the authors to celebrate the publication, and there I was, holy smoke, in the same room with Hugh Garner and Morley Callaghan, etc. One minute after arriving I bent over to pick up a pen and split my pants from belt front to belt back. Consequently I sat down and appeared aloof. Earle Birney offered to lend me his slacks, but I demurred, and when no one was, I hoped, looking, I crab-walked out the door, and drove home to London, Ont. On the way there my car threw a rod on the 401 highway, and I became a very unsuccessful hitchhiker, holding my pants together with one hand but giving the appearance of unsocial behaviour on the roadside. Getting a free drink off Ryerson would have been a fine experience. Seeing those two famous topers lying under a table would have been better. Not walking miles at a two-step to the Forest City would have been better."
[GB Papers, Correspondence Vancouver *Sun*, 10 April 1981, NL]

1967

C8   [Poem] *Commonwealth Poems of Today*. Ed. Howard Sergeant. London, England: The English Association, 1967. Pp. 117–118.
"The Mystery of Moses"

C9   [Poem] *The Enchanted Land: Canadian Poetry for Young Readers*. Compiled by Thelma Reid Lower and Frederick William Cogswell. [Toronto]: W. J. Gage, 1967. Pp. 80–81.
"Vancouver Etude"

C10 [Statement] *The Making of Modern Poetry in Canada: Essential Articles on Contemporary Canadian Poetry in English*. Ed. Louis Dudek and Michael Gnarowski. Toronto: The Ryerson Press, 1967; paperback edition, 1970. Pp. 293–294.
"The Most Remarkable Thing about *Tish*"

"Frank Davey is moving to Victoria. Fred Wah is moving to New Mexico. James Reid promises to leave the continent. Lionel Kearns is going to lock himself in his writing room for a year. I'm moving to Calgary. That leaves Dave Dawson as the new editor of *Tish*, of which I approve heartily. He has a cordon of fresh working poets around him. That's what made *Tish* in the first place."
[From "The Most Remarkable Thing about *Tish*," *Tish* 20, August 1963; see C10 and D159]

C11 [Poems] *Modern Canadian Verse: In English and French*. Ed. A. J. M. Smith. Toronto: Oxford University Press, 1967. Pp. 360–364.
"The Grass"—"Moon Shadow"—"Inside the Tulip"—"Está Muy Caliente"

C12 [Poems] *The Penguin Book of Canadian Verse*. Ed. Ralph Gustafson. Middlesex, England: Penguin Books, 1958; revised edition, 1967. Pp. 257–258.
"Circus Maximus"—"Winter's Dregs"

C13 [Poems] *Poetry Eastwest I: An Anthology of New Poetry 1967*. Ed. Syed Amanuddin. Hyderabad, India: Syed Amanuddin, 1967. Pp. 33–34.
"A Poem That Failed As a Poem"—"Balance My Body"

C14 [Poem] *Un Siècle de Litterature Canadienne/A Century of Canadian Literature*. Ed. Guy Sylvestre and H. Gordon Green. Montreal/Toronto: Editions HMH/The Ryerson Press, 1967. P. 525.
"Red Boots (Kick Coleridge in Wordsworth's Ass)" [Note: prefatory biographical statement says GB was born in 1936]

"I been hobnobbing with the local litry crowd of late, this weekend especially as we had DGJones and wife stay with us, and went for dinner lastnight or all day at FRScott's, old GHBowering and lady friend. But I been very busy lately. Have done 5 small readings in past week, and gave some classes for people, and more this week. Not to mention the fact I've learnt I'm going to be here still in Mtl next year, sounds very exciting, and Angela digs the city, but I aint especially fond of it as a place to live, more a place to visit, but we'll see."
[GB Papers, Correspondence David McFadden, 11 December 1967, Queen's University Archives]

1968

C15   [Poem] *Calico Jam*. Ed. Rose Veighey. Toronto: The Ryerson Press, 1968. P. 12.
       "Friday Afternoon"
C16   [Poem] *The New Romans: Candid Canadian Opinions of the U. S.* Ed. Al Purdy. Edmonton: M. G. Hurtig, 1968. Pp. 116–117.
       "Winning"

"The greatest danger to Canada is, of course, the United States, but the greatest danger to Hawaii is the United States. Our best strength is our best love and beauty—I mean the local, the attention paid to the local, the authentic local object, food or symbol that stays in its place rejecting foreign standards and thus leaping from sea to sea to proclaim its uniqueness that will destroy all isolation.

"As examples I will list 10 of my favorite beautiful wholly Canadian things. A Montreal Canadian sweater. The label on Moose Head Ale. The ceiling of the drugstore in High River, Alberta. The red cliffs on the north shore of PEI. Jack Chambers' painting of the Highway 401 interchange near London, Ont. The Manitoba coat of arms. The way people say 'Jarge' instead of George in Newfoundland and Cape Breton. The scent of the air when you're driving through the Okanagan during apple-blossom time. The wheat elevators that stick up out of Floral, Sask., as you're driving past a mile away on Highway 14. The brave and beautiful name of Snag, Yukon Territory.

"The best thing about Canada is that it is not this. It is this and that."
[From "Confessions of a Failed American"; see D604]

C17   [Poem] *New Voices of the Commonwealth*. Ed. Howard Sergeant. London, England: Evans Brothers, 1968. Pp. 46–47.

"Moon Shadow"

C18   [Poem] *Solitary Walk: A Book of Longer Poems*. Toronto: The Ryerson Press, 1968. Pp. 1–2.
       "Grandfather" [Note: biographical statement and essay on GB; see H65]

1969

C19   [Poems] *Fifteen Winds: A Selection of Modern Canadian Poems*. Ed. A. W. Purdy. Toronto: The Ryerson Press, 1969. Pp. 24–26.
       "Está Muy Caliente"—"The Canada Council Poet"

C20   [Poem] *Only Humans with Songs to Sing*. New York: Smyrna Press, [August 1969]. N. p.
       "Sir George Computer University" [Note on the back of the book: "This anthology was created by mailing out the declaration which appears on the front inside cover to the literary underground. The poems of all those who responded make up the collection." Excerpt from the declaration: "We declare for libertarian communism which is already 12 months pregnant. We declare there are no more poets, only humans with songs to sing."]

C21   [Poem] *60 on the 60's: A Decade's History in Verse*. Ed. Robert McGovern and Richard Snyder. Ashland OH: Ashland Poetry Press, 1969. P. 35.
       "The Grate Society"

C22   [Poems] *Thumbprints: An Anthology of Hitchhiking Poems*. Ed. Doug Fetherling. Toronto: Peter Martin Associates, 1969. Pp. 12–13.
       "The Student of the Road"—"Bright Land"

C23   [Poem] *Upper Reaches: Poetry from* Iconolâtre *Magazine 1963–1968*. Ed. Alex Hand and Alan Turner. Durham, England: Iconolâtre Press, 1969. P. 6.
       "Sullen Poem"

1970

C24   [Poem] *blewointmentpress occupation issew*. [Ed. bill bissett.] [Vancouver]: blewointmentpress, August 1970. P. 55.
       "When I"

C25   [Excerpts from poems] *Canada* [for the 1970 Japan World Exposition]. Ed. Peter Desbarats. Montreal, 1970. Pp. 60, 66, 71, 72, 97.

117

"Forecast" [excerpt]—"Cold Spell" [excerpt]—"Winter Tan, a Joke Poem" [excerpt]—"Angela Sleeping" [excerpt]—"Mud Time" [excerpt] —"Back in Vancouver for a Vancouver Visit" [excerpt] [Note: a Japanese version of the book was also published; see G7]

C26   [Poem] *Canadian Writing Today*. Ed. Mordecai Richler. Middlesex, England: Penguin Books, 1970. P. 232.
    "30 Below"

C27   [Poem] *The Cosmic Chef Glee & Perloo Memorial Society Under the Direction of Captain Poetry Presents An Evening of Concrete Courtesy Oberon Cement Works*. Ed. bp Nichol. [Ottawa]: Oberon Press, 1970. P. 74.
    "Rain Dance" [Note: this book is usually referred to as *The Cosmic Chef: An Evening of Concrete*]

C28   [Poems] *15 Canadian Poets*. Ed. Gary Geddes and Phyllis Bruce. Toronto: Oxford University Press, 1970. Pp. 218–233.
    "The Night Before Morning"—"Grandfather"—"To Cleave"—"The Swing"—"Está Muy Caliente"—"News"—"Circus Maximus"—"Indian Summer"—"Albertasaurus"—"The House"—"The Egg"—"Dobbin"—"Our Triple Birth" [Note: brief bio-critical essay in "Notes on the Poets," pp. 270–272]

"The silence of the dust motes landing, the silence of the dumbfounded—the place to begin'composition, and the state of perfection for which to strive. The process begins when the discursive and orderly mind learns to shut up and the optic heart looks and feels."
[From "Avison's Imitation of Christ the Artist"; see A38 and D601]

C29   [Poem] *Generation Now*. Ed. Richard Woollatt and Raymond Souster. Don Mills ON: Longman, 1970. Pp. 3–4.
    "Grandfather"

C30   [Poem; Statement] *How Do I Love Thee: Sixty Poets of Canada (and Quebec) Select and Introduce Their Favourite Poems from Their Own Work*. Ed. John Robert Colombo. Edmonton: M. G. Hurtig, 1970. P. 107.
    "First Night of Fall, Grosvenor Ave."—["I have been slow in supplying a poem . . ."]

In the blue lamplight
the leaf falls

on its shadow

"During the past few years the main impetus of my composing has been toward longer poems, hopefully serial poems. In the middle of one of these, I took my dogs for a walk around midnight & saw the leaf fall. The poem fell into its place just as quietly & just as surely. I have seldom, lately, witnesst such a short synapse between the eye & the ear."
[GB's "First Night of Fall, Grosvenor Ave." and an excerpt from his comment on it; see C30]

C31   [Poems] *Inside Outer Space: New Poems of the Space Age.* Ed. Robert Vas Dias. New York: Anchor Books, 1970. Pp. 46–47.
       "Round Head"—"Play among the Stars"
C32   [Poem] *Safaris 3.* Ed. J. W. Chalmers and H. T. Coutts. Toronto: J. M. Dent & Sons, 1970. P. 216.
       "The Frost"
C33   [Story; Essay] *Sixteen by Twelve: Short Stories by Canadian Writers.* Ed. John Metcalf. Toronto: The Ryerson Press, 1970. Pp. 157–169.
       "Time and Again"—"Delsing and Me" [Note: photo and short biographical statement on p. 157, which says, "He is currently the Canadian contact for people in the U. S. A. who want to get books to Cuba"; see *Craft Slices*: "Delivering Fiction" and "Delsing and Me"; A44]

Unpublished collage by GB
and David Young; courtesy GB

"My character, George Delsing, has a name somewhat like my own. He is the narrator or central character or minor personage in almost all my fiction, novels and stories. He's not me—I am me. But he is a projection of myself more than anyone else is. His speech is very much like mine. His experiences are similar to mine, with the condition or limitation that they will always be presented through my

119

imagination, even when, as in my novel, *Mirror on the Floor*, the narrator is his best friend, Bob Small. The town of Lawrence is based on the village of Oliver, in the Okanagan Valley of British Columbia, where I grew up. Many of the people in the story (and other stories) are projections of people in Oliver. (In writing this, just now, I accidentally wrote 'Lawrence' instead of 'Oliver'—you see?)

"... I think that my novels and stories are part of an open-ended testament to my lifetime on earth. If there's no end in mind, if I don't know when I will die, I don't know when the Delsing story will end. I must therefore pay attention to both lives moment by moment, and keep on doing so. I can't come back and fix it up when it's over. So I pay attention to the things that define it as I go along. To me that means telling you where I am at the moment, and watching my language as I do."

[From "Delsing & Me," GB's commentary on his story "Time and Again"; see C33]

C34   [Poem] *Solo Flight*. Ed. Maurice Gibbons and James B. Southward. Vancouver: Resource Publications, 1970. N. p.

"The Student of the Road" [Note: this title, presenting a collection of contemporary BC poems for educational use, contains 49 items packaged in a plastic flight bag; the contents consist of various study aids, including four pamphlets; GB's poem is printed in the pamphlet called *Reaching Out*]

C35   [Essay] *Vibrations: Poems of Youth*. Ed. GB. Toronto: Gage Educational Publishing, 1970. Pp. [v–ix].

"Introduction" [to *Vibrations*; see B3]

1971

C36   [Poem] *blewointmentpress oil slick speshul*. [Ed. bill bissett.] [Vancouver]: blewointmentpress, [1971]. P. 21.

"No, Emerson"

C37   [Poem] *Book Cellar's Choice: A Small Anthology of Poems*. Commissioned by Bruce Surtees. Toronto: McClelland and Stewart, 1971. N. p.

"Angela Sleeping" [Note: this anthology celebrates The Book Cellar's 10th year; 100 copies of a numbered set were also issued]

C38   [Poem] *The Broken Ark: A Book of Beasts*. Ed. Michael Ondaatje; drawings by Tony Urquhart. [Ottawa]: Oberon Press, 1971. N. p. Reprinted as *A Book of Beasts*, 1979.

"Dobbin"

C39   [Story] *Fourteen Stories High*. Ed. David Helwig and Tom Marshall. [Ottawa]: Oberon Press, 1971. Pp. 100–102.

"Apples" [Note: note on contributors (p. 172) says GB was born in 1937 in Osoyoos, BC]

C40   [Essay] *Mordecai Richler*. Ed. G. David Sheps. Toronto: Ryerson/ McGraw-Hill, 1971. Pp. 1–14.

"And the Sun Goes Down: Richler's First Novel"

C41   [Poems] *New American and Canadian Poetry*. Ed. John Gill. Boston: Beacon Press, 1971. Pp. 26–33, 260–261.

"The Egg"—"The Beach at Veracruz"—"My Atlas Poet"—"Solid Mountain"—"Smoking Drugs with Strangers"—"Under"—"Grass, Grass" [Note: in a biographical statement (p. 260) GB says, "Born mountains of BC Dec. 1937; education is western Greyhound bus stations and colleges, mainly UBC, Vancouver, early sixties; air force photographer sometimes looking out of planes too low late fifties."]

C42   [Poem] *New Generation: Poetry*. Ed. Fred Wolven and Duane Locke. [Ann Arbor MI]: Ann Arbor Review, 1971. P. 130.

"Past"

C43   [Poems; Statements] *Rhymes and Reasons: Nine Canadian Poets Discuss Their Work*. Ed. John Robert Colombo. Toronto: Holt, Rinehart and Winston, 1971. Pp. 10–19.

"Locus Solus"—"Moon Shadow"—"Inside the Tulip"—"The Grass" —"The Egg"—"Early Afternoon in the Rainy Season" [Note: GB's comments on each of the poems are included in the selection; see *Craft Slices*: "Nature" and "Nature Studies"; A44]

"The Aztecs wrote & drew pictures of men with words, glyphs, in front of their mouths. We with our alphabet tend to abstract too much, locking the words inside our minds, just as we make our cities as colorless as we can, promoting their isolating functions, erecting tall gray buildings instead of the bright-colored ones you see all over Mexico City. This poem tries to give a sense of a city in which people can keep loose because they have so much of the countryside among their buildings. So the words are there, right in front of your face—cactus, rain, clouds, hills, trees, lake, flowers, sky, because they are all around you in the city of seven million people who are also still related to their ancestors.

   ". . . I would like you to read this poem aloud (allowed), & recognize the slight suspension at the end of the line, & I'd like you to do that with all the poems. That is the sound approach."

[GB talking about "Early Afternoon in the Rainy Season," from *Rhymes and Reasons*; see C43]

C44   [Essay; Story] *The Story So Far*. Ed. GB. Toronto: The Coach House
       Press, 1971. Pp. 7–8, 28–37.
       "Preface" [to *The Story So Far*] [Note: see *Craft Slices*: "Stories";
       A44]—"Wild Grapes and Chlorine"

"The contours of a Grecian urn are record of the touching together of hand and
clay in a moment of pushing or turning. The material flesh and the material earth
from which it came meet, and both give with each other's touch. The storyteller
may feel his own skin crawl if he tells a creepy tale."
[From *Craft Slices*: "Stories"; A44; see also B4 and C44]

1972

C45   [Poems] *blewointmentpress poverty issue*. [Ed. bill bissett.] Vancouver:
       blewointmentpress, March 1972. Pp. 22–23.
       "Smoking Drugs with Strangers"—"Quiet Man with Bells"—"An
       Old Ad"

C46   [Translation] *Th Combind Blewoint-
       ment Open Picture Book Nd Th News*.
       [Ed. þill bissett.] Vancouver: blewoint-
       mentpress, December 1972. N. p.
       "The Voices Ignored by the Rich,"
       by Roberto Sosa

C47   [Story] *Forum: Canadian Life and Let-
       ters 1920–1970: Selections from* The
       Canadian Forum. Ed. J. L. Granatstein
       and Peter Stevens. Toronto: University
       of Toronto Press, 1972. Pp. 386–391.
       "The House on Tenth"

C48   [Poem] *Look at the English-Speaking
       World*. By Sigurd Senje. Oslo: Gylden-
       dal Norsk Forlag, 1972. P. 16.
       "30 Below"

C49   [Poems] *Poets of Contemporary Canada
       1960–1970*. Ed. Eli Mandel. Toronto:
       McClelland and Stewart, 1972. Pp. 61–
       69.

GB as a teenager in Oliver, with his
reporter's hat on

       "Inside the Tulip"—"The Grass"—"The Swing"—"Está Muy
       Caliente"—"A Sudden Measure"—"The Blue"—"Indian Summer"—

C65   [Poems] *Canadian Anthology*. Ed. Carl F. Klinck and Reginald E. Watters. Toronto: Gage Educational Publishing; third edition, 1974. Pp. 547–551.
"Grandfather"—"For WCW"—"Cadence"—"News"

C66   [Essay] *Cityflowers*. By Artie Gold. Montreal: Delta, 1974. Pp. 5–6.
Introduction [to *Cityflowers*] [Note: the book is dedicated to Mary Brown and GB; see *Craft Slices*: "Gold"; A44]

C67   [Excerpt from a review; Excerpt from an essay] *Contemporary Literary Criticism*. Vol. 2. Detroit: Gale Research Company, 1974. Pp. 19–20, 29.
"Get Used to It": a review of *Power Politics*, by Margaret Atwood [excerpt]—"Avison's Imitation of Christ the Artist" [excerpt]

C68   [Essay] *From There to Here: A Guide to English-Canadian Literature Since 1960*. By Frank Davey. Erin ON: Press Porcépic, 1974. Pp. 86–91.
"Frank Davey"

Photograph of GB reproduced with a biographic sketch in *The Story So Far*; see C71

C69   [Poems] *It's Gettin Late: And Other Poems from* Ophir. Selected by Walter Saunders and Peter Horn. Johannesburg: Ravan Press, 1974. N. p.
"The Citizens"—"Scars"

C70   [Poem] *Starting Points in Reading: B, Second Book*. By Gladys Whyte and Jessie Shular. [Toronto]: Ginn and Company, 1974. P. 125.
"The Cabin"

C71   [Story] *The Story So Far: 3*. Ed. David Young. Toronto: The Coach House Press, 1974. Pp. 38–47.
"Ebbe's Roman Holiday" [Note: p. 38 is a photo and parodic contributor's note]

"Wondering. What is the status of *The Story So Far*? That is, I dont know. It might have been out for some time. I dont hear much from Coach House these days. Like I was wondering when the Mandel/Creeley BKF [*Beaver Kosmos Folio*] was going to come out & someone says it has. well, I was also wondering whether you cd if yr down there at the CH some time get some copies sent off to me.

"So abt TSSF. Is it still going to come out? I was wondering whether or not to do something else someone else has in mind with the story. I see that Persky has a majority of the work done for the next one . . . .

"Sunday afternoon here, just came in from mowing the lawn, much rather be playing baseball, but a lot of the members of the team are away for the long weekend. Oh well, next week. Roses need trimming, too.

"Aw, it's been a long time since I've heard from Toronto. Like I wrote a poem specially for Saturday Night because I am desperate for some money to pay last May's bills to Angela's various stores. And so they do it, fullpage right at the front of the mag, and what happens, no C-note. Then the rumor comes that SN aint ever going to give me my money because they havent got any. God, I hope CHP is still there. What's yr sense of *Concentric Circles*? What's yr reaction to my suggestion that I send you a short story manuscript? How'd you like a novel MSS? I have a book of essays on hip American and Canadian writers too, want it? How about an enlarged second edition of *Baseball*, another of my late jotted-down ideas? What about my editing a book of essays on Can poetry, to satisfy Victor's notion of having more BKF on Canadian writers, and making this the first 160-pp BKFCHPBook?

"Askt my daughter on her 3rd birthday whether she'd like to be a poet when she grows up and she said, 'Yech, no!' So she's already one.

"Imago 20 still not out, but Dwight [Gardiner] and Talonbooks say they anticipate it any time. Like a week from now? It will cost a fortune, of course. Dwight loves it.

"New Maple Leaf player, named Moffet. Perfect."
[Letter to David Young, 12 October 1974, GB Papers, Correspondence Coach House Press, NL]

1975

C72   [Essay] *The Canadian Novel in the Twentieth Century: Essays from Canadian Literature*. Ed. George Woodcock. Toronto: McClelland and Stewart, 1975. Pp. 219–234.
         "That Fool of a Fear: Notes on *A Jest of God*"
C73   [Excerpt from an essay] *Contemporary Literary Criticism*. Vol. 3. Detroit: Gale Research Company, 1975. Pp. 278–280.
         "That Fool of a Fear: Notes on *A Jest of God*" [excerpt]
C74   [Excerpt from a review] *Contemporary Literary Criticism*. Vol. 4. Detroit: Gale Research Company, 1975. Pp. 64–65.

"Suitcase Poets": a review of *What's So Big about Green?* by Earle Birney [excerpt] [See *Craft Slices*: "Birney's Rage"; A44]

C75   [Poem] *Imagine Seeing You Here: A World of Poetry, Lively and Lyrical*. Ed. Roberta Charlesworth. Toronto: Oxford University Press, 1975. Pp. 218–219.
      "Grandfather"

C76   [Poems] *Mirrors: Recent Canadian Verse*. Ed. Jon Pearce. [Toronto]: Gage Educational Publishing, 1975. Pp. 97–98, 172–174.
      "Grandfather"—"Far from the Shore"

GB during a trip to Arizona, October 1963; see E7 and E8; photograph © LaVerne Clark

C77   [Poems] *Montreal Poems*. Ed. Keitha K. MacIntosh. Dewittville PQ: Sunken Forum Press, 1975. Pp. 8–9.
      "Montreal Poets, 1968"—"The Imperial West"

C78   [Poems] *The Prairie Experience*. Ed. Terry Angus. Toronto: Macmillan, 1975. Pp. 48–49, 109.
      "Grandfather"—"Albertasaurus"

C79   [Essay] *Roy K. Kiyooka: 25 Years*. Exhibition Catalogue. Vancouver: Vancouver Art Gallery, 1975. N. p.
      "Roy Kiyooka's Poetry (an appreciation"

C80   [Poem; Story] *Skookum Wawa: Writings of the Canadian Northwest*. Ed. Gary Geddes. Toronto: Oxford University Press, 1975. Pp. 286, 288–295.
      "News"—"Time and Again"

C81   [Play] *Ten Canadian Short Plays*. Ed. John Stevens. New York: Dell Publishing Co. Inc., 1975. Pp. 147–159.
      The Home for Heroes

C82   [Excerpt from a poem] *These Loved, These Hated Lands*. Ed. Raymond Souster and Richard Woollatt. Toronto: Doubleday Canada, 1975. Pp. 9–11.
      "The Ninth Inning" [from *Baseball*]

C83   [Poems; Reviews; Essays; Statements] *Tish No. 1–19*. Ed. Frank Davey. Vancouver: Talonbooks, 1975.
      [Note: see individual *Tish* entries in section D, September 1961 to August 1963]

"I was sitting in the cafeteria one time and wrote 3 little lyric poems, and Gladys Hindmarch watched me doing it. She knew who I was and she came up and said, 'Oh, are you a writer? I'm a writer' and blah blah blah and that's the way that

GB in Montreal, c.1970

started off. I have no idea where I met Frank Davey. I can't remember at all. I remember meeting Gladys, I remember meeting Lionel [Kearns]. Then all of a sudden there was Frank Davey, Fred Wah, Jamie Reid, David Dawson and all those other guys; and it happened because of Warren Tallman. We were over at Warren Tallman's place one night when *Tish* started. We'd been having regular meetings outside of the university curriculum. We'd been going over to Warren Tallman's every Sunday and saying, 'oh a Robert Duncan book came out—we'll read Robert Duncan, Charles Olson', and so forth. Everybody was from out of town except Jamie Reid who had moved to Vancouver in high school. And we'd been reading *The Floating Bear*—that was our model. LeRoi Jones and Diane DiPrima ran *Floating Bear*, and it was coming in and we thought gee, ya, you can do that." [From an interview by Barry McKinnon; see D885]

1976

C84   [Excerpt from an essay] *Contemporary Literary Criticism.* Vol. 5. Detroit: Gale Research Company, 1976. Pp. 374–375.

"And the Sun Goes Down: Richler's First Novel" [excerpt]

C85   [Excerpt from a review] *Contemporary Literary Criticism.* Vol. 6. Detroit: Gale Research Company, 1976. Pp. 428–429.

"Suitcase Poets": a review of *Sex & Death*, by Al Purdy [excerpt] [See *Craft Slices*: "Purdy" and "Purdy's Process"; A44]

C86   [Poem] *The Face of Poetry: 101 Poets in Two Significant Decades—The 60's & the 70's.* Ed. LaVerne Harrell Clark and Mary MacArthur. Photographic portraits by LaVerne Harrell Clark. Foreword by Richard Eberhart. Arlington: Gallimaufry, 1976. Pp. 36–37.

"AW 6 May 25, 1974"

C87   [Review] *Leonard Cohen: The Artist and His Critics.* Ed. Michael Gnarowski. Toronto: McGraw-Hill Ryerson, 1976. Pp. 32–34.

"Inside Leonard Cohen": a review of *Parasites of Heaven*, by Leonard Cohen

C88   [Essay] *Letters from Geeksville: Red Lane to George Bowering*. Ed. GB. Prince George BC: Caledonia Writing Series, 1976. N. p.

"Some Data" [preface to *Letters from Geeksville*; see B7]

C89   [Excerpt from a novel] *The Story So Four*. Ed. Steve McCaffery and bp Nichol. [Toronto]: The Coach House Press, 1976. Pp. 12–13.

A Short Sad Book: XXIII [Note: chapter is labelled "XVIII" in Contents; "XXIII" with text]

C90   [Poems] *Twelve Prairie Poets*. Ed. Laurence Ricou. [Ottawa]: Oberon Press, 1976. Pp. 38–55.

"Prairie"—"The Oil"—"A Sudden Measure"—"Indian Summer"— "History Is Us"—"Prairie Music"—"CPR Window"—"The Streets of Calgary"—"Cold Spell"—"Mud Time" [Note: a biographic note on p. 38; GB's "A Sudden Measure" is quoted in the introduction]

C91   [Poem] *The West Coast Experience*. Ed. Jack Hodgins. Toronto: Macmillan, 1976. P. 60.

"The Student of the Road"

"I had a David McFadden-type experience this morning. I had said as I was going to sleep last night, I shd send a postcard to Barrie Nichol because we havent heard from each other in the mails for a coupla years.

"& then when I was having Mary Worth and penicillin for breakfast, along came the post, and there was a letter from bp. The letter was H. Of course. I had read his interview in Cap Rev last night, that's why I was thinking of him. The H was made partly of ink and partly of straight pins. That wd be hard to do with Q."

[GB Papers, Correspondence Barry McKinnon, 9 September 1976, NL]

C92   [Statement; Essays] *The Writing Life: Historical & Critical Views of the Tish Movement*. Ed. C. H. Gervais. Introduction by Frank Davey. Coatsworth ON: Black Moss Press, 1976. Pp. 134–135, 208–229.

"The Most Remarkable Thing about *Tish*"—"Poetry and the Language of Sound"—"How I Hear *Howl*"

1977

C93   [Poems] *th blewointmentpress end uv th world speshul*. [Ed. bill bissett.] Vancouver: blewointmentpress, 1977. Pp. 28, 80.

"E"—"Poem for Monica"

C94   [Poems] *Canadian Poetry: The Modern Era*. Ed. John Newlove.
       Toronto: McClelland and Stewart, 1977. Pp. 58–62.
       "Family"—"The Crumbling Wall"—"I Said I Said"—"Poem Written
       For George (1)"—"That Way, in Words"—"First Night of Fall, Gros-
       venor Ave"
C95   [Excerpt from a review] *Contemporary Literary Criticism*. Vol. 7.
       Detroit: Gale Research Company, 1977. P. 472.
       "The Site of Blood": a review of *Blown Figures*, by Audrey Thomas
       [excerpt]
C96   [Poems] *Horizon: Writings of the Canadian Prairie*. Ed. Ken Mitchell.
       Toronto: Oxford University Press, 1977. Pp. 64–65, 237–238.
       "Grandfather"—"The Oil"
C97   [Poem] *The Illustrated Companion History of Sir George Williams Uni-
       versity*. Ed. Ginny Jones and Joel McCormick. Montreal: Concordia
       University, 1977. P. 109.
       "Sir George Computer University"
C98   [Poem] *Learning Language*. By Philip G. Penner and Ruth E. McCon-
       nell. Toronto: Macmillan, 1977. P. 142.
       "The Grass"
C99   [Poem] *Literary Glimpses of the Commonwealth*. Ed. James B. Bell.
       Toronto: Wiley Publishers, 1977. Pp. 71–72.
       "Grandfather"
C100   [Essay] *Margaret Laurence*. Ed. William New. Toronto: McGraw-Hill
       Ryerson, 1977. Pp. 161–176.
       "That Fool of a Fear: Notes on *A Jest of God*"
C101   [Translations] *Modern Romanian Poetry*. Ed. Nicholas Catanoy. Oak-
       ville ON: Mosaic Press/Valley Editions, 1977. Pp. 24–26, 31, 42, 53–54,
       68, 70.
       "Anonymous," by Dan Desliu—"Haven," by A. E. Baconsky—"Wa-
       ters & Dreams," by Emil Botta—"Knight of the Golden Snail," by Emil
       Botta—"The Alibi," by Stefan A. Doinas—"Evening Song," by A. E.
       Baconsky—"Night Harvest," by Florenta Albu—"Your Name," by
       Stefan A. Doinas [Note: the poems were translated from the Romanian
       by J. Ure, A. Bantas, D. Dutescu, and M. Damboiu; GB wrote the poems
       in English from the literal translations]
C102   [Poems; Statement] *New: West Coast: 72 Contemporary British Colum-
       bia Poets*. Ed. Fred Candelaria. Vancouver: West Coast Review
       Books/Intermedia Press, 1977. Pp. 29–30.
       "Last Lyrics: She's Going"—"Last Lyrics: Sitting"—"Last Lyrics:
       Across 37th Avenue"—["I do not compose poetry to show you . . ."]
       [Notes: biographical sketch of GB says he was born in 1934 in West

Summerland; an issue of *West Coast Review*; see D706; see also, for GB's statement, *Craft Slices*: "Adding"; A44]

"I do not compose poetry to show you what I have seen, but rather *because* I have seen. That is, this poet's job is not to tell you what it is like, but to make a poem. If you pick up a book you do not see a red wheelbarrow; you see a 'red wheelbarrow'.

"... The point is that you are, in making a poem (or I am, I guess) not picturing the world—you are adding something to the world, something that was not there before. If you have any good feelings about the world, you will want to add something that will not diminish it in quality.

"For the same reason you would like to utterly destroy most of the pages of any given little poetry magazine."
[From a statement on poetics; see C102 and *Craft Slices*: "Adding"; A44]

"See this is one of the few times when I was born as early as 1934—that's even earlier than the general consensus of my birth."
[GB on the biographic note in *New: West Coast*, Session 9, 18 March 1989]

C103   [Letter] *Nothing Ever Happens in Pointe Claire.* By John McAuley. Montreal: Véhicule Press, 1977. N. p.
      "Dear John" [Note: GB's letter is used as a found poem; see also H249]

C104   [Prose] *The Story, She Said.* Ed. Daphne Marlatt. Vancouver: B. C. Monthly, December 1977.
      [Note: In the spring of 1974 GB was one of several writers who collaborated on a novel during a train trip to Prince George, BC to take part in a literary gathering; other writers included Brian Fawcett, Gerry Gilbert, Carole Itter, Roy Kiyooka, Dwight Gardiner, and Gladys Hindmarch; Marlatt's text works from the manuscript of the collaborative writing; see D728]

"On the long trip up (some fourteen hours), using Gerry's portable typewriter and my notepad, we began writing two separate stories whose pages were passed back & forth among the eight in turn. The stories, being the fiction of so many minds, entered a series of transformations of character & event so complex that no-one could keep them straight, & characters from the typed story began turning up in the handwritten one until one became a version of the other. Since the typewriter was less portable than the notepad (by this time we had arrived & were continuing writing in cars or cabs, in hotel lobbies, on the floor of a radio sound booth, in bars), the handwritten version took over. And took over aspects of our lived life in the parenthesis of a trip away from our daily context

(identity?) so that clearly, some of us *were*, at various times, the characters we were writing out of, or being written about, &, indeed, telling stories on one another which had to do with the actual stories of our lives, both as acted-out narrative & as intimate knowledge of each other that had never been & could hardly be event or outcome."
[From Daphne Marlatt's "how it began," the introduction to *The Story, She Said*; see C104 and D728]

C105   [Excerpt from a poem] *West Coast Works.* Ed. Penny Kemp. London ON: Applegarth Follies, 1977. N. p.
    Allophanes: I–III [Note: the alternate title of this book is *Twelfth Key*, issue No. 0]

C106   [Poems; Interview] *Western Windows: A Comparative Anthology of Poetry in British Columbia.* Ed. Patricia M. Ellis and Sandy Wilson. Vancouver: CommCept Publishing, 1977. Pp. 50–51, 56, 198–205.
    "Grandfather"—"Giant Steps"—"Curiouser & Curiouser," by Marianne Lafon and Ken Norris [Note: the interview was conducted 17 February 1976, in Montreal]

C107   [Poem] *Whale Sounds: An Anthology of Poems about Whales and Dolphins.* Ed. Greg Gatenby. North Vancouver: J. J. Douglas, 1977. P. 30.
    "The Beach at Veracruz" [Note: the book was published in both a trade edition and a limited edition]

C108   [Story] *Wild Rose Country: Stories from Alberta.* Ed. David Carpenter. [Ottawa]: Oberon Press, 1977. Pp. 139–148.
    "The Elevator"

1978

C109   [Poem] *Family Portraits.* By Ian Underhill. Toronto ON: McClelland and Stewart, 1978. Pp. 44–45.
    "Grandfather"

C110   [Poems] *15 Canadian Poets Plus 5.* Ed. Gary Geddes and Phyllis Bruce. Toronto: Oxford University Press, 1978. Pp. 275–291.
    "The Night Before Morning"—"Grandfather"—"To Cleave"—"The Swing"—"Está Muy Caliente"—"News"—"Circus Maximus"—"Indian Summer"—"Albertasaurus"—"The House"—"The Egg"—"Dobbin"—"Our Triple Birth"—"The Breath, Release" [Note: includes a bio-critical essay on GB, pp. 383–384]

C111   [Poem] *Inside Outside.* Ed. Jack Booth. [Toronto]: Holt, Rinehart and Winston, 1978. P. 192.
    "The Cabin"

C112   [Poems] *Literature in Canada: Volume 2.* Ed. Douglas Daymond and Leslie Monkman. Toronto: Gage Educational Publishing, 1978. Pp. 567–577.

"Wattle"—"Grandfather"—"Family"—"For WCW"—"The Swing" —"East to West"—"The Egg"—"Weight"

C113   [Interview; Poems; Excerpt from a poem] *Out-Posts/Avant-Postes.* Ed. Caroline Bayard and Jack David. Erin ON: Press Porcépic, 1978. Pp. 77–99, 100–103.

"George Bowering," interview by Caroline Bayard and Jack David [4 March 1976, at York University]—"Irving Layton"—"AB: The Pope"—"Roy Is Covered" [from *Genève*] [Note: subtitled, "Interviews, Poetry, Bibliographies, & a Critical Introduction to 8 Major Modern Poets"; poets included are Earle Birney, bill bissett, GB, Nicole Brossard, Paul Chamberland, Raoul Duguay, bp Nichol, and Claude P. Lokin (Péloquin)]

GB in his study, 1981; photo by Paul Little for SFU

"... the main twentieth century change from nineteenth century esthetic is that in the nineteenth century all art aimed at rest, finally. When you looked at a painting, you were led by the structure of the painting to having your eyes rest on some area of the painting. And when you taught painting in the academy, you taught where to put the most important material of that painting. And similarly with poetry. You were finally to come to rest. And the main thing that happened in twentieth century art was that you weren't allowed to do that. So Cézanne came along, and your eye doesn't rest anywhere in that painting. And the same thing started to happen with William Carlos Williams. There's one guy who finally cracked through and showed you that where Williams was coming from was from French painting. Not from Whitman or wherever. Gertrude Stein was another one. And that's why I've come back to her. It seems to me that that's the main message of the twentieth century. You can't come to rest—your eye or ear or whatever. So what do you do? You say, OK, very clear articulation of the muscle rather than a golden bird on a golden bough."

[From an interview by Caroline Bayard and Jack David; see C113]

C114   [Essay] *Playback: Canadian Selections*. Ed. Jack David and Michael Park.
        Toronto: McClelland and Stewart, 1978. Pp. 159–164.
        "The Art of the Webfoot"
C115   [Poem] *The Poets of Canada*. Ed. John Robert Colombo. Edmonton:
        Hurtig Publishers, 1978. P. 228.
        "Mouths" [Note: prefatory biographical note says GB was born in
        1938 in Keremeos, BC]
C116   [Excerpt from a novel] *A Political Art: Essays and Images in Honour of
        George Woodcock*. Ed. William H. New. Vancouver: University of
        British Columbia Press, 1978. Pp. 151–152.
        A Short Sad Book: IX
C117   [Poems] *Roman Candles: An Anthology of Poems by Seventeen Italo-
        Canadian Poets*. Ed. Pier Giorgio Di Cicco. Toronto: Hounslow Press,
        1978. Pp. 46–47.
        "Maple" [published under pseud. Ed Prato]—"Immigrant" [pub-
        lished under pseud. Ed Prato]

Ed Prato first submitted poems for *Roman Candles* under the name Ed Pratoverde (i. e. Greengrass in English), but in a letter, 19 April 1977, to editor Pier
Giorgio Di Cicco he wrote: "I think, after thinking about it, I think I'll drop that
dumb pen name, and go with my real name, Ed Prato."
    When two poems were accepted, Prato sent in a brief biography, 25 June
1977: "My parents came here from Trieste in 1951, and I was born a year later, in
Trail, B. C. We moved to San Diego when I was five, and my parents still live
there. I came back to Canada, for obvious reasons, in 1960. I have published a
few poems in very small magazines, but this will be my first publication east of
Saskatoon. I expect to have a book of poems ready in about a year."
[GB Papers, Correspondence Ed Prato, NL]

GB recalled *Roman Candles*: "There were ads looking for Italian Canadian
poets, and Prato said, I could start my literary career in *Roman Candles*, and so
he wrote a bunch of poems in one afternoon—five or six—and shot them to
Giorgio Di Cicco and a couple were published."
[Session 9, 18 March 1989] [Note: poems by Prato were collected in *Seventy-one
Poems for People*; see A45]

C118   [Excerpt from a poem] *Together We Stand*. By Donald G. Swinburne.
        Toronto: Gage Publishing, 1978. P. 40.
        "East to West" [excerpt]
C119   [Poems; Statement] *Transitions III: Poetry: A Source Book of Canadian
        Literature*. Ed. Edward Peck. Vancouver: CommCept Publishing, 1978.
        Pp. 17–18, 51–52, 107, 216–217.

"Grandfather"—"Está Muy Caliente"—"The Blue"—"On 'Grand-father', 'The Blue' and 'Está Muy Caliente' " [Notes: biographic note (p. 315) says GB was born in 1935 in Naramata, BC; see *Craft Slices*: "Anthology Poems"; A44]

"My most often anthologized poem is 'Grandfather'. It fits so nicely into classes organized along thematic lines, and classes that are organized in such a way that students will learn something about this great nation of theirs.

" 'Grandfather' was written during the *Tish* days, when I was a student at UBC, and lived on the third floor of a rickety house on the slopes over False Creek. One night I was trying to get in late, during a rain, but my room-mate had locked the door. I didnt have a key and I had trouble throwing pebbles against the high window because my right hand was in a cast. Eventually I climbed the wooden ladder nailed to the side of the house. I dont know how I made it, because it was still raining, I had my hand in a cast and I was carrying a case of beer. Anyway, out of drunkenness or anger or both plus something else, I wrote, partly with my left hand, a highly rhetorical poem unlike the rest of the poems I was writing for *Tish*. I left it on the kitchen table linoleum and went to bed; and the next day my roomie Willy Trump said it was great. Since then it has been published a few times every year. A real money-maker, that one."
[From "Anthology Poems," in *Craft Slices*; see A44 and C119]

1979

C120   [Poem] *The Alberta Diamond Jubilee Anthology*. Ed. John W. Chalmers. Edmonton: Hurtig Publishers, 1979. Pp. 108–110.
"The Oil" [Note: biographic note says GB was born in 1933 in Penticton, BC]
C121   [Excerpt from a poem] *Amateurs: On the Margin between Work and Leisure*. By Robert A. Stebbins. Beverly Hills/London: Sage Publications, 1979. Pp. 229–231.
Baseball [excerpt]
C122   [Excerpt from an essay] *Contemporary Literary Criticism*. Vol. 10. Detroit: Gale Research Company, 1979. Pp. 288–289.
"Coming Home to the World" [on D. G. Jones] [excerpt]
C123   [Poem] *A Critical (Ninth) Assembling, Precisely: Six Seven Eight Nine*. Compiled and introduced by Richard Kostelanetz. New York: Assembling Press, 1979. N. p.

"e. k." [Note: from the preface, "Also published as *Ninth Assembling Precisely: Six Seven Eight* and *Nine*"]

C124   [Poems] *Explore Express.* Ed. Betty Cooper. Edmonton: Alberta School Broadcast Publications, 1979–1980. Pp. 114, 117.

"Mud Time"—"Albertasaurus"

C125   [Poem] *The Face of Poetry: 101 Poets in Two Significant Decades—The 60's & the 70's.* Ed. LaVerne Harrell Clark and Mary MacArthur. Chico CA: Heidelberg Graphics, 1976; second edition, 1979. Pp. 36–37.

"AW 6 May 25, 1974"

C126   [Story] *Fiddlehead Greens: Stories from* The Fiddlehead. Selected by Roger Ploude and Michael Taylor. [Ottawa]: Oberon Press, 1979. Pp.176–185.

"Flycatcher"

C127   [Essay; Poem] *Great Canadian Sports Stories.* Ed. GB. [Ottawa]: Oberon Press, 1979. Pp. 5–7.

"When Revelation Comes Athlete and Sage Are Merged" [preface to *Great Canadian Sports Stories,* which includes the poem, "A DP in Time"] [See *Craft Slices:* "Sports Fiction"; A44 and B8]

C128   [Poem; Statement] *The Long Poem Anthology.* Ed. Michael Ondaatje. Toronto: The Coach House Press, 1979; reprinted, 1986. Pp. 203–243, 329–331.

Allophanes—"Look into Your Ear & Write: Allophanes" [See *Craft Slices:* "Long Poem"; A44 and A24]

"On the BC Ferry, David McFadden closes his eyes & meditates. In this attitude he hears all the people's voices around him. David is picking up the news & views of the world. He is a good listener.

"I cock my ear. What I want to hear is the voice that enters my secluded study. I dont care, really, to enquire of it where it is coming from. If it is loud enough it is all round one. In this manner I settle the perennial question put to poets: what is your concept of an audience? I am aware of myself as audience. When one plays by ear, it is not to hear what one is putting out. There is enough to do in catching what comes in.

"As I get older, I come more to realize that my activity as a poet composing is an extension of my desirous childhood Christianity. I want like crazy to get here alone & hear God's voice. I mean it. If I hear the gods instead, I am acknowledging, like it or not, my adulthood."

[From "Look into Your Ear & Write: Allophanes"; see A24 and C128]

C129 [Essay] *My Body Was Eaten by Dogs: Selected Poems of David McFadden.* Ed. GB. Toronto/Montreal/New York: McClelland and Stewart/ CrossCountry Press, 1981. Pp. 7–18 [Cdn. ed.]; 9–20 [US ed.]
"Proofing the World: The Poems of David McFadden" [See B11]

C130 [Poem] *Other Canadas: An Anthology of Science Fiction and Fantasy.* Ed. John Robert Colombo. Toronto: McGraw-Hill Ryerson, 1979. Pp. 258–263.
"Windigo"

C131 [Poems] *Panorama: Western Canadian Literature for Youth.* Ed. Theresa M. Ford. Edmonton: Alberta Education, 1979. Pp. 41, 155.
"The Frost"—"Tunnel Mountain"

C132 [Poems] *To Say the Least: Canadian Poets from A to Z.* Ed. P. K. Page. Toronto: Press Porcépic, 1979. Pp. 10, 59, 61, 86.
"Play among the Stars"—"First Night of Fall, Grosvenor Ave."—"The Frost"—"Did"

C133 [Poem] *Western Profiles.* Ed. Theresa M. Ford. Edmonton: Alberta Education, 1979. Pp. 85–86.
"Grandfather"

"No, I am not all those things they say on the back cover, or more properly inside the back cover; that is, I am pisst off that they have me there and in the small ads as Canada's most or one of them 'irreverent' poets, and I know what that is sposed to mean in litsell jargon, but I have been trying to let them and it know for long that I am the opposite, that reverence is what we need around here, and I am interested in what we need, us country."
[GB Papers, Correspondence Margaret Atwood, 19 November 1979, NL]

1980

C134 [Excerpt from a review; Excerpt from an essay] *Contemporary Literary Criticism.* Vol. 13. Detroit: Gale Research Company, 1980. Pp. 357, 538–540.
"A Complex Music": a review of *The Rising Fire*, by Gwendolyn MacEwen [excerpt] [See *Craft Slices:* "MacEwen's Music"; A44]—"Snow Red: The Short Stories of Audrey Thomas" [excerpt]

C135 [Excerpt from a review] *Contemporary Literary Criticism.* Vol. 14. Detroit: Gale Research Company, 1980. P. 377.
Black Night Window, by John Newlove: a review [excerpt]

C136   [Excerpt from a review; Excerpt from an essay] *Contemporary Literary Criticism*. Vol. 15. Detroit: Gale Research Company, 1980. Pp. 9–10, 336–338.
"Acorn Blood": a review of *I've Tasted My Blood*, by Milton Acorn [excerpt]—"Denise Levertov" [excerpt]

C137   [Essay; Story; Statement] *Fiction of Contemporary Canada*. Ed. GB. Toronto: The Coach House Press, 1980. Pp. 7–21, 142–152, 173–175.
"Introductory Notes" [to *Fiction of Contemporary Canada*]—"A Short Story"—"Some Other Rooms in the House" [See B9]

ESSAYING   WAH

The shadows of
the maple tree's leaves

shimmer on the white paper
as I type,

dazing my eyes till

the prose I am trying
turns to poetry.

— G.B.

"Essaying Wah," in GB's handwriting, reproduced in "Poetry and Politics Blend in Bowering"; see D816

"Bowering believes that readers should be reminded that fiction is made of illusion; hence he will often display the carpentry behind the false fronts. He is also interested in the voice of the narrator, sometimes inviting his readers to hear rather than see the story. Often called arch & self-indulgent, he is known for placing the character of the author between the reader & the narrative action."
[From "Introductory Notes"; see B9 and C137]

C138   [Essay] *Loki Is Buried at Smoky Creek: Selected Poems: Fred Wah*. Ed. GB. Vancouver: Talonbooks, 1980. Pp. 9–21.
"The Poems of Fred Wah" [See B10]

C139   [Poem] *Poems of a Snow-Eyed Country*. Ed. Richard Woollatt and Raymond Souster. Don Mills ON: Academic Press, 1980. Pp. 115–116.
"Above Calgary"

"Always swim in water that is over your head. Ski a slope that is frighteningly steep. Keep trying for excellence you think you do not have in you and pay the most intense attention to all your movements. You will know that your limits (or the poem's) are expanding, and all the time you will be reminded of your mortality. There is no time for pride there, but what you will have done will speak of, hint of, perceptions not totally available to human knowledge."
[From "Avison's Imitation of Christ the Artist"; see A38 and D601]

1981

C140   [Poem] *Connections 1: Imagining*. Ed. Richard Davies and Glen Kirkland. Toronto: Gage Publishing, 1981. P. 222.
"News"

C141   [Poem] *Developing Writing Skills*. By William W. West, Stephen D. Bailey and Bernice L. Wood. Scarborough ON: Prentice-Hall; third edition, 1981. Pp. 365–366.
"30 Below"

C142   [Essay] *The Human Elements*. Second Series. Ed. David Helwig. [Ottawa]: Oberon Press, 1981. Pp. 113–131.
"Metaphysic in Time: The Poetry of Lionel Kearns"

C143   [Poem] *Introduction to Literature: British, American, Canadian*. Ed. Gillian Thomas, Richard J. H. Perkyns, Kenneth A. MacKinnon, Wendy R. Katz. Toronto: Holt, Rinehart and Winston, 1981. Pp. 256–257.
"Grandfather"

C144   [Editor; Essay] *Introduction to Poetry: British, American, Canadian*. Ed. Jack David and Robert Lecker. Toronto: Holt, Rinehart and Winston, 1981. Pp. 587–588.
"Introduction: 1945–80" [See *Craft Slices*: "X" and "Xenogenesis"; A44]

C145   [Poem] *The Maple Laugh Forever: An Anthology of Canadian Comic Poetry*. Ed. Douglas Barbour and Stephen Scobie. Edmonton: Hurtig Publishers, 1981. P. 38.
"A Poem for High School Anthologies"

George Bowering was born in
Princeton, British Columbia,
December 1st, 1939, the son of
a high school Latin teacher.
[From "A Poem for High School Anthologies; see C145 and A33]

C146   [Poems] *The Oxford Anthology of Canadian Literature*. Ed. Robert Weaver and William Toye. Toronto: Oxford University Press, 1973; second edition, 1981. Pp. 33–36.
"Grandfather"—"Moon Shadow"—"Prairie"—"Mud Time" [Note: includes a biographical sketch]

C147   [Poem] *Senior High Language Arts*. By Shirley I. Paustian. Calgary: Access, 1981. P. 20.
"Grandfather"

1982

C148   [Poem] *Canada with Love/Canada avec Amour*. Ed. Lorraine Monk. Toronto: McClelland and Stewart, 1982. N. p.
"First Night of Fall, Grosvenor Ave." [Notes: the poem is printed untitled; bilingual edition, translated by Gail Vanstone; see G12]

C149   [Essay] *The Canadian Novel, Volume III: Modern Times: A Critical Anthology*. Ed. John Moss. Toronto: NC Press, 1982. Pp. 209–223.
"Sheila Watson, Trickster"

C150   [Poems] *Canadian Poetry: Volume Two*. Ed. Jack David and Robert Lecker. Downsview/Toronto: ECW Press/General Publishing, 1982. Pp. 153–161.
"Radio Jazz"—"Grandfather"—"The Night Before Morning"— "Está Muy Caliente"—"Circus Maximus"—"Inside the Tulip"— "Daphne Marlatt"—"Did"—"Against Description" [Note: includes a brief essay by Ken Norris, pp. 302–303]

C151   [Story] *Introduction to Fiction*. Ed. Jack David and Robert Lecker. Toronto: Holt, Rinehart and Winston, 1982. Pp. 104–107.
"The Elevator"

C152   [Poems; Excerpt from a poem] *The New Oxford Book of Canadian Verse in English*. Selected by Margaret Atwood. Toronto: Oxford University Press, 1982. Pp. 322–328.
"Grandfather"—"Dobbin"—"The House"—"The Envies"—"From 'Summer Solstice' "—"In the Forest" [Note: date of birth says GB was born in 1938]

C153   [Poem; Letters] *Tasks of Passion: Dennis Lee at Mid-Career*. Ed. Karen Mulhallen, Donna Bennett, and Russell Brown. Toronto: Descant Editions, 1982. Pp. 9, 191–198.
"Detachment from Self"—"Towards Polyphony: Extracts from a Conversation between Dennis Lee and George Bowering" [Note: this book is an issue of *Descant*; see D790]

C154   [Poems] *"Views beside . . . "*. Ed. Fritz Balthaus. Berlin: Ed Vogelsang, 1982. N. p.
"Executive Line"—"Alpha"

C155   [Poem] *Windigo: An Anthology of Fact and Fantastic Fiction*. Ed. John Robert Colombo. Saskatoon: Western Producer Prairie Books, 1982. Pp. 187–191.
"Windigo"

1983

C156   [Poems] *An Anthology of Canadian Literature in English.* Vol. II. Ed. Donna Bennett and Russell Brown. Toronto: Oxford University Press, 1983. Pp. 374–384.
"Harbour Beginnings & That Other Gleam"—"Thru"—"The Raspberries"—"Desert Elm" [Note: includes a brief introductory essay on GB, pp. 374–375]

C157   [Essay] *Approaches to the Work of James Reaney.* Ed. Stan Dragland. Downsview ON: ECW Press, 1983. Pp. 1–31.
"Reaney's Region"

C158   [Excerpts from a poem] *British Columbia: A Celebration.* Ed. George Woodcock. Edmonton: Hurtig Publishers, 1983. P. 42.
George, Vancouver [excerpts]

C159   [Essays; Poems; Excerpt from a poem] *The Contemporary Canadian Poem Anthology.* Four Volumes. Ed. GB. Toronto: The Coach House Press, 1983. Volume 1: pp. 1–3, 53–66. Volume 4: pp. 347–353.
"Unexpected Objects" [preface to *The Contemporary Canadian Poem Anthology*] [See *Craft Slices*: "Unexpected Objects"; A44]—"Rime of Our Time"—"The House"—"Ike & Others" [excerpt]—"The Owl's Eye"—"Feet, Not Eyes"—"James Reaney"—"Poem Written For George (2)"—"Summer Solstice"—"The End of the Line" [Vol. 4] [See B12]

C160   [Story] *Illusion Two: Fables, Fantasies and Metafictions.* Ed. Geoff Hancock. Toronto: Aya Press, 1983. Pp. 25–40.
"Arbre de Décision"

C161   [Poem] *Lords of Winter: And of Love.* Ed. Barry Callaghan. Toronto: Exile Editions, 1983. P. 135.
"Inside the Tulip"

C162   [Essay] *A Place to Stand On: Essays by and about Margaret Laurence.* Ed. George Woodcock. Edmonton: NeWest Press, 1983. Pp. 210–226.
"That Fool of a Fear: Notes on *A Jest of God*"

"Yeah, that picture of me on *Flycatcher* was taken when I was abt 14 I think, and the book I'm reading so seriously is *How to Win Friends and Influence People*—it didn't work. All the time I was in school I was the guy that didnt get invited to parties, remained a virgin, and was pickt last when they were choosing sides for a game. I have been compensating ever since, at this time playing ball twice at least a week, etc. etc. But when I was in school I made up for it, in fact I was romantically glad to be a loner, with abt 3 friends off and on, so that I became a big deal stage actor in school, and wrote sports for all the papers in the South Okanagan etc. and read all the books anyone in that beknighted region cd lay hands on.

Why I became or tried to become a writer. Oak Park, B. C. Manawaga, British Columbia."
[GB Papers, Correspondence Margaret Laurence, 8 July 1975, NL]

C163   [Story] *Short Short Stories: An Anthology*. Ed. Reingard M. Nischik. Paderborn, Germany: Ferdinand Scho-ningh, 1983. Pp. 27–30.
"Apples" [Note: includes a brief essay and biographical note, pp. 25–26]

C164   [Poems] *Through the Open Window*. Ed. Shirley I. Paustian. Toronto: Oxford University Press, 1983. Pp. 43–44.

GB with Allen Ginsberg, Vancouver, c.1979

"Albertasaurus"—"News"

C165   [Story] *West of Fiction*. Ed. Leah Flater, Aritha van Herk and Rudy Wiebe. Edmonton: NeWest Press, 1983. Pp. 329–339.
"A Short Story" [Note: includes a photo and brief biographical sketch, p. 329]

C166   [Poem] *The World of the Novel: The Stone Angel*. Ed. Lillian Perigoe and Beverley Copping. Scarborough ON: Prentice-Hall, 1983. P. 22.
"CPR Window"

1984

C167   [Poem] *The Anthology Anthology: A Selection from 30 Years of CBC Radio's "Anthology."* Ed. Robert Weaver. Toronto: Macmillan, 1984. Pp. 46–50.
"Four Jobs"

C168   [Essays; Poems; Excerpt from a poem] *The Contemporary Canadian Poem Anthology*. Ed. GB. Toronto: The Coach House Press, 1983; second edition, 1984. Pp. 1–3, 53–66, 347–353.
"Unexpected Objects" [preface to *The Contemporary Canadian Poem Anthology*] [See *Craft Slices*: "Unexpected Objects"; A44]—"Rime of Our Time"—"The House"—"Ike & Others" [excerpt]—"The Owl's Eye"—"Feet, Not Eyes"—"James Reaney"—"Poem Written For George (2)"—"Summer Solstice"—"The End of the Line" [See B12]

"If I keep editing, I'll be the John Robert Colombo of the avant-garde."
[GB Papers, c. 1972, NL]

C169   [Poem] *Inside Poetry.* Ed. Glen Kirkland and Richard Davies. Toronto: Academic Press, 1984. P. 79.
"CPR Window"

C170   [Essay] *On the Poetry of Allen Ginsberg.* Ed. Lewis Hyde. Ann Arbor MI: University of Michigan Press, 1984. Pp. 370–378.
"How I Hear *Howl*" [See A8]

C171   [Poems] *The Penguin Book of Canadian Verse.* Ed. Ralph Gustafson. Middlesex, England: Penguin Books, 1958; fourth revised edition, 1984. Pp. 281–283.
"Circus   Maximus"—"Winter's   Dregs"—"In   the   Elevator"—"Against Description"

C172   [Poems] *The Poet's Craft.* Ed. R. J. Ireland. Don Mills ON: Academic Press, 1984. Pp. 65–66, 109–110.
"Grandfather"—"The Crumbling Wall" [Note: the notes to the poems say GB was born in 1938 on p. 66; in 1935 on p. 110]

C173   [Stories] *Shoes & Shit: Stories for Pedestrians.* Ed. Geoff Hancock and Rikki Ducornet. Toronto: Aya Press, 1984. Pp. 78–81, 83–85.
"The Xalapa Handkerchief"—"Constantinople Boots"

"Here's one of the great titles of all time for an anthology. It was perfect because I had a story in which a guy had shit on his shoes, so what could be better?"
[GB on *Shoes & Shit*, Session 9, 18 March 1989; see C173]

C174   [Excerpts from poems] *Vancouver Literary Landscapes.* [Ed. Colin Browne.] Vancouver: SFU, 1984. Pp. 45–48, 155–161.
George, Vancouver [excerpt]—"Elegy Seven" [from *Kerrisdale Elegies*]

1985

C175   [Poems] *Antología de la Poesía Anglocanadiense Contemporánea.* Ed. and trans. Bernd Dietz. Barcelona, Spain: Los Libros de la Frontera, 1985. Pp. 179–185.
"The Grass"—"Indian Summer"—"Forget" [Notes: bilingual edition, translations, pp. 181, 183, 185; includes a brief biography, p. 179; mentions GB in "Introduccion," pp. 9–34] [See G15]

C176   [Translations; Poems] *Grey Matters: The Peace Arts Anthology.* Ed.
        Daniel Brooks and Enda Soostar. Ottawa: Peace Arts Publishers, 1985.
        Pp. 49–51, 69, 110, 116.
        "What Peace Looks Like," by Manuel Pacheco—"What Hunger
        Looks Like," by Manuel Pacheco—"He's Sinking Fast"—"In the Field"

C177   [Poems] *No Feather, No Ink: After Riel.* Saskatoon: Thistledown Press,
        1985. Pp. 143–152.
        Uncle Louis [Note: GB's poem is about Louis St. Laurent, so he
        "could never quite figure out why it was put in that anthology, unless
        somebody thought Uncle Louis referred to Louis Riel, but there's no
        mention of Riel in the poem at all" (Session 9, 18 March 1989); see A34]

C178   [Essay] *Sheila Watson and* The Double Hook. Ed. GB. Ottawa: The
        Golden Dog Press, 1985. Pp. 187–199.
        "Sheila Watson, Trickster" [See B13]

C179   [Essay] *Spider Blues: Essays on Michael Ondaatje.* Ed. Sam Solecki.
        Montreal: Véhicule Press, 1985. Pp. 61–69.
        "Ondaatje Learning to Do"

C180   [Essay] *Towards a Canadian Literature: Essays, Editorials and Manifes-
        toes. Volume II: 1940–1983.* Ed. Leslie Monkman and Douglas Day-
        mond. Ottawa: Tecumseh Press, 1985. Pp. 524–530.
        "Modernism Could Not Last Forever"

C181   [Story] *Vancouver Fiction.* Ed. David Watmough. Winlaw BC: Polestar
        Press, 1985. Pp. 66–80.
        "Ebbe & Hattie"

C182   [Story] *Vancouver Short Stories.* Ed. Carole Gerson. Vancouver: UBC
        Press, 1985. Pp. 111–118.
        "Spans"

1986

C183   [Story] *The Bumper Book.* Ed. John Metcalf. Toronto: ECW Press, 1986.
        Pp. 56–67.
        "Being Audited"

C184   [Essay] *Canada Ieri E Oggi: Atti Del 6° Convegno Internazionale Di
        Studi Canadesi.* Ed. Giovanni Bonnanno. Fasano, Italy: Schena Editore,
        1986. Pp. 15–43.
        "A Great Northward Darkness: The Attack on History in Recent
        Canadian Fiction" [Note: the essay was presented at the sixth Inter-
        national conference on Canadian Studies, 27–31 March 1985, in Solva di
        Fasano]

C185   [Interview; Excerpts from poems; Poem] *Canadian Literature: A Guide*. By the Council of Ministers of Education of Canada. Calgary: Alberta Educational Communications Corporation (Access Network), 1986. Pp. 16–26.

"A Conversation with George Bowering"—"A Poem for High School Anthologies" [excerpt]—*Baseball:* "9th Inning"—"The Flying Dream"—"The Brush Fire"—"Desert Elm" [excerpts] [Note: this guide supplements a series of video programs featuring 24 Canadian writers, including GB; it contains expanded interviews with the writers and the literary material read or produced in the video program. The biographical note on p. 26 says GB was born in 1939] [see E80]

"I feel as if I belong to a tradition, not the whole tradition, and certainly not what some people in eastern Canada would call 'the Canadian tradition'. I feel as if I am doing a big project, or something like that, that's been going on for hundreds of years. And the poets that have delighted me are the poets that I feel that responsibility to, in terms of what they think the relationship between language and a human being in the world is."
[From "A Conversation with George Bowering"; see C185]

C186   [Excerpt from a review] *Contemporary Literary Criticism*. Vol. 38. Detroit: Gale Research Company, 1986. Pp. 135–136.
"Inside Leonard Cohen": a review of *Parasites of Heaven*, by Leonard Cohen [excerpt]

C187   [Story] *Oxford Book of Canadian Short Stories in English*. Selected by Margaret Atwood and Robert Weaver. Toronto: Oxford University Press, 1986. Pp. 279–287.
"A Short Story"

C188   [Poem] *The Swift Current Anthology*. Ed. Frank Davey and Fred Wah. Toronto: The Coach House Press, 1986. P. 19.
"My Father in New Zealand"

C189   [Excerpt from a poem] *Vancouver Poetry*. Ed. Allan Safarik. Winlaw BC: Polestar Press, 1986. Pp. 176–183.
"Elegy Eight" [from *Kerrisdale Elegies*]

C190   [Poem; Excerpt from a poem] *Vancouver: Soul of a City*. Ed. Gary Geddes. Vancouver: Douglas & McIntyre, 1986. Pp. 217–219, 280–284.
"Vancouver Etude"—"Elegy One" [from *Kerrisdale Elegies*]

1987

C191   [Excerpt from a novel] *The CanLit Foodbook*. Compiled and illustrated by Margaret Atwood. Toronto: Totem Books, 1987. Pp. 167–168.

"The Natives Discuss Cannibalism" [from *Burning Water*: 25]

C192   [Prose; Talks] *Future Indicative: Literary Theory and Canadian Literature*. Ed. John Moss. Ottawa: University of Ottawa Press, 1987. Pp. 5–24, 239–245. [Proceedings of a conference, University of Ottawa, 25–27 April 1986]

"Errata 1–11"—"Writer Writing, Ongoing Verb" [with Robert Kroetsch; edited by Betty Schellenberg]—"Present Tense: The Closing Panel" [with Stephen Scobie, Robert

GB with Robert Kroetsch, Geelong, Victoria, Australia, 1986

Kroetsch and Linda Hutcheon] [Note: GB read "Errata 1–11" as part of his talk in "Writer Writing, Ongoing Verb," pp. 6–9]

C193   [Essay] *"Lighting Up the Terrain": The Poetry of Margaret Avison*. Ed. David Kent. Toronto: ECW Press, 1987. Pp. 78–81.

"Margaret, a Vision"

C194   [Poems] *Our American Cousins*. Ed. Thomas S. Axworthy. Toronto: James Lorimer and Company, 1987. Pp. 115–119.

"Above Montana"—"Single World West" [Note: includes introduction and comments on GB's poems, p. 115]

1988

C195   [Excerpt from a story] *Bridges*. Ed. S. D. Robinson *et al.* Scarborough ON: Prentice-Hall, 1988. Pp. 285, 292.

"Time and Again" [Excerpt] [Note: only one sentence cited as an example of a cumulative sentence in this educational text]

C196   [Excerpt from an essay] *Contemporary Literary Criticism*. Vol. 48. Ed. Daniel G. Marowski and Roger Matuz. Detroit: Gale Research Company, 1988. Pp. 248–251.
"Proofing the World: The Poems of David McFadden" [excerpt]

C197   [Poem] *Everyone Leans, Each on Each Other: Words for John Newlove on the Occasion of His Fiftieth Birthday*. [Ottawa]: Bastard Press, 1988. N. p.
"Silver in the Silver Sun" [Colophon: "Published on Canada Day 1988 by the Bastard Press in an edition of 30 copies of which this is No. _."]

C198   [Essay] *Experience and Expression: A Reader for Canadian Writers*. Ed. Alden R. Turner. Toronto: Copp Clark Pitman, 1988. Pp. 4–5.
"Between the Lines"

C199   [Poems] *15 Canadian Poets x 2*. Ed. Gary Geddes. Toronto: Oxford University Press; third edition, 1988. Pp. 341–358.
"Grandfather"—"Está Muy Caliente"—"News"—"Circus Maximus"—"Indian Summer"—"Albertasaurus"—"The House"—"Dobbin"—"Summer Solstice"—"Sequestered Pop & a Stripe"—"Bones along Her Body" [Note: includes a bio-critical essay on GB, pp. 525–527]

C200   [Excerpts from interviews; Poems; Excerpts from poems; Statements; Excerpts from essays; Letters; Prose] *George Bowering Condensed*. By Nicholas Drumbolis. Toronto: Letters Bookstore, [1988]. N. p.
"Curiouser & Curiouser" [excerpts]—"George Bowering" in *Out-Posts* [excerpts]—"At the Intersection"—*Baseball* [excerpt]—*How I Hear* Howl [excerpt]—Letter to Al Purdy, 22 July 1970—"The Owl's Eye"—Letter to Al Purdy, 24 February 1973—"In Answer (to a question from the gathering)" [excerpt]—"Daniel Johnson Lying in State"—"The Old Roue & the Old Hot Number"—"Another Week in the East" [excerpt]—"The Canada Council Poet"—"A Declaration"—"The American Bomb"—"How to Write" [see *Craft Slices*: "How to Write"; A44] [Note: dedications and statements of intent from several of GB's books accompany their entries, as well as reproductions of various book covers; this bibliography, List 67 of Letters Bookstore, was printed in an edition of 40 copies] Special thanks to Nicky Drumbolis for sharing his knowledge of GB's publications during a visit to his Toronto bookstore, Letters Bookstore.

C201   [Excerpts from a poem] *Insight: Canadian Writers View Holland. Volume I: Poetry*. Ed. Hendrika Ruger. Windsor ON: Netherlandic Press, 1988. Pp. 64–67.
"Excerpts from *George, Vancouver: A Discovery Poem*"

C202   [Poems] *The New Canadian Anthology*. Ed. Jack David and Robert Lecker. Scarborough ON: Nelson, 1988. Pp. 207–216.

"Grandfather"—"Against Description"—"The House"—"Thru"—
"Summer Solstice" [Note: includes a prefatory biographical note by Ken
Norris, p. 207]

C203 [Interview] *Strong Voices: Conversations with Fifty Canadian Authors.*
By Alan Twigg. Madeira Park BC: Harbour Publishing, 1988. Pp. 31–34.
"George Bowering," interviewed by Alan Twigg

C204 [Prose] *Tracing the Paths: Reading ≠ Writing* The Martyrology [by bp
Nichol]. Ed. Roy Miki. Vancouver/Burnaby: Talonbooks/Line, 1988.
Pp. 299–300.
"Errata: 58, 67." [Note: this book is an issue of *Line*; see D876]

Section D
Periodicals with Contributions
by George Bowering

Section D lists titles in chronological order by date of publication, starting from Winter in January through to Winter in December. After the genre, the section title is provided where applicable, followed by the title of the periodical, place of publication in parentheses, volume number, issue number, date of publication, page numbers, and title or titles by GB.

The entries begin in 1953, when GB was 17 years old. Material written before, for example, publications in school yearbooks and the sports articles he wrote while in high school and published in the local newspapers, *Oliver Chronicle* and the *Penticton Herald*, are not included. One other area of omission should be noted. When GB served in the RCAF (1954–57) he was for a time the reporter for his section, the photo section, and in that capacity he contributed to the *Rocketeer* at the Macdonald base in Manitoba. That weekly camp newspaper proved too elusive to locate—there is a strong likelihood that it no longer exists—but GB luckily saved a few samples in his scrapbook, and these are included in section D.

Section D attempts to list all of GB's contributions to periodicals from 1953 to 1988, but given the enormous amount he published in such scattered places over this 35-year period, there are undoubtedly stray titles "out there" that have slipped through the network of search and rescue.

For the list of genres, see the introductory note to Section C: Books with Contributions by GB.

1953

D1   [Letter] *Baseball Magazine* (New York NY) 90, No. 1 (Spring 1953): 4.
      "Letter to the Editor"

1956

D2   [Essay] *The Rocketeer* (Mac-
      donald MB), 14 May 1956.
      "Photographs Uncensor-
      ed" [Note: GB was the re-
      porter for the photo section of
      the RCAF camp at Mac-
      donald, and his articles jok-
      ingly—often parodying jour-
      nalistic form—presented news
      and portraits of men in his sec-
      tion]
D3   [Essay] *The Rocketeer* (Mac-
      donald MB), [May or June]
      1956.
      "Strangled Stripper Found
      in Photo Section"

GB in the RCAF, c. 1956

"Why do you find yourself reading this column? Could it be that we caught
your interest with the above headline?
      "Well, do not be so certain of the impossibility of such a situation. Anything
and everything can happen in the photo section and to photographers who are
lucky enough to find employment at Macdonald."
[From "Strangled Stripper Found in Photo Section"; see D3]

D4   [Poem] *The Rocketeer* (Macdonald MB), [May or June] 1956.
      "Camera Fan" [Note: doggerel about men being posted to various
      places]
D5   [Essay] *The Rocketeer* (Macdonald MB), [May or June] 1956.
      "Inside the Photo Section"

"Perhaps many of you people out there have seen Fred Bing of our establishment
wandering about with enough bandages on his person to supply Mayo Clinic for
the next decade. And perhaps you wondered, 'Did those photo types mummify

him?' Well, now for the first time in print the inside story will be revealed. It seems that Fred was galloping down the boulevard in front of the section in quest of a new record for a hundred yards when all at once something snapped and he made a graceful fighter approach upon the unyielding pavement. As a cluster of airmen gathered about screaming at one another to do something, Bing lay there in grotesque repose mumbling things like, 'There's a rhinoceros in my room!' and, 'I wanna wash my car in Benedictine!' Obviously, he was delirious.

"When told that he would have to spend the next few days in the local infirmary, he protested, 'What? And miss duty? No, never! never! You hear? Can I have some pyjamas?' "

[From "Inside the Photo Section"; see D5]

D6   [Poem] *The Rocketeer* (Macdonald MB), 28 June 1956.
      "Camera Clues" [Note: doggerel about Thompson who went to Winnipeg and bought a new Rollei camera]

1957

D7   [Letter] *Hockey Pictorial* (Montreal PQ), April 1957: 30.
      "Aha: A Chief"
D8   [Poem] *Raven* (Vancouver BC), No. 5 (December 1957): 36.
      "The Intellectual Turned Artist"

1958

D9   [Story] *Raven* (Vancouver BC), No. 6 (April 1958): 27–28.
      "Summer: Vancouver"
D10   [Poem] *Hockey Pictorial* (Montreal PQ), November 1958: 4.
      "The ABC's of the NHL"

"The first 2 long poems I ever published were in *Hockey Pictorial*. Hows that for inside Kanadian incunabula?"
[David McFadden Papers, Correspondence GB, 13 February 1968, McMaster University; see D10 and D12]

D11   [Poem] *Raven* (Vancouver BC), No. 7 (November 1958): N. p.
      "Soliloquy on the Rocks" [Notes: GB is listed as a poetry editor; an issue of contributions printed on unbound sheets; see E1]

The ABC's of the NHL

By GEORGE BOWERING, Vancouver, B. C.

A is for Armstrong
George, the Big Chief.
Obviously
A most valuable Leaf

B is for Boom-Boom,
Big noise at the Forum.
If the Habs need six goals,
Bernie will score 'em.

C is for Cullen,
Brian and Barry.
To distinguish between
Is not necessary.

D is for Dickie,
Remarkable Duff.
A young future All-star.
This kid has the stuff.

E is for Evans,
Who looks pretty nice,
Except when you have to
Look up from the ice.

F is for Flaman
And Fernie and fighter,
One of the reasons
The Bruins are brighter.

G is for Godfrey,
A blue line bruiser,
Built on the lines
Of a heavy cruiser.

H is for Howe.
Need we say more?
His efforts so often
Determine the score.

I is for Irvin,
A man we remember,
Whose teams would be twenty
Points up in December.

J is for Johnson,
The Habs unknown man.
He holds them together
If anyone can.

K is for Kelly,
A wizard on skates.
Who keeps Red Wing boosters
Revolving the gates.

L is for Lindsay,
A man of no mystery.
His scoring has made him
Left-winger of history.

M is for Moore,
A high-scoring rage,
Whose fabulous shot
Stuffs the puck in the cage.

N is for Norris,
A recognized name.
The clan owns
50% of the game.

O is for Olmstead,
Who set up the line
That poured all the rubber
Right into the twine.

P is for Plante,
The wandering man,
Who comes up with antics
Nobody else can.

Q is for quality,
This over all
Is the thing you will notice
Of classy Glen Hall.

R is for Rocket,
A fast-moving missile.
The Habs now have two
Who will make your hair bristle.

S is for Sawchuck,
The man in a crouch,
Which never can be
Misconstrued as a slouch.

T is for Topper,
Boston's durable vet.
A good man to have
In front of the net.

U is for Ullman,
A maker of plays.
But scoring would win him
A lot more of praise.

V is for Vasko,
A mountainous guy.
You'll never go through him,
And seldom get by.

W 's for Watson,
A coach full of fire,
Who is pushing the Blueshirts
Higher and higher.

X is for danger,
The dramatists say.
(A tip) Stay out of
Jean Belliveau's way.

Y is for youth,
Which the Leafs have got.
And time will tell
If the team can get hot.

Z is for Zing,
And Zoom as well,
These words sum up
The NHL.

"The ABC's of the NHL"; see D10

1959

D12   [Poem] *Hockey Pictorial* (Montreal PQ), February 1959: 33.
"The ABC's of the NHL Past"

D13   [Poem; Review] *The Ubyssey* (Vancouver BC), 20 March 1959.
"Growl" [a parody of Allen Ginsberg's *Howl*]—"Some Came, Running": a film review

D14   [Poem] *Prism* (Vancouver BC) 1, No. 2 (Winter 1959): 33.
"Soliloquy on the Rocks" [See E1]

1960

D15   [Story] *Raven* (Vancouver BC), No. 8 (January 1960): 10–15.
"The Representative"

D16   [Essays] *The Oliver Chronicle* (Oliver BC), 30 June 1960.
"OBC's [Oliver Baseball Club] Shut Out Kelowna in Best Effort of Season"—"Suddenly It's Summer (As If We Didn't Know)" [Note: the latter is the beginning of a column by GB; editorial note says, "UBC student George Bowering, home in Oliver for a short holiday following his graduation, gives his views on his home town. Any similarity to truth in George's article is strictly co-incidental."]

D17   [Essay] *The Oliver Chronicle* (Oliver BC), 18 August 1960.
"The Heat's On!"

D18   [Essay] *The Oliver Chronicle* (Oliver BC), 8 September 1960.
"Fearless George's Football Predictions." [Note: editor's note says, "A former SOHS (Southern Okanagan High School) High School student and native of Oliver, George Bowering gives us his views on anything and everything as he sees it from UBC."]

D19   [Essay] *The Oliver Chronicle* (Oliver BC), 22 September 1960.
"Sports 'N Snorts" [Note at top of column: "(Memo from Editor: How about doing a regular column on sports?) (Memo to Editor: Yeah, okay, Ed. But

"Soliloquy on the Rocks" by GB; see D14 and E1

let's expand our definition of 'sports' and
lapse into irregularity.)"]

D20   [Essay] *The Oliver Chronicle* (Oliver
BC), 27 October 1960.
  "Sports 'N Snorts" [Note: on a ficti-
tious, but presented as real, baseball
player, Joe Paliacci]

D21   [Story] *Raven* (Vancouver BC), No. 9
(October 1960): 32–34.
  "To Be Dead" [Notes: cover dated
November 1960; taken from "Delsing,"
an unpublished novel, in the GB Papers
at Queen's University Archives and NL]

D22   [Review] *The Ubyssey* (Vancouver BC),
28 October 1960.
  "A Head Full of Fire": a review of
Selected Poems, by Raymond Souster

GB with Jone Payne (then Joan
Huberman), Vancouver, c. 1959

D23   [Review] *The Ubyssey* (Vancouver BC), 18 November 1960.
  "Reveille, I Say!": a review of *A Red Carpet for the Sun*, by Irving
Layton

D24   [Essay] *The Oliver Chronicle* (Oliver BC), 17 November 1960.
  "Sports 'N Snorts: Grey Cup Hangovers"

D25   [Essay] *The Oliver Chronicle* (Oliver BC), 15 December 1960.
  "Sports 'N Snorts: The Big Eye" [Note: on the "apparent demise of
the Okanagan Senior Hockey League"]

D26   [Essay] *The Ubyssey* (Vancouver BC), 2 December 1960.
  "Poetry, Noon Today" [Note: seven student poets, GB, David
Bromige, Maxine Gadd, Lionel Kearns, Grace Kotzer, Mike Sinclair, and
Mike Matthews make a statement on "reasons or non-reasons for writing
poetry"]

"Poetry is going there—(has to go there, as it has to keep mutating itself—) to
that place where it is not only the word-maker in the head that composes, but all
the chambers and throughways of the total psyche contributing themselves to
the spontaneous delivery of (not words from the word-maker) those sporules of
energy that assemble the thing. Will we make it? First we gotta learn to get out of
bed."
[From "Poetry, Noon Today"; see D26]

D27   [Essay] *The Oliver Chronicle* (Oliver BC), 22 December 1960.

"Sports 'N Snorts: Deck the Halls with Bowering's Folly" [Note: predictions for various sports]

1961

D28   [Poem] *The Fiddlehead* (Fredericton NB), No. 47 (Winter 1961): 37.
       "Parallel"
D29   [Essay] *The Oliver Chronicle* (Oliver BC), 5 January 1961.
       "Sports 'N Snorts: Wishes for a Happy New Year"
D30   [Essay] *The Oliver Chronicle* (Oliver BC), 2 February 1961.
       "Sports 'N Snorts: The Foggy Foggy Dew" [Note: on the fog in Vancouver]
D31   [Poem] *The Ubyssey* (Vancouver BC), 3 February 1961.
       "Lord Michael" [Mike Matthews]
D32   [Essay] *The Oliver Chronicle* (Oliver BC), 2 March 1961.
       "Sports 'N Snorts" [Note: on the hockey team, the Trail Smoke Eaters, playing in Europe]
D33   [Review] *The Ubyssey* (Vancouver BC), 24 February 1961.
       "I've Read Prism!": a review of *Prism* 2, No. 2
D34   [Poem; Review] *The Ubyssey* (Vancouver BC), 10 March 1961.
       "A Tribute" [to David Bromige]—"Bone Thoughts": a review of *Bone Thoughts*, by George Starbuck
D35   [Essay] *The Oliver Chronicle* (Oliver BC), 16 March 1961.
       "Sports 'N Snorts" [Note: on the success of his former high school's rink in the Canadian High School Curling Championship]
D36   [Essay] *The Oliver Chronicle* (Oliver BC), 23 March 1961.
       "Sports 'N Snorts" [Note: on the high school basketball tournament at UBC]
D37   [Poems] "Five Poems." *The Canadian Forum* (Toronto ON) 41, No. 1 (April 1961): 10–11.
       "Preventorium"—"House of Commons"—"The Lady and the Love"—"Poemilla"—"Hamlet"
D38   [Essay] *The Oliver Chronicle* (Oliver BC), 6 April 1961.
       "Sports 'N Snorts: Poemsville" [Note: "Your inveterate scribbler serves up a change of pace this week, assailing you with some sportscoops in verse (or worse)."]
D39   [Essay] *The Oliver Chronicle* (Oliver BC), 20 April 1961.
       "Sports 'N Snorts" [Note: comments on the major league baseball schedule just underway]
D40   [Review] *The Oliver Chronicle* (Oliver BC), 27 April 1961.

"U. S. Warned of Attitude toward Castro's Cuba": a review of *Listen, Yankee*, by C. Wright Mills

D41   [Essay] *The Oliver Chronicle* (Oliver BC), 4 May 1961.

"George's Corner: Gostick Address a Sad Affair" [Note: on the anti-Semitic speech by Ron Gostick, a member of the self-styled anti-communist group, the Canadian Intelligence Service, "an organization that depends for its continuance on escaping any intrusions of any degree of intelligence."]

D42   [Essay] *The Oliver Chronicle* (Oliver BC), 11 May 1961.

"George's Corner" [Note: speculates on a "theory of COLD energy" which he will prove in his proposed book, *The Variations of the Bowering Cold Energy Theory*]

D43   [Essay] *The Oliver Chronicle* (Oliver BC), 25 May 1961.

"George's Corner: More on Those UBC Students at Gostick's Meeting"

D44   [Essay] *The Oliver Chronicle* (Oliver BC), 8 June 1961.

"George's Corner: JFK and Johnson Should Ride Freedom Buses" [Note: on the race riots in the American south]

D45   [Essay] *The Oliver Chronicle*, 30 June 1961

"OBC's [Oliver Baseball Club] Extend Home Record As Kelowna Shaded Sunday 3–2" [Note: During July and August 1961, while GB worked as a sports reporter, articles on baseball games appeared on the following dates: 6 July; 13 July; 3 August (two articles); 10 August; 17 August]

D46   [Poems] "Three Poems by George Bowering." *The Fiddlehead* (Fredericton NB), No. 49 (Summer 1961): 20–22.

"The Blood Poem"—"Rain Pain"—"Baghdad Belle"

D47   [Essay] *The Oliver Chronicle* (Oliver BC), 6 July 1961.

"We Should Build a Playpen for Rock-Painters" [Note: attacks those responsible for painting "quasi-Christian messages all over the rockface along B. C. roads"]

D48   [Essay] *The Oliver Chronicle* (Oliver BC), 27 July 1961.

"Hemmingway's [sic] Death a Great Loss to Literature" [Note: also printed in the *Keremeos Courier*, 27 July 1961]

D49   [Poem] *Delta* (Montreal PQ), No. 15 (August 1961): 2–3.

"Letter to Lionel Kearns" [Note: this journal was edited by Louis Dudek]

D50   [Essay] *The Oliver Chronicle* (Oliver BC), 10 August 1961.

"As George Sees It: Our Goodwill Envoy to Note: Japan" [Note: first in a series on the experiences of GB's childhood friend Bill Trump in Japan; Trump received a scholarship to study in Japan]

D51   [Essay] *The Oliver Chronicle* (Oliver BC), 17 August 1961.

"As George Sees It: Toil and Frustration Outlook for Many Japanese Youths"

D52   [Essay] *The Oliver Chronicle* (Oliver BC), 24 August 1961.
      "Bill Trump in Japan: The 'Bomb' Made Japan a Nation of Pacifists"
      [Note: second in a series on Trump]

D53   [Essay] *The Oliver Chronicle* (Oliver BC), 31 August 1961.
      "Bill Trump in Japan: Japanese Chuckle Too When Presley Sings"
      [Note: third in a series on Trump]

D54   [Poems] *Poet* (Madras, India) 2, No. 2 (September 1961): 5–7.
      "Drawn and Quartered"—"The Heart of Lightness"—"The Shouting Genesite"

D55   [Statement; Poems] *Tish* (Vancouver BC), [No. 1] [September 1961]: 4–6.
      ["The best answer anyone ever gave . . ."] [from "Delsing," an unpublished novel]—"Short Cut"—"Poet As Projector"—"Family Group"—"Radio Jazz"

"The poet has a responsibility *to* the whole poetic experience, and it lies in responding to his assumed capacity to re-enact the experience. For while the written poem is only one exposure of the PE [poetic experience], it, like a single neuron, is the most reliable clue to the nature of the greater structure. That is why the smaller parts in the written poem are *things* pertaining to the PE, and not judgements emanating from the interpreting mind of the participant artist. The things themselves participate in the PE."
[From GB's statement of poetics made as an editor for *Tish*, No. 1, subtitled initially "A Magazine of Vancouver Poetry," then changed to "A Poetry Newsletter"; see D55]

D56   [Essay] *The Oliver Chronicle* (Oliver BC), 7 September 1961.
      "Based on Racial Prejudice: Immigration Policy Embarrassing to Bill"
      [Note: fifth and final piece in a series on Trump]

D57   [Essay] *The Ubyssey* (Vancouver BC), 22 September 1961.
      "Placebo" [Note: attacks the arts and literary scene on campus for safe mediocrity]

" 'Placebo' was written for the weekly artistic supplement of *The Ubyssey*. Placebo is a pill you give people to psych them into thinking that they're getting medication, but I wanted to have that double thing where people would say, yeh, I get what's going on, and then say, hey, wait a minute! I also used to say, you're in the wrong place bo, because bo is what you used to call guys."
[On the column "Placebo," Session 12, 28 April 1989]

A MAGAZINE OF VANCOUVER POETRY

TISH 2

October 7
1961

Editor   ·Frank Davey

Contributing Editors   James Reid
George Bowering
Fred Wah
David Dawson

Address all correspondence to TISH, 3591 West 11th Ave.,
Vancouver 8, B.C.,· Canada.

EDITORIAL: VERBATIM FROM A NOTEBOOK

     I have come to realize (as has LeRoi Jones) that poetry
now of us young fellers is the what how of the way we sound.
Heard Br. Antoninus read/ voice like ocean rolling over rocks
and booming into sea caverns/ and read him, knowing how he
sounds, and now have his poetry in. Also discovered how to
read :intonation and breathgroups of Duncan from hearing him
read (he mentioned his similar experience with Edith Sitwell)
and can how to study old Ginsberg and Corso. Ginsberg, whose
breathgroup is formalizing into subdivision lucidity in Kaddish.
Because (Williams) that is how the poem works all right---the
poet's job is to excruciate the natural rhythms, word clusters
of his own culture's idiom, as controlled by the breath,
syntax---to find natural association of object/action/words.

     And furthermore, beauty in poetry today is become synonymous
with appropriateness. All thru English poetry, and this is why
it died with Hardy, the poet has had to go away from life,
its speech and rhythm, to create a beauty for him. All, that is,
except a large part of Blake. Blake said everything is holy,
and that is why he is read today without a need for the reader
to make allowances for background, decorum, and diction. For
Blake, the measure inherent in the iamb-less rhythm of life had
a built-in connection with life's realities, and had to be
breathed into the poem by the man who breathed in sympathy with
Nature. For his, of course, N was God, and poetically he was
right. So what? Take away God, and Nature becomes all the more
powerful. Add man, and it has raison d'etre. But the English
poets have kept ahold of their unnatural iambs, poor souls.

GEORGE BOWERING

TISH, the mag for readers with long letters and small change.

Front cover, *Tish*, No. 2, with GB's editorial; see D59

D58   [Essay] *The Ubyssey* (Vancouver BC), 29 September 1961.
       "Placebo" [Note: criticizes the new Graduate Students' Centre]
D59   [Statement; Poems] *Tish* (Vancouver BC), No. 2 (7 October 1961): 1,
       13–14.
       "Editorial: Verbatims from a Notebook"—"The Sunday Poem"—
       "From 'The Meatgrinder': (1)"
D60   [Review] *The Ubyssey* (Vancouver BC), 13 October 1961.
       "Placebo": a review of *The Distances*, by Charles Olson; *The New
       Book/A Book of Torture*, by Michael McClure
D61   [Essay] *The Ubyssey* (Vancouver BC), 20 October 1961.
       "Placebo" [Note: attacks the RCMP raid on Vancouver bookstores to
       seize copies of Henry Miller's *Tropic of Cancer*]
D62   [Essay] *The Oliver Chronicle* (Oliver BC), 26 October 1961.
       "Naming the Provinces" [Editor's Note: "First of a new series by
       George Bowering"]
D63   [Essay] *The Ubyssey* (Vancouver BC), 27 October 1961.
       "Placebo": a theatre review
D64   [Essay] *Arts Council News* (Vancouver BC) 13, No. 2 (November 1961):
       N. p.
       "B. C. Poets and Their Market"
D65   [Poem] *Canadian Poetry Magazine* (Toronto ON) 25, No. 1 (November
       1961): 16.
       "The Rock Pastorale"
D66   [Essay] *The Oliver Chronicle* (Oliver BC), 2 November 1961.
       "Naming the Provinces" [Note: second in a series]
D67   [Essay] *The Oliver Chronicle* (Oliver BC), 8 November 1961.
       "Naming the Provinces" [Note: third in a series]
D68   [Review] *The Ubyssey* (Vancouver BC), 9 November 1961.
       "Placebo": a review of *Empty Mirror*, by Allen Ginsberg
D69   [Poems] *Tish* (Vancouver BC), No. 3 (14 November 1961): 4, 7.
       "Trail"—"Moment: White"—"Literary Criticism"
D70   [Review] *The Ubyssey* (Vancouver BC), 16 November 1961.
       "Placebo": a review of *Preface to a Twenty Volume Suicide Note*, by
       LeRoi Jones
D71   [Letter] *The Ubyssey* (Vancouver BC), 17 November 1961.
       "More Red Paint" [Note: on propagandist graffiti]
D72   [Review] *The Ubyssey* (Vancouver BC), 23 November 1961.
       "Placebo": a theatre review
D73   [Essay] *The Oliver Chronicle* (Oliver BC), 23 November 1961.
       "Naming the Provinces" [Note: fourth in a series]
D74   [Poem] *The Canadian Forum* (Toronto ON) 41, No. 491 (December
       1961): 197.

"On a Black Painting by Tamayo"

D75   [Review] *The Ubyssey* (Vancouver BC), 1 December 1961.

"Placebo": a review of *Myths and Texts*, by Gary Snyder

D76   [Essay] *The Oliver Chronicle* (Oliver BC), 7 December 1961.

"Naming the Provinces" [Note: last in a series]

D77   [Review; Poems] *Tish* (Vancouver BC), No. 4 (14 December 1961): 5, 6, 7, 14.

"Why Doesn't Somebody Tell the Truth?": a review of *Against a League of Liars*, by Milton Acorn—"Moment: 2 a. m."—"Motor Age"—"A Vigil of Sorts"—"Driving Past"

"Well, when the whole *Tish* thing was happening, we were people who had been deracinated—we didn't get any Canadian writing at school in B. C. Most of the people in *Tish*—Fred Wah and Frank Davey—didn't know anything about Canadian poetry. The only people that knew of Canadian poetry were Lionel Kearns and I, who got together before the *Tish* stuff happened anyway. Lionel had been an exchange student in Quebec and he brought back the Contact Press books and I read them in one of those cabins in the dorms."
[From "George Bowering," an interview by Caroline Bayard and Jack David; see C113]

1962

D78   [Poem] *blue grass* (Dobbs Ferry, NY), [No. 1] (1962): 27.
"Wood"

D79   [Poems] *Sun* (San Francisco CA), No. 8 (1962): 22.
"I Saw Some Wonder at Noon"—"Walking Poem"

D80   [Essay] *The Ubyssey* (Vancouver BC), 12 January 1962.
"Placebo: Dunder on the Right"

D81   [Poems] *Tish* (Vancouver BC), No. 5 (13 January 1962): 4, 14.
"Metaphor 1"—"Telephone Metaphysic"—"The Problem of Margins"

D82   [Essay] *The Ubyssey* (Vancouver BC), 19 January 1962.
"Placebo: Table Scraps" [Note: on "odds and ends"]

"Let me be the first to leak to the public the rumor that *Tish* is soon to venture into the book-publishing game. The poetry newsletter with the most selective and best selective mailing on the continent seems rather secretive on the subject, but my spies have been active and faithful, and I am willing to go out on a

branch. I predict that the inverted phoneticians of aforesaid newsletter will be selling a paperback of poems by a Canadian poet* sometime this spring."
[*like Frank Davey?]
[From "Placebo: Table Scraps"; see D82]

D83   [Review] *The Ubyssey* (Vancouver BC), 26 January 1962.
"Placebo: Kerouac the Dreamer": a review of *Book of Dreams*, by Jack Kerouac

D84   [Play; Statement] *Prism* (Vancouver BC) 3, No. 2 (Winter 1962): 6–15, 58.
The Home for Heroes—["I intend that my theatre . . ."] [Note: the typescript of GB's play says it is "an original half-hour TV tragicomedy" and that it was "finished Sep 10, 1960" (GB Papers, NL)]

D85   [Poem] *Exchange* (Montreal PQ) 2, No. 3 (February/March 1962): 15.
"Moment: Cars"

D86   [Review] *The Ubyssey* (Vancouver BC), 2 February 1962.
"Placebo: Off the Road": a review of a TV version of *On the Road*, by Jack Kerouac

D87   [Review] *The Ubyssey* (Vancouver BC), 9 February 1962.
"Placebo: Ferlinghetti": a review of *Starting from San Francisco*, by Lawrence Ferlinghetti

D88   [Poems; Review] *Tish* (Vancouver BC), No. 6 (14 February 1962): 9, 12–13.
"Dark Around Light"—"Feel of a Leaf"—"A Quarter's Worth of Poetry": a review of *Poems for 27 Cents*, edited by Irving Layton—"Metaphor '2' "

D89   [Essay] *The Ubyssey* (Vancouver BC), 16 February 1962.
"Placebo: Robert Creeley" [Note: introduces a reading by Creeley in downtown Vancouver that night; GB, however, will be in Eugene, Oregon]

D90   [Essay] *The Ubyssey* (Vancouver BC), 23 February 1962.
"Placebo: Eugene, Oregon" [Note: on the visit by GB and David Bromige to the University of Oregon Manuscripts Day for young writers]

D91   [Poem] *The Fiddlehead* (Fredericton NB), No. 52 (Spring 1962): 23.
"The Night Before Morning"

D92   [Story; Statement] *Evidence* (Toronto ON), No. 5 (Spring 1962): 5–10, 78.
"The Promise of the Sky"—[". . . (A) story should tell a story . . ."]
[Note: GB's statement is quoted in the "Notes on Contributors"]

D93   [Poems] *Raven* (Vancouver BC), No. 10 (March 1962): 7, 25, 34, 36.
"Heathcliff"—"Eve's Apples"—"White Cat & a Fly"—"Literary Criticism"

D94   [Poems] *Teangadóir* (Toronto ON) Series 2, 1, No. 3; issue No. 39 (1 March 1962): 102–103.
   "Street Lines"—"White Cat & a Fly"

D95   [Review] *The Ubyssey* (Vancouver BC), 2 March 1962.
   "Placebo: A Rung Higher": a review of *The Jacob's Ladder*, by Denise Levertov

D96   [Review] *The Ubyssey* (Vancouver BC), 9 March 1962.
   "Placebo: Too Much of a Good Thing": a review of an art show

D97   [Poems] *Tish* (Vancouver BC), No. 7 (14 March 1962): 2, 3.
   "L. S." ["Locus Solus"]—"Back from Seattle"—"Tuesday Night"

D98   [Review] *The Sun* (Vancouver BC), 14 March 1962.
   "Important Poets Overlooked in New Canadian Anthology": a review of *Poetry 62*, edited by Eli Mandel and Jean-Guy Pilon

D99   [Letter] *The Ubyssey* (Vancouver BC), 15 March 1962.
   "Indefensible" [pub. under pseud. Helmut Franz] [Note: one of a number of anti-communist letters penned by "Franz" to stir things up and publicize the work of GB's friends]

D100   [Review] *The Ubyssey* (Vancouver BC), 16 March 1962.
   "Placebo: The Mused-Up Mess": a theatre review

D101   [Essay] *The Ubyssey* (Vancouver BC), 23 March 1962.
   "Placebo: *Tish*"

D102   [Poem] *Tish* (Vancouver BC), No. 8 (14 April 1962): 1, 5.
   "P"

D103   [Poem; Review] *The Canadian Forum* (Toronto ON) 42, No. 496 (May 1962): 29, 44.
   "Abort"—*Place of Meeting: Poems 1958–1960*, by Raymond Souster: a review

D104   [Review; Poem] *Tish* (Vancouver BC), No. 9 (14 May 1962): 11–12, 15.
   "The Eyes Are Open the Eyes Are Shut": a review of *Eyes Without a Face*, by Kenneth McRobbie—"(benzedrine)"

D105   [Essay] *The Oliver Chronicle* (Oliver BC), 31 May 1962.
   "Placebo: The Hong Kong Wall"

D106   [Essay] *The Oliver Chronicle* (Oliver BC), 31 May 1962.
   "Record Year Forseen for Trump Plant"

D107   [Essays] *The Oliver Chronicle* (Oliver BC), 7 June 1962.
   "Placebo: Your Voice on the 18th"—"Vernon Batters Clout OBC's [Oliver Baseball Club] for Twin Win Here Sunday"—"Two Oliver Teams Indicate Growing Interest in Fastball" [Note: as a sports reporter GB wrote articles on baseball games on the following dates: 14 June; 5 July; 12 July; 23 August]

D108   [Essays] *The Oliver Chronicle* (Oliver BC), 14 June 1962.

placebo

UNABASHEDLY TO SAY, s will not be a blurb for sh, nor will it be a soliciting moneys or subscriptions; nor ll it be selfconsciously objec- e appraisal of the rise and/or ll of the poetry newsletter. will be an informal descrip- on of the mimeo sheet.

TISH began last summer as idea in the minds of several ets hereabouts who noticed at they were seeing each her often, and were interested exchanging views a b o u t etry, their own and that of e several common interests

—so that this was the origin of **Tish**, and its meaning. **Tish** is not a magazine, truly speak- ing—it is as it calls itself, a poetry newsletter. It exists for the purpose of exchanging poetry and views. The poet in Vancouver can show the poet in Toronto or Philadelphia what he is doing RIGHT NOW, and the poet in Toronto or Phila can tell the Vancouver guy what he thinks of the do- ing RIGHT NOW. With a mag- azine this is impossible, and the air is too thin in any case.

TISH has emerged s e v e n times in the last seven months, and the response has been far greater than the foundling dads could have imagined in their most excited hours. Poems, dol- lars, and letters, not to men- tion scads of magazines and books, come into the **Tish** ori- fices every day. The editors are especially happy about the letters—from the most promi- nent poets in the US and Can- ada. AND from some of the most interesting young writers. This is the answer to **Tish**, the support of its conviction that poems should not be shunted to the pages of professional maga- zines to appear months after they have been written.

THE NEWEST VENTURE for the newsletter is the estab- lishment of a publishing house, the only publishers of poetry in the west, except for the occa- sional Klanak Press. The third galley for Frank Davey's col- lection, **D-Day And After,** are at the Rattlesnake Press now (for the added information of bibliographers, etc.), and the first **Tishbook** should be on the stalls and at the editorial offi- ces in a couple weeks. **Tish** hopes to continue to publish books of this nature, and an- other run—that is, a series of pamphbooks featuring the very long poems and series of poems that magazine publishers sel- dom consider.

IN THE MEANTIME, THE newsletter will try to maintain its monthly pace, and to remain a newsletter, not to be sucked into the magazine business.

Information can be obtained from Tish, 3591 West 11th

GEORGE "HASTY" BOWERI wrapped up in TISH

One of was the an, and the poets involved de- d to bring Duncan to Van- er for a little seminar time he summer, the notion of a try group began to accrue. first it was just a regular nday night meeting, a sort evensong with the emphasis the "song".

UT FIVE OF THE PEOPLE came interested in expand- g the discussion group to in- ude people in farflung places e NY and SF and Mo

"Placebo," 23 March 1962, taken from GB's scrapbook, GB Papers, NL; see D101

"Trump Ltd., Property-Owners Clash Over Closure of Lanes"— "Council Asks to Name Own Chairman"—"Cawston Alfalfa Field Inspiration for Oliver's Irrigated Golf Course"—"Setting of Modern Clubhouse Perfect for Scenic Relaxation"—"500 Cherry Trees Border Course Eighteen-Acre Orchard Adjoins"

D109   [Essay] *The Oliver Chronicle* (Oliver BC), 14 June 1962.
"Local Libraries Starved for Good Books"

D110   [Poem] *Queen's Quarterly* (Kingston ON) 69, No. 2 (Summer 1962): 253.
"A Redemption"

D111   [Review] *Canadian Literature* (Vancouver BC), No. 13 (Summer 1962): 65–67.
"The Canadian Poetry Underground": a review of *Than Any Star*, by Pádraig O Broin; *D-Day and After*, by Frank Davey; *The Drunken Clock*, by Gwendolyn MacEwen; *Poems*, by David A. Donnell

D112   [Essay] *The Oliver Chronicle* (Oliver BC), 12 July 1962.
"Placebo"

D113   [Poems] *Tish* (Vancouver BC), No. 11 (14 July 1962): 6–7.
"The Eyes"—"Anniversary Recall"

D114   [Poems] *Mountain* (Hamilton ON), No. 2 (August 1962): n. p.
"History of Poets: Heathcliff"—"April Weather"—"Vancouver Springtime"—"History of Poets: Ophelia" [Note: this journal was edited by David McFadden]

D115   [Poem] *Evidence* (Toronto ON), No. 6 [Fall/Winter 1962]: 80–81.
"M. M." [Marilyn Monroe]

D116   [Poem] *San Francisco Review* (San Francisco CA) 1, No. 13 (September 1962): 30.
"Academy"

D117   [Poem] *The Canadian Forum* (Toronto ON) 42, No. 500 (September 1962): 140.
"History of Poets: Frederic Henry"

D118   [Poems] *Tish* (Vancouver BC), No. 13 (14 September 1962): 8–9.
"The In the Beginning Sonnet"—"Red Lane"

D119   [Essay] *The Ubyssey* (Vancouver BC), 27 September 1962.
"Placebo: Wring Out the Olde"

D120   [Poems] *Delta (Canada)* (Montreal PQ), No. 19 (October 1962): 3, 7, 10, 12.
"Tuesday Night"—"The Sunday Poem"—"The Hockey Hero"— "Radio Jazz" [Notes: a special issue of Louis Dudek's journal, subtitled "New Vancouver Poetry"; in an introduction, "The Present Scene," Frank Davey describes the poetry scene, concluding: "The past in poetry in Vancouver was never as varied or as promising as this present

generation of young poets. Here we have extremes of engagement, extremes of art, extremes of care, and occasionally various balances of them all, which make for a rich poetry scene . . . ."]

D121   [Review] *The Ubyssey* (Vancouver BC), 4 October 1962.
        "Placebo": a review of a reading by Jamie Reid and John Newlove

D122   [Review] *The Ubyssey* (Vancouver BC), 11 October 1962.
        "Placebo: Cannonball Addles the Inquisition": a review of a jazz concert

D123   [Review; Poems] *Tish* (Vancouver BC), No. 14 (14 October 1962): 5–6, 10–11.
        Big Sur, by Jack Kerouac: a review—"Grandfather"—"Them Bones"

D124   [Review] *The Ubyssey* (Vancouver BC), 18 October 1962.
        "Placebo: Grave Newlove": a review of *Grave Sirs*, by John Newlove

D125   [Essay] *The Ubyssey* (Vancouver BC), 25 October 1962.
        "Placebo: Capaneus Rides Again"

D126   [Letter; Essay] *The Ubyssey* (Vancouver BC), 1 November 1962.
        "Tish, tish" [Note: corrects the implication, in a recent article, that *Tish* was UBC-sponsored]—"Placebo: Irving Layton"

"[Lionel Kearns] came back [from eastern Canada] with some Contact Press books—mainly Contact Press books and a few other things from Montreal (literary stuff from the 40s and 50s), and I started reading those. I found out about Irving Layton and Souster and Dudek, largely, and a few other people. The other *Tish* people didn't know about them. Lionel and I were the only ones who knew about them. Frank and Fred and those people didn't know anything about Canadian writing at all, and it was only a fluke that I did because Lionel had brought these things back with him. I was excited as hell. So for me there were two contiguous lines developing in the things I was reading and being influenced by. *The New American Poetry* was out (that's called *New American Poetry: 1945 to 1960*, but it actually came out in 1959). We got our hands on it in 59, the same time that we got Duncan's book, and so there were those people, and there was also the excitement I was getting from the Contact Press business, but Lionel was not very much influenced at all by the American poets. He was reading them but he didn't care for Olson and Creeley and so forth. I think he liked LeRoi Jones and people like that, so I felt kind of funny because one side of me was the *Tish* guys, and I was saying should I keep the Layton/Souster thing secret from them or shouldn't I? So I said, 'You should listen to some of these younger guys'. We set up a page in *Tish*, in our 14 pages, for stuff from the east. I was mainly in charge of the stuff from the east until Frank began to know people from the east and Frank opened the door to the east."
[From an interview by Barry McKinnon; see D885]

D127   [Review] *The Ubyssey* (Vancouver BC), 8 November 1962.
        "Placebo: Something to Sing about": a review of a folk concert
D128   [Poems; Review; Statement] "Two Deifications." *Tish* (Vancouver BC),
        No. 15 (14 November 1962): 5, 7–8.
        "From Your Son & Lover"—"The Red Hot Element"—"Romance &
        Rice Crispies": a review of *Junge Amerikanische Lyrik*, edited by Greg-
        ory Corso and Walter Hollerer—["The difference between form &
        formalism . . ."] [statement on Dan McLeod]
D129   [Essay] *The Ubyssey* (Vancouver BC), 15 November 1962.
        "Placebo: Look Ma, I'm an Artist"
D130   [Review] *The Ubyssey* (Vancouver BC), 22 November 1962.
        "Placebo: The Language of Man"
D131   [Review] *The Canadian Forum* (Toronto ON) 42, No. 503 (December
        1962): 206.
        "The Well Awake Mind": a review of *Love Is Bright Round My
        Shoulders*, by Luella Booth
D132   [Review; Poem] *Tish* (Vancouver BC), No. 16 (14 December 1962): 2–3,
        5–6.
        "Holes in the San Francisco Fog": a review of *The Heads of the Town
        Up to the Aether*, by Jack Spicer—"Points on the Grid"
D133   [Poem] *South and West* (Fort Smith, AZ) 1, No. 3 (Winter 1962): 6.
        "Ode on Green"

1963

D134   [Poem; Review] *The Canadian Forum* (Toronto ON) 42, No. 504
        (January 1963): 235.
        "The Image"—"Poetry As Recreation": a review of *Five New Bruns-
        wick Poets*, by Elizabeth Brewster, Fred Cogswell, Robert Gibbs, Alden
        Nowlan, and Kay Smith
D135   [Review] *British Columbia Library Quarterly* (Vancouver BC) 26, No. 3
        (January 1963): 35–36.
        Rocky Mountain Poems, by Ralph Gustafson: a review
D136   [Review] *The Ubyssey* (Vancouver BC), 10 January 1963.
        "Placebo: Advise and Consent and So On": a film review
D137   [Poems; Review] *Tish* (Vancouver BC), No. 17 (14 January 1963): 4,
        11–12.
        "Husband"—"For Myself Continuous Discovery": a review of
        Poems for All the Annettes, by Alfred Purdy—"Circus Maximus"
D138   [Essay] *The Ubyssey* (Vancouver BC), 17 January 1963.
        "Placebo: Fanfare & Fooforaw"

George Bowering
Pauline Butling in Campbell Lake

The water of Campbell Lake is very cold,
& Pauline Butling is in it.

Her limbs are long & white, the glacier
is white, her one-piece bathing suit

is pale. She is still here
thirty years after our adult lives began,

doing the breast stroke in Campbell Lake.

I have never been in love with her
but I would kill anyone

who tried to drown her. I would like
the sun to take the time to tan her,

to warm the water a little.

imprimerie dromadaire toronto

"Pauline Butling in Campbell Lake"; see E88

D139 [Essay] *The Ubyssey* (Vancouver BC), 24 January 1963.
"Placebo: Smile, You're Watching Candid Camera"

D140 [Review; Interview] *The Ubyssey* (Vancouver BC), 31 January 1963.
"Why Did They Bring Henry Fourth?": a theatre review—"Clap Hands for George Bowering," by Suzanne Mowat

D141 [Poem] *Campus Canada* (Vancouver BC) 1, No. 1 (February 1963): 36.
"Driving to Kelowna"

D142 [Poems] *Mountain* (Hamilton ON), No. 3 (February 1963): n. p.
"Spring Afternoon"—"The Bread"—"Ex-is Sensual"—"Metaphor 3"—"The Winter's Tale"

D143 [Review] *The Canadian Forum* (Toronto ON) 42, No. 505 (February 1963): 263.
"The Garden or the Gardener": a review of *The Plink Savoir*, by Robin Mathews

D144 [Essay] *The Ubyssey* (Vancouver BC), 7 February 1963.
"Placebo: Shame on You, Mayor Wood"

D145 [Poems] *Tish* (Vancouver BC), No. 18 (14 February 1963): 6–7.
"Thru My Eyes"—"The Candle"

D146 [Poem] *Between Worlds* (Puerto Rico), Spring 1963.
"Metathesis" [Note: published by InterAmerican University]

D147 [Poems] *American Weave: Poems for Enjoyment* (University Heights OH) 27, No. 1 (Spring/Summer 1963): 17–18.
"Memo"—"The Dance"—"Moment: White"

D148 [Excerpt from an essay; Poem] *Tish* (Vancouver BC), No. 19 (14 March 1963): 4–5, 7.
"Some Notes from 'Universal and Particular' "—"The Dance Complete"

"Well, for poetry, in the TISH days, the days when we were all learning to write poetry, that involved making use of the lessons of imagism because when you're an 18-year-old kid you're an automatic Georgian, right? And you start talking about things that must be very important. Teenage poets—untutored—always write about suicides and bodies cut open and blood and death and pain and loneliness—I mean that's what the Georgians were, a bunch of arrested adolescents, right? They would be out in a lake and the lake would just be a backdrop for their own loneliness. That's not what you find in our early poetry. You find an incredible number of proper nouns because proper nouns are the most concrete nouns there are because they verify the existence of something outside your own colorations of the landscape."
[From "14 Plums"; see D748]

D149   [Poem] *The Canadian Forum* (Toronto ON) 43, No. 507 (April 1963): 23.
"Oliver"

D150   [Translations] *Teangadóir* (Toronto ON) Series 2, 1, No. 5 (15 May 1963): 194–195.
"The Cross of Bistolfi," by Gabriela Mistral—"Rodin's Thinker," by Gabriela Mistral

GB with Dan McLeod, Gordon Payne, and Lionel Kearns, 1963

D151   [Essay; Poems; Review] *Evidence* (Toronto ON), No. 7 (Summer 1963): 19–35, 101–104.
"Poetry and the Language of Sound"—"Preserves"—"The Eyes" —"Totems"—"At Victory Square"—"The Brain"—"Lazarus"—"Somnia"—"The Bread"—"Benzedrine"—"Layton Shakes Loose": a review of *Balls for a One-Armed Juggler*, by Irving Layton

D152   [Poem] *Amethyst* (Wolfville NS) 2, No. 4 (Summer 1963): 40.
"The Sons of Freedom"

D153   [Poem] *The Fiddlehead* (Fredericton NB), No. 57 (Summer 1963): 39.
"The Tree"

D154   [Poems] *Genesis West* (Burlingame CA) 1, No. 4 (Summer 1963): 311–318.
"Granville Street Bridge"—"Locus Solus"—"The Winter's Tale"— "Universal & Particular"—"I Think a Head-On Collision"—"Meta Morphosis"—"History of Poets: Jake Barnes"—"Them Bones"— "Spanish B. C."

D155   [Review] *Canadian Literature* (Vancouver BC), No. 17 (Summer 1963): 72–73.
"Hero Without Motive": a review of *The Legend of John Hornby*, by George Whalley

D156   [Review] *The Canadian Forum* (Toronto ON) 43, No. 510 (July 1963): 94–95.
"Poet & Painter": a review of *Jawbreakers*, by Milton Acorn; *A Friction of Lights*, by Eldon Grier

D157   [Poem] *The Sun* (Vancouver BC), 4 July 1963.
"The Hockey Hero"

D158   [Poem] *Wild Dog* (Pocatello ID) 1, No. 4 (13 July 1963): 24–25.
"Grandfather"

"In the early sixties I found this passage somewhere, and assigned it to the Stupid Statements Department: 'Poetry is a manoeuvering of ideas, a spectacular pleasure, achievement and mastery of intractable material, not less than an

attempt to move the world, to order the chaos of man insofar as one is able. Love, harmony, order, poise, precision, new worlds'. Richard Eberhart. In the late eighties, or whenever it is now, there are probably still people, even poets, who think in such terms. I cannot shake the notion that there are essentially two views of poetry. Theirs wants to manoeuver ideas, to show mastery over material, to order chaos. Ours looks after music to shape ideas, offers ourselves as servants rather than masters, and sees no chaos but a multiplicity in order. Eberhart's statement, not an unusual one, sounds in its exuberance, very 'male', like a businessman's, a developer's excitement about his potential world. We others? We sound like girlish priests, I suppose, like insect collectors, roadside talkers."
[*Errata*: "Seventy-one"; see A49]

D159   [Statement; Poem] *Tish* (Vancouver BC), No. 20 (August 1963): 2.
"The Most Remarkable Thing about *Tish*"—"When Visitors Come I Go"

D160   [Poem] *Hawk & Whippoorwill* (Sauk City WI) 4, No. 3 (Autumn 1963): 10.
"The Girl at the Beach"

D161   [Poems] *Canadian Author & Bookman* (Ottawa ON) 39, No. 1 (Autumn 1963): 10.
"Object Lesson for Amy Lowell, and Love for Ami Petersen"—"The Youthful Mother, a Shape upon Her Lap"

D162   [Review] *Canadian Literature* (Vancouver BC), No. 18 (Autumn 1963): 56–58.
"Promises, Promises": a review of *Blind Man's Holiday*, by R. G. Everson; *Flaming City*, by Michael Malus; *Burglar Tools*, by Harry Howith

Cover of *Capilano Review*; see D748; photograph by Nathen Hohn

D163   [Poem] *The Canadian Forum* (Toronto ON) 43, No. 514 (November 1963): 186.
"William Faulkner Dead"

D164   [Letter] *The Herald* (Calgary AB), 15 November 1963.
"Academic Freedom"

D165   [Poems] *Volume 63* (Waterloo ON), No. 1 (December 1963): 51–52.

"Moment: White"—"Wrapt in Black"

D166   [Review; Poems] *Tish* (Vancouver BC), No. 22 (December 1963): 5 [sic;
p. 8], 9.
"Kerouac's Brother": a review of *Visions of Gerard*, by Jack Kerouac
—"In the Sun"—"Leg"

1964

D167   [Poem] *Mother* (Pittsburgh PA), No. 11 [c. 1964]: n. p.
"Above Montana"
D168   [Story] *Evidence* (Toronto ON), No. 8 (1964): 81–90.
"The Representative"
D169   [Poem] *Magazine* (New York NY), No. 1 ([January] 1964): n. p.
"A Sudden Measure"
D170   [Poem] *Tish* (Vancouver BC), No. 23 (January 1964): 6.
"Each Morning"
D171   [Letter] *The Herald* (Calgary AB), 23 January 1964.
"Heavy Hand of the Censor"

"In an article purporting to discuss the dangers of smoking, Rev. Merv Switzer
writes in *The Herald*, Jan. 18:—
" 'Censorship of films is being attacked here in Alberta. In other words,
people are wanting their picture shows more vulgar, debased, and lewd than at
present, so the mind can be filled with what it likes'.
"Then he proceeds to wander off somewhere else, without showing the rea-
soning behind his 'in other words'.
"I would like to suggest, contrary to what Mr. Switzer says, that censorship
and debasement go hand-in-hand. And I would suggest that all one need do to
get an inkling of this is to have a look at current Calgary movie advertising. The
announcer on television leers, 'This is an extremely *adult* picture', signifying that
it sniggers at bedroom peculiarities in the received Doris Day-James Garner
method. Recently, a downtown theatre displayed titanic crimson letters outside
its lobby, announcing, 'Welcome To The Sin Bin'.
"This is the kind of mentality that is produced in a community that supports
censorship of its movies. Without a retired military man with a pair of scissors to
tell us that sex is dirty, we might be allowed to see movies that allow us to think
rather than merely giggle."
[Letter to the Editor; see D171]

D172   [Poem] *Bitterroot* (Brooklyn NY), No. 10 (Winter 1964): 5.
"Angela Sleeping"

D173   [Story] *Wild Dog* (Pocatello ID) 1, No. 5 (30 January 1964): 18–23.
       "The Lawnmower"
D174   [Editor; Statement] *Imago* (Calgary, AB), No. 1 [February 1964]: 2.
       "A Note or Justification" [see B1]
D175   [Poem] *Matter* (Annadale-on-Hudson NY), [No. 1] [February 1964]: 12.
       "The Snow"
D176   [Letter] *The Herald* (Calgary AB), 25 February 1964.
       "The Flag"
D177   [Essay] *Canadian Literature* (Vancouver BC), No. 20 (Spring 1964):
       54–64.
       "Poets in Their Twenties"
D178   [Essay] *Kulchur* (New York NY) 4, No. 13 (Spring 1964): 3–14.
       "Dance to a Measure: Some Words Mainly about Form in the Poetry
       of William Carlos Williams"
D179   [Poems] "Four Poems." *The Tamarack Review* (Toronto ON), No. 31
       (Spring 1964): 68–71.
       "A Corner Store Poem"—"The Dance Complete"—"Rime of Our
       Time"—"Matins"
D180   [Poems] *Theo* (New York NY) 1, No. 1 [March 1964]: n. p.
       "A Bedroom Sound"—"Each Morning"
D181   [Letter] *The Herald* (Calgary AB), 14 March 1964.
       "Air Canada"
D182   [Poems] *el corno emplumado* (Mexico City), No. 10 (April 1964): 94–96.
       "Hideo Kobashi" [sic; "Kobayashi"]—"My Atlas Poet"—"Husband"
       —"A Bedroom Sound" [Note: this journal was edited by Margaret
       Randall and Sergio Mondragón]

"We strongly felt that need to make a kind of publication that would cast some
light on Latin American poetry for us Americans, & *vice versa*. We started to
think about bringing out a magazine, and that's how *El Corno* began, with Sergio
Mondragón, Harvey Wolin, & myself, the three who eventually founded it. And
the name came from Harvey Wolin. He wanted it to represent a combination of
two cultures: the horn, the instrument of American jazz, & the plumes of
Quetzalcóatl, symbol of Mexican culture, or better, of precolumbian Latin
American culture."
[From "The Stormy History of *El Corno Emplumado*," Margaret Randall and
Robert Cohen interviewed by Nils Castro, translated by GB; see D603]

D183   [Poem; Letter] *Wild Dog* (Pocatello ID), No. 7 (5 April 1964): 16, 29–31.
       "Forecast"—"News from the Frozen North" [Letter dated March
       1964, from Calgary]

D184   [Poem] *Sum* (Albuquerque NM), No. 3 (May 1964): 12.
        "When You Run Naked" [Note: this journal, subtitled "A Newsletter
        of Current Workings," was created by former *Tish* editor Fred Wah after
        he left Vancouver to study in New Mexico]
D185   [Poem] *The Canadian Forum* (Toronto ON) 44, No. 520 (May 1964): 38.
        "With Hands and Eyes"
D186   [Poem] *Envoi* (Gloucester, England), No. 23 ([Summer] 1964): 5.
        "Calgary"
D187   [Poems] "Two Poems by George Bowering." *The Fiddlehead* (Frederic-
        ton NB), No. 61 (Summer 1964): 50–51.
        "Hospital"—"Shyly You Are"
D188   [Review] *Canadian Literature* (Vancouver BC), No. 21 (Summer 1964):
        70–71.
        "A Complex Music": a review of *The Rising Fire*, by Gwendolyn
        MacEwen [Note: see *Craft Slices*: "MacEwen's Music"; see A44]
D189   [Review] *Kulchur* (New York NY) 4, No. 14 (Summer 1964): 93–95.
        Natural Numbers, by Kenneth Rexroth: a review [Note: See *Craft
        Slices*: "Rexroth"; see A44]
D190   [Poem] *The Canadian Forum* (Toronto ON) 44, No. 521 (June 1964): 59.
        "Empty Eyeball"
D191   [Poems] *Intrepid* (New York NY), No. 3 (July 1964): n. p.
        "High River, Alberta"—"In the Steambath"
D192   [Poem] *Poetry Review* (University of Tampa FL), No. 2 (August 1964):
        n. p.
        "Thru My Eyes"
D193   [Essay] *Edge* (Edmonton AB), No. 3 (Autumn 1964): 1–4.
        "Some Farsighted Suggestions about Military Reform"
D194   [Essay] *Kulchur* (New York NY) 4, No. 15 (Autumn 1964): 3–15.
        "The New American Prosody: A Look at the Problem of Notating
        'Free' Verse"
D195   [Poem] *Trace* (England), No. 54 (Autumn 1964): 212.
        "Poem" ["potatoes . . . "]
D196   [Poem] *Input* (Valley Stream NY) 1, No. 3 (September 1964): n. p.
        "Lecture by Olson Creeley Duncan Levertov Ginsberg"

They say things
I can't follow
        but I smoke cigarettes
        fast as they do
[from "Lecture by Olson Creeley Duncan Levertov Ginsberg"; see D196]

D197   [Poems] *Literary Times* (New York NY) 3, No. 7 (September 1964): 3.
       "It's the Climate"—"At the Intersection"
D198   [Letter] *The Herald* (Calgary AB), 26 September 1964.
       "Way to Peace"
D199   [Poem; Prose] *Tish* (Vancouver BC), No. 26 (October 1964): 10, 11.
       "Still in the Sky"—"Letter from Hyacinth in Calgary"
D200   [Letter] *The Herald* (Calgary AB), 3 October 1964.
       "History's Lessons"
D201   [Letter] *The Albertan* (Calgary AB), 21 October 1964.
       " 'Catcher' Defended"
D202   [Letter] *The Herald* (Calgary AB), 26 October 1964.
       "Shocked Reaction"
D203   [Editor; Statement; Poem] *Imago* (Calgary AB), No. 2 [November 1964]:
       2, 39–41.
       "About the Cover"—"History Is Us" [see B1]

"Imago 2 held up now, by a guy in the business office of the university here, who thinks it is awful there are dirty words in it; I'm going to see him tomorrow and give him hell. We'll get it out, but Alberta is a terrible place for anyone who wants to say fuck without going to the firing squad."
[From a letter to Margaret Randall, 25 October 1964, in *The Man in Yellow Boots*; see A3 and D262]

GB in Calgary, 1965; publicity photograph used by Coach House Press for *Baseball*

"Imago is now cleard with the censors, i hope, i went in and talkt with the president of the university, I figure thats the direct way, clutch at throat, and I shd have it by two days, lotsa people wondering when it will be in their mailboxes."
[From a letter to Margaret Randall, 2 November 1964, in *The Man in Yellow Boots*; see A3 and D262]

D204   [Letter] *Tish* (Vancouver BC), No. 27 (November 1964): 2–3.
       "Dear Tishers—"
D205   [Poem] *The Atlantic Monthly* (Boston MA) 214, No. 5 (November 1964):
       148.
       "Far from the Shore"
D206   [Poems] *A Poetry Newsletter: Desert Review Press* (Albuquerque NM),
       No. 1 (November 1964): n. p.
       "3:00 a.m."—"New Year Glimpse"

D207   [Letter] *The Albertan* (Calgary AB), 28 November 1964.
        "No Longer a Joke" [GB attacks MLA A. J. Hooke for his puritanical
        and reactionary views on education]
D208   [Poem] *Burning Water* (Princeton NJ), [No. 3] (Winter 1964): 47.
        "Fluff"
D209   [Poems] *Island* (Toronto ON), No. 2 (17 December 1964): 38–41.
        "Social Poem"—"News"—"The Maypole" [Note: this journal was
        edited by Victor Coleman]
D210   [Review] *Kulchur* (New York NY) 4, No. 16 (Winter 1964/65): 86–87.
        Ezra Pound: Translations, by Ezra Pound: a review

1965

D211   [Editor] *Imago* [Calgary AB], No. 3 (1965).
        Listen, George, by Lionel Kearns [See B1]
D212   [Poem] *Marrahawanna Quarterly* (Cleveland OH), No. 3 (1965): n. p.
        "The Simile" [Note: this journal was edited by d. a. levy]
D213   [Poem] *Tlaloc* (Leeds, England) Broadsheet [No. 1] (January 1965): n. p.
        "Poem of Hand"
D214   [Poems; Letter] *el corno emplumado* (Mexico City), No. 13 (January
        1965): 28–33, 182–183.
        "Mexico City Face"—"Making"—"Bum"—"John Kennedy's Grave,
        and the Others"—"News"—"Shelley's Voice"—"The Blood Red Fuck"
        —"To the Editors"
D215   [Poems] *Tish* (Vancouver BC), No. 28 (January 1965): 7, 8.
        "Girls in the Snow"—"The Beach at Veracruz"
D216   [Poem] *The Eventorium Muse* (New York NY), No. 3 (Winter 1965): 5.
        "The Grass"
D217   [Poem] *The Fiddlehead* (Fredericton NB), No. 63 (Winter 1965): 13.
        "The Red Hot Element"
D218   [Poems] *Potpourri* (Tucson AZ) 1, No. 3 (Spring 1965): 4, 25.
        "Over the Rockies"—"Museum Poem"
D219   [Review] *Edge* (Edmonton AB), No. 4 (Spring 1965): 128–131.
        Poetry of Mid-Century, edited by Milton Wilson: a review
D220   [Story] *The Fiddlehead* (Fredericton NB), No. 64 (Spring 1965): 30–36.
        "Flycatcher"
D221   [Poems] *Estro* (Tucson AZ), No. 1 (March 1965).
        "The Road Tells"—"Calgary"—"(Interlude)"—"Alberta"—"The
        Blue"—"I Watch the Storm"—"Prairie"—"The Religious Lake"—
        "Dust" [Note: issued as a single sheet; see E10]
D222   [Poems] *Move* (Preston, Lancs, England), No. 2 (March 1965): n. p.

"Veracruz Visit"—"Phyllis Webb"—"The Boat"

D223   [Poems] "3 Poems by George Bowering." *Fazo* (Burlington ON) 1, No. 1 (March 1965): 4–6.

"The Sea, the Shore"—"Sullen Poem"—"I Watch the Storm"

D224   [Review] *The Canadian Forum* (Toronto ON) 44, No. 530 (March 1965): 282–283.

"Brain Poetry": a review of *Within the Zodiac*, by Phyllis Gotlieb

D225   [Letter] *The Herald* (Calgary AB), 20 March 1965.

"Student Street Demonstrations" [GB and other faculty members at the University of Calgary criticize the Editorial, 16 March 1965, denouncing student demonstrations]

D226   [Poem] *Wild Dog* (San Francisco CA) 2, No. 15 (22 March 1965): 23.

"Dolores Street Music"

D227   [Poem] *Tlaloc* (Leeds, England), No. 7 (28 March 1965): n. p.

"Canadian Cafe"

D228   [Poem] *The Canadian Forum* (Toronto ON) 45, No. 531 (April 1965): 16.

"The Mark"

D229   [Statement] *The Herald* (Calgary AB), 5 April 1965.

"Basic Subject Status Urged for School Sex Education" [Note: GB is quoted as a panel member for a discussion on sex education in schools, 4 April 1965]

"It seems to me a betrayal to suggest that the subject of sexual intercourse between the sexes cannot be a subject of verbal intercourse between the sexes." [GB quoted; see D229]

D230   [Poem] *Canadian Poetry* (Toronto ON) 28, No. 3 (May 1965): 47–48.

"Prairie Music"

D231   [Poems] *Resuscitator* (Paulton, Nr. Bristol, England), No. 4 (May 1965): 20–22.

"Inside the Tulip"—"Frost"—"Now You"

D232   [Poem] *Poetmeat* (Blackburn, Lancs, England), Nos. 9 & 10 ([Summer] 1965): 71.

"At the Round World's [sic; Earth's] Imagined Belly"

D233   [Poem] *Prism International* (Vancouver BC) 5, No. 1 (Summer 1965): 34.

"The Crumbling Wall"

D234   [Poems] *How* (London, England), No. 5 [Summer 1965]: n. p.

"Alberta"—"Prairie"

D235   [Poems] *Potpourri* (Tucson AZ) 1, No. 4 (Summer 1965): 3–4.

"Teotihuacan"—"Poems & Letters"

D236   [Poems] *Work* (Detroit MI), No. 1 (Summer 1965): 16–17.
        "The Beach at Veracruz"—"You Can't Find Your Way"
D237   [Story] *The Dalhousie Review* (Halifax NS) 45, No. 2 (Summer 1965):
        182–188.
        "The Hayfield"
D238   [Excerpt from a novel] *Queen's Quarterly* (Kingston ON) 72, No. 2
        (Summer 1965): 347–354.
        "The Gamin on the Island Ferry" [from *Mirror on the Floor*; A5]
D239   [Poems] *From a Window* (Tucson AZ), No. 2 (June 1965): n. p.
        "A Day in May"—"The Plain"
D240   [Review; Poems] *Tish* (Vancouver BC), No. 30 (June 1965): 5–6, 12–13.
        "Blaser & Levertov": a review of *The Moth Poem*, by Robin Blaser; *O
        Taste and See*, by Denise Levertov—"Greenwood"—"Mexico Walk"
D241   [Letter] *el corno emplumado* (Mexico City), No. 15 (July 1965): 154.
        "Letter to the Editors"
D242   [Poems] *Camels Coming* (Albuquerque NM), No. 1 (August 1965): n. p.
        "Back in Vancouver for a Vancouver Visit"—"On the High Ceiling"
D243   [Poem] *Arts in Mexico* (Mexico City) 2, No. 8 (29 August 1965).
        "Sonata, Opus 722"
D244   [Poem] *Cyclic* (Montreal PQ) 1, No. 2 (Autumn 1965): 13.
        "Right after the Crash"
D245   [Poem] *Evidence* (Toronto ON), No. 9 [Fall 1965]: 36.
        "Shelley's Voice" [Note: the issue contains a letter addressed to Alan
        Bevan, signed "Some Kind of a Nut," attacking GB, Lionel Kearns, and
        Frank Davey for their "total disregard of meter, avoidance of metaphor
        . . . "; see H32]
D246   [Poem] *Potpourri* (Orono ME) 2, No. 1; issue No. 5 (Autumn 1965): 9.
        "A Bicycle"
D247   [Poem] *The Spero* (Flint MI), No. 1 ([Fall] 1965): 31–32.
        "Sally Bowering and the Rooster"
D248   [Poem] *The Tamarack Review* (Toronto ON), No. 37 (Autumn 1965):
        65–69.
        "Windigo"
D249   [Poems; Review] *Canadian Author & Bookman* (Toronto ON) 41, No. 1
        (Autumn 1965): 5, 21.
        "The Picture"—"The Pictures on My Walls"—*City of the Gulls and
        Sea*, by Frank Davey: a review [Note: the review is printed on the inside
        back cover]
D250   [Poems] *Ganglia* (Toronto ON), No. 1 [Fall 1965]: n. p.
        "45 Mex"—"Chihuahua"—"Los Lomas de Mexico"—"Mexican
        Dog" [Note: this journal was edited by bp Nichol and David Aylward]
D251   [Poems] *Intransit* (Eugene OR), No. 1 (Fall 1965): n. p.

"The Silence"—"The Traveler"—"The Cabin"

D252   [Poems] *Poetry Review* (University of Tampa FL), No. 6 ([Fall] 1965): n. p.

"Mexican Dog"—"2nd Thoughts on the Poet"

D253   [Poems] *The Wormwood Review Issue No. 19* (Storrs CT) 4, No. 3 ([Fall] 1965): 11–12.

"Confucius"—"To Margaret Randall de Mondragon"

D254   [Review] *Kulchur* (New York NY) 5, No. 19 (Autumn 1965): 99–100.

A Reconciling of Rivers, by Marguerite Harris: a review

D255   [Poem] *The Canadian Forum* (Toronto ON) 45, No. 536 (September 1965): 143.

"Whose Dwelling Is the Light of the Setting Suns"

D256   [Poems] *Move* (Preston, Lancs, England), No. 4 (September 1965): n. p.

"Greenwood"—"The Cuernavaca Market"

D257   [Poems] "Bowering: Six Poems." *Touchstone* (Toronto ON), No. 2 (September 1965): 16–21.

"Albertasaurus"—"The Graves of Academe"—"After Breakfast"— "The Romantic Agony"—"Poor Man"—"The Internal Internal"

D258   [Poems] "Three Poems." *London Magazine* (London, England) 5, No. 6 (September 1965): 48–50.

"30 Below"—"The Boat"—"Sabino Canyon"

D259   [Essay] *Saturday Night* (Toronto ON) 80, No. 10 (October 1965): 34–36.

"Alberta's War on Intellect" [Note: subtitled, "A Cool Look at the Know-nothings of Canada's Bible Belt"]

"Alberta is spoken of as the Bible Belt, bordered on the west by the Rocky Mountains, and on the east by a province nobody knows anything about. It does sport an entertaining religious community. The religious pages of Calgary newspapers are like movie pages elsewhere. Pictures of guitar-toting evangelists grin over the titles of upcoming sermons. My own favourite is: 'WAS JUDAS A COMMUNIST?' (Calgary *Herald*, March 14, 1964). Informal Christianity is an integral part of the Alberta scene, along with right wing politics, a profusion of chiropractors, and distrust of foreign ideas. Football is very big here.

"But the most frightening thing is that the provincial legislature (59 Social Credit—four Opposition) is the chief source of anti-intellectualism. Here, the government leads."

[From "Alberta's War on Intellect"; see D259]

D260   [Poem] *Camels Coming* (Reno NV), No. 3 (October 1965): n. p.

"The Newspapers"

D261   [Poem] *Resuscitator* (Paulton, Nr. Bristol, England), No. 5 (October 1965): 18.
        "Make It New (Night Thoughts)"
D262   [Poems] *el corno emplumado* (Mexico City), No. 16 (October 1965).
        The Man in Yellow Boots [See A3]
D263   [Poems] *From a Window* (Tucson AZ), No. 3 (October 1965): n. p.
        "Spinning"—"In the Toilet"
D264   [Review] *The Canadian Forum* (Toronto ON) 45, No. 537 (October 1965): 164.
        A Dream of Lilies, by Joan Finnigan: a review
D265   [Review] *The Albertan* (Calgary AB), 21 October 1965.
        "George Bowering Reviews Cat on a Hot Tin Roof"
D266   [Editor; Essay] "The 1962 Poems" [of R. S. Lane]. *Ganglia* (Toronto ON), No. 2 (November 1965): n. p.
        "Introduction" [to "The 1962 Poems"] [Note: an estimated 200 copies were printed]
D267   [Editor; Poem] *Imago* (Calgary AB), No. 4 [November 1965]: 14–19.
        "Red Lane" [See B1]
D268   [Story] *Quarry* (Kingston ON) 15, No. 2 (November 1965): 7–14.
        "Time and Again"
D269   [Review] *The Albertan* (Calgary AB), 4 November 1965.
        "A Winner, Thanks to Sheila Moore": a theatre review of *The Typists* and *The Tiger,* by Murray Shisgal
D270   [Review] *The Albertan* (Calgary AB), 11 November 1965.
        "The Play's At Fault": a theatre review of *Never Too Late,* by Noel Coward
D271   [Review] *The Albertan* (Calgary AB), 17 November 1965.
        " 'Mac' Cast Plays Coward Very Well": a theatre review of *Present Laughter,* by Noel Coward
D272   [Editor; Poems; Essay] *Tlaloc* (Leeds, England), No. 10 [December 1965]: n. p.
        "The Third Blow"—"Wrinkles"—"New Canadian Poets 1960–1965"
D273   [Poems] *Symptom* (University Park NM), No. 2 (December 1965): n. p.
        "Warm February"—"Early Afternoon in the Rainy Season"—"The Graves of Academe"
D274   [Review] *The Canadian Forum* (Toronto ON) 45, No. 539 (December 1965): 209–210.
        "3 Kingston Poets": a review of *The Beast with Three Backs,* by Tom Eadie, Tom Marshall, and Colin Norman
D275   [Review] *The Albertan* (Calgary AB), 2 December 1965.
        "Yvonne Toynbee Show Bright Spot": a review of a musical, *The Sound of Music*

D276 [Poems] *Tish* (Vancouver BC), No. 32 (4 December 1965): 8, 9.
"Grandmother"—"Taps"—"Angela Hand"

D277 [Review] *Kulchur* (New York NY) 5, No. 20 (Winter 1965/66): 91–92.
The Process, by David Meltzer: a review

D278 [Poems] *Alphabet* (London ON), No. 8 (December 1965/March 1966):
25–27.
"The Simile"—"Above Calgary"

D279 [Poems] *Volume 63* (Waterloo ON), No. 4 (Winter 1965): 42–43.
"Fashion Elegy"—"The Road Tells"

D280 [Essay; Poems] *The Aylesford Review* (Aylesford Priory, Nr. Maidstone,
Kent, England) 7, No. 4 (Winter 1965/Spring 1966): 219–236.
"Universal and Particular: An Enquiry into a Personal Esthetic"
[includes poems: "Circus Maximus"—"Universal and Particular"—
"Meta Morphosis"—"Points on the Grid"—"The Skier"—"Hideo
Kobayashi"—"Moment of Truth"] [Note: taken from GB's MA thesis,
"Points on the Grid"; see E4]

"I know for a fact that this winter [1962–63] I have written poems that are pro-
ducts, in part, of my fresh awareness of my place in the natural and human universe. And I am happy that these poems no longer have to worry about the
argument worn to shape in the didactic poems. For the present I am working on
other problems that require new conscious efforts toward resolution, but which
will someday be resolved and turned to my advantage. They will be replaced. I
hope the pattern of problem—resolution—incorporation will continue all my
writing life. The job of writing should always be as hard to do as it was in the
beginning."
[From "Universal and Particular: An Enquiry into a Personal Esthetic"; see
D280 and E4]

1966

D281 [Letter] *The Open Letter* (Victoria BC), No. 1 [1966]: 10.
"An Open Letter to the Former *Tish* Editors & Their Critics" [Note:
this journal, developing from the *Tish* collective, was initiated by its
"Coordinating Editor," Frank Davey; GB is listed as an associate editor,
along with David Dawson and Fred Wah]

"I liked the idea of *Tish*, and I still do. I like the idea of *The Open Letter*, and
would urge the former *Tish* people to keep their noses in this new mag. For one

thing, I want to know what you are all doing, even if it isnt what I'm doing. And I would like to see you quit arguing so much about things that concern the ego. Let's talk about poetry, and remember that good poetry, whatever you think that is, crops up anywhere."
[From "An Open Letter to the Former *Tish* Editors & Their Critics"; see D281]

D282   [Poem] *Pliego* (Orono ME), [No. 7] [1966]: n. p.
        "Divine Poem After Donne" [Note: the poem is the entire issue; see E15]

D283   [Translations] "Two Poems." *Chicago Review* (Chicago IL) 19, No. 1 (1966): 74–75.
        "The Spring," by Sergio Mondragón—"Moaning of the Cow," by Sergio Mondragón

D284   [Poem] *IT: A Stunted Magazine of Poetry* (Detroit MI), No. 3 (January 1966): n. p.
        "As It Was in the Beginning"

D285   [Poem] *The Canadian Forum* (Toronto ON) 45, No. 540 (January 1966): 223.
        "Milton Acorn"

D286   [Poem] *Tish* (Vancouver BC), No. 33 (4 January 1966): 12.
        "Mounties"

D287   [Review] *The Albertan* (Calgary AB), 13 January 1966.
        "NFB Films Praised": a review of five best National Film Board of Canada productions for 1965

D288   [Review] *The Albertan* (Calgary AB), 27 January 1966.
        "Play Lacks Authenticity": a theatre review of *A View from the Bridge*, by Arthur Miller

D289   [Poem] *Ante* (Los Angeles CA) 2, No. 1 (Winter 1966): 59.
        "The Mystery of Moses"

D290   [Poem] *Golden West* (Calgary AB), [No. 2] (January/February 1966): 21.
        "[The] Grass"

D291   [Poem] *Poesia de Venezuela* (Caracas, Venezuela), No. 17 (January/February 1966): n. p.
        "After Breakfast"

D292   [Poem] *Prism International* (Vancouver BC) 5, Nos. 3 & 4 (Winter/Spring 1966): 65.
        "30 Below"

D293   [Poems] "Two Poems." *Ganglia* (Toronto ON), No. 3 (31 January 1966): n. p.
        "You Cant Find Your Way"—"The Name"

D294   [Editor] *Imago* (Calgary AB), No. 5 [Early 1966].

D295   [Review] *The Albertan* (Calgary AB), 3 February 1966.

"Six Characters 'Golden' ": a theatre review of *Six Characters in Search of an Author*, by Luigi Pirandello [Note: no by-line]

D296   [Review] *The Albertan* (Calgary AB), 8 February 1966.

"Spring Thaw Has Plenty of Laughs": a review of a revue, *Spring Thaw 1966*

D297   [Review] *The Albertan* (Calgary AB), 12 February 1966.

"Two Actors Make the Play": a theatre review of *A Man For All Seasons*, by Robert Bolt

---

"Well, you may ask, how did I get to [be] the drama critic for the Calgary *The Albertan*? And how can I stand working in those conditions, where I get to the newspaper right after the play is over, and have a deadline of about 20 minutes, so no revision, no thinking, bat out a few hundred words abt a production of some play, and this about avg once a week here this year. Well, you may ask. Last night I saw "A Man for all Seasons," a play all you dogans are interested [in] whether there in Trinidad or here in this other island. And the audience was full of clergymen dressed in their black business, with coin changers affixed to their belts."

[GB Papers, Correspondence Lionel Kearns, 12 February 1966, Queen's University Archives]

D298   [Review] *The Albertan* (Calgary AB), 24 February 1966.

"Boring Play Well Acted": a theatre review of *The Chalk Garden*, by Enid Bagnold

D299   [Review] *The Albertan* (Calgary AB), 25 February 1966.

"Anything Goes Goes Very Well": a review of a musical, *Anything Goes*, by Cole Porter

D300   [Poem] *Intercourse* (Montreal PQ), [No. 1] (Early Spring 1966): 11–12.
"Oaxaca"

D301   [Letter] *Canadian Author & Bookman* (Toronto ON) 41, No. 3 [Spring 1966]: 1.

["To the Editor"] [Note: a response to Myra Haas' article in 41, No. 1, which mentions "pipe-smoking Tish experimentalists"]

D302   [Letter] *el corno emplumado* (Mexico City), No. 18 (Spring 1966): 235.
["To the Editors"]

D303   [Poem] *Love: (incorporating hate)* (Berkeley CA), No. 1 (Spring 1966): 10–12.
"Time Magazine's Poem"

D304   [Review] *Canadian Literature* (Vancouver BC), No. 28 (Spring 1966): 79–80.

"Sun, Seasons, City": a review of *Ten Elephants on Yonge Street*, by Raymond Souster [Note: see *Craft Slices*: "Souster's Elephants"; A44]

D305   [Review] *The Minnesota Review* (St. Paul MN) 6, No. 1 ([Spring] 1966): 90–93.

"The Smudgy Eye, the Sharp Focus": a review of *The Small Waves*, by Alvin Greenberg

D306   [Letter; Review] *The Open Letter* (Victoria BC), No. 2 (March 1966): 18–20.

"Open Letter: Dear Frank"—*Solitudes Crowded with Loneliness*, by Bob Kaufman: a review

D307   [Poem] *Elizabeth* (New Rochelle NY), No. 9 (March 1966): 39.
"Mud Time"

D308   [Story; Letter] *The Canadian Forum* (Toronto ON) 45, No. 545 (March 1966): 275–278, 281.
"The House on Tenth"—"Letter to the Editor"

D309   [Story] *Gaillardia* (Calgary AB), No. 1 (March 1966): 49–59.
"No No No No No"

D310   [Review] *The Albertan* (Calgary AB), 3 March 1966.
"Two Plays Top Notch": a theatre review of *The Private Ear* and *The Public Eye*, by Peter Shaffer

D311   [Poem] *Tish* (Vancouver BC), No. 35 (4 March 1966): 12.
"Layers [1]"

D312   [Review] *The Albertan* (Calgary AB), 9 March 1966.
"Comediens Superb": a theatre review of *Leçons D'Amour de Monsieur Molière*, presented by Les Jeune Comediens

D313   [Review] *The Albertan* (Calgary AB), 24 March 1966.
"Knack Provides Theatre Bonus": a theatre review of *The Knack and How to Get It*, by Ann Jellicoe

D314   [Poem] *Parallel* (Montreal PQ), No. 1 (March/April 1966): 37.
"Over the Rockies"

D315   [Review] *The Albertan* (Calgary AB), 31 March 1966.
"Rumanian Ballet Happy, Exciting": a review of a performance by the Rumanian Folk Ballet

D316   [Letter; Poems] *The Open Letter* (Victoria BC), No. 3 (April 1966): 3–5.
"Open Letter: Dear Frank & Folk"—"For Victor Coleman"—"On Reading Frank's Book"

D317   [Poem] *The Canadian Forum* (Toronto ON) 46, No. 543 (April 1966): 291.
"A Dead Duck"

D318   [Review] *The Albertan* (Calgary AB), 15 April 1966.
"Great Musical, Top Cast": a review of *Fantasticks*, a musical production by the Manitoba Theatre Centre

D319   [Review] *The Albertan* (Calgary AB), 28 April 1966.
        "Things Went Agley for Mice and Men": a theatre review of *Of Mice
        and Men*, by John Steinbeck

D320   [Poems] "Three Poems." *London Magazine* (London, England) 6, No. 2
        (May 1966): 33–35.
        "The Blue Shirt"—"To My Betrothed on the First Day of WWIII
        (Being Writ during the Cuban Crisis of 1962)"—"Air Photos, Spring
        1957"

D321   [Poem] *Weed* (Kitchener ON), No. 3 (May/June 1966): 2–3.
        "The Universe Begins to Look" [Note: this journal was edited by
        Nelson Ball]

D322   [Review] *The Albertan* (Calgary AB), 5 May 1966.
        "Kaufman Play Spent, Not Well": a theatre review of *The Man Who
        Came to Dinner*, by Moss Hart and George S. Kaufman

D323   [Review] *The Albertan* (Calgary AB), 9 May 1966.
        "Edmonton Hits Home with Play": a theatre review of *Escape*, by
        John Orrell

D324   [Editor] *Imago* (Calgary AB), No. 6 ([Summer] 1966).
        The Scarred Hull, by Frank Davey [See B1]

D325   [Essay] *Canadian Literature* (Vancouver BC), No. 29 (Summer 1966):
        7–17.
        "And the Sun Goes Down: Richler's First Novel"

D326   [Poem] *Intercourse* (Montreal PQ), No. 3 (Summer [1966]): 20.
        "The Bath"

D327   [Poem] *IS* [pronounced "eyes"] (Toronto ON), No. 1 [Summer 1966]: n.
        p.
        "Once in a While You Catch Yourself" [Note: this journal was edited
        by Victor Coleman]

D328   [Poem] *Potpourri* (Milwaukie OR) 1, Nos. 7 & 8; 2, Nos. 3 & 4 (Summer
        1966): 11.
        "Coltrane"

D329   [Poem] *Tlaloc How* (Leeds, England), No. 12; (London, England), No. 6
        [Summer 1966]: n. p.
        "Mud Time" [Note: a joint publication]

D330   [Poem] *Volume 63* (Waterloo ON), No. 5 (Summer 1966): 4–5.
        "History of Poets: John the Baptist"

D331   [Poems] *Iconolâtre* (Durham, England), No. 16 [Summer 1966]: 3–4.
        "The Sea, the Shore"—"Sullen Poem"

D332   [Review] *Western Humanities Review* (Salt Lake City UT) 20, No. 3
        (Summer 1966): 261–262.
        English Poetry in Quebec, edited by John Glassco: a review [Note: see
        Craft Slices: "Quebec Anglos"; A44]

D333   [Story] *The Tamarack Review* (Toronto ON), No. 40 (Summer 1966): 21–29.
"The Elevator"

D334   [Letter] *The Open Letter* (Victoria BC), No. 4 (June 1966): 19.
"Open Up, Letter"

D335   [Poems] *LitQuiz Weekly* (Bombay, India), No. 1 [23 June 1966]: 1.
"Snow Tired on a City Bus"—"History of Poets: Tess"—"Patrol"

D336   [Poems; Editor; Excerpt from a letter] *el corno emplumado* (Mexico City), No. 19 (July 1966): 23–61, 191–192.
"Hamatsa"—"Calle Triangulo"—"Thirteen Canadian Poets" [Note: "Notes on contributors" contains an excerpted letter from "George Bowering, who rounded up this selection of Canadian Poetry for us," which was titled "Thirteen Canadian Poets"]

OKANAGAN STORM
by George Bowering

forks of standing lightning
on the mountain crests
   as the dark rolling storm
   thunders on the edges of the valley
   overlooking mountains
light the night
and fill the forest with morning
in a second
   Valley is refuge
   a trench in the storm
   a dark
   blue
      balls of orange rain cloud
      drifting west
      up the hills
   Letting up the pressure
   for the first rain
   creeping fast across the lake
   and the lightning
   goes out

Hudson's Bay Company
INCORPORATED 2ᴺᴰ MAY 1670
presents this work as one of a new series written by Canadian poets

"Okanagan Storm"; see D345, D416, and E16

D337   [Poem] *Quarry* (Kingston ON) 15, No. 4 (August 1966): 21.
"The Silence"

D338   [Poems] *Camels Coming* (Reno NV), No. 5 (August/September 1966): n. p.
"The Streets of Calgary"—"Confidence"—"Calgary Now"

D339   [Poem; Stories] *Edge* (Edmonton AB), No. 5 (Fall 1966): 67–69, 71.
"Colonel Fleming et Jules et Jim"—"Two Grave News Stories: The Towers; The Deputy Sheriff" [Note: the stories were taken from an unpublished novel, "What Does Eddie Williams Want?"]

D340   [Poem] *The Grande Ronde Review* (Lagrande OR), No. 6 ([Fall] 1966): n. p.
"Gas Station Town"

D341   [Poem] *Twentieth Century* (Victoria, Australia) 20, No. 3 (Autumn 1966): 214.
"Tunnel Mountain"

D342   [Translation] *Prism International* (Vancouver BC) 6, No. 2 (Autumn 1966): 94.
"To Be Poet," by Manuel Pacheco

D343   [Poem] *Saturday Night* (Toronto ON) 81, No. 9 (September 1966): 44.
"It Was in the Newspaper"

D344   [Poem] *Delta* (Montreal PQ), No. 26 (October 1966): 17–18.
"East to West"

D345   [Poem] *Quarry* (Kingston ON) 16, No. 1 (October 1966): [back cover].
"Okanagan Storm" [Note: Hudson's Bay Company ad; see D416 and
E16]

D346   [Review] *The Canadian Forum* (Toronto ON) 46, No. 549 (October
1966): 166–167.
Energy=Mercy Squared, by Mervyn Procope: a review

D347   [Editor; Poem] *Imago* (London ON), No. 7 [December 1966]: 26–28.
[See B1]
"The House"

D348   [Poem] *The Canadian Forum* (Toronto ON) 46, No. 550 (November
1966): 188.
"To Gordon"

D349   [Translation] *The Open Letter* (Victoria BC), No. 5 (November 1966): 4.
"World," by Raquel Jodorowsky

D350   [Poems] *New Measure* (Oxford, England), No. 4 (Winter 1966/67):
31–32.
"Money"—"That Girl Walks with Her Back to Me"

1967

D351   [Story] *Talon* (Vancouver BC) 4, No. 4 [1967]: 24–32.
"Have You Seen Jesus?"

D352   [Letter] *The Canadian Forum* (Toronto ON) 46, No. 552 (January 1967):
219.
"The Editor"

D353   [Poem] *Manhattan Review* (New York NY) 1, No. 3 ([January] 1967):
19–20.
"Back in Vancouver for a Vancouver Visit"

D354   [Review] *Guerrilla* (Detroit MI) 1, No. 1 (January 1967): 11.
"On War: Robert Duncan": a review of *Of the War*, by Robert
Duncan [Notes: GB is listed as a contributing editor; see *Craft Slices*:
"Duncan's War"; A44]

D355   [Statement; Poems] *20 Cents Magazine* (London ON) 1, No. 5 (January
[1967]): n. p.
"What the Student for Peace Wants"—"Even Los Angeles"—"The
Late News"—"Winning"

D356   [Poem] *Latitudes* (Houston TX) 1, No. 1 (February 1967): 23.

"Pancakes"
D357   [Poems; Letter] *The Open Letter* (Victoria BC), No. 6 [February/March 1967]: 7, 16–19.
"The Cup"—"Even Los Angeles"—"Winning"—"The Late News"—"O I Pen You a Letter or 2"
D358   [Review] *Edge* (Edmonton AB), No. 6 (Spring 1967): 114–119.
"Canadian Novel Chronicle": a review of *Beautiful Losers*, by Leonard Cohen; *Amongst Thistles & Thorns*, by Austin C. Clarke; *A Gift of Echoes*, by Robert Harlow; *In Praise of Older Women*, by Stephen Vizinczey; *We Always Take Care of Our Own*, by C. J. Newman [Note: see *Craft Slices*: "Ugly Winner," "Thorny," and "Remember Newman"; A44]
D359   [Poem] *Move* (Preston, Lancs, England), No. 7 (March 1967): n. p.
"History Is Us"

"I have been writing letters tonight, putting off the essay I'm typing on William Carlos Williams, wch I have been writing while putting off my travel book wch I have been writing while putting off my novel, wch I have been working on while putting off my epic poem. And all this time I am supposed to be writing an essay on Shelley wch I have put off in order to work on an essay on Denise Levertov."
[GB Papers, Correspondence David McFadden, 5 March 1967, Queen's University Archives]

GB and AB in London ON, 1967

D360   [Letter] *el corno emplumado* (Mexico City), No. 22 (April 1967): 141–142.
"To Margaret Randall, Editor"
D361   [Poem] *Poetry* (Chicago IL) 110, No. 2 (May 1967): 88.
"The White Station Wagon Strophes"

"I might be considered a romantic poet in that I believe nature to be the best instructor. Romantic poets tend to join primitives, children, & crazy people in believing that the natural environment is trying to tell them something. Instead of praying or preaching I now write poems. I think that the poetic act is largely in realizing the common energy that runs through the nature in me & the nature I find myself among. A great number of my poems deal with that realization, & most of them are informed by it. I think that poems, souls, governments, & families begin to fail when there is something thrust between them & the details of

the natural world."
[From a statement for *Rhymes and Reasons*; see C43]

D362　[Review] *20 Cents Magazine* (London ON) 1, No. 9 (May [1967]): n. p.
"America's Angels": a review of *Hell's Angels*, by Hunter S. Thompson

D363　[Poem] *Quarry* (Kingston ON) 16, No. 4 (Summer 1967): 15.
"Duluth, Midway"

D364　[Poems] *The Avalanche* (Berkeley CA), No. 3 (Summer 1967): n. p.
"On the Radio"—"Because I Dig"

D365　[Review] *Canadian Literature* (Vancouver BC), No. 33 (Summer 1967): 71–72.
"Inside Leonard Cohen": a review of *Parasites of Heaven*, by Leonard Cohen

D366　[Story] *The Fiddlehead* (Fredericton NB), No. 72 (Summer 1967): 6–18.
"Looking for Ebbe"

D367　[Poem] *Poetry Australia* (Sydney, Australia), No. 16 (June 1967): 10–11.
"Animals That Eat"

D368　[Review] *Guerrilla* (Detroit MI) 1, No. 2 (1 June 1967): 11.
"Pennies in a Stream": a review of *To Come to Have Become*, by Theodore Enslin

D369　[Review] *The Canadian Forum* (Toronto ON) 47, No. 557 (June 1967): 71–72.
"If That's Christ, I'll Take Vanilla": a review of *A Christ of the Ice-Floes*, by David Wevill [Note: see *Craft Slices*: "The League"; A44]

D370　[Essay; Poems] *Parallel* (Montreal PQ) 2, No. 7 (June/July 1967): 42, 44–45.
"The Valley" [Note: this essay includes the poems "Gas Station Town" —"Locus Solus"—"Locus Primus"—"Patrol"—"Driving to Kelowna" —"Okanagan Winter Scenario"—"Old Umbrella Tree"]

Gas station town
sports a new sidewalk
and the Village Commissioners
have stopt wearing suspenders

walking the short street

I look down at
the tops of heads
　　　　　and these
　　　　　were the men
　　　　　who taught

me in school
branded me a fool
(tho dangerous)
handed me a rolled up paper
diploma

And forgot
as fast as they could
walking the short street
I look down at

my initials
in the cement

["Gas Station Town," in "The Valley"; see D370]

D371   [Review] *The Globe and Mail* Supplement, 8 July 1967.
"A Dream Dies in Grass-Roots Rot": a review of *When She Was Good*, by Philip Roth

D372   [Poem] *The Canadian Forum* (Toronto ON) 47, No. 559 (August 1967): 119.
"The Second Runner"

D373   [Review] *Guerrilla* (Detroit MI), No. 3 (August 1967).
Zacapa, by Donn Munson: a review

D374   [Letter] *Kayak* (San Francisco CA), No. 11 ([Summer] 1967): 28.
"To the Editor"

D375   [Poem] *The Dalhousie Review* (Halifax NS) 47, No. 3 (Autumn 1967): 447.
"Elementary School, Oak Lake, Man."

D376   [Poem] *The University of Windsor Review* (Windsor ON) 3, No. 1 (Fall 1967): 18–19.
"Grass, Grass"

D377   [Poems] *Camels Coming* (Reno NV), No. 7 ([Summer] 1967): 4–5.
"Delicate Deer"—"The Covenant"

D378   [Story] *Quarry* (Kingston ON) 17, No. 1 (Fall 1967): 16–30.
"The White Coffin"

D379   [Review] *The Globe and Mail* Supplement, 23 September 1967.
"A Lyrical Boom in Slim Volumes": a review of *The Unquiet Bed*, by Dorothy Livesay; *North of Summer*, by Al Purdy; *Journeying & the returns*, by bp Nichol; *Poems, New and Collected*, by A. J. M. Smith; *Between the Wars*, edited by Milton Wilson [Note: see *Craft Slices*: "Say Live," "Purdy's North," and "bp's Returns"; A44]

D380   [Poem] *The Canadian Forum* (Toronto ON) 47, No. 561 (October 1967): 154.
      "Actual Love, Leonard"

D381   [Review] *el corno emplumado* (Mexico City), No. 24 (October 1967): 145–147.
      "Two Canadian Poets": a review of *What They Say*, by John Newlove; *The Poem Poem*, by David McFadden

---

"Want to tell you before I forget, that THE POEM POEM is just great great, and I yam done a review of it for El Cornhole Emplumado, wch shd be in the 24th issue, the 23rd having just arrived here. I reviewed it along with Nolove's book, but gave gave THE POEM POEM the most space space. Concongratsgrats!

"I have been idiotically going to movies in the afternoons of late, since finishing the ms for my Vancouver poem [*George, Vancouver*], and with no publisher to send it to. When I was a sophomore in cawlitch after the air farce I used to go to doublefeatures about 3 afternoons a week, it was insane. It is naturally just a phase I'm going under. glub"
[GB Papers, Correspondence David McFadden, 9 August 1967, Queen's University Archives]

D382   [Translation] *Poet* (Madras, India) 8, No. 10 (October 1967): 6–7.
      "At the Ear of Christ," by Gabriela Mistral

1968

D383   [Poem] *Guerrilla* [Free Newspaper of the Streets] (New York NY) 2, No. 2 (1968): n. p.
      "A Declaration"

D384   [Poem; Excerpt from a poem] "Two Poems by George Bowering." *Ahora* (Albuquerque NM), [No. 1] [January 1968]: n. p.
      "Sonata, Opus 722"—"For George" [excerpt from "Poem Written For George (2)"]

D385   [Poem] *Mainline* (Windsor ON), No. 1 [January 1968]: n. p.
      "Friday Afternoon"

D386   [Poem] *The Malahat Review* (Victoria BC), No. 5 (January 1968): 120–122.
      "Sekhemab & Perabsen"

D387   [Review] *The Canadian Forum* (Toronto ON) 47, No. 564 (January 1968): 235.

D388   "Footprints on the Dashboard Upside Down": a review of *Total War*, by Harry Howith [Review] *The Globe and Mail* Supplement, 13 January 1968.

"A Focus on All That Is Rotten": a review of *The Temple on the River*, by Jacques Hébert

D389   [Poem; Translations] *The Fiddlehead* (Fredericton NB), No. 74 (Winter 1968): 26–30.

"Friday Afternoon"—"Good Night," by Manuel Pacheco— "Poem for the 'Gospel According to Saint Matthew'," by Manuel Pacheco—"The Appearance of a Burial," by Manuel Pacheco —"The Appearance of Happiness," by Manuel Pacheco

D390   [Story] *West Coast Review* (Burnaby BC) 2, No. 3 (Winter 1968): 12–21.

"Ricardo and the Flower"

D391   [Editor; Poem] *Imago* (Montreal PQ), No. 8 [February 1968]: 31–37.

"Renunciation of Old Poetics III" [See B1]

D392   [Interview; Poem] *The Montrealer* (Montreal PQ) 42, No. 2 (February 1968): 8–9.

"George Bowering, Resident Writer," by Ted Ferguson [Note: contains "Under the Spreading Chestnut Legs," printed untitled]

A DECLARATION

WHEREAS the government of the United States of America forces men to carry weapons & learn to kill with them, &

WHEREAS that government imprisons the bodies of men who resist the enforced carrying of weapons & killing of other men, acting in fact as hired killers, & thus doing ungodly injury to their immortal souls, &

WHEREAS that same government employs those hired killers to destroy the lands & properties of smaller nations in all parts of the world that is by no legal or moral right the preserve of the United States of America, &

WHEREAS that same government uses its hired killers to destroy the economies of other nations in order to enrich the economy of the United States of America, &

WHEREAS the government of those United States uses its hired killers to take away the lives of men, women & children in any nation of the world it may want to terrorize at any given moment, some of those nations having been:

MEXICO · LAOS · VIET NAM · CUBA · GUATEMALA · LEBANON CAMBODIA · NICUARAGUA · THE DOMINICAN REPUBLIC · &

WHEREAS the United States government openly encourages & supports dictators in their suppression of human rights & dignity in the nations where the United States has not yet or recently sent its armed killers, some of these nations being:

SPAIN · PORTUGAL · FORMOSA · COLOMBIA · ECUADOR BOLIVIA · &

WHEREAS the United States uses its financial good fortune to coerce & influence the governments that are not dictatorships but which may ignore the urgins of moral & social improvement in favor of economic bribery by the United States, some of these governments ruling in:

CANADA – THE UNITED KINGDOM · JAPAN · PANAMA AUSTRALIA · NEW ZEALAND · &

WHEREAS the United States government declares that human life outside its boundaries is less important than the American notion of economy, so that Indians & Nigerians starve while American farmers destroy their own crops, & so that Vietnamese babies are burned to death by the machines of the Boeing Aircraft Corporation, &

WHEREAS the United States government seeks by unilateral actions of violence & terror to destroy the efforts toward peace & world order & justice, those efforts made by international bodies such as the United Nations, & agreements to seek peace, such as those of 1954 in Geneva,

I DO SOLEMNLY, & from this moment forward,
                                                                                                    Declare war
on the government of the United States of America.
                                                                        —George Bowering

"A Declaration"; see D383, D430, D439, and C200

"Oh, how I dreaded that second year at Western [University of Western Ontario]. I wanted badly to begin writing again and I could see myself spending the whole winter memorizing answers to questions like 'When was the first bilingual essay printed in Upper Canada?' "
[from "George Bowering, Resident Writer"; see D392]

D393   [Review] *The Globe and Mail* Supplement, 24 February 1968. "Good. But Canadian? Come Now": a review of *Canadian Winter's Tales*, edited by Norman Levine

D394   [Essay] *Canadian Literature* (Vancouver BC), No. 36 (Spring 1968): 40–49.
"Why James Reaney Is a Better Poet: 1) Than Any Northrop Frye Poet; 2) Than He Used to Be"

D395   [Poem] *Prism '68* (Montreal PQ), (Spring 1968): 63–64.
"Gil"

D396   [Poem] *The Ant's Forefoot* (Toronto ON), No. 2 (Spring 1968): 39.
"Round Head"

GB in Montreal, 1970

D397   [Poems] "Two Poems." *Quarry* (Kingston ON) 17, No. 3 (Spring 1968): 29.
"Elsy"—"The Pear"

D398   [Poem] *Kauri* (Washington DC), No. 25 (March/April 1968): 15.
"Layers [9]"

D399   [Review] *The Globe and Mail* Supplement, 9 March 1968.
"In the Good Old Pre-Beat Days": a review of *Vanity of Duluoz*, by Jack Kerouac [Note: see *Craft Slices*: "Vanity"; A44]

D400   [Poems] *Noose* (New York NY), No. 1 (23 March 1968): n. p.
"Coltrane & Che"—"Talent"—"Where It Comes from"—"Round Head"

D401   [Review] *The Globe and Mail* Supplement, 6 April 1968.
"A Luminous Sharing of Insights in Collision": a review of *T.V. Baby Poems*, by Allen Ginsberg [Note: see *Craft Slices*: "Ginsberg's VW"; A44]

D402   [Poem] *Ann Arbor Review* (Ann Arbor MI), No. 4 (Summer 1968): 4.
"Brook Water"

D403   [Review] *Canadian Literature* (Vancouver BC), No. 37 (Summer 1968): 87–88.

A. J. M. Smith and GB at F. R. Scott's cottage in the Eastern Townships, Quebec, 1968

193

"Unit Structures": a review of *Pointing*, by Lionel Kearns
D404   [Review] *The Fiddlehead* (Fredericton NB), No. 76 (Summer 1968): 85–87.

"Red Lane's Poems": a review of *The Collected Poems of Red Lane*, by Red Lane
D405   [Translation] *Apple* (Springfield IL), No. 2 (Summer 1968): 3.

"Summer on the Shoulders," by Sergio Mondragón
D406   [Editor] *Imago* (Montreal PQ), No. 9 [June 1968].

The Saladmaker, by David McFadden [See B1]
D407   [Poem] *Mainline* (Windsor ON), No. 2 (June 1968): n. p.

"Community"
D408   [Poem] *0 to 9* (New York NY), No. 4 (June 1968): 95–97.

"No Time Left"
D409   [Review] *The Canadian Forum* (Toronto ON) 48, No. 569 (June 1968): 70.

The Last of the Crazy People, by Timothy Findley: a review
D410   [Poems] *Hyphid* (Toronto ON), No. 2 (July 1968): 30–33.

"For Ronnie Carter"—"My Garden"—"Secret Purr"—"City Stones" —"Bells"
D411   [Statement] *The Georgia Straight* (Vancouver BC) 2, No. 23 (26 July–8 August 1968): 16.

"Fellatio Rock" [Note: on pop music]
D412   [Poem] *Canadian Poetry* (Ottawa ON) 31, No. 4 (August 1968): 67.

"I Am Told Wordsworth" [pub. under pseud. E. E. Greengrass] [Note: this is the first public appearance of E. E. Greengrass, launching his poetic career with a poem written back in March 1965]

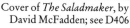

Cover of *The Saladmaker*, by David McFadden; see D406

"Edward Eytan Greengrass—I don't remember when I first created him. I may have created him for a purpose, for instance, to write a book review when I said I wouldn't write book reviews, or to enter a contest, or to write a letter to an editor. I kept him going because I said I wasn't writing lyric poems anymore but I still wanted to write some. I also liked the idea of making the scene uncertain. E. E. Greengrass was there to make it a bit more worrisome.

"Someone came along and said, I get it, e. e. cummings, but that had not entered my mind at all. E. E. Greengrass came simply from his initials, EEG, which stands for electroencephalogram. When we were doing *Tish*, Frank [Davey] and I had an office at UBC that used to be an EEG testing area where they put electrodes in monkey heads. There were still rusty knives lying around and boxes that said EEG stuff on them. So the letters EEG stuck in my head. "Greengrass is a Jewish name. I remember one time getting a letter after I moved to Vancouver from a woman in Montreal saying that she had been tracking down all the people with that name.

"The other source of the name was a baseball player named Greengrass in the major leagues when I was a kid. There was another ball player, at the same time, I don't know if he was Jewish or not, whose name was Delsing. So Greengrass and Delsing [a main figure in much of GB's fiction] were both, in the 50s, kind of journeymen ball players in the major leagues."
[Session 14, 26 May 1989]

D413　[Poem] *The Far Point* (Winnipeg MB) No. 1 (Fall/Winter 1968): 26.
　　　"Printers of Books"
D414　[Essay] *The Georgia Straight* (Vancouver BC) 2, No. 27 (30 August–5 September 1968): 12.
　　　"It's Canada's 101st Birthday, Hurrah"
D415　[Poem] *The Minnesota Review* (St. Paul MN) 8, No. 2 ([Summer] 1968): 192.
　　　"First Line Writ in London, the Rest in Istanbul"
D416　[Poem] *The Tamarack Review* (Toronto ON), No. 48 ([Fall] 1968): [back cover].
　　　"Okanagan Storm" [Note: a drawing with poem, produced by the Hudson's Bay Company; see D345 and E16]
D417　[Review] *Edge* (Edmonton AB), No. 8 (Fall 1968): 143–148.
　　　"Canadian Fiction Chronicle II": a review of *Girls of Two Summers*, by Gerald Taaffe; *The Road Past Altamont*, by Gabrielle Roy; *A Jest of God*, by Margaret Laurence; *Watcha Gonna Do, Boy . . . Watcha Gonna Be?*, by Peter Taylor; *Whirlpool*, by Diane Giguère; *Place d'Armes*, by Scott Symons; *The Personnel Man*, by Michael Sheldon; *Scratch One Dreamer*, by David Lewis Stein; *Honey in the Rock*, by Christine Van der Mark
D418　[Review] *The Globe and Mail* Supplement, 31 August 1968.
　　　"Exigencies with Myths Making It Bravely": a review of *Bending the Bow*, by Robert Duncan; *The Back Country*, by Gary Snyder; *Airplane Dreams*, by Allen Ginsberg
D419　[Essay] *The Georgia Straight* (Vancouver BC) 2, No. 28 (6–12 September 1968): 9.
　　　"The Indecent Treatment of Indecent Exposure"
D420　[Poem] *grOnk* (Toronto ON) 2, No. 2 (October 1968): n. p.

"The American Bomb"

D421   [Poems] *Ninth Circle* (University Park NM), No. 4 (October 1968): n. p.
        "On a Brown Painting by Rivera"—
        "A Beginning"—"Round"

D422   [Statement] *The Georgia Straight* (Vancouver BC) 2, No. 31 (4–10 October 1968): 3.
        "How to Become a Responsible Citizen"

D423   [Statement] *The Georgia Straight* (Vancouver BC) 2, No. 32 (11–17 October 1968): 3.

GB and AB at Île d'Orléans, Quebec, summer 1968

        "Smut Science Rhetoric"

D424   [Poem] *The Nation* (New York NY) 207, No. 14 (28 October 1968): 446.
        "The Grate Society"

D425   [Poem] *Mainline* (Windsor ON), No. 3 (November 1968): 6–7.
        "Election Poem"

D426   [Poems] *The Open Letter* (Victoria BC), No. 8 (November 1968): 22–24.
        "Poem Written for George (1)"—"Poem Written for George (2)"—
        "A Thames Bridge"

D427   [Poems] "Two Poems by George Bowering." *Elizabeth* (New Rochelle NY), No. 12 (November 1968): 25–26.
        "Open"—"On Reading Some Words"

D428   [Review] *The Canadian Forum* (Toronto ON) 48, No. 574 (November 1968): 187–188.
        Black Night Window, by John Newlove: a review

D429   [Essay] *The Georgia Straight* (Vancouver BC) 2, No. 35 (1–7 November 1968): 13.
        "Would You Rather Be Bitten by a Nark or a Shark?"

D430   [Poem] *Open City* (Los Angeles CA), No. 78 (15–21 November 1968): 1.
        "A Declaration"

"The American Bomb"; see D420

D431   [Statement] *The Georgia Straight* (Vancouver BC) 2, No. 37 (15–21 November 1968): 5.
        "25 Things to Shoot Back at Cops Who Are Shooting Mace at You"

D432   [Poem] *The South Florida Poetry Journal* (Tampa FL) 1, No. 2 (Winter 1968): 39.
        "The Sun Also Rises"

D433   [Essay] *Artscanada* (Toronto ON) 25, No. 5; issue No. 124/127 (December 1968): 76–77.
       "Kiyooka's Sculpture" [Note: see *Craft Slices*: "Kiyooka's Sculpture"; A44]

D434   [Poem] *Alphabet* (London ON), No. 15 (December 1968): 4–6.
       "Goodbye Middlesex County"

D435   [Poems] *Hyphid* (Toronto ON), No. 4 (December 1968): 8.
       "River Rhine"—"Strangers & Friends" [Note: "River Rhine" comes from an unpublished travelogue, "Eye-Kicks in Europe" (1966)]

D436   [Poems] *Liontayles* (Waterloo ON) 2, No. 1 (December 1968): 8–9.
       "The Rabbit on the Roof" [pub. under pseud. E. E. Greengrass]— " 'Mr. Pearson' (The Movie)" [pub. under pseud. E. E. Greengrass]

D437   [Review] *The Canadian Forum* (Toronto ON) 48, No. 575 (December 1968): 212–213.
       Shapes and Sounds, by W. W. E. Ross: a review [Note: see *Craft Slices*: "W. W. E. Ross"; A44]

D438   [Essay] *The Georgia Straight* (Vancouver BC) 2, No. 42 (20 December 1968–2 January 1969): 4.
       "Johnny Flag & the Welfare Commandoes"

D439   [Poem] *The Fifth Estate* (Detroit MI) 3, No. 17 (26 December 1968–8 January 1969): n. p.
       "A Declaration" [Note: a folded insert, the first page from *Open City*; see D430]

D440   [Review] *Canadian Dimension* (Winnipeg MB) 5, No. 7 (December 1968/January 1969): 43–44.
       "Why Poets Are Poor": a review of *Kingdom of Absence*, by Dennis Lee; *From the Portals of Mouseholes*, by Seymour Mayne; *Letters from the Savage Mind*, by Patrick Lane

1969

D441   [Poems] *Abyss* (Dunkirk NY) 2, No. 2 (1969): 56, 58.
       "Reading the Book"—"That Wind"

D442   [Editor; Poem] *Imago* (Montreal PQ), No. 10 [January 1969]: 35–37.
       "Single World West" [See B1]

D443   [Poem] *The Nation* (New York NY) 208, No. 2 (13 January 1969): 58.
       "Man with Broom"

D444   [Poem] *Duel* (Montreal PQ), No. 1 (Winter 1969): 64.
       "Particulars on the Picture Cards"

D445   [Poem] *Potpourri* (Portland OR), No. 17 (Winter 1969): 20.
       "The Water Flame"

D446   [Poems] "Three Poems." *Quarry* (Kingston ON) 18, No. 2 (Winter 1969): 32–33.
        "Beer in Cans"—"Dont Think That Way"—"Beardsley"

D447   [Review] *Canadian Literature* (Vancouver BC), No. 39 (Winter 1969): 74–76.
        "Eli and Irving": a review of *An Idiot Joy*, by Eli Mandel; *The Shattered Plinths*, by Irving Layton [Note: see *Craft Slices*: "Mandel's Shift"; A44]

D448   [Poem] *Black Moss* (Windsor ON) 1, No. 1 [February 1969]: 11.
        "Coltrane & Che"

D449   [Poems] *Noose* (New York NY), No. 12 (8 February 1969): n. p.
        "A Comment on the Singular"—"The Rites of Passage, Book of the Real"—"Mountain I Burn"—"Nearing Britain" [Note: "Nearing Britain" is a revision of material in an unpublished travelogue, "Eye-Kicks in Europe" (1966)]

D450   [Poems] *Black Moss* (Windsor ON) 1, No. 2 (Spring 1969): 16–18.
        "Silent Night Explosions"—"Prizren"—"For Angela, Sheila, Marian, Sarah, Aviva, Magdalein, etc."—"An Introduction" [Note: "Prizren" was part of an unpublished travelogue, "Eye-Kicks in Europe" (1966)]

D451   [Poems] "Four Poems." *Sumac* (Fremont MI) 1, No. 3 (Spring 1969): 31–33.
        "Stan"—"Footfalls"—"The Ground of Lincoln County"—"Coming to London from Toronto"

D452   [Essay] *The Georgia Straight* (Vancouver BC) 3, No. 47 (28 February–6 March 1969): 4.
        "Notes on the Sir George Computer" [Note: an unsigned report on the student sit-in and fire at Sir George Williams University computer centre, and the arrest of 100 people]

D453   [Essay] *Walt Whitman Review* (Detroit MI) 15, No. 1 (March 1969): 13–26.
        "The Solitary Everything"

D454   [Poem] *The Fiddlehead* (Fredericton NB), No. 79 (March/April 1969): 90.
        "Western Ontario Music"

D455   [Statement] *Direction One* (Montreal PQ), single issue newsletter [March 1969]: 2.
        "Notes on the Sir George Computer"

D456   [Poem] *Poesia de Venezuela* (Caracas, Venezuela), No. 36 (March/April 1969): n. p.
        "History of Poets: Plastic Man"

D457   [Essay] *The Georgia Straight* (Vancouver BC) 3, No. 49 (14–20 March 1969): 12.

"Montreal Police Support Our Boys in Viet Nam"

D458   [Essay; Poems] *The Open Letter* (Victoria BC), No. 9 (1 April 1969): 14–16, 16–18.

"Serving or Filling Orders" [Note: see *Craft Slices*: "Orders Filled" and "Orders Served"; A44]—"Calm After"—"Fast"

D459   [Poem] *Intercourse* (Montreal PQ), No. 11 (April 1969): 6.

"The Glass Ball" [pub. under pseud. E. E. Greengrass]

D460   [Poem] *IS* (Toronto ON), No. 6 (April 1969): 2–8.

"Ike & Others"

D461   [Poem] *Mainline* (Windsor ON), No. 4 (April 1969): n. p.

"God's Creature in Calgary"

D462   [Poem] *Ophir* (Pretoria, South Africa), No. 8 (April 1969): 10.

"The Window"

D463   [Essay] *The Georgia Straight* (Vancouver BC) 3, No. 53 (11–17 April 1969): 4.

"Throwing a Few Stiff Cheques in Montreal"

D464   [Poems] *Poetry* (Chicago IL) 114, No. 2 (May 1969): 78–79.

"On Quadra Island"—"Passport Doves"

D465   [Translations] *The Fiddlehead* (Fredericton NB), No. 80 (May/June/July 1969): 53–57.

"Two Little Elegies," by David Fernández—"Militia Man," by David Fernández—"Contemporary History," by David Fernández—"New Woman," by David Fernández

D466   [Poem] *The Dalhousie Review* (Halifax NS) 49, No. 2 (Summer 1969): 259.

"Fredericton Houses"

D467   [Poems] *Ballsout* (Vancouver BC) 1, No. 2 (Summer 1969): n. p.

"Leather" [pub. under pseud. E. E. Greengrass]—"What Are You Serving, Irving?" [pub. under pseud. E. E. Greengrass]—"Love Poem" [unsigned]—"A Few Words about My Dearly Beloved Self" [unsigned]

D468   [Poems] *Salt* (Moose Jaw SK), No. 2 (Summer 1969): 6–7.

"Bending Over" [pub. under pseud. E. E. Greengrass]—"Ballad of the Mosquito's Bite" [pub. under pseud. E. E. Greengrass]

D469   [Poems] *Twentieth Century* (Victoria, Australia) 24, No. 2 (Summer 1969): 168–169.

"The Snowfall"—"Open"

D470   [Editor; Excerpts from a poem] *Imago* (Montreal PQ), No. 11 [June 1969]: 26–29.

"Poundmaker" [excerpts] [See B1]

GB with Warren Tallman, Montreal, May 1970

D471   [Review] *The Globe and Mail* Supplement, 7 June 1969.
        "A Poet's Peregrinations for Non-Specialists": a review of *Vision Fugitive: Ezra Pound and Economics*, by Earle Davis [Note: see *Craft Slices*: "Social Cantos"; A44]

D472   [Interview by] *The Georgia Straight* (Vancouver BC) 3, No. 61 (11–17 June 1969): 7–8.
        "Sleep for Peace": an interview with John Lennon and Yoko Ono

D473   [Review] *The Globe and Mail* Supplement, 14 June 1969.
        "A Singing Hydrant Doesn't Slum": a review of *I've Tasted My Blood*, by Milton Acorn [Note: see *Craft Slices*: "Romantic Carpenter"; A44]

D474   [Poem] *The Georgia Straight* (Vancouver BC) 3, No. 65 (9–15 July 1969): 12.
        "Sir George Computer University"

D475   [Translation] *The Georgia Straight* (Vancouver BC) 3, No. 68 (30 July–6 August 1969): 4.
        "Psalm Five," by Ernesto Cardenal

D476   [Essay; Poems] *The Five Cent Review* (Montreal PQ) 1, No. 2 (August 1969): 18–19; Poems
        "Five Cents' Worth of Sports" [Notes: GB is listed as an associate editor; contains poems, "Ted Williams," "For Ronnie Carter," and "AB: The Pope"]

"When I was a kid in school my geography teacher askt me where Pittsburgh was, & I answered correctly, 'Eighth place'.

"A couple of years ago some friends of mine who are not the least interested in baseball as the world's national game publisht my book called *Baseball*. They knew it wasnt just a book about Babe Ruth & Cal Griffith. They knew it was my metaphor. Every poet has a metaphor, or a Metaphor. Try as you might with the stuff you learn in school & college, you cant get away from your Metaphor. For Wordsworth it was a woodlot. For Hugh Hefner it was a can of Carnation Milk."
[From "Five Cents' Worth of Sports"; see D476]

D477   [Poem] *The Canadian Forum* (Toronto ON) 49, No. 583 (August 1969): 109.
        "The Artisans"

D478   [Poem] *Sumac* (Fremont MI) 2, No. 1 (Fall 1969): 48.
        "The Cup, Though"

D479   [Poem] *The University of Windsor Review* (Windsor ON) 5, No. 1 (Fall 1969): 44.
        "Pussywillow"

D480 [Poems; Review] *Stony Brook: America a Prophecy* (Stony Brook NY), Nos. 3 & 4 (Fall 1969): 113–115, 191–201.
"The Mysteries"—"Building"—"Before the Revolution"—"A Tainted Memory"—"Weight"—"*On the Road*: & the Indians at the End": a review of *On the Road*, by Jack Kerouac

D481 [Poems] *IS* (Toronto ON), No. 7 (Fall 1969): [9–19].
"Touch"

D482 [Poems] *Salt* (Moose Jaw SK), No. 3 (Autumn 1969): 7–8.
"The Wave" [pub. under pseud. E. E. Greengrass]—"Frost Bite" [pub. under pseud. E. E. Greengrass]

D483 [Poems] *The Ant's Forefoot* (Toronto ON), No. 4 (Fall 1969): 31.
"The McFadden Shopping Bag"—"Time Capsule" [Note: error in page numbers; GB's poem is on what should be p. 33, numbered p. 31]

D484 [Review] *Canadian Literature* (Vancouver BC), No. 42 (Autumn 1969): 84–86.
"Acorn Blood": a review of *I've Tasted My Blood*, by Milton Acorn [see *Craft Slices*: "Romantic Carpenter"; A44]

D485 [Story] *Quarry* (Kingston ON) 19, No. 1 (Fall 1969): 11–21.
"Ebbe & Hattie"

D486 [Poem] *New: American and Canadian Poetry* (Trumansburg NY), No. 10 (September 1969): 31.
"Of My Age" [pub. under pseud. E. E. Greengrass]

D487 [Poem] *Floorboards* (Fredericton NB), No. 2 (October 1969): 25.
"U. S. Asia" [pub. under pseud. E. E. Greengrass]

D488 [Review] *The Five Cent Review* (Montreal PQ) 1, No. 3 (October 1969): 10–11.
The Long Count, by Mel Heimer: a review

D489 [Poem] *The Nation* (New York NY) 209, No. 13 (20 October 1969): 416.
"Adonai"

D490 [Poem] *The Fiddlehead* (Fredericton NB), No. 82 (November/December 1969): 52–60.
"Stab"

D491 [Essay] *The Georgia Straight* (Vancouver BC) 3, No. 84 (19–26 November 1969): 16.
"Capital Punishment Is Not Enough"

D492 [Poem] *New Measure* (Northwood, Middlesex, England), No. 10 (Late final issue, 1969): 5.
"A Woman Is Water"

D493 [Poems] *New: American and Canadian Poetry* (Trumansburg NY), No. 11 (December 1969): 21–22.
"I Ask Her" [pub. under pseud. E. E. Greengrass]—"We" [pub. under pseud. E. E. Greengrass]

D494   [Poems] "George Bowering: Three Poems." *Ophir* (Pretoria, South Africa), No. 10 (December 1969): 2–3.
        "History of Poets: Lord Jim"—"Remember Them Alive"—"The Citizens"

1970

D495   [Essay] *The Windsor Star* (Windsor ON), c. 1970.
        "[New Windsor Poets] Are Showing Their Salt" [Note: GB's manuscript was titled, "Poets on the Border"]
D496   [Poem] *The South Florida Poetry Journal* (Tampa FL), Nos. 4 & 5 (1970): 25.
        "Layers 3"
D497   [Poems] *Ann Arbor Review* (Ann Arbor MI), Nos. 8 & 9 (1970): 12, 38.
        "I Saw" [pub. under pseud. E. E. Greengrass]—"AB: The Pope" [pub. under pseud. E. E. Greengrass]
D498   [Poems] *Anonym* (Buffalo NY), Nos. 5 & 6 (1970): 78–83.
        "The Law, Taken"—"Making a Virtue of Necessity"—"Even the Public Conveyances Sing"—"Ghosts"—"Tan"—"The Eucharist"
D499   [Prose] *Center* (Woodstock NY), No. 1 (1970): n. p.
        "Excerpts ... from Quick Canada" [Note: this became "Match-Boxes"]
D500   [Editor; Poems] *Imago* (Montreal PQ), No. 12 [January 1970].
        Sitting in Mexico [See A11 and B1]
D501   [Poem] *Intercourse* (Montreal PQ), Nos. 12 & 13 (January 1970): 12.
        "The Critics" [pub. under pseud. E. E. Greengrass]
D502   [Poems] *West Coast Review* (Burnaby BC) 4, No. 3 (January 1970): 34, 36.
        "Slot" [pub. under pseud. E. E. Greengrass]—"How They Get Fat Bellies"
D503   [Interview; Excerpts from a poem] *The Montreal Star* (Montreal PQ), Writing Supplement, 24 January 1970.
        "George Bowering," interviewed by John Richmond—"Solid Mountain" [excerpts] [Note: part of a special section on West Coast Poets; see also H100]
D504   [Essay] *Canadian Literature* (Vancouver BC), No. 43 (Winter 1970): 24–35.
        "Purdy: Man and Poet"
D505   [Poem] *Hanging Loose* (Brooklyn NY), No. 9 (Winter 1970): 16.
        "Steak & Gravy"

D506   [Poem] *Io* (Somesville ME), No. 7 (Winter 1970): 192.
        "Onion Skins"
D507   [Talk] *SGWU* [Sir George Williams University] *Issues & Events* (Montreal PQ) 1, No. 19 (5 February 1970): 1–4.
        "What Are George Bowering, Peter London, David McKeen and Michael Sheldon Doing in the Gallery? Discussing Creativity"
D508   [Poems] *The Georgia Straight* (Vancouver BC) 4, No. 98 (25 February–4 March 1970): 9.
        "Branches (for Ron Loewinsohn)"—"Otherwise Nobody Would Ever Have Remembered Joe"
D509   [Essay] *IS* (Toronto ON), No. 8 (Spring 1970): n. p.
        "How to Write" [Note: see *Craft Slices*: "How to Write"; A44]
D510   [Poem] *Seven* (Toronto ON), No. 1 [Spring 1970]: n. p.
        "Branches (for Ron Loewinsohn)"
D511   [Review] *Quarry* (Kingston ON) 19, No. 3 (Spring 1970): 62–64.
        "4 More, But We Should Be for More": a review of *Man: Unman*, by Glen Siebrasse; *Images*, by Gerald Robitaille; *I've Laughed and Sung the Whole Night Long Seen the Sunrise in the Morning*, by Raymond Fraser; *Manimals*, by Seymour Mayne [Note: see *Craft Slices*: "Like Siebrasse"; A44]
D512   [Editor] *Imago* (Montreal PQ), No. 13 [Early 1970]. [See B1]
D513   [Review] *The Globe and Mail* Supplement, 25 April 1970.
        "Squirmy Lessons for Prof-Crits": a review of *Shake It for the World, Smartass*, by Seymour Krim
D514   [Statement] *The Georgia Straight* (Vancouver BC) 4, No. 107 (29 April–6 May 1970): 5.
        "Loyola Doesn't Understand English"
D515   [Poem] *Elizabeth* (New Rochelle NY), No. 15 (May 1970): 44.
        "Already Markt"
D516   [Poems] "4 Poems." *Vigilante* (Calgary AB), No. 1 (May 1970): 7–12.
        "That Old Testament"—"A Man Is No Boat"—"Little Treatise on Time"—"Apollo Eleven"
D517   [Review] *The Globe and Mail* Supplement, 2 May 1970.
        "To Share the World Or Despair of It": a review of *The Happy Hungry Man*, by George Jonas; *The Journals of Susanna Moodie*, by Margaret Atwood
D518   [Essay] *Harbinger: Coach House Writing Supplement* (Toronto ON) 3, No. 5 (May 1970): 9.
        "How to Write" [Note: see *Craft Slices*: "How to Write"; A44]

Out of his rotting bones
he builds moonlit stairs to
the sky above us. The government
will not feed him; he must
cut off pieces from time to time,
hope to win cigarette contests,
cutting off piece by piece, selling
them one at a time, for bread
to make bones. His country
will not pay to bury his
boneless flesh.

["Poet Laureate," from *Another Mouth*, written May 1970, in response to receiving the 1969 Governor General's Award for Poetry; see A33]

"Since I won an award all kinds of squares are suddenly recognizing my talent."
[GB Papers, Correspondence Victor Coleman, 20 June 1970, NL]

D519   [Excerpt from a poem] *The Ant's Forefoot* (Toronto ON), No. 6 (Summer 1970): 24.
            "I'd Forgotten Too Much" [from *Genève*]

D520   [Poems] "Two Poems." *Tuatara* (Victoria BC), No. 2 (June 1970): 23–24.
            "Place Names in the Global Village"—"LeRoi the Bird"

D521   [Essay] *Gumbo* (Montreal PQ) 1, No. 2 (3 July 1970): 14–15.
            "New Jazz and Montreal"

D522   [Essay] *The Georgia Straight* (Vancouver BC) 4, No. 119 (15–22 July 1970): 17.
            "New Jazz and Montreal"

D523   [Statement] *The Georgia Straight* (Vancouver BC) 4, No. 119 (22–29 July 1970): 18.
            "Montrealities" [Note: an unsigned column with news from Montreal]

D524   [Statement] *The Georgia Straight* (Vancouver BC) 4, No. 120 (29 July–5 August 1970): 14.
            "Montrealities" [Note: "Youth Acted Strange After Pop Festival," a column by GB with news from Montreal]

D525   [Poems] *Poetry Australia* (Five Dock, New South Wales, Australia), No. 35 (August 1970): 22–23.
            "Classic Poetry & Its Laws"—"Smoking Mirror in Alberta"—"George Speaking"

D526   [Review] *The Globe and Mail* Supplement, 8 August 1970.

"Pleasure in Massive Detail": a review of *The Life of Ezra Pound*, by Noel Stock

D527   [Poem] *Black Moss* (Windsor ON), No. 5 [Fall 1970]: n. p.

"I Said I Said"

D528   [Poem] *The Dalhousie Review* (Halifax NS) 50, No. 3 (Autumn 1970): 377.

"Post-Darwinian Herrick"

D529   [Poems] *Intercourse* (Montreal PQ), No. 14 (Fall 1970): 6, 12.

"Gun Man"—"Layers 10"—"The Known Universe"

D530   [Poems] "Three Poems." *Vigilante* (Calgary AB), No. 2 (Fall 1970): 51–53.

"The Ribbon"—"Precious"—"Moisture"

D531   [Poem] *Ophir* (Pretoria, South Africa), No. 12 (September 1970): 9.

AB with Ted Berrigan, Montreal, c. 1970

"Scars"

D532   [Editor; Poem] *Imago* (Montreal PQ), No. 14 [Late 1970]: 13–19.

"Mars" [See B1]

D533   [Poem] *The McGill Daily* Supplement (Montreal PQ), 16 October 1970.

"No Solitudes"

D534   [Review] *The Globe and Mail* Supplement, 24 October 1970.

"Opening a Window into Will's World": a review of *Shakespeare*, by Anthony Burgess

D535   [Interview by] *Copperfield* (Hamilton ON), No. 3 [November 1970]: 77–82.

"It's a Funny Thing": an interview with David McFadden

D536   [Poem] *The Orange Bear Reader* (Windsor ON), No. 7 [November 1970]: n. p.

"The Owl's Eye" [Note: the poem is the entire issue; the magazine consists of regular issues of broadsides printed by Coach House Press, Toronto; see E31]

D537   [Poem] *The Canadian Forum* (Toronto ON) 50, Nos. 598 & 599 (November/December 1970): 289.

"Hope-Princeton Highway" [pub. under pseud. E. E. Greengrass]

D538   [Review] *The Georgia Straight* (Vancouver BC) 4, No. 136 (18–25 November 1970): 20.

"Cancer Rising": a review of *Cancer Rising*, by David Cull

D539   [Poem] *Saturday Night* (Toronto ON) 85, No. 12 (December 1970): 39.

"North Shore, PEI"

D540   [Poems] *The Mysterious East* (Fredericton NB), (December 1970): 5, 10, 33.
       "Nine Holes"—"No Solitudes"—"Out"
D541   [Statement] *SGWU* [Sir George Williams University] *Issues & Events* (Montreal PQ) 2, No. 13 (11 December 1970): n. p.
       " 'Peace Sucks' . . . Mackenzie Kink" [Note: a statement against the invoking of the War Measures Act]
D542   [Statement; Review] *The Georgia Straight* (Vancouver BC) 4, No. 140 (16–23 December 1970): 5, 21.
       " 'Peace Sucks' . . . Mackenzie Kink"—"Loony Tunes": review of *Luna*, by David Meltzer

---

"Born mountains of BC Dec. 1937; education is western Greyhound bus stations and colleges, mainly UBC, Vancouver, early sixties; air force photographer sometimes looking out of planes too low late fifties . . . . At the moment trying to take major change in life, follow Olson's advice to get away

GB with Frank Davey and
David McFadden, 1970

from slop of existentialism, renew my eyes and will as source of history, no force entrapping us. Also influenced by Greg Curnoe, Heraklitus, Albert Ayler, Phil Whalen, William Eastlake. Soon to edit collection of Canadian poems to be published California. Am highranking officer of Nihilist Party of Canada."
[From contributor's note to *New American and Canadian Poetry*; see C41]

1971

D543   [Excerpt from a poem] *Rain* (Wilmette IL), Nos. 1 & 2 (1971): 115.
       "I Know These Warriors" [from *Genève*; A14]
D544   [Poem] *Scrip* (Derbyshire, England), No. 37 (1971): 16.
       "The Weight"
D545   [Poems] *First Encounter* (Sackville NB), [1971]: 52.
       "Arrival Time"—"Not Salesmen"
D546   [Poems] *Gnosis* (Brooklyn NY), No. 6 (1971): n. p.
       "Layers 6"—"Layers 8"
D547   [Poems] "Two Poems." *The Fiddlehead* (Fredericton NB), No. 88 (Winter 1971): 59.
       "Frame"—"Apparent"
D548   [Editor] *Imago* (Montreal PQ), No. 15 ([Early] 1971).
       Back East, by Victor Coleman [See B1]

D549   [Poem] *Mainline* (Windsor ON), No. 8 (February 1971): 23.
       "Lines from Hollo"
D550   [Poems] *Ganglia* (Orangeville ON) 2, No. 2 (February 1971): n. p.
       "Yes I Sold"—"Jesus & Paul"
D551   [Poem] *Blackfish* (Burnaby BC), No. 1 (Spring 1971): 12.
       "Indulgence"
D552   [Poem] *The* (Boulder CO), No. 8
       ([Spring] 1971): 16.
       ["Why given round heads ... "]
       [Note: from *Autobiology*, "Chapter 21:
       Come"; A17]
D553   [Review] *UBC Alumni Chronicle* (Van-
       couver BC) 25, No. 1 (Spring 1971):
       30–31.

GB in front of his childhood house
in Greenwood BC, 1976

       "Birney Steps into the Dada Border-
       blur": a review of *Rag and Bone Shop*, by Earle Birney [Note: see *Craft
       Slices*: "Birney's Advent"; A44]
D554   [Story] *The Antigonish Review* (Antigonish NS) 2, No. 1 (Spring 1971):
       21–26.
       "Constantinople Boots" [Note: story was drawn from an unpublished
       book "Eye-Kicks in Europe" (1966); see also A23]
D555   [Poems] "3 Poems." *Tuatara* (Victoria BC), No. 4 (March 1971): 1–3.
       "Thoughts off the Concrete Isle"—"In a Bower"—"Flowery Verse
       for A"
D556   [Poem] *Jewish Di'al-og* (Toronto ON), (Passover, 1971): 16.
       "Mouth" [Note: poem is printed untitled]
D557   [Poems] "Two Poems by George Bowering." *Black Moss* (Fergus ON),
       No. 6 (May 1971): n. p.
       "Among Friends"—"Not to Describe"
D558   [Poems] *Georgia Straight Writing Supplement* (Vancouver BC), No. 7
       (May 1971): 13.
       "The Raspberries"—"The Verandah"
D559   [Prose] "Ripoff of the Month." *COSMEP Newsletter* (San Francisco
       CA) 2, No. 8 (May 1971): n. p.
       "Excerpts ... from Quick Canada" [excerpt] [Note: this became
       "Match-Boxes"]
D560   [Poem] *Canadian Author & Bookman* (Toronto ON) 46, No. 4 (Summer
       1971): 11.
       "Top Top Cafe" [pub. under pseud. E. E. Greengrass]
D561   [Poems] *IS* (Toronto ON), No. 10 (Summer 1971): n. p.
       "The Teeter Totter"—"The Raspberries"

D562   [Poem] *Out of Sight* (Wichita KS), No. 9 [June 1971]: 3.
        "Apparent"

D563   [Interview] *Alphabet* (London ON), Nos. 18 & 19 (June 1971): 18–21.
        "Cutting Them All Up": an interview with bp Nichol [Note: drawn from a CBC radio series "Young Canadian Poets," hosted by GB; see E27]

Contract

— It is hereby certified —

That   George Mr. Whip Bowering

on   July 9 1972

Has entered into an exclusive arrangement with THE GRANVILLE GRANGE ZEPHYRS in return for the sum of $70,000.00. This agreement gives sole playing rights of the above mentioned player to THE ZEPHYRS unless waived by either the general manager or the unanimous consent of the team.

The above player will recieve in the way of added bonuses $2000.00 if his batting average is over 400 at the end of the playing season $600.00 if his H.R. is maintained and a Governor General's Award if he wins the Miss Kosmic League contest.

Michael Quigley (G.M.)   George Mr. Whip Bowering

Dated this __ day of _____ 19 7?

Engledink Birdhumper (O.Ed.K.)

Killer Kelly Kiley (O.K.L.V.K.)

GB's contract to play on the Granville Grange Zephyrs baseball team, GB Papers, NL

D564   [Review] *The Georgia Straight* (Vancouver BC) 5, No. 171 (1–4 June 1971): 21.
        "Some Flowers for Davey": a review of *Weeds*, by Frank Davey

D565   [Essay] *The Georgia Straight* (Vancouver BC) 5, No. 178 (25–29 June 1971): 19.
        "Black Mountain College" [Note: talks about *Letters for Origin* and *The Special View of History*, by Charles Olson; *The Black Mountain Book*, by Fielding Dawson]

"I'm . . . typing out the last copy of my book I wrote over the last year, 48 chapters, called *Autobiology*. Watch for it. I'm afraid that it is going to be part one of a trilogy, so there go two more years of my short life."
[GB Papers, Correspondence David McFadden, 1 July 1971, NL]

D566   [Essay] *The Georgia Straight* (Vancouver BC) 5, No. 181 (6–10 July 1971): 18.
        "Zephyrs Gust into First Place" [pub. under pseud. Erich Blackhead]

"The Granville Grange Zephyrs took over full possession of first place in the Kosmik Softball league Sunday evening, with a convincing 20–10 defeat of a hard-dying Moose Valley Farms nine . . . .
    "Another highlight of the game was the rookie umpire, Ronnie. She brought unaccustomed dazzle to the area behind the plate, and withstood the rude verbal

attacks of the less civilized Zephyr players. Her only bad moment came when she was booed by women's lib members in the crowd for sweeping off home plate.

ZEPHYRS   120 323 630—20 16 5
FARMERS   110 035 000—10 11 9

"THREE STARS, as picked by the editors of Beaver Kosmos. (1) G. Bowering, whose four hits, including a titanic triple, and many runs batted in, led his team thru rally after rally. He also set a record for shortshops by catching three popups in one inning, pounding his mitt before each. His only lapse was when he committed his first error of the season, letting a weak grounder by little Phyllis skip by him with two out and the bases loaded in the big Farmer sixth inning . . . . "
[From "Zephyrs Gust into First Place"; see D566]

D567   [Essay] *The Georgia Straight* (Vancouver BC) 5, No. 184 (16–20 July 1971): 3.

   "Coquitless Cop" [Note: an account of being stopped and questioned in Coquitlam BC by an RCMP officer, during a trip to Vancouver from Montreal]

D568   [Essay; Review] *The Georgia Straight* (Vancouver BC) 5, No. 187 (27–30 July 1971): 14, 21.

   "Zephyrs Storm Back to Rout Rats" [pub. under pseud. Erich Blackhead]—"Happy Birthday, Bob": a review of *St. Martin's*, by Robert Creeley [Note: see *Craft Slices*: "Creeley's Holiday"; A44]

"The pseudonym Erich Blackhead was conceived in relation to Eric Whitehead, the sports columnist for the Vancouver *Province*, who was also the stepfather of Daphne Marlatt's former husband, Al Marlatt."
[Session 14, 26 May, 1989]

"Well, when I was a kid, after I gave up the idea of wanting to be a policeman, I decided I wanted to be a baseball writer. As a matter of fact, when I was a kid in school, grades 10, 11, 12, I was a baseball writer for newspapers and weekly newspapers in the Okanagan . . . . "
[From "Curiouser & Curiouser"; see C106 and D680]

Sweat all over my face, eyes squinting

thru the chicken wire, preparing
batting averages & story for

the *Oliver Chronicle.*

[From *Baseball*; see A6, A15, A25, and A36]

D569   [Editor; Poem] *Imago* (Montreal PQ), No. 16 [August 1971]: 39–40.
       "The Breath, Release" [See B1]

D570   [Essay; Review] *The Georgia Straight* (Vancouver BC) 5, No. 190 (6–10 August 1971): 11, 17.
       "Late Chinook Melts Punks—Zephyrs Hobble to Surprise Victory" [pub. under pseud. Erich Blackhead]—"And Away He Run": a review of *Green*, by Tom Clark

---

"The Zephyrs are one of the banner teams in the famed Kosmik League, the community alternative to the professional sports run by foreign businessmen in Vancouver. The freak spirit prevails on the diamond, where the scores are soon forgotten, the standings are not kept or published, and all the ballplayers with their funny names share a joint with the second baseman when they manage to hit a double. The scene is not Jarry Park and it is not Grossman's Tavern. But then the *Grape Writing Supplement* is not the *Tamarack Review*.

GB's baseball team, the Granville Grange Zephyrs, at Nat Bailey Stadium (then called Capilano Stadium), Vancouver, 1971; back row, l. to r.: Brad Robinson, Glen Toppings, team manager, GB, Lionel Kearns; centre row, l. to r.: Gary Lee Nova, Jerry Nairn, Dwight Gardiner, Brian Fisher, Dennis Vance, Lanny Beckman; front row, l. to r.: Liam Kearns, Frank Kearns

"I suppose a lot of readers will know that *Tamarack* is the archetypal establishment literary magazine in Canada, or at least Toronto. There a subscriber will find most of the big names in Canadian poetry and fiction, and sometimes a poem or story. More readers will know that *Grape* is Vancouver's belabored Freak newspaper. Probably a very few in eastern Canada will know about the *Writing Supplement*. *Writing Supplement* is simply the literary magazine with the largest circulation in the country. The usual press run is about 20,000 compared with 2,000 for *Tamarack* and 300 for the average little mag. Furthermore, all copies are given away free; many stuffed into *Grape*, others passed out at schools or on the beach.

"*Writing Supplement* is printed in tabloid format, designed for offset, and given to, again, cooperative production. It has the highest quality work of any litmag in the country. But its most interesting feature is its timeliness. Because an issue can be gathered and distributed on short notice, it can be planned to coincide with any event of literary interest. When American poet Ed Dorn and English poet Jeremy Prynne visited the city for a series of lectures and readings, the *WS* put out a Dorn-Prynne issue, with photos, poems, criticism and notices of the public readings."
[From "The Art of the Webfoot"; see D623]

D571   [Essay] *Canadian Literature* (Vancouver BC), No. 50 (Autumn 1971): 41–56.
　　　　"That Fool of a Fear: Notes on *A Jest of God*"
D572   [Essay] *The Antigonish Review* (Antigonish NS), No. 7 (Autumn 1971): 76–87.
　　　　"Denise Levertov"
D573   [Excerpt from a poem] *Blue Pig: Sleeping Sickness* (Northampton MA), No. 16 [Fall 1971]: n. p.
　　　　"I Always Lookt" [from *Genève*]
D574   [Letter] *English Quarterly* (Waterloo ON) 4, No. 3 (Fall 1971): 77–78.
　　　　"Our Colonial English Profs" [Note: on the absence of Canadian writers in university courses]
D575   [Story] *The Fiddlehead* (Fredericton NB), No. 91 (Fall 1971): 78–83.
　　　　"How Delsing Met Frances & Started to Write a Novel" [Note: a story based on GB's return to a scene from "Delsing," his first novel, unpublished, in the GB Papers at Queen's University and NL]

"As you know, Delsing was a poet before death, or so he convinced himself and a few others, but once he tried to write a novel about his traditional U. S. coming of age, all that sobbing tormented youth bit, at least he thought about writing the novel, sitting around drinking beer with Bob Small in Vancouver 1960 or thereabouts and beginning in 1947, knowing, he said later, that he wasn't a U. S. kid at all but only an early captive of their radio stations on the west coast." [Opening sentences of "How Delsing Met Frances and Started to Write a Novel"; see D575 and A23]

D576   [Poem] *Miss Chatelaine* (Toronto ON) 8, No. 5 (5 October 1971): 65.
"The Student of the Road"

D577   [Poems] *Punk Iron* (Port Moody BC), No. 13 (November 1971): n. p.
"The Fourth Town"—"The First City"—"The Extractions"—"The Next Place"

D578   [Editor] *Georgia Straight Writing Supplement* (Vancouver BC), No. 10 (Mid-November 1971).
"Ontario Issue: bp Nichol, Victor Coleman, Robert Hogg, Michael Ondaatje, and Greg Curnoe" [Note: a note on the bottom of the last page says, "most of this issue was put together by George Bowering"]

D579   [Poems] *Man-Root* (San Francisco CA), No. 5 (Late 1971): 77–79.
"Hands & Nets"—"Feet, Not Eyes"—"The River of Her Dreams"

D580   [Essay; Statement] *Open Letter* (Toronto ON) Second Series, No. 1 (Winter 1971/72): 45–47, 48.
"Delsing and Me" [Note: see *Craft Slices*: "Delivering Fiction" and "Delsing and Me"; A44]—"A Note on Poetry & Calendars" [Note: see *Craft Slices*: "Poetry and Calendars"; A44]

"We became poets when we learned to resist time. Each time we write we are trying to push the pen thru into the open space of God's eye, in eternity. & if we finally give in & say that we cant live forever, then, like all parents, we try to get for our children what we couldnt have, in this case immortality for our poems.

"The moments of delight, then, are moments when we see light thru the membrane. Moments of hope, that our line, our race, has a chance. Poets, resisting time, are prisoners in the past, cruel past, where people die. My great rage is that some dirty bastard in the future will get eternal life, while his world feeds on the molecules of my dead body."
[Dated July 1967, from "A Note on Poetry & Calendars"; see D580 and *Craft Slices*: "Poetry and Calendars"; A44]

D581   [Essay; Poem] *Io* (Cape Elizabeth ME), No. 10 [Winter 1971/72]: 109–120.
"Baseball Notes"—*Baseball* [Note: "Baseball Notes" is also in *The Five Cent Review* under title, "Five Cents' Worth of Sports"; see D476]

1972

D582   [Poem] *Oasis* (London, England), No. 7 (1972): 46.
"Losing & Getting, to Be Getting"

D583   [Poem] *Scrip* (Derbyshire, England), No. 40 [1972]: 6.
"A Grammar Lesson"

D584   [Poems] "Four Poems." *The Antigonish Review* (Antigonish NS), No. 8 (Winter 1972): 73–76.
"Place of Birth"—"The Code"—"The Trees"—"Working & Wearing"

D585   [Editor; Poem] "From *Curious.*" *Imago* [Vancouver BC], No. 17 [Spring 1972]: 42–43.
"Jack Spicer" [See B1]

D586   [Poem] *Naissance* (Winchester, England), Nos. 5 & 6 [Spring 1972]: n. p.
"A Comment on the Singular"

D587   [Poems] *The Capilano Review* (North Vancouver BC) 1, No. 1 (Spring 1972): 28–30.
"Layers 5"—"It's There You Can't Deny It"—"The Bars"

D588   [Review] *Canadian Literature* (Vancouver BC), No. 52 (Spring 1972): 91–92.
"Get Used to It": a review of *Power Politics*, by Margaret Atwood

D589   [Statement] *The New York Post* (New York NY), 28 March 1972.
["When I was a kid . . . "] [Note: from "Five Cents' Worth of Sports"; see D476]

D590   [Interview] *Quill & Quire* (Toronto ON) 38, No. 5 (May 1972): 3, 14–15.
"Don Cameron Interviews George Bowering"

"Sometimes it happens that you think you're writing about one thing and you're writing about something else or else you are really writing about both of them—and sometimes it literally happens—I mean it really sounds so corny—but it happens that I don't know *what* I'm writing about. I often just get a kind of tune in my head when I start writing—much more often than I get an image to take off from or a subject to take off from or anything like that. I get a kind of a tune going and the tune may resolve itself into a line with words in it and then take off from that. I don't write occasional poems very much anymore, but when I do, it seems almost always to happen that the first part of that poem comes while I'm on my way home, with all the strange rhythms of going down the escalator, walking to the subway, going down to the subway, taking the subway, getting out, taking the bus and going out and all that . . . .

"That's not the way I write any prose though. Prose is more like—hmm, what *is* it like? Well, this prose I'm writing now [GB was writing *Autobiology*] is like—I don't know why I'm wanting to say it is *like* something, because I hate

comparisons—but I sit down and I don't know what the subject is. I get ready to start moving and if a useful line comes along, one that I haven't made up, then I can keep going. If I make up the line it's usually a case of writing it down on an index card and throwing it in my desk drawer and then later either throwing it out or selling it to the university library."
[From "Don Cameron Interviews George Bowering"; see D590 and C57]

D591   [Translations] *Karaki* (Victoria BC), No. 3 (May 1972): 30–31.
        "The Cloisters," by Roberto Sosa—"The Appearance of Hunger," by Manuel Pacheco

D592   [Poem] *Miss Chatelaine* (Toronto ON) 9, No. 3 (9 May 1972): 102.
        "News"

D593   [Poems] *Repository* (Seven Persons AB), No. 3 [Summer 1972]: 15–17.
        "Divine Poem After Donne" [pub. under pseud. E. E. Greengrass]—"Noel" [pub. under pseud. E. E. Greengrass]

D594   [Poems] "Three Poems." *Quarry* (Kingston ON) 21, No. 3 (Summer 1972): 12–14.
        "Fainting"—"The Cloves"—"The Fingers"

D595   [Reviews] *Open Letter* (Toronto ON) Second Series, No. 2 (Summer 1972): 59–64, 82–84.
        The San Francisco Poets, edited by David Meltzer; *Revenge of the Lawn: Stories 1962–1970*, by Richard Brautigan; *Some Poems/Poets: Studies in American Underground Poetry Since 1945*, by Samuel Charters: a review; *Monotones*, by bp Nichol: a review [Note: see *Craft Slices*: "A Nicholodeon"; A44]

D596   [Story] *Journal of Canadian Fiction* (Fredericton NB) 1, No. 3 (Summer 1972): 14–15.
        "Wings"

D597   [Poems] *Athanor* (Clarkson NY), No. 3 (Summer/Fall 1972): 46–47.
        "Building"—"The Dear Path"

D598   [Review] *The B. C. Monthly* (Vancouver BC) 1, No. 1 (June/July 1972): 36–37.
        "Too Much Telling about": a review of *Relation*, by Kenneth Irby [Note: GB is listed as a contributing editor for this first issue]

D599   [Poems] *The Literary Half-Yearly: Canadian Number* (Mysore, India) 13, No. 2 (July 1972): 15–18.
        "The Pen"—"Two People"—"Panting"—"The Snowfall"—"In to It"

D600   [Poems] "Four Poems by E. E. Greengrass," "Four Poems by George Bowering." *Black Moss* (Windsor ON), [No. 9] (July 1972): n. p.
        "No Luggage" [pub. under pseud. E. E. Greengrass]—"In Sickness & in Health" [pub. under pseud. E. E. Greengrass]—"The Knowledge"

[pub. under pseud. E. E. Greengrass]—"My 6-Pound Dog" [pub. under pseud. E. E. Greengrass]—"In the Middle of Jewish Montreal"—"Health"—"Late Spring, New Week"—"Not Salesmen"

D601 [Essay] *Canadian Literature* (Vancouver BC), No. 54 (Autumn 1972): 56–69.

"Avison's Imitation of Christ the Artist"

D602 [Poems] "4 Poems." *Tuatara* (Victoria BC), Nos. 8 & 9 (Fall 1972): 25–28.

"The Childhood"—"St. Louis"—"The Fruit Ranch"—"Roger Falling"

D603 [Translation; Review] *Open Letter* (Toronto ON) Second Series, No. 3 (Fall 1972): 5–21, 81–83.

"The Stormy History of *El Corno Emplumado*," Margaret Randall and Robert Cohen, interviewed by Nils Castro—*A Book of Occasional*, by Dwight Gardiner: a review [Note: see *Craft Slices*: "Serial Gardiner"; A44]

D604 [Essay] *Maclean's* (Toronto ON) 85, No. 11 (November 1972): 79–81.

"Confessions of a Failed American" [Note: subtitled "How Jack Armstrong Became Johnny Canuck in the Okanagan Valley"]

"In school the little bit of Canadian history I was exposed to was the ringing of the names Cartier, Champlain, Dollard and Cabot, all those Europeans who visited the waters dumped down the St. Lawrence. After I had spent one year in college and a few in the air force, my old girl friend, who was at UBC, mentioned Earle Birney in a letter. I had never heard of him, my own province's most famous poet (if you don't count Pauline Johnson, the lady on the chocolate boxes). A similar education was experienced by the other BC poets of my generation. For that reason we had to discover—and invent—our land for ourselves.

"For instance, Frank Davey began from the geography and dug into the records to write his book of verse about shipwrecks around Cape Flattery and Victoria. I read, among other things, Menzies' 18th-century journal and traveled on the waters myself in order to write my book on Captain Vancouver's visit to our coast. We had to cover the ground ourselves and bring any myths to life, not out of books but from the very soil and water and air. This is the reality for a western artist, and is why his work is so much different from the Jungians and Frye-heads in the east."

[From "Confessions of a Failed American"; see D604]

D605 [Poem] *Center* (Woodstock NY), No. 4 (November 1972): 69.

"Denise Levertov"

D606   [Poem] *The B. C. Monthly* (Vancouver BC) 1, No. 2 (November 1972): 85.

    "Lionel Kearns"

D607   [Letter] *Blackfish* (Burnaby BC), Nos. 4 & 5 (Winter 1972/Spring 1973): n. p.

    "Dear AS [Allan Safarik]" [Note: GB's response, 22 July 1972, to Milton Acorn's "Avoid the Bad Mountain"; Acorn answers GB in "Bowering: The Laws of Language? Or of Empire?" immediately following GB's letter; see H164]

1973

D608   [Poem] *The B. C. Monthly* (Vancouver BC) 1, No. 4 (January 1973): 98.

    "George Stanley"

D609   [Editor; Poems] *IS* (Toronto ON), Nos. 12 & 13 (Winter 1973): n. p.

    "Gerry Gilbert"—"Jack Spicer"—"David McFadden" [Note: GB co-edited this issue on west coast writing with Victor Coleman]

"At about the time I turned thirty I moved from the West to southern Ontario. I found it difficult to keep on writing lyrics. I found it difficult but I did it, I kept on writing lyrics. But the poems were different from those that had come before. In my twenties in the West I'd been learning to write lyrics by finding my voice as it sounded according to my sense of place, in Vancouver, by the sea, the mountain valleys of B. C., the snows of Alberta's crumpled plains. But in southern Ontario there is no place. At least not the kind you can get lost in & find your way in. So I didnt quite know what I was doing, but I began to look elsewhere, inward, as they say, & into my personal time, around me in dreams, over my shoulder at the approach of the dentist & his friend the man in alligator shoes.

"In your twenties, I was saying, you are a cell, interacting. In your thirties you enter time, that is not only yours. In your thirties you become all ways aware of your life as a drama, of the cycle, the place in the pattern your life is now taking, who's been there & who's coming. You see that where you are is where Gilgamesh was. The passion takes over, & in art the passion takes over from mere worship, what you were doing in your lyrical twenties. To think that for thirteen years I was completely convinced that I'd die at twenty-nine!

"As it shows up in the art, it makes itself known in the emotions. My experience is that I feel things more deeply since turning thirty. Sometimes I think, my god, can this growth in feeling go on forever? There were feelings in the previous decade, obviously, but the senses were so busy taking in details that I was always saying or learning to say, oh, there it is out there. After thirty I said, oh,

here it is in here. It was as if the language was not going out to meet the objects, but was being said by them from inside up to my larynx & out there."
[From "I Never Felt Such Love," the preface to *In the Flesh*; see A21]

D610   [Editor] *Imago* (Vancouver BC), No. 18 [Spring 1973].
         Five Books of a Northmanual, by Brian Fawcett [See B1]

D611   [Poem] *The Dalhousie Review* (Halifax NS) 53, No. 1 (Spring 1973): 149.
         "Louis Dudek"

D612   [Poem] *The Antigonish Review* (Antigonish NS), No. 13 (Spring 1973): 84.
         "Stephen Spender"

D613   [Poems; Review] *Open Letter* (Toronto ON) Second Series, No. 4 (Spring 1973): 56–57, 71–74.
         "Robert Duncan"—"Gerry Gilbert"—"Where Does the Truth Lie": a review of *Lies*, by John Newlove

D614   [Poem] *The B. C. Monthly* (Vancouver BC) 1, No. 5 (March 1973): 107.
         "Gladys Hindmarch"

D615   [Poems; Translation] "Poems." *The Canadian Forum* (Toronto ON) 52, No. 626 (March 1973): 26–28.
         "To You & You"—"Just A"—"April 25, 1972"—"Open Mind"—"Ascension"—"Barber Chair"—"Careering"—"That Way, in Words"—"Losing & Getting, to Be Getting"—"The Indians," by Roberto Sosa—"York Ave"—"Already Markt"

D616   [Review] *The Georgia Straight* (Vancouver BC) 7, No. 289 (19–26 April 1973): 16.
         "Kerouac's Big Book of Love": a review of *Visions of Cody*, by Jack Kerouac

D617   [Poem] *Alive* (Guelph ON), No. 28 ([May] 1973): 25.
         "The Scattered Blintz" [pub. under pseud. E. E. Greengrass]

D618   [Poem] *Impulse* (Toronto ON) 2, Nos. 3 & 4; *Porcépic* (Erin ON) 1, No. 2 (May 1973): 37–38.
         "David McFadden"

D619   [Poem] *Saturday Night* (Toronto ON) 88, No. 5 (May 1973): 4.
         "Raymond Souster"

D620   [Interview; Review] *Open Letter* (Toronto ON) Second Series, No. 5 (Summer 1973): 30–39, 95–98.
         "Jewish Layton Catholic Hood Protestant Bowering," by Kerry Allard—*Visions of Cody*, by Jack Kerouac: a review [Note: the transcription and editing for the interview were done by GB; the tape is in the GB Papers, NL; see E28]

D621   [Poems] *is* (Clarksville TN), [No. 1] (Summer 1973): n. p.

"Jack Spicer"—"George Stanley"—
"Robin Blaser" [Note: the journal is sub-
titled "A Printed Occurrence in Time &
Place"]

D622 [Poems] "Three Poems by E. E. Green-
grass." *Elfin Plot* (Wood Mountain SK),
No. 13 (Summer 1973): n. p.
"The Lodge" [pub. under pseud. E. E.
Greengrass]—"SF" [pub. under pseud.
E. E. Greengrass]—"Berkeley Letter"
[pub. under pseud. E. E. Greengrass]

D623 [Essay] *Maclean's* (Toronto ON) 86, No.
6 (June 1973): 47, 58–59, 62.
"The Art of the Webfoot: Baseball,
Poetry and Other Cultures" [Note: GB's
manuscript title was "The Poetic Community of Cloud Cuckoo Coast"]

D624 [Poem] *Grain* (Saskatoon SK) 1, No. 1
(June 1973): 51.
"Daphne Marlatt"

D625 [Poems] *High Iron* (Vancouver BC), No.
14 [July 1973]: n. p.
"David Bromige"—"Robert Hogg"
—"Jamie Reid"—"Bill Bissett"

GB as a child in Greenwood,
c. 1943

D626 [Review] *The Georgia Straight* (Vancouver BC) 7, No. 304 (2–9 August
1973): 19–20.
"Jazz Recordings: Yesterday, Today & Tomorrow": a review of
Charles Mingus and Friends in Concert, by Charles Mingus; *Cosmic
Furnace,* by Roger Powell; *Bap-Tizum,* by the Art Ensemble of Chicago

D627 [Editor; Poems] "3 from *Curious." Imago* (Vancouver BC), No. 19 [c.
Summer 1973]: 38–43.
"Victor Coleman"—"Margaret Avison"—"Margaret Randall"

D628 [Poems] *Repository* (Seven Persons AB), No. 8 (Fall 1973): 38–39.
"The Final Agony" [pub. under pseud. E. E. Greengrass]—"Cultural
Exchange" [pub. under pseud. E. E. Greengrass]

D629 [Poems] *Star-Web Paper* (Laurinburg NC), No. 3 (Autumn 1973): n. p.
"Robert Creeley"—"Charles Reznikoff"

D630 [Story] *The Capilano Review* (North Vancouver BC), No. 4 (Fall/Winter
1973): 52–58.
"The Big Leagues" [excerpts]

D631 [Letter] *University Affairs* (Ottawa ON) 14, No. 7 (September 1973): 12.
"Writers Are Viewed Seriously in Canada"

D632   [Review] *The Georgia Straight* (Vancouver BC) 7, No. 318 (8–15 November 1973): 19, 22.

      Duke Ellington Presents Ivie Anderson, by Ivie Anderson; *The Great Paris Concert*, by Duke Ellington: a review [Note: unsigned]

D633   [Poems] "Two Portraits." *Tuatara* (Victoria BC), No. 11 (Winter 1973): 18–19.

      "bpNichol"—"Margaret Atwood"

D634   [Poem] *Grain* (Saskatoon SK) 1, No. 2 (December 1973): 17.

      "Nausea Nostalgia" [pub. under pseud. E. E. Greengrass]

D635   [Poem] *Ophir* (Braamfontein, South Africa), No. 18 (December 1973): 29.

      "Düsseldorf" [Note: says November 1973 on cover]

D636   [Poem] *Out of Sight* (Wichita KS), No. 70 (December 1973): n. p.

      "Midnight Lunch"

D637   [Poems] *Athanor* (Clarkson NY), No. 5 (Winter 1973): 48–50.

      "William Carlos Williams"—"Ed Dorn"

D638   [Review] *The Georgia Straight* (Vancouver BC) 7, No. 322 (6–13 December 1973): 19–20.

      The Beginning And the End, by Clifford Brown; *Straight Life*, by Freddie Hubbard: a review [Note: unsigned; see *Craft Slices*: "Trumpet"; A44]

" . . . when you sit down and write your attention is not towards the thing that you're writing about, you're not writing something that will provide a window through which the reader can see the world, but the attention is to the page that the words are going down on. If it is a window it's a window that you look at for its own sake, like a cut-glass window. I mean, writing is writing—sculpture doesn't try to pretend it's not there. None of the other arts try to pretend they're not there, so why should prose?"
[From "Footnote 2, An Interview with George Bowering"; see D755]

1974

D639   [Poem] *Strange Faeces* (Oakland CA), No. 15 [1974]: n. p.

      "What the Poet Does" [Note: listed in table of contents as "What a Poet Does"]

D640   [Poem] *Unmuzzled Ox* (New York NY) 2, No. 3 (1974): 67–68.

      "George Oppen"

D641   [Review] *Open Letter* (Toronto ON) Second Series, No. 7 (Winter 1974): 84–86.

"Tragic Jack": a review of *Kerouac*, by Ann Charters [Note: "Spring 1974" on cover; "Winter 1974" on title-page]

D642   [Poem] *Waves* (Downsview ON) 2, No. 2 (Winter 1974): 64.

"Black Eyed Girl" [pub. under pseud. E. E. Greengrass]

D643   [Poems] "Two Poems." *The Antigonish Review* (Antigonish NS), No. 20 (Winter 1974): 65–66.

"From the Window Light" [pub. under pseud. E. E. Greengrass]—"It Is a Kind of Pressure" [pub. under pseud. E. E. Greengrass] [Note: the notes on contributors (p. 113) say E. E .G. teaches English at UBC]

D644   [Story] *Journal of Canadian Fiction* (Montreal PQ) 3, No. 1 (Winter 1974): 21–23.

"The Xalapa Handkerchief"

D645   [Poems] "Two Poems." *Quarry* (Kingston ON) 23, No. 2 (Spring 1974): 4–5.

"Frank Davey"—"Al Purdy"

D646   [Review] *Canadian Literature* (Vancouver BC), No. 60 (Spring 1974): 112–114.

"A Singular Voice": a review of *Waiting for Wayman*, by Tom Wayman [Notes: "Winter 1974" on the title-page; see *Craft Slices*: "Still Waiting"; A44]

D647   [Talk] *Waves* (Downsview ON) 2, No. 3 (Spring 1974): 4–7.

"Little Competing Nations of Perception," transcribed from tape by Barry McKinnon [Notes: originally a statement for a panel discussion on "The Future of Poetry in Canada," with Irving Layton and Earle Birney, at the Canadian Writers and Critics Conference, University of Calgary and Banff School of Fine Arts, 11 February 1973; see *Craft Slices*: "Post Lyric"; A44]

GB with Fred Miller, c. 1952

"There is a typical Canadian poem. You pick up a little mag that is 50 pages long and see 48 poems dealing with an injured dog on the street or a naked man in a bath. That's okay; you still have to learn how to do it if you are a new poet. Now each of us has written a couple hundred lyric poems, and something else has been

beginning for a decade or more. It is a poem that is larger, looks for a larger experience. I hesitate to give it a name, although sometimes it tends toward epic, and other times it tends toward the cosmic. There might be a case for saying that in the east it tends toward something like the epic, a poem containing history. In Vancouver, particularly, it tends toward something that can contain a cosmos, or something that can contain the clues to a cosmos. Perhaps the hero of the west coast poets I am interested in would be Hesiod, whereas in the east it might be Homer. This is tangential."
[From *Craft Slices*: "Post Lyric"; A44; see also D647]

D648   [Poem] *Tens* (Vancouver BC), No. 5 (April 1974): n. p.
       "Anselm Hollo"
D649   [Essay; Review] *Open Letter* (Toronto ON) Second Series, No. 8 (Summer 1974): 37–47, 94–99.
       "That Was Ida Said Miss Stein"—"Lines on the Grid": a review of *Among*, by Fred Wah; *Vancouver Poems*, by Daphne Marlatt; *Rat Jelly*, by Michael Ondaatje [Note: see *Craft Slices*: "Kootenai Wah" and "Marlatt's Vancouver"; A44]
D650   [Poem] *Tuatara* (Victoria BC), No. 12 (Summer 1974): 46.
       "Marianne Moore"
D651   [Review] *Canadian Literature* (Vancouver BC), No. 61 (Summer 1974): 95–100.
       "Suitcase Poets": a review of *Sex & Death*, by Al Purdy; *What's So Big about Green?*, by Earle Birney [Note: see *Craft Slices*: "Birney's Rage," "Purdy," and "Purdy's Process"; A44]
D652   [Story] *Center* (Woodstock NY), No. 6 (July 1974): 90.
       "The Minnesota Twins" [from "The Big Leagues"]
D653   [Poem] *Saturday Night* (Toronto ON) 89, No. 8 (August 1974): 2.
       "A Poem for High School Anthologies"
D654   [Poems] *Boundary 2* (Binghamton NY) 3, No. 1 (Fall 1974): 92–95.
       "Radio Jazz"—"Circus Maximus"—"Giant Steps"—"Composition" [Note: "A Canadian Issue," edited by Robert Kroetsch; GB's poems are part of "Poets of the Sixties/Vancouver," selected by Warren Tallman and arranged by AB]

"I'm always wondering if I'm finished as a poet, whether I'll ever write poems again. One time I didn't write any for nine months. I just said no writing for nine months."
[GB recalling the nine months prior to starting *Allophanes* in September 1974, Session 2, 9 March 1988; see A24]

D655   [Review] *Open Letter* (Toronto ON) Second Series, No. 9 (Fall 1974): 117–119.
  "Mr. Joy": a review of *The Sun Rises into the Sky*, by Fielding Dawson [Note: see *Craft Slices*: "Fielding"; A44]

D656   [Essay] *Update: Newsletter of the B. C. English Teachers' Association* (Vancouver BC) 15, No. 1 (September 1974): 2.
  "What Elementary and Secondary School English Should Be about" [Note: see *Craft Slices*: "School English"; A44]

D657   [Poem] *Out of Sight* (Wichita KS), No. 94 (September 1974): n. p.
  "Ride"

D658   [Editor; Statement; Poems] *Imago 20* (Vancouver BC), No. 20 (October 1974): 9–11, 90–93.
  "Preface" [to *Imago 20*]—"Poet Meets Euterpe"—"Mais le rien perce"—"Reconsiderations IV"—"AW AUG 17/74" [See B1 and B6]

D659   [Poem] *Man-Root* (San Francisco CA), No. 10 (Late Fall 1974/Winter 1975): 15.
  "Jack Spicer"

1975

D660   [Poem] *Iron II: River* (Vancouver BC), No. 1 (1975): 49.
  "Ranchero"

D661   [Poem] *Unmuzzled Ox* (New York NY) 3, No. 2; issue No. 10 (1975): 111.
  "Jack Spicer"

D662   [Poem] *Workshop* (Brattleboro VT), No. 24 (January 1975): n. p.
  "In the Forest"

D663   [Poems] *Descant* (Toronto ON), No. 13 (Early Winter 1975): 35–36.
  "The Bottles" [pub. under pseud. E. E. Greengrass]—"Bomb Run" [pub. under pseud. E. E. Greengrass]

D664   [Poem] *The Peak* (Burnaby BC) 39, No. 4 (30 January 1975): 14.
  "The Smooth Loper"

D665   [Poems] *CrossCountry* (Woodhaven NY/Montreal PQ), No. 1 (Winter 1975): 30–33.
  "Poet Laureate"—"Did"—"Beyond"—"New Love"

D666   [Poem; Statement] *The Capilano Review* (North Vancouver BC), No. 7 (Spring 1975): 165–174, 220.
  "Desert Elm"—["You are, for instance, already putting out a magazine which . . . "] [Note: brief statement used as an ad for the journal]

D667   [Poem] *Rune* (Toronto ON), No. 2 (Spring 1975): 5.
  "Onion Skins"

D668   [Poems] *Alive* (Guelph ON), No. 42 [Spring 1975]: 34.
        "Two People"—"Panting"
D669   [Essay; Review] *Canadian Literature* (Vancouver BC), No. 65 (Summer 1975): 7–27, 86–90.
        "Coming Home to the World" [on D. G. Jones]—"The Site of Blood": a review of *Blown Figures*, by Audrey Thomas
D670   [Poem] *Repository* (Prince George BC), No. 15 (Summer 1975): 20.
        "El Paso" [pub. under pseud. E. E. Greengrass]
D671   [Poems] "Three Poems." *Prism International* (Vancouver BC) 14, No. 2 (Summer 1975): 7–9.
        "Advice, As If"—"Poet Laureate"—"The Mask of"
D672   [Translations] *Invisible City* (Fairfax CA), Nos. 16 & 17 (June 1975): 6, 38.
        "Sometimes . . . ," by Nicolas Guillen—"The Grain Cut by the Peasants" by Roberto Sosa—"Malign Headless Dancers," by Roberto Sosa

---

"I havent done any writing really since December. I vowed on NY day not to write for 2 years, so I spent most of the time since editing and teaching. But lately I have been showing signs of wanting to break the vow, 8 months old now, and find that I cant anyway, because I'm too busy at University. Gad. I have in mind a novel, dont tell anyone, written against Capt George Vancouver. Safe target, eh? been dead 125 years.
"Or more."
[GB Papers, Correspondence Margaret Randall, 11 August 1975, NL]

D673   [Interview by; Reviews] *Open Letter* (Toronto ON) Third Series, No. 2 (Fall 1975): 26–38, 112–121.
        "Keep Witnessing": a review/ interview of *Steveston*, by Daphne Marlatt and Robert Minden— "Studying Hawkes": a review of *Comic Terror: The Novels of John Hawkes*, by Donald J. Greiner [review pub. under pseud. E. E. Greengrass]—"Mother Stein Anderson": a review of *Sherwood Anderson/Gertrude Stein, Correspondence and Personal Essays*,

GB with his father Ewart Bowering and his grandfather Jabez Harry Bowering, c. 1955

edited by Ray Lewis White [review pub. under pseud. E. E. Green-
grass]—"The Politics of Pound and Possum": a review of *The Political
Identities of Ezra Pound and T. S. Eliot*, by William M. Chace [review
pub. under pseud. E. E. Greengrass] [Notes: cover dated "Spring";
title-page "Fall"; see *Craft Slices*: "Hawkes," "Eliot," and "Eliot's Politics"; A44]

D674   [Poems] *Davinci* (Montreal PQ) 2, No. 1; issue No. 4 (Autumn 1975):
        16–19.
            "New Love"—"Western Town Around"—"Sunday Driver"—"Spell-
        ing/Rule"

D675   [Statement; Poem] *Olson* (Storrs CT), No. 4 (Fall 1975): 70–75, 86–87.
            "Some Notes from Vancouver 1963 Poetry Conference"—"Charles
        Olson"

"Here are some pieces re 1963. I was going thru my diary on the time, and it is
not useful at all (a) because most of my attention went, apparently to Ginsberg
and Whalen there. And the pieces I send here from my notebook are not writing,
werent set up to be, that came elsewhere, but just little notes to me, sitting there
in thr [sic] odd-ience. but I send them anyway, to see whether they offer you a
checkover on the others' memories. I snd [sic] write sometime my memories on
all that, but not for now."
[GB Papers, Correspondence George Butterick, 22 April 1975, NL]

D676   [Translation] *The Antigonish Review* (Antigonish NS), No. 23 (Autumn
        1975): 48–49.
            "The Color of Color," by Manuel Pacheco
D677   [Excerpts from a poem] *The Capilano Review* (North Vancouver BC),
        Nos. 8 & 9 (Fall 1975/Spring 1976): 198–201.
            Allophanes: V–VII
D678   [Excerpt from a poem] *Asphodel* (Burton OH), Asphodel Book Shop
        Catalogue No. 45 (November 1975): n. p.
            Allophanes: IV
D679   [Poem] *Canadian Review* (Ottawa ON) 2, No. 4 (Christmas 1975): 31.
            "Pacific Grey" [pub. under pseud. E. E. Greengrass]

1976

D680   [Poems; Interview] *CrossCountry* (Woodhaven NY/Montreal PQ), No.
        5 (1976): 4–19.

"Smoking Mirror"—"Curiouser & Curiouser," by Marianne Lafon and Ken Norris [Note: the interview was taped 17 February 1976, at McGill University, Montreal]

D681 [Story] *Journal of Canadian Fiction* (Montreal PQ), No. 16 (1976): 7–15.

"Re Union"

D682 [Excerpts from a poem] *Wrought Iron* (North Vancouver BC) Second Series, No. 2 (January 1976): n. p.

Allophanes: VIII–X

D683 [Review] *Canadian Literature* (Vancouver BC), No. 71 (Winter 1976): 92–95.

"I's and Eyes": a review of *Virgins and Vampires*, by Joe Rosenblatt; *Name*, by Seymour Mayne; *A Knight in Dried Plums*, by David McFadden [review pub. under pseud. E. E. Greengrass; misspelled "Greenglass"] [Note: see *Craft Slices*: "Joe's Head," "Seymour's Similes," and "McFadding"; A44]

D684 [Reviews] *Open Letter* (Toronto ON) Third Series, No. 4 (Winter 1976): 96–103.

"Love in a White Coat": a review of *William Carlos Williams: The Knack of Survival in America*, by Robert Coles [review pub. under pseud. E. E. Greengrass]—"The Strange Posthumous Life of the American Novel": a review of *Literary Disruptions: The Making of a Post-Contemporary American Fiction*, by Jerome Klinkowitz [review pub. under pseud. E. E. Greengrass] [Notes: cover dated "Spring 1976"; title-page says "Winter 1976"; see *Craft Slices*: "Posthumous Fiction," "Undone Tradition," and "Uprooting"; A44]

D685 [Essay] *Essays on Canadian Writing* (Downsview ON), No. 4 (Spring 1976): 16–18.

"Robert Duncan in Canada" [Note: see *Craft Slices*: "Duncan in Canada" and "Duncan in Vancouver"; A44]

D686 [Excerpts from a novel] *Longhouse* (100 Mile House BC), No. 1 (Spring 1976): n. p.

A Short Sad Book: I–II

D687 [Excerpt from a novel] *NMFG* (Vancouver BC), No. 3 (April 1976): n. p.

A Short Sad Book: III

D688 [Essay; Review] *Open Letter* (Toronto ON) Third Series, No. 5 (Summer 1976): 28–39, 100–103.

"Snow Red: The Short Stories of Audrey Thomas"—"Eros and Thanatos Again": a review of *John Hawkes and the Craft of Conflict*, by John Kuehl [pub. under pseud. E. E. Greengrass]

D689 [Excerpt from a novel] *IS* (Toronto ON), No. 18 (Summer 1976): 30–31.

A Short Sad Book: IV [Note: this issue was called "A Document of the 1975 Writers' Tour of the Northwest Territories," edited by Victor

Coleman and Linda McCartney; includes "Showering Bowering Reads Writing," a review of GB's reading by Ken Coach; see H236]

D690   [Letter] *SFU Week* (Burnaby BC) 5, No. 5 (3 June 1976): 4.

"Boring Subject": to the editor

D691   [Excerpt from a novel] *NMFG* (Vancouver BC), No. 6 (18 June 1976): n. p.

A Short Sad Book: XXXVI

D692   [Excerpts from a novel] *NMFG* (Vancouver BC), No. 7 (July 1976): n. p.

A Short Sad Book: XL–XLI

D693   [Excerpts from a novel] *NMFG* (Vancouver BC), No. 8 (August 1976): n. p.

A Short Sad Book: XLII–XLIII

D694   [Poems] "Two Poems from *The Concrete Island.*" *Echo* (Vancouver BC), No. 2 (Fall 1976): 17.

"Mandatory Spring Poem"—"Silver & Gold, the Trees"

D695   [Story; Poems] *IS* (Toronto ON), Nos. 19 & 20 (Fall 1976): n. p.

"A Short Hagiography of Old Quebec"—"Provender" [pub. under pseud. E. E. Greengrass]—"The Poem" [pub. under pseud. E. E. Greengrass]

D696   [Story] *Event* (New Westminster BC) 5, No. 3 [Fall 1976]: 10–14.

"Highway Three"

D697   [Translation; Story] *Black Moss* (Coatsworth ON) Series 2, No. 2 (Fall 1976): 27, 41–43.

"Knight of the Golden Snail," by Emil Botta—"Protective Footwear"

D698   [Excerpts from a novel] *NMFG* (Vancouver BC), No. 9 (September 1976): n. p.

A Short Sad Book: XLIV–XLV

D699   [Excerpts from a novel] *NMFG* (Vancouver BC), No. 11 (November 1976): n. p.

A Short Sad Book: XLVI–XLVII [Note: contents lists "*A Short Sad Novel*" as the book title]

D700   [Statement; Excerpt from a novel] *Iron Without Measure* [*Iron II*] (Vancouver BC), No. 4 (November 1976): 4.

["The real difference is not prose & poetry . . . "]—*A Short Sad Book*: V [Note: the statement is an epigraph for this special prose issue: "The real difference is not prose &

GB and his family, c. 1953; back row, l. to r.: GB, Pearl (mother), Ewart (father), Sally (sister); front row, l. to r.: Roger and Jim (brothers)

poetry the real difference is prose & verse, both of which can be poetry or might not be."]

D701   [Excerpts from a novel] *NMFG* (Vancouver BC), No. 12 (December 1976): n. p.
       A Short Sad Book: XLVIII–XLVIX

"A couple of years ago when I read in Medicine Hat I was the first poet to read there since Rudyard Kipling, literally. They dont have a heavy program. I asked how Rudyard's reading went. No one seemed to have attended it."
[GB Papers, Correspondence Victoria Walker, 14 December 1976, NL]

D702   [Poem; Excerpts from a poem; Talk] *The B. C. Monthly* (Vancouver BC) 3, No. 3 (December 1976): n. p.
       "She Pulled My Skin"—*Allophanes*: XI–XIII—"Vancouver Poetry in the Early 60s" (with Lionel Kearns and Gerry Gilbert) [See E52]
D703   [Story] *Descant* (Toronto ON), No. 16 (Winter 1976/77): 26–33.
       "Spans"

1977

D704   [Poem] *CrossCountry* (Woodhaven NY/Montreal PQ), Nos. 8 & 9 (1977): 77.
       "Northern Ont CP Air"
D705   [Poem] *The B. C. Monthly* (Vancouver BC) 2, No. 2 (February 1974–1977): n. p.
       ["Frame of Film the . . . "] [Note: one of nine folded sheets comprising the issue; see E44]
D706   [Poems; Statement] *West Coast Review* (Burnaby BC) 12, No. 2 (1977): 29–30.
       "Last Lyrics: She's Going"—"Last Lyrics: Sitting"—"Last Lyrics: Across 37th Avenue"—["I do not compose poetry to show you . . . "]
       [Notes: see *Craft Slices*: "Adding"; A44; this issue was published as a book, *New: West Coast: 72 Contemporary British Columbia Poets*, edited by Fred Candelaria; see C102]
D707   [Excerpt from a novel] *NMFG* (Vancouver BC), No. 13 (January 1977): n. p.
       A Short Sad Book: L [Note: contributor's note says "next month will feature sections of *NMFG* George's new sociological novel *The Function of Rocksalt within the Kerrisdale Psychological Club*"]
D708   [Excerpt from a novel] *The Malahat Review* (Victoria BC), No. 41 (January 1977): 150–151.

A Short Sad Book: XX ("Basic Victim Positions")

D709   [Excerpts from a poem] *A Hundred Posters* (Boston MA), No. 13 (January 1977): n. p.

Allophanes: XIV–XVI

D710   [Story] *The Capilano Review* (North Vancouver BC), No. 11 ([January] 1977): 16–21.

"The Creator Has a Master Plan"

"Well, what am I up to?

"I have finally come to what I have been coming to for the past 5 years or so, aaaabandoning verse, and being what I wanted to be at the first, a prose writer. But I made the error of trying to write realist prose earlier, and the poetry and then the later events like *Autobiology* taught me to come at it from he the I mean, floor up, or the syllable up. So I am writing prose with a pen with black ink, instead of the typewriter, wch I may trust myself to later on, so everything is short & sparse. If you use a pen then you can not get the energy to make all those adjectives and dialogue. Once rid of them, you can write prose.

"He said.

"Or rather she said.

"Now I wonder what it is about all you Maritimes people who retreat to the earth, get trucks, build boats and woodsheds, surround yrselvs with dogs and chickens, smoke pipes, and eat fish grown in yr own garden. Is this a conscious effort to be a Canadian?

"That's the sort of thing I'm writing now."

[GB Papers, Correspondence Donald Cameron, 30 March 1977, NL]

D711   [Poem] *Repository* (Prince George BC), Nos. 21 & 22 (Winter/Spring 1977): 5.

"Dark Alley Dream" [pub. under pseud. E. E. Greengrass]

D712   [Excerpt from a novel] *Longhouse* (100 Mile House BC), No. 2 (Winter 1977): n. p.

A Short Sad Book: VIII

D713   [Letter] *The Canadian* (Toronto ON), 5 February 1977: 20.

"Re the People's Poet" [Note: a short letter praising Milton Acorn]

D714   [Excerpt from a novel] *Periodics* (Vancouver BC), No. 1 (Spring 1977): 15–16.

A Short Sad Book: XXXII [Note: this journal was edited by Daphne Marlatt and Paul de Barros]

D715   [Review; Letter] *Contemporary Verse II* (Winnipeg MB) 3, No. 1 (Spring 1977): 27, 52.

"The Upper Canada Book of the Dead": a review of *I Ching Kanada*, by David Godfrey [pub. under pseud. E. E. Greengrass]—"That Puzzling Voice, Some (In)formal Assumptions" [pub. under pseud. E. E. Greengrass] [Note: see *Craft Slices*: "I Ching"; A44]

D716   [Review] *Canadian Fiction Magazine* (Vancouver BC), No. 27 ([Spring] 1977): 153–156.

Agent Provocateur, by David Young: a review [Note: published in *The Mask in Place* as "Genreflect"; A41; see also D719 and E49]

D717   [Statement] *Canadian Literature* (Vancouver BC), No. 72 (Spring 1977): 95–96.

"Symbolism and Imagism" [pub. under pseud. E. E. Greengrass]

D718   [Poem] *Maker* (Montreal PQ), No. 2 [March 1977]: n. p.

"Gwendolyn" [pub. under pseud. E. E. Greengrass]

D719   [Review] *NMFG* (Vancouver BC), No. 15 (April 1977): n. p.

"Genreflect": a review of *Agent Provocateur*, by David Young

D720   [Story] *The Canadian Forum* (Toronto ON) 57, No. 670 (April 1977): 31–34.

"The Wallet: An Exercise in Sixties West Coast Bourgeois Realism" [Note: the story was drawn from an unpublished novel, "What Does Eddie Williams Want?"]

D721   [Reviews] *Open Letter* (Toronto ON) Third Series, No. 7 (Summer 1977): 117–126.

"Image Picking": a review of *The Cantos of Ezra Pound: The Lyric Mode*, by Eugene Paul Nassar—"Williams' Dualities": a review of *The Early Poetry of William Carlos Williams*, by Rod Townley—"The Academy vs. William Carlos Williams": a review of *William Carlos Williams: Poet from Jersey*, by Reed Whittemore [all pub. under pseud. E. E. Greengrass]

D722   [Letters] *Contemporary Verse II* (Winnipeg MB) 3, No. 2 (Summer 1977): 63–64.

"For the Record"—"Responding to a Base Canard" [pub. under pseud. E. E. Greengrass] [Note: "For the Record" is a response to Robin Mathews' "Seeing Through a Greenglass Clearly" in the previous issue]

"I take typewriter in lap to reply to the base canard from Robin Mathews (which is probably a pseudonym for Seymour Mayne) wherein he accuses me of being George Bowering.

"I may be a lot of things, but I am not an ex-Tisher. The accusation bothers me for various reasons. I am not a birthright citizen of B. C., but an immigrant from N. D. G. Bowering is about seven years older than I am. He is clearly and obviously a WASP, while I ain't. And I refuse to take the responsibility for his poems, which are pretty ordinary, or his 'critical' statements, which are incomprehensible except on occasion.

"Now if Robin (Seymour) had said that I am a pen-name for Artie Gold, that would be a different matter. He's about five years younger than I am.

"Eytan Edward Greengrass would like to retain his name, Seymour. My uncle was an outfielder and first-baseman in the major leagues. I don't remember any Maynes playing there."

["Responding to a Base Canard"; see D722]

D723   [Poem] *Origins* (Hamilton ON) 7, No. 2 (June 1977): 7.
        "Alden's Beard" [pub. under pseud. E. E. Greengrass]
D724   [Poem] *A Hundred Posters* (Boulder CO), No. 19 (July 1977): n. p.
        "The Middle-aged Poet Dumpt at Last into the Iambic"
D725   [Statement] *Center* (Hattiesburg MS), No. 10 [July 1977]: 53.
        "Stained Glass Prose" [Note: see *Craft Slices*: "Stained Glass"; A44]

"I can read fiction that acts like a window on the world once in a while, at bedtime, perhaps, as a kind of relaxation something like crime thrillers on TV. But I dont anymore want to write it, & I dont want to find it in prose that purports to be serious & contemporary. Prose is no longer interesting just because it offers a slice of life. If you want to see what a South Chicago street looks like, take a 747 to Chicago. I dont want to look thru a novel at it. If I find some fiction I want it to look like fiction. If it is a window it is a stained glass window. You dont look thru a stained glass window. It has to be interesting itself.

"Of course a stained glass window looks better when there is some outside light coming thru. But the glass uses that light for its own purpose. And the eye inside is a careful reader, not a passive customer of the wares 'outside'."

["Stained Glass Prose"; see D725]

D726   [Poem] *Mamashee* (Inwood ON) 1, No. 3 [Fall 1977]: n. p.
        "Ditch on US 99" [pub. under pseud. E. E. Greengrass]
D727   [Poems; Translation] *Bezoarrr* (Gloucester MA) 11, No. 1 (Last call of 1977): n. p.
        "Kits Beach"—"Cicatrice"—"The Tree," by Nicolas Guillen
D728   [Story] *The B. C. Monthly* (Vancouver BC) 3, No. 8 (December 1977).
        The Story, She Said, by Daphne Marlatt [Note: GB was one of several contributing writers; see C104]

1978

D729   [Excerpts from a novel] *CrossCountry* (Woodhaven NY/Montreal PQ), Nos. 10 & 11 (1978): 5–15.
"The Black Mountain Influence" [chapters XXXII–XXXIX from *A Short Sad Book*]

D730   [Poem] *Canadian Author & Bookman* (Toronto ON) 53, No. 2 (January 1978): 40.
"The Social Sciences" [pub. under pseud. E. E. Greengrass]

D731   [Poem] *The Capilano Review* (North Vancouver BC), No. 13 ([January] 1978): 136–138.
"Which Poesy"

D732   [Excerpt from a novel] *Periodics* (Vancouver BC), No. 3 (Spring 1978): 5–8.
"The Dead Sailors": 2 [earlier title of *Burning Water*]

D733   [Essay] *The University of Windsor Review* (Windsor ON) 13, No. 2 (Spring/Summer 1978): 24–36.
"The Painted Window: Notes on Post-Realist Fiction"

D734   [Poems] *Credences* (Kent OH) 2, Nos. 3 & 4; issue Nos. 5 & 6 (March 1978): 88–98.
"Smoking Mirror"

D735   [Story] *The Malahat Review* (Victoria BC), No. 46 (April 1978): 77–83.
"A Tale Which Holdeth Children from Play"

D736   [Interview] *The Albertan* (Calgary AB), 12 April 1978.
"Money Is Least Important," by Bob Bergen

D737   [Excerpt from a novel; Statement] *Open Letter* (Toronto ON) Third Series, No. 9 (Fall 1978): 68–70, 87.
"The Dead Sailors": 1—"Reading Before *TISH*" [Note: chapter 1 of "The Dead Sailors" was the original chapter of the manuscript for *Burning Water*; it was removed but in revision GB blended it into the "Prologue" and chapters 1 and 2]

D738   [Excerpts from a novel] *Periodics* (Vancouver BC), No. 4 (Fall 1978): 35–41.
"The Dead Sailors": 21, 26 [*Burning Water*: 20, 25]

D739   [Excerpt from a novel] *Island* (Lantzville BC), Nos. 5 & 6 (Fall 1978/Spring 1979): 29–31.
"The Dead Sailors": 35 [*Burning Water*: 34]

D740   [Poem] *The Chelsea Journal* (Saskatoon SK) 4, No. 5 (September/October 1978): 215.
"At the Vet" [pub. under pseud. E. E. Greengrass]

D741   [Editor; Translations] "David Iron" (Vancouver BC), No. 20 ([November] 1978): n. p.

"I Say to Begin," by David Fernández—"This Man," by David Fernádez [Note: a special issue of *Iron*, edited by GB, published by Beaver Kosmos; see B2]

D742   [Poem] *West Coast Review* (Burnaby BC) 13, No. 2 (October 1978): 16–17.

"Another Week in the East"

D743   [Essay] *The Ubyssey* (Vancouver BC), 17 October 1978: 8.

"George Bowering" [Note: published in section called "The Lost Years: 1950–1962"; see *Craft Slices*: "Ubyssey"; A44]

"Damn, we were good! The downtown papers read everything we had to say, and quoted us whenever they needed any wit to support their columns. [Mike] Matthews was the ne plus ultra of the hyperbolic rant. [David] Bromige brought with him an acerbity learned in British schools and Saskatchewan loony bins.

"I loved the power and freedom of my arts column called Placebo. I loved the responses and smirks I received the rest of the week, in classrooms and in the The Georgia. I loved the free tickets to plays and jazz concerts. And I loved the way those tickets and my flashy note-taking impressed my date.

"I remember thinking over and over: Oh God, if I have but one life to live, I hope this is it."

[From "The Lost Years"; see D743]

D744   [Poems] "Two Poems by George Bowering." *Dandelion* (Calgary AB), No. 4 (Winter 1978): 42–43.

"Thinning Apples"—"Trucking Peaches" [Note: these are from the sequence "Four Jobs"]

D745   [Letter] *Books in Canada* (Toronto ON) 7, No. 10 (December 1978): 40.

"On Cohen and Ajzenstadt"

1979

D746   [Poem] *CrossCountry* (Woodhaven NY/Montreal PQ), No. 12 (1979): n. p.

"Against Description" [Note: a special postcard issue; see E60]

D747   [Statement] *Unmuzzled Ox: The Poets' Encyclopedia* (New York NY) 4, Nos. 4 & 5 (1979): 130.

"Iamb"

D748   [Poems; Excerpt from a novel; Story; Interview] *The Capilano Review* (North Vancouver BC), No. 15 ([January] 1979): 51–107.

"West Window"—"Old Standards"—"The Dead Sailors": 38, 39 [*Burning Water*: 37 and variant of 38]—"Carter Fell"—"14 Plums," interview by Bill Schermbrucker, Sharon Thesen, David McFadden, and Paul de Barros [Note: GB is featured in this issue]

"In poetry I like some kind of arbitrary structure that will then free you in your response to it, whereas in prose I like total control on the part of the author. I like the author to assert his independence of causality as much as possible in the prose, in the causality of the novel."
[From "14 Plums"; see D748]

D749   [Statement; Essay] *Books in Canada* (Toronto ON) 8, No. 1 (January 1979): 4, 7–9.
"Overrated & Underrated of Canadian Fiction, Non-fiction and Poetry"—"English, Our English"

D750   [Essay; Poem] *West Coast Review* (Burnaby BC) 13, No. 3 (February 1979): 20–25, 39–42.
"The Three-Sided Room: Notes on the Limitations of Modernist Realism"—"Poundmaker"

D751   [Letter] *The Daily Colonist* (Victoria BC), 20 February 1979.
"Pip-pip Pap Still Flowing from Pens" [pub. under pseud. E. E. Greengrass]

D752   [Editor; Essay; Interviews] *Three Vancouver Writers. Open Letter* (Toronto ON) Fourth Series, No. 3 (Spring 1979): 5–181.
"Preface" [to *Three Vancouver Writers*]—"Songs & Wisdom: An Interview with Audrey Thomas"—"Given This Body: An Interview with Daphne Marlatt"—"Starting at Our Skins: An Interview with Frank Davey" [Notes: the entire issue consists of the interviews by GB; see A32; also see *Craft Slices*: "Three Vancouvers"; A44]

D753   [Translation; Poems] *Star-Web Paper* (La Mesilla NM), No. 7 (Spring 1979): n. p.
"Marvelous Chickenshit Country," by Roberto Mckay—"How They Get Fat Bellies"—"A Clean Park"

D754   [Review] *West Coast Review* (Burnaby BC) 14, No. 1 (June 1979): 43–46.
Two-Headed Poems, by Margaret Atwood; *Poems New & Selected*, by Patrick Lane: a review [pub. under pseud. Edward Prato] [Notes: see *Craft Slices*: "Pat"; A44; a response to Prato's review, "Prato vs Pat Lane: A Review Reviewed," by Alice Van Wart, appeared in 15, No. 3 (Winter 1981): 82–84]

D755   [Interview] *V. P. C.* [Vancouver Poetry Centre] *Newsletter* (Vancouver BC) 1, No. 10 (16 August 1979): 2–3.
"Footnote 2, An Interview with George Bowering," by Eric Eggertson [Note: the newsletter, edited by Warren Tallman, was a vehicle for

the reading series "Writing in Our Time," at the Italian Cultural Centre, Vancouver; for GB's reading, 6 April 1979, see E61]

"I'm writing much less verse now than I used to. When I was very young I wanted to be a prose writer, and I became a poetry writer partly because your attention span and how excited you get about the world when you're in your twenties seem to lead almost inevitably towards writing lyrics.

"I did write prose in those days but I was all wrong about how to do it. I was trying to write realist prose from the samples that I saw in a small-town bookstore. I was paying more attention to the world which needs to be remembered and described. Meanwhile, I spent 15 years writing poetry which was getting longer and longer and larger and larger and more and more narrative in some sense. It just turned inevitably into what I'm more interested in, and that's fiction."
[From "Footnote 2"; see D755]

D756   [Essay] *Concerning Poetry* (Bellingham WA) 12, No. 2 (Fall 1979): 3–13. "The Poems of Fred Wah"

D757   [Excerpt from a novel] *Periodics* (Vancouver BC), No. 6 (Fall 1979): 69–72.
        "The Dead Sailors": 16 [*Burning Water*: 15]

D758   [Essay] *Books in Canada* (Toronto ON) 8, No. 10 (December 1979): 6–7.
        "*Tish* Tectonics" [Note: subtitled "Being a nostalgic history of how the bare hills around Oliver and Osoyoos gave birth to the Brown Mountain Poets"; see *Craft Slices*: "Brown Mountain" and "Brown Tish"; A44]

"As many readers may be tired of hearing, I was born and brought up in the Okanagan Valley. The more I read Canadian literature, the more I am convinced that being shaped in the Okanagan has to be a disadvantage for a Canadian writer. As I was growing up I learned every day that what seemed to me a pretty normal place to live was for outsiders a kind of Eden, a sun-washed vacation land of desert lakes, generous fruit trees, and top-notch baseball. Hence I was late to discover that I had missed out on the most valuable experience for a Canadian writer—harsh, unforgiving Nature.

GB with his daughter Thea, D. G. Jones, and Margaret Atwood, 1979

"Even people from the Coast spilled into the Okanagan Valley, gladly throwing off their clothes, because in that northernmost tip of the Great Sonora Desert

filled with aliens, we Okanagan kids just naturally took to the hills. The hills around Oliver and Osoyoos are bare and brown. We thought of ourselves as the Brown Mountain Boys. Later, when we were too old to play cowboys, we started taking our Mammoth Scribblers up the hills with us, where we would light a sagebrush campfire, and write poems as the sky darkened. We called ourselves the Brown Mountain Poets."
[From "*Tish* Tectonics"; see D758]

D759   [Poem] *Yang 91: Made in Canada* (Ghent, Belgium), No. 6 (December 1979): 146.
        "The Egg" [Note: a bilingual edition, edited by Eli Mandel and Achilles Gauthier; see G11]
D760   [Essay] *Canadian Fiction Magazine* (Toronto ON), Nos. 32 & 33 (1979/80): 4–9.
        "Modernism Could Not Last Forever"

1980

D761   [Poems] *CrossCountry* (Woodhaven NY/Montreal PQ), Nos. 13–15 (1980): 62–64.
        "A Typewritten Poem"—"Essaying Wah"—"Thirty-one at Sex"— "Thousand Souls"
D762   [Excerpt from a novel] *Writing* (Nelson BC), No. 1 (Summer 1980): 8–9.
        "The Dead Sailors": 30 [*Burning Water*: 29]
D763   [Review] *Canadian Literature* (Vancouver BC), No. 85 (Summer 1980): 142–144.
        "Nichol's Prose": a review of *Journal* and *Craft Dinner*, by bp Nichol [review pub. under pseud. E. E. Greengrass]
D764   [Translations] *The Antigonish Review* (Antigonish NS), No. 42 (Summer 1980): 41–42.
        "Christmas Carol for a Child of Vietnam," by Manuel Pacheco— "The Appearance of Rain," by Manuel Pacheco—"The Tree," by Nicolas Guillen
D765   [Review] *The Vancouver Free Press* (Vancouver BC) 2, No. 61 (1–8 August 1980): 9.
        "Famous Marriage": a review of *Straight Hearts' Delight*, by Allen Ginsberg and Peter Orlovsky
D766   [Letter] *Books in Canada* (Toronto ON) 9, No. 7 (August/September 1980): 40.
        "Purdy's Moose" [pub. under pseud. E. E. Greengrass]

"Sir:

"I notice in the June-July issue that Al Purdy makes this claim: 'After reading eight times in three days to audiences near Sudbury, Ont., a large moose appeared at the window whenever I spoke'.

"I think I have an idea why that happened. If this moose was smart enough to give poetry readings outside town, presumably in the Ontario woods, he was probably thinking that he might move into the Canada Council reading circuit, where poets, mooses or Purdies, are allowed to read indoors, and he was peeking inside to see how it is done.

"I hope that he succeeds, and if he does, I hope that he passes on some advice to a bear I know. He has written a cycle of love poems about a bad-tasting but energetic lady who seduced him in the bushes a few summers ago.

"E. E. Greengrass

"Vancouver"

[Letter to *Books in Canada*; see D766]

D767   [Essay] *Canadian Poetry* (London ON), No. 7 (Fall/Winter 1980): 38–48.

    "Proofing the World: The Poems of David McFadden"

"Sometimes I think I am just Canadian Poetry, a kind of walking Geddes anthology. Actually. But the real truth is that I keep writing away, not doing anything that can be understood on Front St or the rest of Toronto or whatever that province back there is called, and so they pass me off with a sentence that doesnt say anything abt me but lots about them."

[GB Papers, Correspondence David McFadden, 4 October 1980, NL]

D768   [Poem] *Toronto Life* (Toronto ON), (October 1980): 118.
    "This Is One of Those Days"

D769   [Interview] *Books in Canada* (Toronto ON) 9, No. 9 (November 1980): 30–31.
    "Why Problem-Solver George Bowering Vows Never to Write Another Historical Novel," by Linda M. Leitch

D770   [Review] *Canadian Literature* (Vancouver BC), No. 87 (Winter 1980): 103–105.
    "A Net Full of Ondaatje": a review of *There's a Trick with a Knife I'm Learning to Do*, by Michael Ondaatje [review pub. under pseud. Ed Prato]

D771   [Story] *Writing* (Nelson BC), No. 2 (Winter 1980/81): 23.
    "Stuffed Horse"

D772 [Story] *Island* (Lantzville BC), Nos. 8 & 9 (Winter 1980/Spring 1981): 69–76.
"Match-Boxes"

1981

D773 [Essay] *Studies in Canadian Literature* (Fredericton NB) 6, No. 1 (1981): 39–52.
"Margaret Atwood's Hands"

D774 [Translation] *The World* (New York NY), No. 35 (1981): 85.
"You & You Alone" ["A Usted Solamente," by "Anonimo, Chile"] [Note: published in Spanish in *Cuadernos Universitarios* (University of San Carlos, Guatemala), No. 2 (May/ June 1979)]

GB with Fred Wah, Nelson BC, c. 1981

D775 [Excerpts from a poem] *Ink* (Buffalo NY), Nos. 4 & 5 (1981): 21–22.
"Old Standards" [excerpts]

D776 [Story] *Rampike* (Toronto ON) 1, Nos. 2 & 3 (Spring 1981): 20.
"Road Games"

D777 [Interview] *Louis Dudek: Texts & Essays*. Ed. Frank Davey and bp Nichol. *Open Letter* (Toronto ON) Fourth Series, Nos. 8 & 9 (Spring/Summer 1981): 9–39.
"Questions (Some Answers)" [Note: Louis Dudek is interviewed, through an exchange of letters, by GB, Frank Davey, Steve McCaffery, and bp Nichol]

D778 [Poem; Excerpt from a letter] *Epoch* (Ithaca NY) 30, No. 3 (Spring/Summer 1981): 161–174.
"Uncle Louis" [Note: the poem is followed by GB's notes on Canadian places and persons in the poem, for his American readers; also includes an excerpt from GB's letter to the editor]

D779   [Statement] *Academy of Canadian Writers Newsletter* (Hamilton ON) 2, No. 3 (May 1981): 1.
"Canada Day 1981 Thunder Bay"

D780   [Essay] *Writing* (Nelson BC), No. 3 (Summer 1981): 15–17.
"The Heart of Diane Jones" [Note: this was part of a radio script; see E51]

D781   [Excerpt from a novel] *Comment* (Burnaby BC), Farewell edition (Summer/Fall 1981): 10–11.
Burning Water: 32 [Note: a publication of the SFU Alumni Association]

D782   [Poem] *Zest* (Nelson BC), No. 1 (28 October 1981): n. p.
"Alpha"

D783   [Statement] *Books in Canada* (Toronto ON) 10, No. 9 (November 1981): 41.
"Results of CanWit No. 65" [pub. under pseud. Ed Prato] [Note: a winning entry for "typographically mangled titles" of Canadian Books]

Coming Through Laughter: Michael Ondaatje Meets the Happy Hooker
The Circe Game: A New Collaboration by Margaret Atwood and Aritha van Herk
[From "CanWit No. 65"; see D783]

D784   [Essay] *Periodics* (Vancouver BC), Nos. 7 & 8 (Winter 1981): 178–179.
"Who Is Your Favorite Novelist? A Questionaire [sic] for Poets"

D785   [Essay] *UBC Alumni Chronicle* (Vancouver BC) 35, No. 4 (Winter 1981): 11.
"Writing from Outside: The Personal View of George Bowering" [Note: "The First in a Series of Essays by Distinguished University of British Columbia Alumni"; see *Craft Slices*: "Creative Writhing" and "Creative Writing"; A44]

"When university students, thinking that I teach creative writing, tell me they want to study such a thing because of their desire to express themselves, my heart shrinks. Poetry is not yourself, I tell them; poetry does not come from inside. It comes as it always has, from the world. The poet's job is not to disgorge, but to read all the great and good writing that

GB with Governor General Edward Schreyer, 1981, receiving the 1980 Governor General's Award for *Burning Water*

has been granted to the human race, to learn all the mechanics of our language, tune his body, and then listen. The poet is not an ex-presser but a reacher. The poet, Jack Spicer, was one of our teachers beyond the creative writing department. Poetry-writing is what Jack Spicer called it, the practice of outside."
[From "Writing from Outside"; see D785 and D788; see also *Craft Slices*: "Creative Writhing" and "Creative Writing"; A44]

D786   [Poem] *Zest* (Nelson BC), No. 4 (15 December 1981): n. p.
         "Aram Saroyan"
D787   [Story] *Writing* (Nelson BC), No. 4 (Winter 1981/82): 5–6.
         "Comparative Public Deaths"

1982

D788   [Essay] *Helix* (Ivanhoe, Australia), Nos. 11 & 12 (1982): 183, 186–187.
         "Writing from Outside" [Note: the essay is part of a section, "An Exchange on Creative Writing"; see *Craft Slices*: "Creative Writhing" and "Creative Writing"; A44; see also D785]
D789   [Poems] *Rampike* (Toronto ON) 2, Nos. 1 & 2 (1982): 42.
         "Again Obscurity & Ambiguity"—"Songbird"
D790   [Poem; Letters] *Descant* (Toronto ON), No. 39 (Winter 1982): 9, 191–198.
         "Detachment from Self"—"Towards Polyphony: Extracts from a Conversation between Dennis Lee and George Bowering" [Notes: titled in table of contents, "Selections from the Dennis Lee/George Bowering Correspondence"; this issue was published as a book, *Tasks of Passion*; see C153]

"Yes, and I am of course prejudiced, the long poem seems not only possible but called fr in the modernist and later period. That is to say, after the little rueful lyrics are all done with their job is over, goodbye to all that, and then you have to say: is there history? Is my one mind in any way determined by it or now lately a determinant? I take a lot of sustenance from Olson's *Special View of History*, of course, mainly because it puts to rest my feeling of obligation to the existential view; he attacks existentialism naturally from his view that it is a human universe, that history, as we live IN it rather than at its end or as effect of it, is created by our wills attacht to intelligence, i.e., the gathering man, now not of crops but of knowledge."
[From GB to Dennis Lee in "Towards Polyphony"; see D790]

D791   [Review] *Brick* (Ilderton ON), No. 14 (Winter 1982): 57–58.
        "Love in a White Coat": a review of *William Carlos Williams: The Knack of Survival in America*, by Robert Coles
D792   [Statement] *Books in Canada* (Toronto ON) 11, No. 1 (January 1982): 34.
        "CanWit No. 67" [pub. under pseud. Ed Prato]
D793   [Letter] *Interface* (Edmonton AB) 5, No. 2 (February 1982): 18.
        "Reply and Response: Getting the Facts Straight": To the Editor [Note: to correct numerous errors in a review by George McWhirter of the Talonbooks series of selected writings, including GB's *Particular Accidents*; see H408]
D794   [Poem] *Zest* (Nelson BC), No. 5 (2 February 1982): 7.
        "Franco P. and Others" [pub. under pseud. Ed Prato]
D795   [Essay] *The Review of Contemporary Fiction* (Elmwood Park IL) 2, No. 1 (Spring 1982): 83–87.
        "Douglas Woolf's 'Bank Day' "
D796   [Poems] *Writing* (Nelson BC), No. 5 (Spring 1982): 24.
        "Essaying Wah"—"Poem" ["A Typewritten Poem"]
D797   [Story] *Pig Iron* (Youngstown OH), No. 9 ([Spring] 1982): 57.
        "Road Games" [Note: an issue on baseball]
D798   [Poem] *Zest* (Nelson BC), No. 7 (April 1982): [2].
        "He's Sinking Fast"
D799   [Essay] *Open Letter* (Toronto ON) Fifth Series, No. 3 (Summer 1982): 5–10.
        "The End of the Line"
D800   [Story] *Prism International* (Vancouver BC) 20, No. 4 (Summer 1982): 74–82.
        "The Clam Digger & the Turtle" [Note: this is a children's story, part of a section called "A Selection of Writing for Children"]
D801   [Poems] *Zest* (Nelson BC), No. 8 (June 1982): 8.
        "Wed 1953"—"Breakfast 1953"—"I'm"
D802   [Essay] *Books in Canada* (Toronto ON) 11, No. 6 (June/July 1982): 4–5.
        "Diamonds Are Forever" [Note: originally titled "Poets Are the Unacknowledged Shortstops of the World"]

"Waiting on the balls of your feet. That is the stance of any writer who is not a hack. Baseball differs from the other sports in that the ball is not put into play by the offensive side. Neither are the people who put it into play defending a territory; rather they are covering a ground, the vast majority of which the other side has no interest in occupying."
[From "Diamonds Are Forever"; see D802]

D803   [Statement] *Books in Canada* (Toronto ON) 11, No. 7 (August/September 1982): 41.
        "CanWit No. 73" [pub. under pseud. Ed Prato]

D804   [Essay] *The Globe and Mail*, 28 August 1982.
        "Maybe Commissioner of Taste?" [Note: on tasteless attire, including license plates and bumper stickers, written for the regular feature, "The Mermaid Inn"; a note describes GB as "one of Vancouver's finest dressers"]

"I am more or less middle-aged, and no one has yet called me a tastemaker in print, but I do have a deep sense of civic responsibility. Therefore I wish I could be named by Order-in-Council to a position from which I could impose a general Canadian dress code. Or to put it more precisely, I'd like to have the power to enact a proscription list against certain moronic wearables.

"My first action would be taken against that jersey with the word HAWAII across the front of it with a two-digit number just below. In the first place, the University of Hawaii must have a feckless football team, because you never hear of them, even at Bowl time; and in the second place, who could believe that some mouse-faced runt in Weyburn, Saskatchewan, was even an early cut from a mid-Pacific gridiron squad?"

[From "Maybe Commissioner of Taste?"; see D804]

D805   [Poems] "Two Poems." *Epoch* (Ithaca NY) 32, No. 1 (Fall 1982): 82–83.
        ["If you are squeamish . . . "]—"Last Lyrics: From the Mystery"

D806   [Poems] *Rampike* (Toronto ON) 2, No. 3 (1982): 49, 55.
        "Strange Lady" [pub. under pseud. Ed Prato]—"The Grate Society"
        —"He's Sinking Fast"

"bp Nichol says I write fiction like an essayist, and criticism like a fiction writer; and I think he is right."
[GB Papers, Correspondence Eli Mandel, 31 October 1982, NL]

D807   [Poem] *Zest* (Nelson BC), No. 10 (November 1982): 17.
        "Phones Ring Out"

D808   [Story] *Prism International* (Vancouver BC) 21, No. 2 (Winter 1982): 51–57.
        "Four California Deaths" [Note: cover is dated December]

1983

D809   [Poem] *Helix* (Ivanhoe, Australia), No. 16 (1983): 24.

"Ice in Italy"
D810   [Poem] *Rampike* (Toronto ON) 3, No. 1 (1983): 36.
"The Ballad of the Little Shoemaker's Friend"
D811   [Poems] "Four Poems." *The Camrose Review* (Camrose AB), No. 4
[1983]: 28–29.
"Falling Thru"—"Valour Calls"—"Cool Streets"—"Mirrors Show"
D812   [Poem] *Zest* (Nelson BC), No. 11 (January 1983): 8.
"Tongue on Pollen"
D813   [Poems] *Brick* (Ilderton ON), No. 17 (Winter 1983): 40.
"Grace Requires Age"—"Pastoral Music"—"Monsieur Has Made"—
"Just As We Lose" [Note: poems are printed on back cover]
D814   [Essay] *Epoch* (Ithaca NY) 32, No. 2 (Winter/Spring 1983): 159–165.
"Ondaatje Learning to Do"
D815   [Essay] *The Review of Contemporary Fiction* (Elmwood Park IL) 3, No.
1 (Spring 1983): 55–62.
"Portrait of a Horse with Twenty-six Artists" [on William Eastlake's
Castle Keep]
D816   [Poem; Interview] *MRC* [Mount Royal College] *Reporter* (Calgary AB),
28 February 1983.
"Essaying Wah"—"Poetry and Politics Blend in Bowering," by Pat
Slater

"Biographically I have always been a loner. Friends tell me that I am a lone kind
of figure. Perhaps that is an inevitable outcome when you grow up smart in a
small town . . . .

"One of my favorite experiences is to be in a city all by myself knowing
nobody. I feel just as connected to people I don't know as to people I do know . . . .

"I don't hold for the American perception of the rugged individual. While an
artist is being an artist he may need to be rugged. But an artist is not an artist all
the time."
[GB quoted in "Poetry and Politics Blend in Bowering"; see D816]

D817   [Review] *Line* (Burnaby BC), No. 1 (Spring 1983): 89–93.
"Modernist Lives": a review of *Three on the Tower: The Lives and
Works of Ezra Pound, T. S. Eliot and William Carlos Williams,* by Louis
Simpson
D818   [Statement] *Books in Canada* (Toronto ON) 12, No. 5 (May 1983): 34.
"CanWit No. 81" [pub. under pseud. Ed Prato]
D819   [Review] *The Reader* (Vancouver BC) 2, No. 2 (June 1983): 6–8.
Incognito, by David Young: a review

D820   [Poem; Story] *The Literary Half-Yearly: Canadian Number* (Mysore, India) 24, No. 2 (July 1983): 67, 196–207.

        "Thea in Oliver"—"Old Bottles"

D821   [Statement] *Books in Canada* (Toronto ON) 12, No. 7 (August/September 1983): 41.

        "CanWit No. 83" [pub. under pseud. Ed Prato]

D822   [Essay] *Brick* (Ilderton ON), No. 19 (Fall 1983): 10.

        "Apt ology" [Note: subtitled "(being a preface that didn't make it into a book of essays)"; intended as a preface to *A Way with Words* (A38); see *Craft Slices*: "Tradition"; A44]

D823   [Excerpt from a poem] *Writing* (Nelson BC), No. 7 (Fall 1983): 14–19.

        "Elegy Three" [from *Kerrisdale Elegies*]

D824   [Review] *Line* (Burnaby BC), No. 2 (Fall 1983): 122–124.

        "Recent Reading" [on *Company*, by Samuel Beckett; *H. D.: The Life and Work of an American Poet*, by Janice S. Robinson; *Mantissa*, by John Fowles; *Plutonian Ode and Other Poems, 1977–1980*, by Allen Ginsberg]

D825   [Poems; Talk; Essay] "Five Poems." *Credences* (Buffalo NY) 2, Nos. 2 & 3 (Fall/Winter 1983): 19–21, 211–228, 276–288.

        "A Typewritten Poem"—"Lou"—"Stuck Wasps"—["When I/ take off my glasses . . . "]—["If you are squeamish . . . "] [Note: the untitled poems and part of "Stuck Wasps" are printed on the same page]—"The Roots of Present Writing" [GB with Daphne Marlatt, Fred Wah, Robert Creeley, Peter Culley, Victor Coleman, Steve McCaffery, bp Nichol, Joel Oppenheimer, and Robert Bertholf, 20 October 1980]—"Reaney's Region" [Note: this is the special "Canadian Poetry Festival" issue, a gathering held in Buffalo NY, 15–21 October 1980; organized by Robert Creeley and Warren Tallman]

D826   [Poems] *Zest* (Nelson BC), No. 15 (September 1983): 7, 27.

        "9/8/83"—"Bare E"

D827   [Poem] *The B. C. Monthly* (Vancouver BC), No. 33 (October 1983): n. p.

        "The Pope's Pennies"

1984

D828   [Excerpt from a poem] *True North/Down Under* (Lantzville BC), Annual No. 2 (1984): 5–16.

        "Elegy Two" [from *Kerrisdale Elegies*]

D829   [Poem; Excerpt from a poem] "Handling It." *The Canadian Forum* (Toronto ON) 63, No. 735 (January 1984): 22–23.

        "Yes, I Sold"—"Elegy One" [from *Kerrisdale Elegies*]

D830   [Poem; Translation] *Contemporary Verse II* (Winnipeg MB) 7, No. 4
        (January 1984): 28.
        "In the Field"—"Psalm Five," by Ernesto Cardenal

D831   [Letter] *Books in Canada* (Toronto ON) 13, No. 2 (February 1984): 33.
        "Sins of Omission" [pub. under pseud. Ed Prato]

D832   [Review] *American Poetry* (Albuquerque NM) 1, No. 3 (Spring 1984):
        90–91.
        H. D.: The Life and Work of an American Poet, by Janice S. Robinson:
        a review

D833   [Review] *Brick* (Ilderton ON), No. 21 (Spring 1984): 11–12.
        "Mom, Baseball and Beaver Pie": a review of *Cheering for the Home
        Team*, by William Humber

D834   [Statements] *Line* (Burnaby BC), No. 3 (Spring 1984): 34, 40.
        "Cuban Letter from Lionel Kearns": prefatory and concluding state-
        ments

D835   [Essay] *B. C. Studies* (Vancouver BC), No. 62 (Summer 1984): 9–28.
        "Home Away: A Thematic Study of Some British Columbia Novels"

D836   [Essay] *Books in Canada* (Toronto ON) 13, No. 6 (June/July 1984): 4–5.
        "Balancing the Books"

D837   [Excerpt from a novel] *Writing* (Vancouver BC), No. 10 (Fall 1984):
        30–32.
        Caprice [excerpt]

D838   [Poems; Excerpts from a novel] *Span* (Christchurch, New Zealand), No.
        19 (October 1984): 8–25.
        "The Pope's Pennies" [subtitled, "an attempt at an end to writing
        verse"]—*Caprice* [excerpt]

"Thea, do your piano practice! Oh, excuse me, I was sposed to shout that, not
type it. I am an automatic narrative plunker-down. I cant help myself, a slave of
Gutenburg or Cupertino."
[GB Papers, Correspondence Michael Ondaatje, 25 December 1984, NL]

D839   [Translation; Poem] *Rampike* (Toronto ON) 3, No. 3; 4, No. 1 (1984/85):
        17.
        "Spanish Burial" [adapted from Manuel Pacheco]—"Election Poem"

D840   [Statement; Excerpts from a novel] "Special Section: from *Caprice*."
        Epoch (Ithaca NY) 34, No. 2 (1984/85): 138–149.
        "What do readers have to know about the novel, *Caprice*?"—from
        Caprice: "Caprice Practises," "The First Indian Tells a Coyote Story,"
        "A Lesson on Race Relations," "Frank Spencer Has a Drink" [Note:

excerpts are titled here, but untitled in the book; includes a prefatory essay by editor, C. S. Giscombe, p. 138]

D841   [Story] *Prism International: 25 Years in Retrospect* (Vancouver BC) 23, No. 2 (Winter 1984): 180–186.

"Four California Deaths"

D842   [Excerpt from a poem] "Two Sections from 'Delayed Mercy'. *Epoch* (Ithaca NY) 34, No. 3 (1984/85): 165–178.

"Delayed Mercy": IV, V

1985

D843   [Interview] *Island* (Lantzville BC), Nos. 15 & 16 (1985): 23–34.

"Bowering on George Bowering's *Particular Accidents*," by Roy Miki

D844   [Essay] *Line* (Burnaby BC), No. 5 (Spring 1985): 38–58.

"A Great Northward Darkness"

"In Canada we were too young, too new for international Modernism. Nature was right outside the window. History had just recently put us here. Instead of the Imagists our poets copied the Georgians until the middle of the twentieth century. Our novelists were not interested in the Modernist game of stray fragments falling into patterns in the imagination. We had a land to people and a half-continent to name. We wrote well-constructed novels and moved in."
[From "A Great Northward Darkness"; see C184, D844, and A50]

D845   [Essay] *Books in Canada* (Toronto ON) 14, No. 3 (April 1985): 4–5.

"Between the Lines" [Note: GB's manuscript is titled, "There's Handwriting on My Manuscript"; also read on "Anthology" (CBC); see E78]

"This is a true story: yesterday an English professor asked me how I decided on the length of the lines in my poems. I said that it depended on two things—how I hear what's being said, and what size paper I'm writing on.

"In all the years that I have devoted to writing and reading literature, I have read only one discussion of the effect of the writing surface on the writing. That was the transcript of a discussion between Allen Ginsberg and Robert Creeley at the 1963 summer poetry extravaganza at the University of British Columbia.

"But I know from personal experience and talking with other writers, that critics are missing the boat because they dont consider such mundane things as whether the author wrote his novel in a stenographer's pad or on custom-made vellum."
[From "Between the Lines"; see D845 and E78]

D846   [Poem] *Canadian Literature* (Vancouver BC), No. 105 (Summer 1985): 68.
"Brown Cup, Dirty Glasses"

D847   [Poem] *Prism International* (Vancouver BC) 23, No. 4 (Summer 1985): 49.
"Bushy Considerations"

D848   [Essay; Talk] *Long-liners Conference Issue.* Ed. Frank Davey and Ann Munton. *Open Letter* (Toronto ON) Sixth Series, Nos. 2 & 3 (Summer/Fall 1985): 85–90, 120–124, 131–144, 153–164, 278–298.
"Stone Hammer Narrative"—Participation in various discussions [Note: The "Long-liners Conference on the Canadian Long Poem" was held in Toronto at York University, 29 May–1 June 1984; organized by Frank Davey, Ann Munton, and Eli Mandel]

D849   [Poems] *Origin* (Kyoto, Japan) Fifth Series, No. 6 (Fall 1985): 74–80.
"The Pope's Pennies"

D850   [Talk] *Line* (Burnaby BC), No. 6 (Fall 1985): 21–44.
" 'Syntax Equals the Body Structure': bpNichol, in Conversation with Daphne Marlatt and George Bowering," edited by Roy Miki

D851   [Interview] *Westerly* (Nedlands, Western Australia) 30, No. 4 (December 1985): 75–81.
"George Bowering: The Fact of Place on the Canadian West Coast," by Reginald Berry [Interviewed in Christchurch, New Zealand, 20 May 1984]

"Most of us in Vancouver who were doing the experimental writing and actually joining together in order to do so and work out some kind of poetic every day had to cross a whole pile of streets that had Spanish names. But none of us would be able to tell each other why those Spanish names were there, whether they were names of ships or people, or Spaniards back home. What were they? So, being pretty new to the working out of poetics coincided with being pretty new to that area, because none of us were from Vancouver—we were all from other places in the Interior, and on Vancouver Island, or up north, who had converged there at the same time. We got into history not the way a historian would but the way an archaeologist would—a street name is a

GB reading his paper at the Long-liners Conference, Toronto, 1984; see D848; drawing by James Reaney

finding, right? Then we'd go and dig and try to fill *up* the holes from there."
[From "GB: The Fact of Place on the Canadian West Coast"; see D851]

D852   [Review] *The Citizen* (Ottawa ON), 14 December 1985.
        "Two Short-Story Anthologies Show Canadians Equal to World's
        Best": a review of *85: Best Canadian Stories*, edited by David Helwig and
        Sandra Martin; *The New Press Anthology No. 2: Best Stories*, edited by
        John Metcalf and Leon Rooke
D853   [Poem] *Rampike* (Toronto ON) 4, Nos. 2 & 3 (1985/86): 8.
        "On the Radio"

1986

D854   [Essay] *Brick* (Toronto ON), No. 27 (Spring 1986): 17–18.
        "Western Writing" [Note: later adapted as part of *Caprice*]
D855   [Essay] *Canadian Literature* (Vancouver BC), No. 108 (Spring 1986):
        115–124.
        "Baseball and the Canadian Imagination"
D856   [Essay] *Room of One's Own* (Vancouver BC) 10, Nos. 3 & 4 (March
        1986): 86–98.
        "Munchmeyer and the Marys" [Note: a special issue on Audrey Thomas]
D857   [Excerpt from a poem; Poem] *Span* (Christchurch, New Zealand), No. 22
        (April 1986): 32–40.
        "Delayed Mercy": VII—"Paulette Jiles in Whitehorse"
D858   [Essay] *Read the Way He Writes: A Festschrift for bp Nichol*. Ed. Paul
        Dutton and Steve Smith. *Open Letter* (Toronto ON) Sixth Series, Nos. 5
        & 6 (Summer/Fall 1986): 7–20.
        "bpNichol on the Train"
D859   [Prose] *Brick* (Toronto ON), No. 28 (Fall 1986): 56–57.
        Errata: 1–10
D860   [Poem] *Landfall* (Christchurch, New Zealand) 40, No. 3; issue 159
        (September 1986): 281.
        "My Father in New Zealand"
D861   [Poems; Excerpts from a novel] *The Malahat Review* (Victoria BC), No.
        86 (September 1986): 135–151.
        "Berlin: Wish I Were"—"Birds in the Tiergarten"—"Every Night"—
        "The Difference"—"Personal Narrative"—"Hitler's Bunker"—"To Live
        In"—"Ku'damm Eck"—"Commonwealth Conference, Jagdschloss
        Glienicke"—from *Caprice*: "Telling Stories in the Old West"—"Where
        the Indians Came from" [Note: excerpts from *Caprice* are titled here, but
        untitled in the book]

1987

D862   [Poem] *Pig Iron* (Youngstown OH), No. 14 (1987): 76.
"Jacket Too Big"

D863   [Essay] *Australian-Canadian Studies* (Nathan, Queensland, Australia) 5, No. 1 (1987): 5–11.
"bpNichol on the Train"

D864   [Prose; Poems] *Mattoid*, Canadian Supplement (Victoria, Australia), No. 27 (1987): 24–33.
Errata: 1–10—"Paulette Jiles in Whitehorse"—"Pauline Butling in Campbell Lake"—"Constance Rooke in Sydney"—"Smaro Kamboureli in the Foothills" [Note: includes an introductory essay by Brian Edwards, "Here Come the Canadians," pp. 2–9]

D865   [Statement] *Books in Canada* (Toronto ON) 16, No. 1 (January/February 1987): 8–11.
"Writer's Writers" [Note: a collection of statements by writers on writers they are reading and why]

D866   [Prose] *Brick* (Ilderton ON), No. 29 (Winter 1987): 52–53.
Errata: 11–20

D867   [Essay] *Canadian Literature* (Vancouver BC), No. 112 (Spring 1987): 216–218.
"Milton Acorn (1923–1986)"

D868   [Prose] "Tributes from *Warren's Book.*" *Line* (Burnaby BC), No. 9 (Spring 1987): 8.
Errata: 31 [Note: *Warren's Book* is a single-copy volume of tributes to Warren Tallman on his retirement from UBC, compiled and produced by Peter Quartermain]

D869   [Essay; Excerpts from a novel] *Descant* (Toronto ON) 18, Nos. 1 & 2; issue Nos. 56 & 57 (Spring/Summer 1987): 101–116.
"I Would Even Wear One of Their Hats If It Wasn't So Dumb"—from *Caprice*: "The Elks Come to Town"—"Conversations About Caprice"—"A Rifle in Deep Center" [Note: excerpts from *Caprice* are titled here, but untitled in the book]

D870   [Prose] *Update: Newsletter of the B. C. English Teachers' Association* (Victoria/Duncan BC) 29, No. 3 (April 1987): 7–8.
Errata: 48, 49 [Note: placed in a section, "Margaret Laurence: Tributes to the First Lady of Canadian Literature"]

D871   [Story] *Rampike* (Toronto ON) 5, No. 3 ([Summer] 1987): 32–33.
"Spread Eagle"

D872   [Poem] *University of Toronto Review* (Toronto ON), No. 11 (Summer 1987): 2.
"Pauline Butling in Campbell Lake"

D873   [Essay] *The Whig-Standard Magazine* (Kingston ON), 11 July 1987.
        "The Hits and Myths of Baseball"
D874   [Poem] *Last Issue* (Calgary AB) 5, No. 1 (Autumn 1987): 28.
        "Time Magazine's Poem"
D875   [Prose] "Further Adventures of Errata." *Brick* (Toronto ON), No. 31 (Fall 1987): 48–50.
        Errata: 21–30

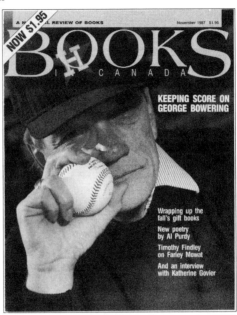

D876   [Prose] "Errata." *Line* (Burnaby BC), No. 10 (Fall 1987): 299–300.
        Errata: 58, 67. [Note: this issue was co-published with Talonbooks as a book, *Tracing the Paths*; see C204]
D877   [Poem] *Nexus* (Burnaby BC) 2, No. 3 (October 1987): 20.
        "Here in Attachment"
D878   [Letter] *The Sun* (Vancouver BC), 10 December 1987.
        "Not a Whole Lot Grammatical": To the Editor

GB on cover of *Books in Canada*, November 1987; see H604

D879   [Prose] "Selections from *Errata.*" *Prairie Fire* (Winnipeg MB) 8, No. 4 (Winter 1987): 6, 8.
        Errata: 1, 30, 46, 63, 65 [Note: part of a special feature on Robert Kroetsch]

1988

D880   [Prose] "Errata: A Continuing Story." *Brick* (Toronto ON), No. 32 (Winter 1988): 46–48.
        Errata: 31–40 [Note: listed in the table of contents as "The Further Adventures of Errata"]
D881   [Editor; Essays] *Sagetrieb* (Orono ME) 7, No. 1 (Spring 1988): 7–10, 131–141.

"Do You Know Who the Canadian Poets Are?"—"Language Women: Post-anecdotal Writing in Canada" [Note: a "Special Canadian Issue," co-edited by GB and Ken Norris]

D882   [Story; Interview] *West Coast Review* (Burnaby BC) 23, No. 1 (Spring 1988): 33–73.

"Staircase Descended"—"Extra Basis: An Interview with George Bowering," by Peter Quartermain and Laurie Ricou

D883   [Essay] *reVision* (Castlegar BC), (May 1988): 53, 62.

"Bring Back the WHA"

D884   [Excerpt from a poem] "Acrostic #4." By Mary Trainer. *Simon Fraser Alumni Journal* (Burnaby BC) 6, No. 1 (Summer 1988): 23.

"Elegy One" [excerpt] [see H618]

D885   [Interview; Statements] *Poets and Print: Barry McKinnon Talks with 10 British Columbia Poet/Publishers. Open Letter* (Toronto ON) Seventh Series, Nos. 2 & 3 (Summer/Fall 1988): 8–28.

"George Bowering," by Barry McKinnon [Note: includes reproductions of "Verbatims from a Notebook" from *Imago* 1; "A Note or Justification" from *Imago* 2; the cover of *Listen, George*; and "Preface" to *Imago* 20.

D886   [Prose] *Secrets from the Orange Couch* (Killam AB) 1, No. 2 (August 1988): 39–40.

Errata: 39, 40, 66, 71

D887   [Essay] *Descant* (Toronto ON) 19, No. 3 (Fall 1988): 18–24.

"Desire and the Unnamed Narrator" [in Margaret Atwood's *Surfacing*] [Note: GB, in conversation, referred to this title as a story written as an essay]

Section E
Other Works by George Bowering:
Audio-Visual, Broadsides, MA Thesis,
Postcards,
Dust Jacket Statements, etc.

Note on Audio-Visual entries:

Since the early 1960s, GB has appeared on many radio programs in various cities, often for only a brief reading or interview. The items listed here, although limited by the sources consulted, include the important entries for tapes and programs that are publicly accessible. GB's public readings were often recorded privately by individuals or institutions, so it was not feasible to list all of these. Tapes of readings housed in SFU's Contemporary Literature Collection, many of which were copied from GB's collection, are listed. Also listed are a selection of tapes in the GB Papers at the NL, especially those of readings on radio or at a significant literary event.

1958

E1   [Broadside] "Soliloquy on the Rocks." *Raven* (Vancouver BC), No. 7 (November 1958).
     9 x 12 in.; 22.5 x 30.5 cm. Black italicized print on a white background; poem is printed beside a drawing of an orange sun over an expanse of water. [Note: this issue consists of individual sheets in a folder; see D11]

1961

E2   [Video: Poem] CBC, 7 October 1961.
     "The Sunday Poem"

1962

E3   [Audio: Poems] "Anthology." CBC, 16 March 1962.
     "Locus Solus"—"Locus Primus"—"Telephone Metaphysic"—"Academy" [Note: this program featured GB, Lionel Kearns, David Bromige, and Gerry Gilbert]

1963

E4   [Essay; Poems; Excerpt from a poem] "Points on the Grid." By GB. Vancouver: UBC, MA thesis, 1963.
     "Universal and Particular: An Enquiry into a Personal Esthetic"—"Universal & Particular"—"Meta Morphosis"—"Circus Maximus"—"Points on the Grid"—"The Skier"—"Hideo Kobayashi"—"Moment of Truth"—"Husband"—"Leg"—"Poem for My Wife Angela"—"The Candle"—"The Sea Shore"—"Thru My Eyes"—"What Is It"—"Ed Dorn"—"In Your Yellow Hair"—"Rime of Our Time"—"Love & War Is Kind"—"The Critics"—"The Dance Complete"—"The Youthful Mother, a Shape upon Her Lap"—"My Garden"—"Forest Fire Summer"—"Vancouver Etude"—"Brave Horse Dream"—"For WCW" [excerpt]

E5   [Audio: Poems] "Wednesday Night." CBC, 27 March 1963.
     "The Sea Shore"—"The Dance Complete"—"The Youthful Mother, a Shape upon Her Lap"—"Rime of Our Time"—"In Your Yellow Hair"—"Thru My Eyes"

E6   [Audio: Poems] "New Canadian Writing." CBC, 13 August 1963.

"The Bread"—"Totems"—"Telephone Metaphysic"—"At Victory Square"

E7   [Audio: Poems] "Reading at University of Arizona" (Tucson AZ), 30 October 1963.

    60 minute tape. NL #12.

    Contents: GB reads "Situation," by Lionel Kearns—"Mount Norquay"—"Vancouver Island"—"The Measurer"—"Rime of Our Time"—"For WCW"—"Vancouver Etude"—"Thru My Eyes"—"Vancouver–Courtenay–Calgary"—"Divine Poem after Donne"—"East to West"—"Calgary"—"High River, Alberta"—"Park Love Poem"—"Inside the Tulip"—"Pender St. Sapphic"—"The Descent"—"Points on the Grid"—"My Garden"—"Steps of Love"—"Grandfather"—"Spanish B. C."—"The Sunday Poem" [Note: a program was printed; see E8]

E8   [Poems in a program] *George Bowering Reading Selections from His Poetry.* Program for GB's reading at the University of Arizona (30 October 1963); see E7. 11 pages; mimeo, stapled.

    "The Measurer"—"Vancouver Island"—"Ed Dorn"—"Rime of Our Time"—"For WCW"—"Vancouver Etude"—"My Garden"—"Forest Fire Summer"—"Family"—"Vancouver–Courtenay–Calgary"

1964

E9   [Poem in a program] *Poets at le Metro* (149 Second Avenue, New York NY), No. 12 (March 1964): n. p.

    "Open My Heart"

    Colophon: handwritten by the authors and published unedited and indiscriminately by Dan Saxon

1965

E10   [Broadside] *Estro* (Tucson AZ), No. 1 (March 1965).

    "Rocky Mountain Foot".

    $10^3/_4$ x $17^1/_4$ in.; 27.5 x 44 cm. Printed two-sided on brown cartridge paper with black print. Also printed one-sided: $17^1/_2$ x $22^1/_2$ in.; 44.5 x 57.4 cm. The first of a projected regular issue of broadsides.

    Contents: "The Road Tells"—"Calgary"—"(Interlude)"—"Alberta"—"The Blue"—"I Watch the Storm"—"Prairie"—"The Religious Lake"—"Dust"

E11   [Video: Play] "Shoestring Theatre." CBC, Montreal, 28 March 1965.

"What Does Eddie Williams Want?" [Note: according to a letter, 10 December 1974, from the CBC to GB, the kinescope of this play was not found and presumed destroyed. (GB Papers, Correspondence CBC, NL)]

E12   [Video: Play] CBC, Ottawa, c. August 1965. "What Does Eddie Williams Want?" [See E11]

E13   [Audio: Poems] "New Canadian Writing." CBC, 19 September 1965.
"The Name"—"To Gordon"

E14   [Audio: Essay] "Trans-Canada Matinée." CBC, 21 October 1965.
"On Not Being a Gringo in Mexico" [a travel piece]

GB at Harbourfront reading, Toronto, 1965; photograph by Karl Jirgens

1966

E15   [Broadside] *Pliego* [Orono ME], [No. 7] [1966].
"Divine Poem After Donne"
8¹/₂ x 17 in.; 21.5 x 43.3 cm. Printed on blue typewritten mimeo sheets. [See D282]

E16   [Poem in an ad] Hudson's Bay Company, c. 1966
"Okanagan Storm"
Black print on a white background with a sketch of a storm; sketch by Les Simoens; designed as a page-size ad for magazines; see D345 and D416.

E17   [Statement] *A Breakfast for Barbarians*. By Gwendolyn MacEwen. Toronto: Ryerson, 1966.
["A young woman with ... "] [on back cover]

E18   [Audio: Poems] "Anthology." CBC, 20 October 1966.
"The Grass"—"Albertasaurus"—"Tunnel Mountain" [Note: part of a program on new Canadian poetry, introduction and commentary by John Robert Colombo]

E19   [Audio: Poems] *Canadian Poets #1*. CBC, November 1966. Poets chosen by Robert McCormack, Robert Weaver, and William Young. Produced by Janet Sommerville.
12 in. LP; 33¹/₃ rpm.
"Breaking Up, Breaking Out"—"The Descent"—"Grandfather"— "Moon Shadow" [Note: this album was aired on "The Best of Ideas," 14 November 1966; also included Earle Birney, Leonard Cohen, Irving

Layton, Gwendolyn MacEwen, John Newlove, Alfred Purdy, and Phyllis Webb. The CBC ad for the record says, "Priced at $7.50, the album includes notes by Robert McCormack and pictures and biographies of the eight poets."]

E20   [Audio: Poems] "The Perceiving Self." "Ideas," Part 2. CBC, 4 November 1966. [Note: GB and Gwendolyn MacEwen read their poems on the CBC record *Canadian Poets #1*; see E19]

1967

E21   [Video: Poems] "Extension: Modern Canadian Poetry. Program 3: The Sixties." CBC, 14 May 1967, Toronto and Ottawa; 9 July 1967, Montreal.

"The Sunday Poem"—"The Hockey Hero" [Note: program 3 is part of a 13 week series, produced by John Kennedy and Terri Thompson; written, organized, and hosted by Phyllis Webb. GB was on with Earle Birney, Victor Coleman, and bp Nichol. The program notes say that these poets "talk about the 'Concrete Poetry Movement', the impact of American writers, the significance of little magazines and private presses—and they read their poems."]

GB, 1971

E22   [Audio: Interview] "Anthology." CBC, 10 August 1967.

GB interviewed by William French

E23   [Audio: Poems] "Anthology." CBC, 17 August 1967.

"Continental Drift"—"If I Fall Asleep"—"Stampede"—"Trees in Geneva"—"Even Los Angeles"—"If the Brain" [Note: the poems were read by Bruno Gerussi]

E24   [Broadside] *Quarry* Poster Series (Kingston ON), No. 4 (November 1967).

"Poem Written For George (2)."

37¹/₂ x 25 in.; 95 x 63 cm. Silkscreen poster with a drawing of black and purple concentric rings. Designed by David Brown.

E25   [Poems in a program] *Angry Arts Happening*. Montreal: Sir George Williams University, [1967]. Pp. 2–5.

"The Doubts"—"Animals That Eat"—"Winning"

1969

E26   [Card] Toronto: Ganglia, c. 1969.
"An Old Add"
3¹/₈ x 4¹/₄ in.; 8 x 10.8 cm. Printed on folded white bond paper.
Designed by bp Nichol.
Colophon: #28 in Ganglia's programme of presenting the other side of
some of Canada's better known sportswriters. A slice of 5¢ mom &
applepie madness from 29 gerrard west toronto canada. [Note: the word
"Ad" was changed to "Add" for this publication, the influence of bp
Nichol; see "An Old Ad," C45]

E27   [Audio: Interviews by] *Young Canadian Poets*. CBC radio series aired
Fridays, 18 April, 25 April, 2 May 1969, with GB as host and interviewer.
Poets interviewed were bp Nichol, David McFadden, Seymour
Mayne, Lionel Kearns, Pat Lane, and Gwendolyn MacEwen. A printed
program also exists.

E28   [Audio: Talk] CBC, 5 October 1969.
"Bowering: Speaking of Books" [GB
talks with Irving Layton and Hugh
Hood, moderated by Kerry Allard]
30 minute tape. GB Papers, NL #12.
[Note: the tape was transcribed and
edited by GB and published as "Jewish
Layton Catholic Hood Protestant Bowering," in *Open Letter*; see D620]

E29   [Audio: Poems; Story] "Bowering: The
Spoken Word." Agnes Etherington Art
Gallery, Queen's University, Kingston
ON, 27 November 1969. Taped for later
broadcast on CFRC arts program, "The
Spoken Word."

GB reading a book on William
Carlos Williams, with Michael
Ondaatje reading a TV guide,
Montreal, c. 1969

57 minute tape. GB Papers, NL #13.
"Far from the Shore"—"Inside the Tulip"—"The Dance Com-
plete"—"The Snow"—"The Beginning of"—"A Man Is No Boat"—
"Room & Alma"—"Constantinople Boots"—"Spelling/Rule"—"Frame"
—"Mouths"—"Otherwise Nobody Would Ever Have Remembered Joe"
—"Branches (for Ron Loewinsohn)"—"The Owl's Eye"—"Our Triple
Birth"—"Dobbin"—"Thru"—"The Mysteries"—"The Smooth Loper"
—"You Too"—"Play among the Stars"—"I Said I Said"—"Touch"

E30   [Audio: Poems; Story] "Anthology." CBC, 6 December 1969.

"My Real True Canadian Prophecy Poem"—"This Time"—"Poems Come Seven"—"Diem's Machine"—"The Smoking Mirror"—"The Footprint"—"The Water Flame"—"Constantinople Boots"

1970

E31   [Broadside] *The Orange Bear Reader* (Windsor ON), No. 7 [November 1970].
"The Owl's Eye"
10 x 13 in.; 25.4 x 33 cm. Printed in purple ink on white paper sheets flecked with purple; wrapped in a dark taupe folder.
Colophon: THE ORANGE BEAR READER issues monthly 500 copies of a new poem on individually wrapped broadsides. Individual Numbers 75¢, sets of 12, $6. Hand printed at The Coach House Press, Toronto.

1971

E32   [Video: Film] "Canadian Writers Series: George Bowering." TVOntario, 1971. BPN 3806.
28:10 minutes. Produced by Elizabeth Whelpdale and Kerry Feltham; directed by Graeme Gibson. [Note: filmed in Montreal]

E33   [Audio: Interview] "Poets of Canada: 1920 to the Present." "Anthology." CBC, 15 May 1971.
GB and many other writers talk about the creative process with Allan Anderson, in a seven part series; in same series, 22 May 1971, on what makes poets and their poetry Canadian; in same series, 12 June 1971, on young poets and the magazines *IS* and *Tish*; in same series, 26 June 1971, on the practical aspects of being a poet.

E34   [Audio: Poem] "Canadian Poets Reading." "Anthology." CBC, 6 November 1971.
"The House" [Note: a program on Canadian poets reading their favourite poems]

E35   [Audio: Poems] "George Bowering Reading in Vanier Hall" (Prince George BC), College of New Caledonia, 23 November 1971.
60 minute tape. SFU #223.
"As Introduction"—"Locus Solus"—"Grandfather"—"Far from the Shore"—"The Oil"—"The Cabin"—"Está Muy Caliente"—"The Beach at Veracruz"—*Baseball*—"Play among the Stars"—"Pharoah Sanders, in the Flesh"—"Single World West"—"The Raspberries"—"The Teeter

Totter"—"The Pollywogs"—"The Flying Dream"—"The Pool"—"The Gun"—"It"—"The Breaks"—"The Verandah"—"The Breaks"—"The Operation"—"The Flesh"—"The Scars"—"The Body"

1972

E36 [Audio: Poem] "Anthology." CBC, 12 February 1972.
George, Vancouver (a play for voices)
30 minute tape. GB Papers, NL #7. [Note: an adaptation of *George, Vancouver*, read by GB, Robert Clothier, and Peter Haworth, with GB also talking about writing the poem; see A12]

E37 [Audio: Poems] "Reading" (Medicine Hat AB), 23 February 1972.
60 minute tape. GB Papers, NL #6.
"The Snow"—"The Grass"—"The Crumbling Wall"—"The Cabin" —"The Oil"—"The Raspberries"—"The Teeter Totter"—"The Pollywogs"—"The Childhood"—"St. Louis"—"Place of Birth"—"The Breaks"—"Some Deaths"—"Composition"—"The Breaks"—"The First Two Towns"—"The Flying Dream"—"The Cloves"—"The Fingers"—"The Joints"—"Marianne Moore"—"bpNichol"—"Earle Birney"—"Stephen Spender"—"William Carlos Williams"

E38 [Audio: Talk; Poems] "The Practice of Poetry" (Burnaby BC), SFU, 27 July 1972.
108 minute tape. SFU #447. [Note: a panel discussion with GB, Fred Candelaria, Lionel Kearns, Stanley Cooperman, and Robin Blaser; moderated by Evan Alderson; GB talks about writing and reads "Composition," "The Code," "The Acts," and "It"]

1973

E39 [Audio: Talks] "Lectures for ENGLISH 414" (Burnaby BC), SFU, 11 September–6 December 1973.
29 tapes, 50 minutes each. SFU #660–688. [Note: twenty-nine lectures for a course on American poetry; topics include: Imagism, H. D.'s early poems and *Trilogy*, Gertrude Stein's writing, William Carlos Williams' *Paterson* and Charles Olson's *The Maximus Poems*]

E40 [Audio: Poems; Story] "George Bowering Reading at Capilano College" (North Vancouver BC), 24 October 1973.
46 minute tape. SFU #133; GB Papers, NL #14.

"Letter to Richard Nixon"—"The Big Leagues"—"The Bigamist"—"The Window"—"Nine Holes"—"Coltrane & Che"—"That Old Testament"—"Losing & Getting, to Be Getting"—"The Horse"—"Apparent"—"Frame"—"Sit Down"—"Strangers & Friends"—"The Ground of Lincoln County"—"Place Names in the Global Village"—"Smoking Drugs with Strangers"—"Indulgence"—"Take Me, She Said, Smiling Inwardly"—"Careering"—"The Breath, Release"—"While"—"To You & You"

E41   [Audio: Poem] "Anthology." CBC, 8 December 1973.

   Sitting in Mexico [Note: an adaptation of *Sitting in Mexico*, read by Anna Hagen and Ted Stidder; see A11]

1974

E42   [Audio: Interview] "This Country in the Morning." CBC, 30 January 1974.

   GB interviewed by Peter Gzowski

E43   [Audio: Talk] "This Country in the Morning." CBC, 20 February 1974.
   "Chinook Day"

E44   [Broadside] Western Front (Vancouver BC), 15 April 1974.
   ["Frame of Film the . . . "]
   9^{12}/₁₆ x 6⁷/₈ in.; 24.5 x 17.5 cm. White sheet folded in half as a card. One of nine in a folder, the other broadsides by Victor Coleman, Bill Hutton, David Cull, Barry McKinnon, Brad Robinson, Audrey Thomas, Fred Wah, Gerry Gilbert, and Carole Itter, with a Rick Simon print. Issued as *The B. C. Monthly* 2, No. 2 (February 1974–1977); see D705

E45   [Audio: Excerpts from a poem] "Radio International." CBC, 15 November 1974.
   Sitting in Mexico [excerpts]

1975

E46   [Audio: Interview; Prose] "GB Interviewed by Elizabeth Hay." CBC (Yellowknife NWT), [August 1975].
   15 minute tape. GB Papers, NL #1.

E47   [Audio: Poems; Excerpts from a novel] "George Bowering Reading His Poetry at Langara College" (Vancouver BC), 27 November 1975.
   50 minute tape. SFU #170; GB Papers, NL #9.

"Charles Olson"—"George Stanley"—"bpNichol"—"Gladys Hind-march"—"David McFadden"—"Alden Nowlan"—"Bill Bissett"—*A Short Sad Book*: I–X

1976

E48　[Postcard] *52 Pickup*, Card #19. Toronto: Dreadnaught Press, 1976.
"Daniel Johnson Lying in State"
6¼ x 4¾ in.; 15.9 x 12.1 cm. Printed on stiff white paper with a drawing of a receding trail of motorcycles at right. [Note: part of a deck of postcard poems]

E49　[Review in an ad] *Wanna Lift?* Toronto: The Coach House Press, 1976.
"Genreflect"
8½ x 11 in.; 22.5 x 28 cm. Two lime green sheets with black type, folded, unstapled. [Note: GB's re-view of David Young's *Agent Provocateur*, reprinted to advertise the novel; see A41, D716, and D719]

E50　[Broadside] Vancouver: Cobble-stone Press, 1976.
"My Lips Were Red"　　　　"Daniel Johnson Lying in State"; see E48
9⅜ x 15 in.; 23.7 x 38 cm. Letterpress on cream paper.
Colophon: Printed at Cobblestone Press for W. Hoffer in an edition of one hundred & twenty-six copies. April 7th, 1976.

E51　[Audio: Essay] "Rebound." CBC, 3 July 1976.
Profile of Diane Jones [See D780]

E52　[Audio: Talk] "Rap Session with GB, Lionel Kearns and Gerry Gilbert" (Burnaby BC), SFU, 23 November 1976.
55 minute tape. SFU #452.
[Notes: on early 60s in Vancouver writing and *Tish*; GB reads Kearns' "Top Coat"; Kearns reads GB's "Motor Age"; partly transcribed and published as "Vancouver Poetry in the Early 60s" in *The B. C. Monthly*; see D702]

1977

E53　[Audio: Talk] "Writer's Conference Panel on Fiction" (Nanaimo BC) Malaspina College, 25 March 1977.

Panel discussion with GB, Gladys Hindmarch, and Robert Kroetsch; moderated by John Harris.

90 minute tape. SFU #232A.

1978

E54   [Audio: Talk; Prose] "Bowering on Sunrise CFRO" (Vancouver BC), Spring 1978.

30 minute tape. GB Papers, NL #14.

[Note: on writing stories, early career, *Tish*, teaching poetry; reads "The Detroit Tigers"]

E55   [Audio: Poems] "Heritage Writers' Festival, Poetry Festival Night" (Burnaby BC), SFU, 27 May 1978.

GB reading with Robin Blaser, Brian Fawcett, Lionel Kearns, Daphne Marlatt, and Fred Wah; introductory remarks by Roy Miki and Warren Tallman.

120 minute tape. SFU #87.

"Last Lyrics: From the Mystery"—"Another Week in the East"—"Myself in the Capital"—"He in the Forest"—"They All Over Mexico"—"Which Poesy"—"Four Jobs" [excerpt]—"e.k."

[Note: for a review see H308; see also E56]

E56   [Broadside] *Six B. C. Poets.* Vancouver: Talonbooks, 1978.

"Last Lyrics: From the Mystery"

10 x 13 in.; 25 x 33 cm. Broadside #1 of a series enclosed in a folder. Printed on cream paper. Designed by Karl Siegler; edited by Roy Miki.

Colophon: SIX B.C. POETS | a series of six broadsides | limited to an edition of 350 copies | published by Talonbooks | especially for | the B.C. Heritage Poetry Festival |

LAST LYRICS: FROM THE MYSTERY

Thru the windows come
the low sun of March second
lies warm on my neck
white on the page

of soft hand-made paper
in the afternoon late
where poems are & shadow
of a vine, of my hair

where violins strive
around a gift the old stereo
gives, a note to envalue
the day, stolen

from notions of winter
two thousand miles east
& death someway old news
somehow familiar, remember

I said this
I was saying this

George Bowering

"Last Lyrics: From the Mystery"; see E56

---

held in the Simon Fraser University pub | on May 27, 1978 | as part of the Heritage Writers Festival | presented by the Department of English | and

Continuing Studies, Simon Fraser University. [Note: biographic sketch says GB was born in West Summerland BC in 1934]

E57   [Audio: Talk] "Heritage Writers' Festival Panel: Problems of the B. C. Writer" (Burnaby BC), SFU, 13 June 1978.
GB with John Mills and Audrey Thomas; moderated by Bruce Nesbitt.
103 minute tape. SFU #448.
[Note: comments by GB on *Burning Water*]

E58   [Audio: Poem] "Anthology." CBC, 14 October 1978.
"Four Jobs": "Thinning Apples"—"Trucking Peaches"—"Taking Pictures"—"Cleaning the Pool" [Note: published in *The Anthology Anthology*; see C167]

E59   [Performance: Play] Waterloo, Ontario, December 1978.
The Home for Heroes, performed by the Tabard Players

1979

E60   [Postcard] *CrossCountry* (Woodhaven NY/Montreal PQ), No. 12 (1979).
"Against Description"
5 x 6¹/₂ in.; 12.6 x 16.3 cm. Printed in two different colour designs: white card with title inset on a navy rectangle, poem printed in green; navy card with title on a green rectangle, poem printed in white. 750 copies printed. [Note: a special postcard issue; see D746]

E61   [Audio: Story] "Reading at Italian Cultural Centre" (Vancouver BC), 6 April 1979.
"Carter Fell"
30 minute tape. GB Papers, NL #8.

1980

E62   [Broadside] Prince George BC: 1980.
"Stuck Wasps"
9 x 12 in.; 22.7 x 30.5 cm. Printed on pale grey-green paper, with title and author's name printed in purple ink. Designed and printed by Barry McKinnon.
Colophon: 150 copies printed for WORDS LOVES | in Prince George B. C. 2.8.80.

E63   [Audio: Story] "Sunday Morning." CBC, 5 October 1980.
"Why Did It Have to be Mike Schmidt?"

1981

E64   [Audio: Excerpt from a novel] "Morningside." CBC, 1 April 1981.
        Burning Water: 33

E65   [Audio: Poems; Story; Essay; Excerpt from a novel] "The Coast Is Only
        a Line: Reading Series" (Burnaby BC), SFU, 4–5 August 1981.
        80 minute tape. SFU #343.
        "When I"—"Stuffed Horse"—"Brown Mountain"—"Match-Boxes"
        —"Spread Eagle"—"E"—"Talent 1967"—"The House"—"The White
        Station Wagon Strophes"—"The Believer"—"Mars"—"The Acts"—
        "The Scars"—"Fred Wah"—"Frank Davey"—*Allophanes*: IV, XII,
        XXVI—*A Short Sad Book*: XIX—"Old Standards" [excerpts]
        [Note: introductory and concluding remarks by Warren Tallman]

1982

E66   [Performance: Play] Sears Drama Festival, 12 February 1982.
        The Home for Heroes, performed by Guelph Centennial C. I.

E67   [Statement] *My Career with the Leafs & Other Stories*. By Brian Fawcett.
        Vancouver: Talonbooks, 1982.
        ["It is a relief and a joy . . . . "] [on back cover]

E68   [Broadside] Mission BC: Barbarian Press, 1982.
        "Just Five"
        6¹/₄ x 6¹/₄ in.; 15.8 x 15.9 cm. Letterpress on ice blue paper.
        Colophon: here first printed for the | *Pacific Northwest Library
        Association Conference* | August 25 to 27, 1982 | | *in an edition of one
        hundred copies* | by Crispin & Jan Elsted at Barbarian Press. [Note: "This
        is actually a William Hoffer, Bookseller, publication. It was organized for
        distribution at the PNLA Conference, but the Association declined to
        pay the hundred dollars the edition of 100 cost to print. As I was
        addressing a panel at the conference I decided to have it printed anyway,
        on the condition that I would come
        into the undistributed copies. It took
        six months to get them from the not too
        terribly lamented former librarian or-
        ganizer, and my stash of copies is now
        lost" (from *William Hoffer Catalogue:
        List 67*).]

E69   [Song lyric] *Too Much Isn't More*. By
        Gary Cramer.
        "Eat Your Brain"

> Just five old men are shaping all our graces
> and living known to few upon the land;
> churls of our time don't see their faces,
> knowing neither art nor artist's hand.
>
> Some fall into our favour only once;
> he shakes the country's spirit every year,
> and then few know of our deliverance
> denied the eyes of reason or of fear;
> but working close to heaven he persists,
> on matter made of earth his finger races;
> little do the dolts care of his fists
> that rime our pummelled earth with heaven's graces.

"Just Five"; see E68

12 in. LP; 33¹/₃ rpm. RQ [Red Queen] 1001. Produced and designed by Gary Cramer. Recorded and mixed at Offerman Music, RR #1, Nelson BC, 10–12 September 1979.

E70   [Audio: Quiz show] "Look That Up." CBC (Vancouver BC), 17 October 1982–4 January 1983; 6 December 1983–27 March 1984.
[Note: GB was a panelist on this weekly quiz program, hosted by Chuck Davis]

1983

E71   [Poster] *Writers in Hawaii.* University of Hawaii, 24 February 1983.
"In the Forest"
8¹/₂ x 14 in.; 21.7 x 35 cm. White paper with black print; poem framed by scrollwork triangles.
[Note: produced to advertise a reading]

1984

E72   [Poem in a calendar] *Poetry Agenda/Poésie.* Ed. Endre Farkas and Lucien Francoeur. Ste. Anne de Bellevue, Quebec: The Muses' Company/La Compagnie Des Muses, 1984. n. p.
"Easter Parade"

E73   [Audio: Talk] "Anthology." CBC, 10 March 1984.
"Bowering and Wedde": Marion Fraser moderating a talk with GB and New Zealand writer Ian Wedde

E74   [Audio: Essay] "Anthology." CBC, 7 April 1984.
"Serious Book Reviews" [Note: published in *Books in Canada* as "Balancing the Books"; see D836]

E75   [Audio: Essay] "Sunday Morning." CBC, 14 October 1984.
"Deadman Falls"

E76   [Performance: Play] Lethbridge, Alberta, November 1984.
The Home for Heroes, performed at the University of Lethbridge

E77   [Audio: Interview] "Anthology: B. C. Writing." CBC, 8 December 1984
GB with Phyllis Webb, Anne Cameron, P. K. Page, Daphne Marlatt, W. D. Valgardson, and Jack Hodgins, interviewed by Eleanor Wachtel

E78   [Audio: Essay] "Anthology." CBC, 15 December 1984.
"There's Handwriting on My Manuscript" [Note: published as "Between the Lines"; see D845]

" . . . when you are planning to write a novel you know you are in for a routine that will dominate your days for a year or two. With novels I like to set myself a routine I havent learned before. Maybe I think that will make it impossible to write the same book over and over.

"My first novel I just sat and typed with a manual typewriter on the kitchen table. When I was ready to do a novel about Captain Vancouver I took my index-card notes, bought three beautiful bound notebooks in Chinatown, and ten of my favourite German felt pens, and flew to Trieste. There I sat every day and wrote a thousand-word chapter, or as I like to think of it, ten pages of ink.

"My next one I did at home, on the same black no-nonsense hardback scribblers I do my diary in. Then I typed it up on my new word processor. It looked a lot different on the screen.

"This year I decided to write the novel I have been thinking of for seven years—a western that takes place in the Thompson Valley of British Columbia in 1889. Again I stayed home, but for a reason the reviewers will never bother to think of. I wrote it right on the computer screen. Every morning when I got up I looked forward to those hours at the quiet machine. Every time I had saved a chapter to disk I rewarded myself with a nice game of 'Frogger'.

"Now I am shopping for a little portable computer. The next novel is going to be written on the road somewhere. Maybe I can take it to the ballpark with me."
[From "There's Handwriting on My Manuscript"; see E78 and D845]

E79   [Audio: Poems] "Anthology." CBC, 19 January 1985.
       "B. C. Writing/Delayed Mercy"
       From *Delayed Mercy*: "A Pendulous Lip"—"Open Biology"—"Pen in Hand, Beard on Head"—"The Sink's Leaking"—"After the Dance"—"A Camera Sitting Idle"—"A Mask Over the Eyes"—"French Something in the Oven"—"Not an Equinox"—"Gross Herbs"—"A Swing in the Rain"—"Brown Socks in Bed"—"Late Romantic Broom"—"Motel Consideration"—"Facial Massage"

1985

E80   [Video: Interview; Excerpts from poems; Poem] "George Bowering."
       Canadian Literature (Author) Series. Council of Ministers of Education of Canada, 1985.
       "A Poem for High School Anthologies" [excerpt]—*Baseball*: "9th Inning"—"The Flying Dream"—"Desert Elm" [excerpt]
       15 minutes. [Note: part of a series of 25 programs featuring Canadian writers, packaged with *Canadian Literature: A Guide*; "GB" was

produced by the Provincial Educational Media Centre (PEMC) in BC, and features GB in Greenwood where he lived as a child and Oliver where he grew up and became a writer; see also C185 and E83]

1986

E81   [Statement] *Cambodia*. By Brian Fawcett. Vancouver: Talonbooks, 1986.
["Nowhere in Canada is there . . . ."]
[on back cover]

E82   [Statement] *Sitting in the Club Car Drinking Rum and Karma Cola*. By Paulette Jiles. Winlaw BC: Polestar Press, 1986.
["Paulette Jiles the fiction writer . . . ."]
[on back cover]

E83   [Video: Interview; Excerpts from poems; Poem] "George Bowering." *The Academy on Canadian Literature*. Produced by Michael McManus. The Ontario Educational Communications Authority, 1986.
30 minutes. BPN 271209.
"A Poem for High School Anthologies" [excerpt]—"The Brush Fire"—*Baseball*: "9th Inning"—"The Flying Dream"—"Desert Elm" [excerpt]
[Note: same video program as for E80, but packaged by TVOntario for a 10 program series on Canadian Literature, of which the GB program is number 9; the program includes an interview with Frank Davey by Sandra Martin, who hosts the series; see also H555 and C185]

E84   [Audio: Radio program] "State of the Arts." CBC, August 1986.
"Music in the Park"

E85   [Audio: Poem] "State of the Arts." CBC, December 1986.
"Post-Christmas Poem"

GB being filmed at the baseball field in Oliver BC, September 1983; see E80 and E83

1987

E86   [Statement] *Music at the Heart of Thinking*. By Fred Wah. Red Deer AB: Red Deer College Press, 1987.
["The word 'heart' contains . . . ."] [on back cover]

E87   [Statement] *Questions I Asked My Mother*. By Di Brandt. Winnipeg: Turnstone Press, 1987.

["She writes with a . . . ."] [on back cover]
E88   [Broadside] Toronto: Imprimerie Dromadaire, 14 March 1987.
"Pauline Butling in Campbell Lake"
7¹/₂ x 11¹/₈ in.; 18 x 28.2 cm. Letterpress on white paper; title printed in blue, figure of a diver in yellow under the title. Designed and printed by Glenn Goluska. Approximately 125 copies printed, of which 60 are numbered and signed.
[Note: part of *Nine Poets*, a series of broadsides produced for the Salon/Letters Reading Series: with GB, Stephen Rodefer, Phyllis Webb, Kate Van Dusen, Peter Culley, Gerry Gilbert, David Bromige, Victor Coleman, and August Kleinzahler]

E89   [Audio: Poems; Excerpts from a novel] "George Bowering Reading." NL, Ottawa, 14 May 1987.
56 minute tape. NL.
"Thanks, Bob"—"My Father in New Zealand"—"Thea in Oliver"—"Late Romantic Broom"—"Hardware Disguise"—"Glycerine Travel"—"Mop & Sky"—"Fair Cucumbers"—"Motel Consideration"—"Facial Massage"—*Caprice* [excerpts]—"Takhini" [Note: includes comments by GB on the writing of *Caprice*]

1988

E90   [Statement] *Anahistoric.* By Daphne Marlatt. Toronto: The Coach House Press, 1988.
["For years we have . . . ."] [on back cover]

Section F
Major Manuscript Collections
of George Bowering

The major collections of GB's papers are located in two places: Queen's University Archives and the Literary Manuscripts Division, National Library.

F1 Queen's University Archives:

The GB Papers at Queen's University were purchased in 1970 and consist, for the most part, of work during the period from 1958 to 1969. There is correspondence with various writers, including David McFadden, D. G. Jones, Al Purdy, John Newlove, and Margaret Randall, but the greater portion of the papers consists of manuscripts, working drafts, and typescripts of unpublished and published books, essays, stories, and poems.

The papers contain manuscripts of *George, Vancouver, Al Purdy* [called "The Man and the Poet"], and typescripts of *Baseball, Mirror on the Floor, The Silver Wire, Rocky Mountain Foot,* and *Points on the Grid.* There are also two unpublished novels, "Delsing" and "What Does Eddie Williams Want?", part of an unfinished novel, "Looking for Ebbe," and an unpublished travel narrative, "Eye-Kicks in Europe." The collection also includes some reviews of GB's publications.

Reference: *George Bowering Papers: Preliminary Inventory* (Kingston: Queen's University).

F2 National Library of Canada:

By far the most substantial collection of GB's papers is located in the NL. Among the wide array of materials, dated through to 1984, is an enormous correspondence between GB and friends, family, writers, magazines, and presses. GB started keeping copies of his correspondence in c. 1966, so the files from then on often contain letters to and from.

There are 55 boxes, which occupy 11 metres of shelf space, plus tapes and records, of which half contain correspondence to an amazing number of friends, writers, literary acquaintances, magazines, and presses, i. e. to and from virtually all quarters of his writing and life. The correspondence with individuals includes letters to and from Milton Acorn, Margaret Atwood, Margaret Avison, Nelson Ball, Earle Birney, bill bissett, Victor Coleman, Greg Curnoe, Frank Davey, Lionel Kearns, Robert Kroetsch, Red Lane, Margaret Laurence, Dorothy Livesay, Gwendolyn MacEwen, David McFadden, Barry McKinnon, John Newlove, bp Nichol, Al Purdy, Margaret Randall, Fred Wah, Phyllis Webb, and many others.

GB kept a record of poems written from 1955 on, with the date of composition noted, and these were kept in three-ring binders with 100 poems in each. Each binder is assigned a title; for instance, the first 100 are called "The Immaterialist"; the second 100 are "The Adventurist"; the third 100 are "The Palmodist." By

Ch. 14 – Composition

Consciousness is how it is composed. Consciousness is how it is composed. I told the Jungian professor there is no such thing as the subconscious. I decided to appear at his window where the blackness was to shout there is no subconscious. Consciousness is how it is composed. We cant go asleep I said to find out what we are thinking because then we are asleep. Or are we asleep. Consciousness is how it is composed. We are sometimes composed when we are awake. I think we are always being composed when we are awake and consciousness is how it is composed & we are it too because we are nobody's dream. When we dream we are awake. It is composed & not by us because we are in the composition. I say consciousness is how it is composed. Composition is how it is composed & that is how we are conscious so we never were asleep composing. I wanted to appear at his window before he fell asleep & tell him I was no dream. I may be romantic but I am no dream. That is simply the way I am composed. I am composed

Manuscript page, *Autobiology*; see A17

272

Manuscript: page 1, chapter 1, *A Short Sad Book*; see A29

25 November 1984, the last entry before GB sent his papers to the National Library, he had reached the seventeenth 100th, called "The Supertextualist."

For a long time, GB listed his poems separately, creating other lists for stories, essays, plays, and reviews, but in 1973 he started to list all his work, regardless of form, in one list. At the end of the three-ring binder recording his writing, GB also noted dates and places of publication.

Along with the three-ring binders of writing, the GB Papers contain notebooks with miscellaneous essays and reviews, manuscripts or typescripts of stories, plays, essays, and reviews, starting from university writing in the late 1950s and early 1960s through to 1984.

There are typescripts for most of GB's books, as well as manuscripts of *Genève*, *Autobiology*, "Irritable Reaching," *Kerrisdale Elegies*, *A Short Sad Book*, *Allophanes*, and *Burning Water*. Two unpublished novels, also in the GB Papers at Queen's University, are housed in the collection: "Delsing" (dated Vancouver 1961) and "What Does Eddie Williams Want?" (dated 1967).

Finally, the GB Papers contain files with reviews of his works, correspondence and material related to his teaching career and to his reading tours, and radio work.

Reference: *George Bowering Papers: Finding Aid* (Ottawa: National Library, 1987).

F3   Other Sources:

GB letters, manuscripts, and typescripts can be found in the papers of numerous writers and presses, for instance, in the Earle Birney Papers at the University of British Columbia, the Al Purdy Papers at Queen's University, the David McFadden Papers and the McClelland and Stewart Papers at McMaster University, the Papers of *El Corno Emplumado*, edited by Margaret Randall and Sergio Mondragón, at the University of Texas, to name but a few of many sources. A comprehensive listing of available GB papers has yet to be compiled.

Section G
Translations of Works
by George Bowering

1965

G1   [Poems in translation; Letters in translation] *The Man in Yellow Boots.* Trans. Sergio Mondragón. Mexico City: *el corno emplumado* No. 16, October 1965. Pp. 7, 9, 11, 13, 15, 17, 19, 21, 23, 25, 27, 29, 31, 35, 37, 39, 41, 43, 45, 47, 49, 51, 53, 55, 57, 59, 61, 63, 65, 67, 69, 71, 73, 75, 77, 79, 81, 83, 85, 87, 89, 91, 101–105.

"Penetrar" ["To Cleave"]—"Despues del Desayuno" ["After Breakfast"]—"La Maquina de Escribir" ["The Typewriter"]—"Poema para Mi Esposa Angela" ["Poem for My Wife Angela"]—"Que Pasa?" ["What Is It?"]—"Dentro del Tulipan" ["Inside the Tulip"]—"Helada" ["Frost"] —"Limite" ["The Measurer"]—"Sombra de Luna" ["Moon Shadow"]— "Pobre Hombre" ["Poor Man"]—"David"—"La Hierba" ["The Grass"] —"Vox Crapulous (titulo opcional: J. Edgar Hoover)" ["Vox Crapulous (alternate title: J. Edgar Hoover)"]—"El Dia Anterior a la Bomba de los Chinos" ["The Day Before the Chinese A-Bomb"]—"Su Acto Fue una Bomba" ["Her Act Was a Bomb"]—"Para WCW" ["For WCW"]— "Cafe Canadiense" ["Canadian Cafe"]—"Domingo en Calgary" ["Calgary Downtown Sunday"]—"El Buen Futuro" ["The Good Prospects"] —"El Columpio" ["The Swing"]—"Antigua Foto del Presente" ["Old Time Photo of the Present"]—"Mesa de Cocina" ["The Kitchen Table"] —"Recarga" ["Recharge"]—"Veranillo de San Martin" ["Indian Summer"]—"Old Cracker Barrel"—"Está Muy Caliente"—"El Muro Derruido" ["The Crumbling Wall"]—"Profesores de Ingles" ["The English Teachers"]—"El Descenso" ["The Descent"]—"Aire Moviente" ["The Shifting Air"]—"Deshaciendose, Liberandose" ["Breaking Up, Breaking Out"]—Cartas de George Bowering *al corno emplumado* [Letters from George Bowering to *el corno emplumado*] [Note: see A3 and D262]

1966

G2   [Poem in translation] *Parva* (Mexico), No. 5 (May/June 1966): 14–15.

"Paisaje en Tlalpan" ["Tlalpan Scene," trans. Jose Ma. de la Pena]

G3   [Poem in translation] *Revista de los Viernes* (Montevideo, Uruguay) [c. November 1966]

"Vox Crapulous"

G4   [Poem in translation] *Les Lettres Nouvelles: Ecrivains du Canada* (Paris, France), numéro special (Décembre 1966/Janvier 1967): 31.

"Canadian Pacific Railway" ["CPR Window," trans. Serge Fauchereau] [Note: edited by Maurice Nadeau]

1969

G5   [Essay in translation] *Ellipse* (Sherbrooke PQ), No. 1 (Fall 1969): 48–51.
"Quelques bénis parmi les maudits," trans. Raynald Desmeules
[Note: GB's English title on the manuscript is "A Few Blesst among Les
Maudits"; published only in French, this essay provides a brief overview
of postwar English-Canadian poetry]

G6   [Poem in translation] *Cormoran y delfin* (Buenos Aires, Argentina), No.
19 (October 1969): 115.
"Déjenme Entrar Déjenme Salir" ["Let Me In Let Me Out," trans.
Manuel Betanzos Santos]

1970

G7   [Excerpts from poems in translation] *Canada* [for the 1970 Japan World
Exposition]. Ed. Peter Desbarats. Montreal, 1970. Pp. 65, 70, 73, 76, 104.
"Forecast" [excerpt]—"Cold Spell" [excerpt]—"Winter Tan, a Joke
Poem" [excerpt]—"Angela Sleeping" [excerpt]—"Mud Time" [ex-
cerpt]—"Back in Vancouver for a Vancouver Visit" [excerpt] [Note:
trans. into Japanese]

1971

G8   [Essay in translation] *Ellipse* (Sherbrooke PQ), Nos. 8 & 9 (1971):
128–140.
"Ce Hurlement que j'entends" ["How I Hear *Howl*," trans. Marc
Lebel]

1973

G9   [Essay in translation] *Ellipse* (Sherbrooke PQ), No. 13 (1973): 82–103.
"D. G. Jones: 'Etre chez soi dans le Monde' " ["D. G. Jones: 'Coming
Home to the World'," trans. Rodolphe Lacasse]

1977

G10   [Poems in translation] *Înţelegînd Zapada: Antologie a poetilor canadieni
de limbă engleză*. Ed. and trans. Virgil Teodorescu and Petronela Ne-
gosanu. Bucureşti: Editura Univers, 1977. Pp. 164–167.

"Istoria Poeţilor: Heathcliff" ["History of Poets: Heathcliff"]—
"Noaptea Dinaintea Dimineţii" ["The Night before Morning"] [Note:
bio-bibliography on p. 164]

1979

G11   [Poem in translation] *Yang 91: Made in Canada* (Ghent, Belgium), No. 6
        (December 1969): 146–147.
        "Het Ei" ["The Egg," trans. Achilles Gauthier] [See D759]

1982

G12   [Poem in translation] *Canada with Love/Canada avec Amour.* Ed. Lor-
        raine Monk. Toronto: McClelland and Stewart, 1982. N. p.
        "First Night of Fall, Grosvenor Ave." [trans. Gail Vanstone; see C148]
G13   [Novel in translation] *En eaux troubles.* [Montreal]: Quinze, 1982.
        Burning Water [trans. L.-Philippe Hébert; see A35]

1983

G14   [Poems in translation] *Gótika a va-*
        donban: Kanadai angol nyel-
        vükötök. [Ed. Köpeczi Béla]. Trans.
        Györe Balázs [Budapest, Hungary]:
        Európa Könyvkiadó, 1983. Pp. 193–
        200.
        "Nagyapa" ["Grandfather"]—
        "A Hinta" ["The Swing"]—"Hi-
        rek" ["News"]—"W. C. W.–Nek"
        ["For WCW"]—"Igy, a szavak-
        ban" ["That Way, in Words"]

GB with the author, in the back yard of
GB's childhood home in Greenwood BC,
September 1983

1985

G15   [Poems in translation] *Antología de la Poesía Anglocanadiense Contem-*
        poránea. Ed. and trans. Bernd Dietz. Barcelona, Spain: Los Libros de la
        Frontera, 1985. Bilingual edition. Pp. 181, 183, 185.

"La Hierba" ["The Grass"]—"Veranillo Indio" ["Indian Summer"]—
"Olvidamos" ["Forget"] [See C175]

1986

G16   [Excerpt from a novel in translation] *Die Horen* (Hanover, Germany) 31,
No. 1; issue no. 141 (1986): 35–37.
"Ein Kurzes, Trauriges Buch" [*A Short Sad Book*: XXI, trans. Michael
Mundhenk] [Notes: a special issue on Canada, edited and translated by
Michael Mundhenk; contributor's note on p. 212 says GB was born in
Okanagan Falls BC]

G17   [Story in translation] *Erkundungen: 26 Kanadische Erzähler*. Ed. Karla
El-Hassan and Helga Militz. Berlin: Verlag Volk und Welt, 1986. Pp.
85–92.
"Der Rasenmäher" ["The Lawnmower," trans. Andrea Sachs]

1987

G18   [Essay] *Merian* (Hamburg, Germany) 40, No. 6 (June 1987): 98.
"Bedrohtes Paradies" ["Paradise Threatened," trans. Michael Mund-
henk] [Note: on Malcolm Lowry]

G19   [Poems] *Luceaiárul*, 8 August 1987.
"Párul lui Artaud" ["Artaud's Hair"]—"Red Lane"—"Istorie Con-
temporaná" ["Contemporary History"]—"Poem Social Pentru Robert
Lindner" ["Social Poem for Robert Lindner"] [Note: "Revistá Editatá de
Uniunea Scriitorilor din Repubica Socialista Romania"]

G20   [Essay in translation] *Nuit Blanche* (Quebec City PQ), No. 29 (Oc-
tober/November 1987): 44–48.
"Le Baseball et L'Imaginaire Canadien" ["Baseball and the Canadian
Imagination," trans. Sylvie Chaput; see D855]

1988

G21   [Poems in translation] *Iton 77* (Israel), No. 10 (March/April 1988): 34.
"Inside the Tulip"—"The Grass" [Note: produced by the Beit-Berl
Kibbutz]

Section H
Works on George Bowering

Section H contains a substantial, but not exhaustive, list of works on GB. Some reviews, especially those published outside of North America, could not be located to verify by the time of publication, and others were too trivial to be included. Nevertheless, the list incorporates a wide range of material: reviews, essays, newspaper profiles, bibliographies, and essays and books where GB is discussed with other writers. By December 1988, no book length study of GB has been published.

The following categories, placed in brackets at the beginning of each entry, are used to describe the type of work: Review, Essay, Letter, Poem, Statement (includes a creative prose piece that is not poetry or fiction), Interview, Bibliography, Bio-critical sketch, Biographic sketch.

To help readers make more efficient use of Section H, three types of references have been isolated: 1) short reviews that are both short in length and slight in content; 2) reviews that are, in substance and scope, essays; 3) reviews, essays, and books that do not focus primarily on GB but provide a contextual understanding of his work, even in cases where the comments on GB may be minimal. These special references appear with the category of the entry, following a slash: e. g. [Review/Short], [Review/Essay], [Essay/Context]. The term "Essay" is used in the broadest sense to refer not only to standard critical essays, but also to journalistic profiles.

1961

H1   [Letter] Hermont, Pete. "Join MUSSOC Mr. Bowering?" *The Ubyssey* (Vancouver BC), 6 October 1961: 5. [Note: a response to GB's recent "Placebo," inviting him to join a campus theatre group]

H2   [Essay] [Bromige, David]. " 'Pish', by George Boring." *The Ubyssey* (Vancouver BC), 1 December 1961: 8. [Note: a pseudonymous parody]

H3   [Essay] "Bowering's Writing Gaining Acclaim." *The Oliver Chronicle* (Oliver BC), 19 January 1961.

1962

H4   [Letter] Purdy, Al. "Dear *Tish*." *Tish* (Vancouver BC), No. 15 (13 January 1962): 2. [Note: criticizes GB's review of Milton Acorn's *Against a League of Liars* in the last issue]

H5   [Poem] Davey, Frank. "A Repudiation For GB." *Tish* (Vancouver BC), No. 7 (14 March 1962): 5.

H6   [Essay] Creeley, Robert. "Preface." *Sticks & Stones*. By GB. Vancouver: Tishbooks, [c. May 1962]. Pp. 3–5. [See A1]

H7   [Essay/Context] Davey, Frank. "Anything But Reluctant." *Canadian Literature* (Vancouver BC), No. 13 (Summer 1962): 39–44. Also in *The Making of Modern Poetry in Canada* and *The Writing Life*; see H44 and H231

H8   [Letter] Mayne, Seymour. *The Canadian Forum* (Toronto ON) 42, No. 499 (August 1962): 111. [To the editor: a response to GB's review of Raymond Souster's *Place of Meeting* in the May issue]

H9   [Poem] Lane, R. S. "Big Benzedrine (an open letter to George Bowering)." *Tish* (Vancouver BC), No. 12 (14 August 1962): 4.

H10   [Letter] Chamberlin, Ted. "Grand Slam." *The Ubyssey* (Vancouver BC), 16 November 1962: 4. [To the editor: a response to GB's reviewing]

1963

H11   [Letter] Bromige, David. "Bricks from Bromige." *The Ubyssey* (Vancouver BC), 14 February 1963: 4. [To the editor: on the Suzanne Mowat interview of GB]

H12   [Letter] Bromige, David. "Boring/Much." *The Ubyssey* (Vancouver BC), 21 February 1963: 4–5. [To the editor: lampoon of the Mowat interview of GB]

H13   [Letter] Duncan, Robert. *Genesis West* (Burlingame CA) 1, No. 4 (Summer 1963): 319. [Note: primarily a statement about *Genesis West* to explain why Duncan would not write an introduction to GB's poems]

H14   [Statement] Childs, Barney. *Genesis West* (Burlingame CA) 1, No. 4 (Summer 1963): 309–310. [Note: introduces the GB poems in the issue]

H15   [Essay/Context] Newlove, John. "The Poetry Scene: It's Alive, Man, in B. C.—But the Poets Are Unknown." *The Sun* Supplement (Vancouver BC), 26 July 1963. [Note: includes a biographical note]

1964

H16   [Review/Context] McCarthy, Brian. *Evidence* (Toronto ON), No. 8 (1964): 127–133. Review of *Poetry '64* [Note: brief comment on *Tish* poets]

H17   [Essay/Context] Bergé, Carol. *The Vancouver Report*. New York: Fuckpress, February 1964. [Colophon: "A FUCK YOU press publication printed, published & zapped by Ed Sanders at a secret location in the lower east side New York City, U. S. A. February 1964 year of the writhing squack."] [Note: a report on the 1963 Poetry Conference at UBC; also in *The Writing Life*; see H231]

H18   [Review] Webb, Phyllis. *The Canadian Forum* (Toronto ON) 44, No. 520 (May 1964): 46. Review of *Poetry '64* [Note: GB contributed ten poems; Webb comments on GB, Davey, and Kearns and quotes from GB's "Eyes That Open"]

H19   [Review] Fiamengo, Marya. "Perennial Puritanism." *Canadian Literature* (Vancouver BC), No. 21 (Summer 1964): 71–72. Review of *Points on the Grid*

H20   [Review] Webb, Phyllis. "Bowering's Poems Show Real Energy." *The Sun* Supplement (Vancouver BC), 10 July 1964. Review of *Points on the Grid*

H21   [Review] Howith, Harry. *Canadian Author & Bookman* (Toronto ON) 40, No. 1 (Autumn 1964): 17. Review of *Points on the Grid*

H22   [Review] Purdy, Alfred W. "Western and Montreal." *The Fiddlehead* (Fredericton NB), No. 62 (Fall 1964): 65–68. Review of *Points on the Grid* [and *That Monocycle the Moon*, by Seymour Mayne]

H23   [Review] Sowton, Ian. "Moving from Word to Word." *Edge* (Edmonton AB), No. 3 (Autumn 1964): 119–122. Review of *Points on the Grid*

H24   [Statement] Stevens, Peter. "A Counterblast to Mr. Bowering." *Canadian Literature* (Vancouver BC), No. 22 (Autumn 1964): 78–80. [Note: a response to GB's "Poets in Their Twenties"; see D177]

1965

H25   [Review] Gnarowski, Michael. *Culture* (Quebec City PQ), No. 26 (1965): 335–336. Review of *Points on the Grid*

H26   [Poem] Kearns, Lionel. "Listen, George . . . " *Tish* (Vancouver BC), No. 28 (January 1965): 3–5. [Note: a sequence on trains, from the longer work with the same title; see B1 and D211]

H27   [Review/Short] McCloskey, Mark. *Poetry* (Chicago IL), No. 105 (January 1965): 270–273. Review of *Points on the Grid* [and six other books]

H28   [Essay/Context] Davey, Frank. "Black Days on Black Mountain." *The Tamarack Review* (Toronto ON), No. 35 (Spring 1965): 62–71. [Note: also in *The Writing Life*; see H231]

H29   [Review] Dawson, David. "Notes: in Reaction/Response." *Tish* (Vancouver BC), No. 29 (March 1965): 9–10. Review of *Points on the Grid*

H30   [Review] Wilson, Milton. "Letters in Canada 1964: Poetry." *University of Toronto Quarterly* (Toronto ON) 34, No. 4 (July 1965): 349–370. Review of *Points on the Grid* [and other books of poetry in 1964]

H31   [Essay] Randall, Margaret. "George Bowering: One of the Few of Our Generation Who Shall Be Remembered." *Arts in Mexico* (Mexico City) 2, No. 8 (29 August 1965). [Note: GB's poem, "Sonata, Opus 722," is published at the end of the article; see D243]

H32   [Letter] Signed, Some Kind of a Nut. *Evidence* (Toronto ON), No. 9 [Fall 1965]: 129. [To the editor: on poems by GB and Lionel Kearns and GB's essay, in No. 7; see D151]

H33   [Review] Nava, Thelma. "Notas de Poesía." *El Dia* (Mexico City), 8 October 1965. Review of *The Man in Yellow Boots*

H34   [Review/Short] Fulford, Robert. *The Star* (Toronto ON), 13 October 1965. Review of *The Man in Yellow Boots*

H35   [Review/Short] Randall, Margaret. *Kulchur* (New York NY) 5, No. 20 (Winter 1965/66): 92–93. Review of *Listen, George*, by Lionel Kearns [Note: includes a lengthy passage from *Listen, George*]

1966

H36   [Review/Short] *Poésie Vivante* (Geneva, Switzerland), No. 16 (January 1966): 21. Review of *The Man in Yellow Boots* [Note: GB's poem "What Is It"/"Que Pasa?" is published alongside the review]

H37   [Review/Short] Coleman, Victor. "Now We Are Six." *The Canadian Forum* (Toronto ON) 45, No. 542 (March 1966): 283–284. Review of *The Man in Yellow Boots* [and *The Gathering*, by David Bromige; *Bridge Force*, by Frank Davey]

H38   [Essay/Context] Dudek, Louis. "Poetry of the Sixties: The Little Decade of the Children's Crusade." *Parallel* (Montreal PQ), No. 1 (March/April 1966): 32–33.

H39   [Letter] Davey, Frank. "Dear George." *The Open Letter* (Victoria BC) First Series, No. 3 (April 1966): 14–16. [Note: an open letter to GB on *The Man in Yellow Boots*]

H40   [Review] Grier, Eldon. "Emotional Postcards." *Canadian Literature* (Vancouver BC), No. 29 (Summer 1966): 69–70. Review of *The Man in Yellow Boots*

H41   [Essay] Lyttik, George. "George Bowering: Portrait of a Poet As an Alive Man." *The Albertan* (Calgary AB), 27 August 1966.

H42   [Review] Lacey, Edward A. (pseud.) "Poetry Chronicle." *Edge* (Edmonton AB), No. 5 (Fall 1966): 97–107. Review of *The Man in Yellow Boots* [and five other books, including *The Cariboo Horses*, by Alfred Purdy]

1967

H43   [Essay/Context] Davey, Frank. "How to Use a University." *Evidence* (Toronto ON), No. 10 (1967): 119–123.

H44   [Essay/Context] Davey, Frank. "Anything But Reluctant." *The Making of Modern Poetry in Canada: Essential Articles on Contemporary Canadian Poetry in English*. Ed. Louis Dudek and Michael Gnarowski. Toronto: The Ryerson Press, 1967. Pp. 222–227. Also in *Canadian Literature* and *The Writing Life*; see H7 and H231

H45   [Review] Harrison, Keith. "Poetry Chronicle." *The Tamarack Review* (Toronto ON), No. 42 (Winter 1967): 74–76. Review of *The Silver Wire* [and other books]

H46   [Review/Context] Weaver, Robert. "Steeling Themselves." *The Tamarack Review* (Toronto ON), No. 42 (Winter 1967): 92–93. Review of *Modern Canadian Stories*

H47   [Review/Short] Dodsworth, Martin. *London Magazine* (London, England) Second series, 7, No. 1 (April 1967): 111–114. Review of *The Silver Wire* [and three other books]

H48   [Review/Short] "Some Novel Novels and Non-Novels." *The Montreal Star* Supplement (Montreal PQ), 22 April 1967. Review of *Mirror on the Floor* [and three other books]

H49   [Review] Fess, Craig W. *The London Evening Free Press* (London ON), 29 April 1967. Review of *Mirror on the Floor*

H50   [Review/Short] Evans, Eleanor. *Commentator* (Toronto ON) 11, No. 5 (May 1967): 30. Review of *Mirror on the Floor*

H51 [Review] Godfrey, W. D. "Andrea or Andre." *The Canadian Forum* (Toronto ON) 47, No. 556 (May 1967): 45–46. Review of *Mirror on the Floor* [and *Place D'Armes*, by Scott Symons]

H52 [Review] Grosskurth, Phyllis. "New Canadian Novels." *Saturday Night* (Toronto ON) 82, No. 5 (May 1967): 39, 41. Review of *Mirror on the Floor* [and *The Last of the Crazy People*, by Timothy Findley; *Willows Revisited*, by Paul Hiebert]

H53 [Review] Vincent, Don. *20 Cents Magazine* (London ON) 1, No. 9 (May [1967]): n. p. Review of *Mirror on the Floor*

H54 [Review] Parton, Lorne. "The Written Word." *The Province* Supplement (Vancouver BC), 5 May 1967. Review of *Mirror on the Floor*

H55 [Review] Clute, John. "Pro Poet But Novice Novelist." *The Globe and Mail* Supplement, 6 May 1967. Review of *Mirror on the Floor*

H56 [Review] Kattan, Naim. "De la Colombie-Britannique au Nouveau Brunswick." *Le Devoir* (Montreal PQ), 27 May 1967. Review of *Mirror on the Floor* [and *Watcha Gonna Do Boy—Watcha Gonna Be?*, by Peter Taylor; *Willows Revisited*, by Paul Hiebert]

H57 [Review] MacCallum, Hugh. "Letters in Canada 1966: Poetry." *University of Toronto Quarterly* (Toronto ON) 36, No. 4 (July 1967): 354–379. Review of *The Silver Wire* [and other books of poetry in 1966]

H58 [Review] Spray, Carole. *The Fiddlehead* (Fredericton NB), No. 72 (Summer 1967): 87–88. Review of *Mirror on the Floor* [and *In the Balance*, by Violet Anderson]

H59 [Review] Gerwing, Howard B. *B. C. Library Quarterly* (Vancouver BC) 31, No. 1 (July 1967): 29. Review of *Mirror on the Floor*

H60 [Review] Dalt, Gary Michael. "Fiction Chronicle." *The Tamarack Review* (Toronto ON), No. 45 (Autumn 1967): 114–117, 120–122. Review of *Mirror on the Floor* [and other novels]

H61 [Review] Dudek, Louis. "Trouncing the Younger Poets." *Canadian Literature* (Vancouver BC), No. 34 (Autumn 1967): 80–84. Review of *The Silver Wire* [and *During Rain, I Plant Chrysanthemums*, by M. Lakshmi Gill; *The Scarred Hull*, by Frank Davey]

H62 [Review] Kask-Rapoport, Janet. *Our Generation* (Montreal PQ) 5, No. 2 (September 1967): 124–127. Review of *Mirror on the Floor* [and *The Day Is Dark*, by Marie-Claire Blais; *Place D'Armes*, by Scott Symons]

H63 [Review/Short] "Capsule Reviews." *Canadian Author & Bookman* (Toronto ON) 43, No. 2 (Winter [December] 1967): 24. Review of *Mirror on the Floor*

H64 [Review] Gwinn, Claudia. "Poet's Words in a Novel." *The Sun* Supplement (Vancouver BC), 15 December 1967. Review of *Mirror on the Floor*

1968

H65   [Statement] Toppings, Earle. "Grandfather." *Solitary Walk: A Book of Longer Poems*. Toronto: The Ryerson Press, 1968. Pp. 35–40. [Note: a brief biographic sketch precedes, and notes to GB's poem "Grandfather" follow; see C18]

H66   [Review] Bernstein, John. "Protest and Pain." *The Minnesota Review* (St. Paul MN) 8, No. 2 (1968): 186–187. Review of *Mirror on the Floor*

H67   [Review] Greenberg, Alvin. *El Corno Emplumado* (Mexico City), No. 25 (January 1968): 143–144. Review of *Mirror on the Floor*

H68   [Review/Short] Bell, Marvin. "Nine Canadian Poets." *Poetry* (Chicago IL) 111, No. 5 (February 1968): 323–328. Review of *The Silver Wire* and *The Man in Yellow Boots* [and eight other books, including *The Scarred Hull*, by Frank Davey]

H69   [Review] Woodcock, George. "Mod Murders." *Canadian Literature* (Vancouver BC), No. 36 (Spring 1968): 74–77. Review of *Mirror on the Floor* [and *Alley Jaggers*, by Paul West]

H70   [Review] Duncan, Chester. "New Canadian Poetry." *Canadian Dimension* (Winnipeg MB) 5, No. 4 (April/May 1968): 39–40. Review of *The Silver Wire* [and *Selected Poems*, by F. R. Scott; *New Wings for Icarus*, by Henry Beissel]

H71   [Review] Draayer, Ken. *Quarry* (Kingston ON) 17, No. 4 (Summer 1968): 46–47. Review of *Mirror on the Floor*

H72   [Review/Short] MacCallum, Hugh. "Letters in Canada 1967: Poetry." *University of Toronto Quarterly* (Toronto ON) 37, No. 4 (July 1968): 359–382. Review of *Baseball* [and other books of poetry in 1967]

H73   [Review/Short] Stedmond, J. M. "Letters in Canada 1967: Fiction." *University of Toronto Quarterly* (Toronto ON) 37, No. 4 (July 1968): 382–390. Review of *Mirror on the Floor* [and other books of fiction in 1967]

H74   [Review/Short] Randall, Margaret. *El Corno Emplumado* (Mexico City), No. 27 (July 1968): 148. Review of *Baseball* [and *The Dainty Monsters*, by Michael Ondaatje]

H75   [Review] Benedikt, Michael. "The Shapes of Nature." *Poetry* (Chicago IL) 113, No. 3 (December 1968): 188–215. Review of *Baseball* [and other books of poetry]

1969

H76   [Statement] "Bowering, George 1935– (The Panavision Kid)." *Contemporary Authors*. Vols. 21–22. Detroit: Gale Research Company, 1969. P. 68.

H77   [Review/Context] Livesay, Dorothy. *The Far Point* (Winnipeg MB), No. 2 (Spring/Summer 1969): 51–57. Review of *The Collected Poems of Red Lane*, by Red Lane

H78   [Review] Stainsby, Don. "The Poet Who Knows Alberta." *The Sun* (Vancouver BC), 14 March 1969. Review of *Rocky Mountain Foot*

H79   [Review] Pearson, Alan. "A Poet's Love of the Land." *The Montreal Star* Supplement (Montreal PQ), 22 March 1969. Review of *Rocky Mountain Foot*

H80   [Review] Schroeder, Andreas. "Would-Be Poets Who Are Deluding Themselves." *The Province* Supplement (Vancouver BC), 28 March 1969. Review of *Rocky Mountain Foot*

H81   [Review] Law, Carl. "A Canadian Accent on Poetry." *The Gazette* (Montreal PQ), 29 March 1969. Review of *Rocky Mountain Foot*

H82   [Review/Short] Weaver, Robert. "Irving Layton Refuses to be Pushed Aside by a New Generation." *The Star* (Toronto ON), 29 March 1969. Review of *Rocky Mountain Foot* [and *The Whole Bloody Bird*, by Irving Layton; *Passage of Summer*, by Elizabeth Brewster]

H83   [Review] Brewster, Elizabeth. "New Collection of Poems of Special Interest Here." *The Edmonton Journal* (Edmonton AB), 3 April 1969. Review of *Rocky Mountain Foot*

H84   [Review] Stubbs, Roy St. George. "Imagination and Judgment." *The Winnipeg Free Press* Supplement (Winnipeg MB), 12 April 1969. Review of *Rocky Mountain Foot*

H85   [Review] Van Steen, Marcus. "Love Poems Inspired by Province of Alberta." *The Citizen* (Ottawa ON), 3 May 1969. Review of *Rocky Mountain Foot*

H86   [Review] Downes, G. V. "Calgary Poems Become a Social Documentary." *Victoria Daily Times* (Victoria BC), 10 May 1969. Review of *Rocky Mountain Foot*

H87   [Review] Hamilton, Jacques. "A Young Poet's Bitter-Sweet Look at Calgary." *The Herald* Supplement (Calgary AB), 16 May 1969. Review of *Rocky Mountain Foot*

H88   [Review] Fetherling, Doug. "Poems and Poets, Good and So-So." *The Globe and Mail* Supplement, 24 May 1969. Review of *Rocky Mountain Foot* [and three other books]

H89   [Review] Barbour, Douglas. *The Dalhousie Review* (Halifax NS) 49, No.
       2 (Summer 1969): 289–295. Review of *Rocky Mountain Foot* [and five
       other books, including *Frames*, by Daphne Marlatt]
H90   [Review] Hunt, Russell A. *The Fiddlehead* (Fredericton NB), No. 80
       (May/July 1969): 99–101. Review of *Rocky Mountain Foot*
H91   [Review/Short] J. W. C. [John W. Chalmers] "New Books of Poetry."
       Canadian Author & Bookman (Toronto ON) 44, No. 4 (Summer 1969):
       18, 20, 22. Review of *Rocky Mountain Foot* [and other books]
H92   [Review/Short] Fetherling, Doug. *The Five Cent Review* (Montreal PQ)
       1, No. 1 (June 1969): 6–7. Review of *Rocky Mountain Foot*
H93   [Review/Short] S. A. "Alberta Poetry." *The Star-Phoenix* (Saskatoon
       SK), 13 June 1969. Review of *Rocky Mountain Foot*
H94   [Review] Gustafson, Ralph. "Virtue Is Not Enough." *Canadian Litera-
       ture* (Vancouver BC), No. 42 (Autumn 1969): 72–77. Review of *Rocky
       Mountain Foot* [and four other books, including *The Whole Bloody Bird*,
       by Irving Layton]
H95   [Review] Harris, David W. "From the Silver Quarry." *Alphabet* (London
       ON), No. 16 (September 1969): 64–65. Review of *The Silver Wire*
H96   [Essay] McFadden, David. "Poets Influenced by Kerouac." *The Specta-
       tor* (Hamilton ON), 1 November 1969. [Note: profile of GB]

1970

H97   [Bibliography; Bio-critical sketch] "Bowering, George." *Contemporary
       Poets*. Ed. Rosalie Murphy and James Vinson. New York: St. Martin's
       Press, 1970. Pp. 122–123. [Note: says GB was born in Keremeos BC on 1
       December 1938; see also H210]
H98   [Essay/Context] Jones, D. G. "Chapter 7: An Ancient Slang Or a Mod-
       ern." *Butterfly on Rock: A Study of Themes and Images in Canadian
       Literature*. Toronto: University of Toronto Press, 1970. Pp. 163–192.
H99   [Review] Purdy, Al. *Wascana Review* (Regina SK) 5, No. 2 (1970): 53–63.
       Review of *The Gangs of Kosmos* [and five other books, including *The
       Journals of Susanna Moodie*, by Margaret Atwood]
H100   [Essay/Context] Mortimer, Hilda. "The West Coast Poets." *The Mon-
       treal Star* Supplement (Montreal PQ), 24 January 1970.
H101   [Review] van Huyse, Nadine. "Book's Mood Like a Trip." *The Daily
       Ryersonian* (Toronto ON), 6 February 1970. Review of *The Gangs of
       Kosmos*
H102   [Review] Brewster, Elizabeth. "Bowering's Best Poetry." *The Edmonton
       Journal* (Edmonton AB), 20 February 1970. Review of *The Gangs of
       Kosmos*

H103   [Review] John, Brian. "Canadian Poets Excel." *The Spectator* (Hamilton ON), 28 February 1970. Review of *The Gangs of Kosmos* [and *Year of the Quiet Sun*, by Ian Young]

H104   [Review] Barbour, Douglas. "The Young Poets and the Little Presses, 1969." *The Dalhousie Review* (Halifax NS) 50, No. 1 (Spring 1970): 112–126. Review of *The Gangs of Kosmos* [and other books of poetry in 1969]

H105   [Review] Heyen, William. "Sensibilities." *Poetry* (Chicago IL) 115, No. 6 (March 1970): 426–429. Review of *Rocky Mountain Foot* [and three other books]

H106   [Review] Cooke, Peter. "Enough to Make Portnoy Complain." *The Gazette* (Montreal PQ), 11 April 1970. Review of *The Gangs of Kosmos*

H107   [Essay] "Montreal Poet Wins Top Award." *The Gazette* (Montreal PQ), 14 April 1970. [Notes: on winning the Governor General's Award for Poetry in 1969, for *Rocky Mountain Foot* and *The Gangs of Kosmos*; see also the news article, "Literary Award Presentations Held Under Tight Security," *The Ottawa Journal*, 12 May 1970; the awards ceremony was held on May 11, and officials expected nationalist students to protest the presence of an American on the Canada Council jury, namely Warren Tallman from BC, but the protest did not occur]

H108   [Review] Duncan, Chester. "Two Books of Poetry." *The Winnipeg Free Press* Supplement (Winnipeg MB), 18 April 1970. Review of *The Gangs of Kosmos* [and *Year of the Quiet Sun*, by Ian Young]

H109   [Review] Gibbs, Robert. *The Fiddlehead* (Fredericton NB), No. 85 (May/June/July 1970): 108–110. Review of *The Gangs of Kosmos*

H110   [Review/Short] McCarthy, Brian. "Less Than Meets the Eye." *The Montreal Star* Supplement (Montreal PQ), 9 May 1970. Review of *Rocky Mountain Foot* and *The Gangs of Kosmos* [and eight other books]

H111   [Essay/Context] Sypnowich, Peter. "Our Literary Prize-Givers Just Love the Controversy." The Star (Toronto ON), 12 May 1970. [Note: on the Canada Council awards]

Photograph of GB reproduced with Frank Davey's "Play Ball!"; see H112

H112   [Essay] Davey, Frank. "Play Ball! The Message of George Bowering." *UBC Alumni Chronicle* (Vancouver BC) 24, No. 2 (Summer 1970): 13–15.

H113   [Review/Short] Marshall, Tom. "Canpo: A Chronicle." *Quarry* (Kingston ON) 19, No. 4 (Summer 1970): 50–54. Review of *The Gangs of Kosmos* and *Sitting in Mexico* [and other books of poetry]

H114   [Review/Short] Hornyansky, Michael. "Letters in Canada 1969: Poetry." *University of Toronto Quarterly* (Toronto ON) 39, No. 4 (July 1970): 324–337. Review of *Rocky Mountain Foot* [and other books of poetry in 1969]

H115   [Letter] Abbey, Lloyd. "The Organic Aesthetic." *Canadian Literature* (Vancouver BC), No. 46 (Autumn 1970): 103–104. [Note: a response to GB's "Why James Reaney Is a Better Poet"; see D394]

H116   [Review] Swaine, Mary. *The McGill Daily* Supplement (Montreal PQ), 16 October 1970. Review of *Two Police Poems* [Note: "No Solitudes" by GB is published with the review; see D533]

1971

H117   [Poem] McFadden, David. "History of Poets: George Bowering." *Poems Worth Knowing*. Toronto: The Coach House Press, 1971. N. p. Also in *Open Letter* (Toronto ON) Second Series, No. 4 (Spring 1973): 58.

H118   [Review/Short] Shucard, Alan. "The O-Zone And Other Places." *Canadian Literature* (Vancouver BC), No. 48 (Spring 1971): 80–82. Review of *The Gangs of Kosmos* [and three other books]

H119   [Review] May, Scott. "Sensitivity in Evidence in Bowering's Verse." *The Albertan* (Calgary AB), 20 March 1971. Review of a reading

H120   [Review] Vernon, Lorraine. "The Craftsman Poet." *The Sun* Supplement (Vancouver BC), 8 April 1971. Review of *Al Purdy*

H121   [Review/Short] Fetherling, Doug. "Poetic Journal." *The Tamarack Review* (Toronto ON), No. 57 (Second Quarter 1971): 80–84. Review of *George, Vancouver* [and other books]

H122   [Review] Rose, Mildred A. *Skylark: The Official Publication of the Saskatchewan English Teachers' Association* (Saskatoon SK) 7, No. 4 (Summer 1971): 60. Review of *Vibrations*, edited by GB

H123   [Review] Stevens, Peter. "Essence and Breath As Signs of Life." *The Globe and Mail* Supplement, 28 August 1971. Review of *Touch* [and *Collected Poetry*, by Louis Dudek]

H124   [Review] Moss, John G. *The Fiddlehead* (Fredericton NB), No. 91 (Fall 1971): 107–109. Review of *The Story So Far*, edited by GB

H125 [Essay] Jankola, Beth. "Don't Ever Call Me 'Chicken' Again, George Bowering." *The Georgia Straight* (Vancouver BC) 5, No. 197 (31 August–3 September 1971): 20. [Note: essay includes "Roger Falling" from *Autobiology*]

H126 [Review/Short] *Choice* (Middletown CT) 8, No. 8 (October 1971): 1009. Review of *Al Purdy*

H127 [Review] Morley, Patricia. "To Intensify Life." *The Ottawa Journal* (Ottawa ON), 9 October 1971. Review of *Touch*

H128 [Review] Van Steen, Marcus. "Anti-Devices Device Flops." *The Citizen* (Ottawa ON), 9 October 1971. Review of *Touch*

H129 [Review] Calder, Margaret. *The Gateway* (Edmonton AB) 62, No. 10 (13 October 1971): 9. Review of *Touch*

H130 [Review] Lynd, Ted. "Language Lifted Out of the Ordinary." *The Ubyssey* (Vancouver BC), 15 October 1971: 6. Review of *Touch*

H131 [Review] Davey, Frank. *The Varsity* (Toronto ON), 22 October 1971. Review of *Genève* and *Touch*

H132 [Review] Garnet, Eldon. "Two Bowerings Embrace Past, Present, Future." *Saturday Night* (Toronto ON) 86, No. 11 (November 1971): 46, 49–50. Review of *Genève* and *Touch*

H133 [Review] Stephen, Sid. *The Gateway* (Edmonton AB), 25 November 1971: 13. Review of *Genève*

H134 [Review/Short] Stevens, Peter. "Creative Bonds in the Limbo of Narcissism." *The Globe and Mail*, 4 December 1971. Review of *Genève* [and five other books, including *Selected Poems*, by Phyllis Webb]

H135 [Review] Nugent, John L. *The Fiddlehead* (Fredericton NB), No. 93 (Winter 1971): 109–110. Review of *Touch* [Note: both No. 88 and No. 93 were labelled "Winter 1971," and with this issue the magazine commenced numbering the last issue of the year "Winter," instead of the first]

H136 [Review] Davey, Frank. "A Note on Bowering's *Genève*." *Open Letter* (Toronto ON) Second Series, No. 1 (Winter 1971/72): 42–44. Review of *Genève*

1972

H137 [Bibliography; Bio-critical sketch] Cameron, Donald. "Bowering, George." *Contemporary Novelists*. Ed. James Vinson. New York: St. Martin's Press, 1972. Pp. 142–145. [Note: says GB was born in Keremeos BC on 1 December 1938]

H138 [Essay/Context] Mitchell, Beverley Joan. "A Critical Study of the *Tish* Group, 1961–1963." MA Thesis, University of Calgary, 1972.

H139   [Biographic sketch; Poem] Geggie, Mary, and Peter Whalley. "Splurge Sowering"—"Inside the Pickled Walnut." *Northern Blights.* Morin Heights PQ: Upbank Press, 1972. P. 38. [Note: also includes an introductory essay with comments on Splurge Sowering's book on Ab Surdy]

H140   [Poem] McFadden, David. "George Bowering." *Intense Pleasure.* Toronto/Montreal: McClelland and Stewart, 1972. P. 72.

H141   [Review] Lawrance, Scott. "George Bowering's 'George Vancouver'." *Raincoast Chronicles* (Madeira Park BC), No. 1 (1972): 30–31. Review of *George, Vancouver*

H142   [Review/Short] Aspinall, Dawn. "Made in Canada: New Books, 1971." *Canadian Dimension* (Winnipeg MB) 8, Nos. 4 & 5 (January 1972): 54–55. Review of *The Story So Far*, edited by GB, *Touch*, and *Genève* [and other books]

H143   [Review] Kasper, Michael. *B. C. Library Quarterly* (Vancouver BC) 35, No. 3 (January 1972): 44–46. Review of *Touch*

H144   [Review/Short] Lawford, Diane. *Quarry* (Kingston ON) 21, No. 1 (Winter 1972): 75–80. Review of *The Story So Far*, edited by GB [and *The Fruit Man, the Meat Man and the Manager*, by Hugh Hood; *Fourteen Stories High*, edited by Tom Marshall and David Helwig; see C39]

H145   [Review/Short] Moss, John G. "Five Canadian Short Story Anthologies." *Journal of Canadian Fiction* (Fredericton NB) 1, No. 1 (Winter 1972): 79–81. Review of *The Story So Far*, edited by GB [and four other books, including *Sixteen by Twelve*, edited by John Metcalf; see C33]

H146   [Essay] Van Luven, Lynne. "Ceaseless Search for the 'Perfect' Poem." *The Red Deer Advocate* (Red Deer AB), 26 February 1972. [Note: report of a visit by GB to Red Deer College, including transcribed comments by GB]

H147   [Review] Francis, Wynne. "The Distinctive Voice of George Bowering." *Monday Morning* (Toronto ON) 6, No. 7 (Spring 1972): 23. Review of *Touch*

H148   [Review] Kennedy, Murray. "Throw Da Ball." *The Grape* (Vancouver BC), No. 9 (16–23 March 1972): 21. Review of *Autobiology*

H149   [Review/Short] Vernon, Lorraine. "8 From Weed/Flower." *The Sun Supplement* (Vancouver BC), 14 April 1972. Review of *George, Vancouver* [and seven other books, including *The Other Side of the Room*, by bp Nichol]

H150   [Review] Barbour, Douglas. *The Canadian Forum* (Toronto ON) 52, No. 616 (May 1972): 68–69. Review of *Al Purdy* [and *Earle Birney*, by Frank Davey; *A. M. Klein*, by Miriam Waddington]

H151   [Review] Coleman, Victor. *Open Letter* (Toronto ON) Second Series, No. 2 (Summer 1972): 80–81. Review of *Autobiology*

H152   [Review] Gairdner, William D. *Open Letter* (Toronto ON) Second Series, No. 2 (Summer 1972): 64–70. Review of *The Story So Far*, edited by GB

H153   [Review/Short] Hornyansky, Michael. "Letters in Canada 1971: Poetry." *University of Toronto Quarterly* (Toronto ON) 41, No. 4 (Summer 1972): 325–341. Review of *Genève* and *Touch* [and other books of poetry in 1971]

H154   [Review/Short] Rudzik, O. H. T. "Letters in Canada 1971: Fiction." *University of Toronto Quarterly* (Toronto ON) 41, No. 4 (Summer 1972): 308–318. Review of *The Story So Far*, edited by GB [and other books of fiction in 1971]

H155   [Review] Green, Paul. "Cold Touch from Bowering." *The Sun* Supplement (Vancouver BC), 7 July 1972. Review of *Touch* and *Genève*

H156   [Interview/Context] Robinson, Brad and Stan Persky. *An Oral History of Vancouver: Stan Persky's Section*. Vancouver: Beaver Kosmos, [c. August] 1972. Also in *The Writing Life*; see B2 and H231

H157   [Review] Frazer, Ray. "Lip Projects." *Books in Canada* (Toronto ON) 1, No. 9 (August 1972): 26–27. Review of *Autobiology* [and *The Day*, by Stan Persky]

H158   [Review] Sutherland, Fraser. "Foreign Fabulous Free." *Books in Canada* (Toronto ON) 1, No. 10 (August 1972): 19–21. Review of *The Story So Far*, edited by GB [and three other books]

H159   [Review] New, William H. "Poet and Person." *Canadian Literature* (Vancouver BC), No. 54 (Autumn 1972): 90–92. Review of *Al Purdy* [and *Margaret Avison*, by Ernest Redekop]

H160   [Review] Purdy, Al. "The Woman of Barrie." *Canadian Literature* (Vancouver BC), No. 54 (Autumn 1972): 86–90. Review of *Touch* [and three other books, including *Nobody Owns th Earth*, by bill bissett]

H161   [Review] Scobie, Stephen. "You Gotta Have Heart." *Books in Canada* (Toronto ON) 1, No. 11 (October 1972): 31–32. Review of *Touch* and *Genève*

H162   [Review] Kearns, Lionel. "Recycled Self." *The B. C. Monthly* (Vancouver BC) 1, No. 2 (November 1972): 84–85. Review of *Autobiology*

H163   [Essay/Context] Stevens, Peter. "The State of Canadian Poetry." *Quill & Quire* (Toronto ON) 38, No. 12 (December 1972): 2–3.

H164   [Letter] Acorn, Milton. "Bowering: The Laws of Language? Or of Empire?" *Blackfish* (Burnaby BC), Nos. 4 & 5 (Winter 1972/Spring 1973): n. p. [Note: a response to GB's response to Acorn's "Avoid the Bad Mountain"; see D607]

1973

H165   [Essay/Context] Denham, Paul. "Introduction." *The Evolution of Canadian Literature in English 1945–1970.* Ed. Paul Denham. Toronto: Holt, Rinehart and Winston, 1973. Pp. 6–7. [Note: GB's "A Sudden Measure" is quoted]

H166   [Review] Wagner, Jeanie M. *Wascana Review* (Regina SK) 8, No. 1 (Spring 1973): 62–67. Review of *Al Purdy* [and *Earle Birney*, by Frank Davey; *Margaret Avison*, by Ernest Redekop; and *A. M. Klein*, by Miriam Waddington]

H167   [Essay/Context] Gervais, C. H. "Vancouver's *Tish* Movement." *Alive* (Guelph ON), No. 26 ([March] 1973): 31–35. Also in *The Writing Life* and published as a chapbook, *Tish: A Movement*; see H175 and H231

H168   [Review] Harlow, Robert. "Confections Beyond Our Bestsellers." *Maclean's* (Toronto ON) 86, No. 3 (March 1973): 96. Review of *The Story So Far*, edited by GB [and *72: New Canadian Stories*, edited by David Helwig and Joan Harcourt; *Columbus and the Fat Lady*, by Matt Cohen]

H169   [Review] Brett, B. T. "Is George Bowering a Fool?" *The Peak* (Burnaby BC), 7 March 1973: 8. Review of *Imago* 17, edited by GB

H170   [Review/Short] Hornyansky, Michael. "Letters in Canada 1972: Poetry." *University of Toronto Quarterly* (Toronto ON) 42, No. 4 (Summer 1973): 366–380. Review of *The Sensible* [and other books of poetry in 1972]

H171   [Review/Short] Klepac, Walter. "Getting It All Apart." *Books in Canada* (Toronto ON) 2, No. 3 (July/September 1973): 11–12. Review of *IS* 12 & 13, edited by GB and Victor Coleman [and *File* Magazine; *International Image Exchange Directory*] [See D609]

H172   [Letter] Woodcock, George. *Maclean's* (Toronto ON) 86, No. 8 (August 1973): 18. [To the Editor: a response to GB's "The Art of the Webfoot"; see D623]

H173   [Review] Doyle, Mike. "Perhaps Profound." *Canadian Literature* (Vancouver BC), No. 58 (Autumn 1973): 108–109. Review of *George, Vancouver* [and *Old Friend's Ghosts*, by Victor Coleman]

1974

H174   [Essay; Bibliography] Davey, Frank. "George Bowering." *From There to Here*. By Frank Davey. Erin ON: Press Porcépic, 1974. Pp. 57–62.

H175   [Essay/Context] Gervais, C. H. *Tish: A Movement*. Guelph ON: Alive Press, 1974. Pp. 5–21. Also in *Alive* and *The Writing Life*; see H167 and H231

H176   [Review] Fulford, Robert. "Canadian Poetry Resembles Forsyte Saga." *The Star* (Toronto ON), 16 February 1974. Review of *Curious*

H177   [Review] Gervais, Marty. "Bowering on a See-Saw." *The Windsor Star* (Windsor ON), 16 February 1974. Review of *Curious* and *In the Flesh*

H178   [Review] Pearson, Alan. "Curious Indeed These Wisps of Words, This Dual Bowering." *The Globe and Mail* Supplement, 16 February 1974. Review of *Curious* and *In the Flesh*

H179   [Review] J. W. R. R. "Bowering's Poetic View after 30." *The Star-Phoenix* (Saskatoon SK), 22 February 1974. Review of *In the Flesh*

H180   [Review] Whitney, Paul. *B. C. Library Quarterly* (Vancouver BC) 37, No. 4 (Spring 1974): 56–57. Review of *Curious*

H181   [Poem] Hanson, Joan. "Bowering." *The Canadian Forum* (Toronto ON) 53, No. 638 (March 1974): 30.

H182   [Review] Barbour, Douglas. "Publish Frequently, Be Damned Frequently." *The Edmonton Journal* (Edmonton AB), 2 March 1974. Review of *Curious*, *In the Flesh*, and *Layers 1–13*

H183   [Review] Wyatt, Louise. "Unmemorable Poetry Worth Second Reading." *The London Evening Free Press* (London ON), 9 March 1974. Review of *In the Flesh*

H184   [Review] Suknaski, Andrew. "George Bowering Unfolding." *The Albertan* Supplement (Calgary AB), 9 March 1974. Review of *In the Flesh*

H185   [Review] McFadden, David. "Bowering Eyes Pro Ranks." *The Spectator* (Hamilton ON), 16 March 1974. Review of *Curious* and *In the Flesh* [and four other books, including *A Choice of Dreams*, by Joy Kogawa]

H186   [Review] Kidd, Z. Chilko. "ZCK Curious (Chartreuse)." *The Peak* (Burnaby BC), 20 March 1974. Review of *Curious*

H187   [Review/Short] "Naked to the World." *The Sheaf* (Saskatoon SK), 27 March 1974. Review of *In the Flesh*

H188   [Review] Nodelman, Perry. "Two Books of Poems." *The Winnipeg Free Press* Supplement (Winnipeg MB), 6 April 1974. Review of *In the Flesh* [and *A Choice of Dreams*, by Joy Kogawa]

H189   [Review] Roney, Stephen. "Clearing His Throat." *The Whig-Standard* (Kingston ON), 25 April 1974. Review of *In the Flesh*

H190   [Review] Bragg, Bob. "A Poignant Awareness of Life." *The Herald* Supplement (Calgary AB), 26 April 1974. Review of *In the Flesh* [and *Snakeroot*, by Gary Geddes; *Songbook*, by Douglas Barbour]

H191   [Review] Riter, Roberta. "Poet Recaps UBC Scene." *The Sun* Supplement (Vancouver BC), 26 April 1974. Review of *Curious* and *In the Flesh*

H192   [Review/Essay] Douglas, Charles. "Between the Landscape & the Scene." *The Lakehead University Review* (Thunder Bay ON) 7, No. 1 (Summer 1974): 123–130. Review of *Curious* and *In the Flesh*

H193   [Review] Sorestad, Glen. *Skylark: The Official Publication of the Saskatchewan English Teachers' Association* (Saskatoon SK) 10, No. 4 (Summer 1974): 54. Review of *In the Flesh*

H194   [Review] Lacey, Edward. "Canadian Bards and South American Reviewers." *Northern Journey* (Ottawa ON), No. 4 (June 1974): 82–120. Review of *In the Flesh* and *Curious* [and other books, including *The Clallam*, by Frank Davey; *A Choice of Dreams*, by Joy Kogawa] [Note: the review of *Curious* is written as a parody of Lionel Kearns' *Listen, George*]

H195   [Review/Short] Bradbury, Maureen. *Quill & Quire* (Toronto ON) 40, No. 7 (July 1974): 20. Review of *Curious* and *In the Flesh*

H196   [Review] Musgrave, Susan. *The Malahat Review* (Victoria BC), No. 31 (July 1974): 161–165. Review of *In the Flesh* [and *Rat Jelly*, by Michael Ondaatje; *Sex & Death*, by Al Purdy; *A Choice of Dreams*, by Joy Kogawa]

H197   [Review] Musgrave, Susan. "Language Used As Dangerous Weapon." *The Victoria Times* (Victoria BC), 27 July 1974. Review of *In the Flesh*

H198   [Essay] Tallman, Warren. "Wonder Merchants: Modernist Poetry in Vancouver During the 1960's." *Boundary 2* (Binghamton NY) 3, No. 1 (Fall 1974): 57–89. Also in *Open Letter* and *The Writing Life*; see H230 and H231

H199   [Review] Alpert, Barry. "Procedures." *Open Letter* (Toronto ON) Second Series, No. 9 (Fall 1974): 99–101. Review of *Genève* and *Curious* [and *Ten Years in the Making* and *Birds of the West*, by David Bromige; *A Paleozoic Geology of London Ontario*, by Christopher Dewdney]

H200   [Review] E. A. B. [Elizabeth Barnes] *Quarry* (Kingston ON) 23, No. 4 (Autumn 1974): 79. Review of *Curious*

H201   [Review] Langmaid, Bob. *Alive* (Guelph ON), No. 36 (September 1974): 15. Review of *Curious*

H202   [Review/Short] Powell, D. Reid. *Alive* (Guelph ON), No. 36 (September 1974): 15. Review of *Curious*

H203   [Review] Simpson, Leo. "Short Stories Thrive in the Country in a Novel Disguise." *The Globe and Mail*, 12 October 1974. Review of *Flycatcher* [and *The Skating Party*, by Merna Summers; *Bodyworks*, by George McWhirter]

H204   [Review] Diotte, Robert. "Boring Bowering Book Boasts Banalities." *The Ubyssey* (Vancouver BC), 8 November 1974: 2. Review of *Flycatcher*

H205   [Review] Stevens, Peter. "Bowering and Summers: Keep It Short." *The Windsor Star* (Windsor ON), 9 November 1974. Review of *Flycatcher* [and *The Skating Party*, by Merna Summers]

H206   [Review] Boyd, Marion. *The Oliver Chronicle* (Oliver BC), 21 November 1974. Review of a reading in Oliver BC

H207   [Review/Short] Chadbourne, Eugene. "Lurching Syncopation." *The Herald* Supplement (Calgary AB), 29 November 1974. Review of *Flycatcher*

H208   [Review] Ricou, Laurie. *Quill & Quire* (Toronto ON) 40, No. 12 (December 1974): 21–22. Review of *Flycatcher*

H209   [Review] Rix, Beverly. "Oberon, an Adventurous Publisher." *The Citizen* (Ottawa ON), 14 December 1974. Review of *Flycatcher* [and *74: New Canadian Stories*, edited by David Helwig and Joan Harcourt; *Bodyworks*, by George McWhirter]

1975

H210   [Bibliography; Bio-critical sketch] Colombo, John Robert. "Bowering, George." *Contemporary Poets*. Ed. Rosalie Murphy. New York: St. Martin's Press, second edition 1975. Pp. 154–156. Third edition. Ed. James Vinson. London: MacMillan Press, 1980. Pp. 147–149. [Note: says GB was born in Keremeos BC on 1 December 1938]

H211   [Review] Smith, Michael. "Ampersands and Aquafans." *Books in Canada* (Toronto ON) 4, No. 1 (January 1975): 20–21. Review of *Flycatcher* [and *Bodyworks*, by George McWhirter]

H212   [Review] Nodelman, Perry. "Two Types of Fiction." *The Winnipeg Free Press* Supplement (Winnipeg MB), 18 January 1975. Review of *Flycatcher* [and *Bodyworks*, by George McWhirter]

H213   [Review] Oughton, John. "Writers Enter Gap in Reality." *The Star* (Toronto ON), 24 January 1975. Review of *Flycatcher* [and *In the Belly of the Whale*, by Don Bailey]

H214   [Review] Thompson, Eric. "Between Two Worlds." *Canadian Literature* (Vancouver BC), No. 63 (Winter 1975): 111–112. Review of *In the Flesh* [and *A Choice of Dreams*, by Joy Kogawa]

H215   [Review] White, Doug. *Quarry* (Kingston ON) 24, No. 1 (Winter 1975): 74–75. Review of *Flycatcher*

H216   [Essay] Johnston, George. "Are Poems Artifacts? (A Riposte to George Bowering)." *Open Letter* (Toronto ON) Third Series, No. 2 (Spring 1975): 87–88. [Notes: a response to GB's review of Michael Ondaatje's *Rat Jelly*; see D649; the cover says Fall 1975]

H217   [Review/Essay] Alberti, A. J. *Rune* (Toronto ON) No. 2 (Spring 1975): 70–78. Review of *In the Flesh* and *Curious*

H218   [Review/Short] Stephens, Donald. "Insistent Fluidity." *Canadian Literature* (Vancouver BC) No. 64 (Spring 1975): 101–104. Review of *Flycatcher* [and six other Oberon books]

H219   [Review] Crowell, Peter. "Books." *Revue* (Vancouver BC) 1, No. 3 (May 1975): 2. Review of *At War with the U. S.*

H220   [Review/Short] Barbour, Douglas. "The Poets and Presses Revisited: Circa 1974." *The Dalhousie Review* (Halifax NS) 55, No. 2 (Summer 1975): 338–360. Review of *At War with the U. S.* [and other books]

H221   [Review/Short] Ireland, G. W. *Queen's Quarterly* (Kingston ON) 82, No. 2 (Summer 1975): 300–303. Review of *In the Flesh* [and three other books]

H222   [Review/Short] Rudzik, O. H. T. "Letters in Canada 1974: Fiction." *University of Toronto Quarterly* (Toronto ON) 44, No. 4 (Summer 1975): 304–315. Review of *Flycatcher* [and other books of fiction in 1974]

H223   [Review] Novik, Mary. "Talon Is Grasping Some Good Work." *The Sun* (Vancouver BC), 4 July 1975. Review of *At War with the U. S.* [and *Love: A Book of Remembrances*, by bp Nichol; *Speech Sucks*, by Victor Coleman]

H224   [Review/Short] Barras, Leonard. *The Sunday Times* (London, England), 20 July 1975. Review of *Flycatcher*

H225   [Review] Baxter, Marilyn. "Six Firsts from Oberon." *The Canadian Forum* (Toronto ON) 55, No. 657 (December 1975/January 1976): 48–51. Review of *Flycatcher* [and six other books from Oberon Press]

1976

H226   [Bibliography] Woodcock, George. "Bowering, George." *Canadian Poets 1960–1973: A Checklist.* Ottawa: The Golden Dog Press, 1976. Pp. 8–9.

H227   [Biographic sketch] Colombo, John Robert. "Bowering, George." *Colombo's Canadian References.* Toronto: Oxford University Press, 1976. P. 52.

H228   [Essay] Galvin, Robert. "George Bowering: The Seventies." *Cross-Country* (Woodhaven NY/Montreal PQ), No. 5 (1976): 20–23.

H229   [Essay/Context] Richardson, Keith William. *Poetry and the Colonized Mind:* Tish. Preface by Robin Mathews. Oakville/Ottawa: Mosaic Press/Valley Editions, 1976. [Note: originally a thesis for Carleton University]

H230   [Essay/Context] Tallman, Warren. "Wonder Merchants: Modernist Poetry in Vancouver During the 1960's." *Godawful Streets of Man. Open Letter* (Toronto ON) Third Series, No. 6 (1976): 175–207. Also in *Boundary 2* and *The Writing Life*; see H198 and H231

H231   [Essays/Context] Davey, Frank. "Introduction"—"Black Days on Black Mountain"—"Anything But Reluctant"—"Introducing *Tish*." *The Writing Life.* Ed. C. H. Gervais. Coatsworth ON: Black Moss Press,

1976. Pp. 15–24, 117–127, 136–142, 150–161. "Black Days" is also in *The Tamarack Review* [see H28]; "Anything But Reluctant" is also in Canadian Literature [see H7]; "Introducing *Tish*" combines the "Introduction" to *Tish No. 1–19* [see C83] and *"Tish, B. C., and After"* in *Western Windows* [see C106 and H247]

Drawing with Frank Davey, Red Lane, GB, and Robert Hogg, after a slide owned by Frank Davey; postcard of cover for *The Writing Life*; see H231; drawing by Craig Robinson

H232 [Review] Beardsley, Doug. "War and Other Measures." *Contemporary Verse II* (Winnipeg MB) 2, No. 1 (January 1976): 21. Review of *At War with the U. S.* [and *Virgins & Vampires*, by Joe Rosenblatt]

H233 [Review/Short] MacKendrick, Louis K. *The University of Windsor Review* (Windsor ON) 11, No. 2 (Spring/Summer 1976): 107–108. Review of *Flycatcher* [and four other books by Oberon Press]

H234 [Review] Aspden, Lorraine. "They Like His Poems—When 'He' Reads." *Kamloops News* (Kamloops BC), 15 March 1976. Review of a reading in Kamloops BC

H235 [Review/Context] Downes, G. V. "Two Sides of the Coin." *Contemporary Verse II* (Winnipeg MB) 2, No. 2 (May 1976): 46–47. Review of *Boundary 2*, A Canadian Issue, and *From There to Here*, by Frank Davey

H236 [Review] Coach, Ken. "Showering Bowering Reads Writing." *IS* (Toronto ON), No. 18 (Summer 1976): 32. Review of a reading in Yellowknife NWT. [Note: reprinted from *News of the North* (Yellowknife NWT), 27 August 1975; GB was part of the Writers' Tour of the Northwest Territories in 1975]

H237 [Essay] Sandler, Linda. "Romantic Anarchy in Art and Life." *Quill & Quire* (Toronto ON) 42, No. 8 (June 1976): 26.

H238 [Review] McDonald, David. "Ebbe-Tied." *Northern Journey* (Ottawa ON), No. 6 (June 1976): 138. Review of *Flycatcher*

H239 [Statement/Context] McFadden, David. "The Black Mountain Influence (for George Bowering)." *NMFG* (Vancouver BC), No. 6 (18 June 1976): n. p.

H240 [Review/Context] Gervais, Marty. *Essays on Canadian Writing*, No. 5 (Fall 1976): 90–92. Review of *Tish 1–19*, edited by Frank Davey.

H241 [Review] Rosenblatt, Joe. "No Bowering Toady He." *Books in Canada* (Toronto ON) 5, No. 10 (October 1976): 29–30. Review of *The Catch*

H242 [Review/Short] Adachi, Ken. "Poet Al Purdy's Tough-Guy Pose Just a Mask." *The Star* (Toronto ON), 6 November 1976. Review of *The Catch* [and *Sundance at Dusk*, by Al Purdy]

H243   [Review] Geddes, Gary. *The Globe and Mail*, 20 November 1976. Review of *The Catch*

H244   [Review] Petrusiak, Bill. "George Bowering Extends Boundaries of Poetry." *The Sarnia Observer* (Sarnia ON), 20 November 1976. Review of *The Catch*

H245   [Review] Geddes, Gary. "Uneven Fishing in Sea of History." *The Edmonton Journal* (Edmonton AB), 22 November 1976. Review of *The Catch*

H246   [Review] Leigh, Simon. "Two Minor Talons and a Tidal Borealis." *The Fiddlehead* (Fredericton NB), No. 108 (Winter 1976): 120–124. Review of *At War with the U. S.* [and *Speech Sucks*, by Victor Coleman]

1977

H247   [Essay/Context] Davey, Frank. "*Tish*, B. C., and After." *Western Windows*. Ed. Patricia M. Ellis and Sandy Wilson. Vancouver: CommCept Publishing, 1977. Pp. 194–198. Also in *The Writing Life* as part of "Introducing *Tish*"; see H231

H248   [Essay] Farkas, Andre and Ken Norris. "Introduction." *Montreal: English Poetry of the Seventies*. Montreal: Véhicule Press, 1977. Pp. ix–xii. [Note: comments on GB's creative writing classes and the influential reading series he helped organize at Sir George Williams University (now Concordia University)]

H249   [Poem] McAuley, John. "Dear John." *Nothing Ever Happens in Pointe Claire*. Montreal: Véhicule Press, 1977. N. p. [Note: a found poem, written from a letter GB sent to McAuley; see also C103]

H250   [Review] Brandeis, Robert C. *Canadian Book Review Annual 1976*. Ed. Dean Tudor, Nancy Tudor, and Linda Biesenthal. Toronto: PMA Books, 1977. P. 174. Review of *The Catch*

H251   [Review] Holland, Patrick. *Canadian Book Review Annual 1976*. Ed. Dean Tudor, Nancy Tudor, and Linda Biesenthal. Toronto: PMA Books, 1977. P. 180. Review of *Allophanes*

H252   [Review/Context] Norris, Ken. *CrossCountry* (Woodhaven NY/Montreal PQ), Nos. 8 & 9 (1977): 103–104. Review of *Letters from Geeksville*, edited by GB, and *Tish 1–19*, edited by Frank Davey [and *Godawful Streets of Man*, by Warren Tallman; *Poetry and the Colonized Mind: Tish*, by Keith Richardson]

H253   [Review] Gervais, Marty. *Quill & Quire* (Toronto ON) 43, No. 1 (January 1977): 31. Review of *The Catch*

H254   [Review] Pearson, Ian. *Quill & Quire* (Toronto ON) 43, No. 1 (January 1977): 31. Review of *Poem and Other Baseballs*

H255   [Review] McKinnon, Barry. *Repository* (Prince George BC), Nos. 21 & 22 (Winter/Spring 1977): 73–78. Review of *The Catch*. Also in *Caledonian* 6, No. 3 (April 1977): 40–47.

H256   [Review] Harris, John. *Repository* (Prince George BC), Nos. 21 & 22 (Winter/Spring 1977): 69–72. Review of *Letters from Geeksville*, edited by GB. Also in *Caledonian* 6, No. 3 (April 1977): 18–23.

H257   [Review] McAuley, John. "Poems from the Bottom Drawer." *Contemporary Verse II* (Winnipeg MB) 3, No. 1 (Spring 1977): 22–23. Review of *The Concrete Island*

H258   [Statement] Mathews, Robin. "Seeing Through a Greenglass Clearly." *Contemporary Verse II* (Winnipeg MB) 3, No. 1 (Spring 1977): 52. [Note: a reply to GB, to which GB responded with two letters, "For the Record," and "Responding to a Base Canard"; see D722]

H259   [Review] Novik, Mary. "A Fine Catch." *The Sun* (Vancouver BC), 4 March 1977. Review of *The Catch*

H260   [Essay] Gervais, Marty. "George Bowering: A Poet on His Way." *The Windsor Star* (Windsor ON), 26 March 1977.

H261   [Review] Amprimoz, Alexandre. " . . . But Why and Where?" *The Windsor Star* (Windsor ON), 26 March 1977. Review of *The Catch*

H262   [Review/Context] Stevens, Peter. "And Then There Was *Tish*." *The Windsor Star* (Windsor ON), 26 March 1977. Review of *Poetry and the Colonized Mind:* Tish, by Keith Richardson [and *A Stone Diary*, by Pat Lowther]

H263   [Review/Short] Lincoln, Bob. *Quill & Quire* (Toronto ON) 43, No. 6 (May 1977): 43. Review of *Allophanes*

H264   [Review] Peirce, J. C. *The Dalhousie Review* (Halifax NS) 57, No. 2 (Summer 1977): 381–383. Review of *The Catch*

H265   [Review] Barbour, Douglas. "Poetry Chronicle IV." *The Dalhousie Review* (Halifax NS) 57, No. 2 (Summer 1977): 355–371. Review of *The Catch* and *Poem and Other Baseballs* [and many other books of poetry]

H266   [Review/Short] Brewer, Barry F. *Canadian Materials* (Toronto ON) 5, No. 3 (Autumn 1977): 122. Review of *The Catch*

H267   [Poem] Grassnake, A. A. "Up Yours So to Speak." *NMFG* (Vancouver BC), No. 16 (June 1977): n. p. [Note: "A. A. Grassnake is a protégé of George Bowering"]

H268   [Review] Boland, Viga. *Quill & Quire* (Toronto ON) 43, No. 10 (August 1977): 38. Review of *The Concrete Island*

H269   [Review] Nabhan, Gary. *Western American Literature* (Logan UT) 12, No. 3 (Fall 1977): 244–246. Review of *The Catch* [and *Petroglyphs*, by Sam Hamill; *Selected Poems*, by Lucien Stryk] [Note: "November" on cover; "Fall" on title-page]

H270   [Review/Context] Davey, Frank. "Tish, Tish." *Essays on Canadian Writing* (Toronto ON), Nos. 7 & 8 (Fall 1977): 126–129. Review of *Poetry and the Colonized Mind*: Tish, by Keith Richardson

H271   [Review/Context] Whiteman, Bruce. "Criticizing the Wonder Merchants." *Essays on Canadian Writing* (Toronto ON), Nos. 7 & 8 (Fall 1977): 130–134. Review of *Poetry and the Colonized Mind*: Tish, by Keith Richardson

H272   [Review/Context] Hogg, R. L. "This Vital Point." *Essays on Canadian Writing* (Toronto ON), Nos. 7 & 8 (Fall 1977): 135–142. Review of *The Writing Life*, edited by C. H. Gervais

H273   [Review] Demels, M. *Essays on Canadian Writing* (Toronto ON), Nos. 7 & 8 (Fall 1977): 143–144. Review of *Yankee Poetry in British Columbia: The Curious Case of the Tish Magazine*, by Metro Paserik (Dos Equis Press) [Note: a pseudonymous review of GB's title for a non-existent book by a non-existent writer from a non-existent press]

H274   [Review] Garebian, Keith. "Guaranteed to Offend." *The Montreal Star* (Montreal PQ), 1 October 1977. Review of *The Catch*

H275   [Review/Short] Gasparini, Len. "Here's a Delightful Tale of First Love." *The Star* (Toronto ON), 26 November 1977. Review of *A Short Sad Book* [and *Sidehill Gouger*, by Shane Dennison; *Bearwalk*, by Lynne Sallot and Tom Peltier]

H276   [Review] Finnie, John. "Sadly, the Man's Right!" *The Edmonton Journal* (Edmonton AB), 28 November 1977. Review of *A Short Sad Book*

H277   [Review] McKay, Don. "Two Voices: Purdy and Bowering." *The University of Windsor Review* (Windsor ON) 13, No. 1 (Fall/Winter 1977): 99–104. Review of *The Catch* and *Poem and Other Baseballs* [and *Sundance at Dusk*, by Al Purdy]

H278   [Review] Wagner, Linda W. "The Most Contemporary of Poetics." *The Ontario Review* (Windsor ON), No. 7 (Fall 1977/Winter 1978): 88–95. Review of *The Catch* [and six other books]

H279   [Review] Twigg, Alan. "A Deep Affinity for the Land." *The Georgia Straight* (Vancouver BC) 11, No. 524 (1–8 December 1977): 23. Review of *A Short Sad Book*

H280   [Review] Yaffe, Virginia. " 'Short, Sad Book' Is Long on Allusions." *The Gazette* (Montreal PQ), 3 December 1977. Review of *A Short Sad Book*

H281   [Review] Whiteman, Bruce. "A Seat on His Language." *Essays on Canadian Writing* (Toronto ON), No. 9 (Winter 1977/78): 83–88. Review of *The Catch* and *Allophanes*

1978

H282 [Bibliography] Gnarowski, Michael. "Bowering, George." *A Concise Bibliography of English-Canadian Literature.* Toronto: McClelland and Stewart, 1973; revised edition 1978. Pp. 16–18.

H283 [Bibliography] Stevens, Peter. "Bowering, George Harry (1935–)." *Modern English-Canadian Poetry.* Detroit: Gale Research Company, 1978. Pp. 162–165.

H284 [Essay] Norris, Ken. "The Poetry of George Bowering." *Brave New Wave.* Ed. Jack David. Windsor ON: Black Moss Press, 1978. Pp. 83–107. Excerpted in *Contemporary Literary Criticism.* Volume 15. Detroit: Gale Research Company, 1980. Pp. 81–84

H285 [Poem] McFadden, David. "Vancouver Lights." *On the Road Again.* Toronto: McClelland and Stewart, 1978. P. 37.

H286 [Statement] Randall, Margaret. "Parallel George." *We.* New York: Smyrna Press, 1978. Pp. 25–26.

H287 [Review] Gifford, Tony. *Canadian Book Review Annual 1977.* Ed. Dean Tudor, Nancy Tudor, and Linda Biesenthal. Toronto: PMA Books, 1978. P. 110. Review of *A Short Sad Book*

H288 [Review] Lincoln, Robert. *Canadian Book Review Annual 1978.* Ed. Dean Tudor, Nancy Tudor, and Linda Biesenthal. Toronto: PMA Books, 1978. P. 155. Review of *The Concrete Island*

VANCOUVER LIGHTS

George was driving me around town
telling me stories
midnight
me as relaxed as a fish
at the bottom of lovely Lake Erie
and for some reason I looked up
and shouted
hey
what are those lights in the sky
(there shouldn't be lights in the sky
except for stars and the moon you know)
and he laughed and said oh
you people from Ontario
that's not the sky
it's the ground
this is BC.

"Vancouver Lights," by David McFadden; see H285

H289 [Statements; Bibliography] David, Jack and Caroline Bayard. [Statements on] "Irving Layton," "AB: The Pope," and "Roy Is Covered"—"Bibliography of George Bowering." *Out-Posts/Avant-Postes.* Erin ON: Press Porcépic, 1978. Pp. 101, 102, 103, 104–106.

H290 [Review] Davey, Frank. "Swift Currents." *Books in Canada* (Toronto ON) 7, No. 1 (January 1978): 14–15. Review of *A Short Sad Book*

H291 [Review] McKellar, Iain. "Novel Much in Need of Its Own Program." *The Citizen* (Ottawa ON), 4 January 1978. Review of *A Short Sad Book*

H292 [Review] Cook, Barrie. "Oblique, Complex, Fanciful." *The Province* (Vancouver BC), 13 January 1978. Review of *A Short Sad Book*

H293 [Review] Crowell, Peter M. *Quill & Quire* (Toronto ON) 44, No. 2 (February 1978): 39. Review of *A Short Sad Book*

H294 [Review/Short] Dempster, Barry. *Quill & Quire* (Toronto ON) 44, No. 2 (February 1978): 38–39. Review of *Concentric Circles*

H295   [Review] McKim, David. "Profound & Preferred." *Books in Canada* (Toronto ON) 7, No. 2 (February 1978): 17–18. Review of *Concentric Circles* [and *The Search for Sarah Grace*, by Eugene McNamara]

H296   [Review/Short] Barbour, Douglas. "Poetry Chronicle V." *The Dalhousie Review* (Halifax NS) 58, No. 1 (Spring 1978): 149–169. Review of *Allophanes* [and other books]

H297   [Review/Short] Davies, Gwendolyn. "Something's Happening in Montreal." *Essays on Canadian Writing* (Toronto ON), No. 10 (Spring 1978): 82–87. Review of *The Concrete Island* [and seven other books]

H298   [Review] Fawcett, Brian. *Periodics* (Vancouver BC), No. 3 (Spring 1978): 74–78. Review of *A Short Sad Book*

H299   [Review] Dudley, Wendy. "Canada's History: Short and Sad." *The Gauntlet* (Calgary AB), 7 March 1978. Review of *A Short Sad Book*

H300   [Review] Cruikshank, John. "No Eastern Corral for This Western Poet." *The Whig-Standard* (Kingston ON), 18 March 1978. [Note: a profile in which GB is quoted]

H301   [Review/Essay] French, William. "What Happens When the Muse Passes a Poet By?" *The Globe and Mail*, 21 March 1978. Review of *A Short Sad Book* [Note: includes a profile of GB]

H302   [Review] Adachi, Ken. "Stories Hold Promise But They Don't Deliver." *The Star* (Toronto ON), 25 March 1978. Review of *Protective Footwear* [and *Splendid Lives*, by Penelope Gilliatt]

H303   [Review] Barbour, Doug. *Pacific Northwest Review of Books* (Seattle WA) 1, No. 1 (April 1978): 17. Review of *Concentric Circles* and *A Short Sad Book*

H304   [Review] Fulford, Robert. "Bowering, Me, and the Robertian Conspiracy." *Saturday Night* (Toronto ON) 93, No. 3 (April 1978): 14. Excerpted in *Contemporary Literary Criticism*. Volume 15. Detroit: Gale Research Company, 1980. P. 81. Review of *A Short Sad Book*

H305   [Review] Engel, Marian. *The Globe and Mail*, 8 April 1978. Review of *Protective Footwear*

H306   [Review] Novak, Barbara. "Bowering Draws Reader Artfully into Tales." *The London Free Press* (London ON), 22 April 1978. Review of *Protective Footwear*

H307   [Review] Pearson, Ian. *Quill & Quire* (Toronto ON) 44, No. 7 (May 1978): 42. Review of *Protective Footwear*

H308   [Review] Persky, Stan. "At the Heritage Reading." *NMFG* (Vancouver BC), No. 22 (May 1978): n. p. Review of "Heritage

Drawing of GB
by Greg Curnoe

Writers' Festival poetry reading"; see E55 [Note: Daphne Marlatt responds in *NMFG*, No. 24]

H309 [Review] Langmaid, Bob. "Short Stories on People Are Engaging Entertainment." *News Advertiser* (Ajax ON), 10 May 1978. Review of *Protective Footwear*

H310 [Review] Hatch, Ronald. "Bowering: Shucking the Old Razzmatazz." *The Sun* (Vancouver BC), 12 May 1978. Review of *Protective Footwear*

H311 [Review] Fisher, Joan. "Harmonics Link Vision and Style." *The Peak* (Burnaby BC), 31 May 1978: 11. [Review of "Heritage Writers' Festival poetry reading"; see E55]

H312 [Review] Runkle, Helen. *BCSLA Reviews* (Vernon BC) 3, No. 3 (June 1978): 3–4. Review of *A Short Sad Book*

H313 [Review] Fisher, Joan. "Love Affair Fails Insight." *The Peak* (Burnaby BC), 12 July 1978: 14. Review of *A Short Sad Book*

H314 [Review] McKim, David. "Once Upon an Instance." *Books in Canada* (Toronto ON) 7, No. 7 (August/September 1978): 21–22. Review of *Protective Footwear*

H315 [Review] Kellythorne, Walt. "His Wit Gets in Way of Feeling." *The Victoria Times* (Victoria BC), 4 August 1978. Review of *Protective Footwear*

H316 [Review/Short] Baird, Nora. *Canadian Materials* (Toronto ON) 6, No. 4 (Autumn 1978): 200. Review of *A Short Sad Book*

H317 [Review/Short] Barbour, Douglas. "Canadian Poetry Chronicle VI." *The Dalhousie Review* (Halifax NS) 58, No. 3 (Autumn 1978): 555–578. Review of *The Concrete Island* [and many other books of poetry] [Note: "Autumn 1979" on cover; "Autumn 1978" on title-page]

H318 [Review] Cohen, Matt. "Bowering's Act of Faith." *Essays on Canadian Writing* (Toronto ON), No. 12 (Fall 1978): 51–55. Review of *Protective Footwear*

H319 [Review] Needham, Alan. "Poet's Meandering with Prose Weak." *The Citizen* (Ottawa ON), 2 September 1978. Review of *Protective Footwear*

H320 [Review/Short] Thompson, Eric. "The Uses of Reflection." *The University of Windsor Review* (Windsor ON) 14, No. 1 (Fall/Winter 1978): 76–78. Review of *Protective Footwear* [and *Dark Must Yield*, by Dave Godfrey; *Over by the River, and Other Stories*, by William Maxwell]

H321 [Review] Chodan, Lucinda. "Taking a Run at Prose." *The Edmonton Sun* Supplement (Edmonton AB), 17 December 1978. Review of *Protective Footwear*

H322 [Review] Oliver, Michael Brian. "Clever, Curious, Sometimes Composed George." *The Fiddlehead* (Fredericton NB), No. 116 (Winter 1978): 158–164. Review of *The Concrete Island*, *Allophanes*, and *The Catch*

1979

H323   [Bibliography] Tata, Sam. "George Bowering, Vancouver 1973." *Canadian Fiction Magazine* (Toronto ON), No. 29 (1979): 68–69. [Note: part of a section of portraits by Tata of prominent figures]

H324   [Essay] Clark, LaVerne Harrell. "George Bowering." *Focus 101: An Illustrated Biography of 101 Poets of the 60's and 70's.* Chico CA: Heidelberg Graphics, 1979. Pp. 8–9. [Note: says GB was born in Keremeos BC on 1 December 1935]

H325   [Review] Labonté, Ronald. *Canadian Fiction Magazine* (Toronto ON) Nos. 30 & 31 (1979): 213–217. Review of *A Short Sad Book* and *Protective Footwear*

H326   [Review] Reid, Robbie. *Canadian Book Review Annual 1978.* Ed. Dean Tudor, Nancy Tudor, and Linda Biesenthal. Toronto: PMA Books, 1979. Pp. 154–155. Review of *Protective Footwear*

H327   [Review] Cutt, Joanne. *Quarry* (Kingston ON) 28, No. 1 (Winter 1979): 91–94. Review of *Protective Footwear*

H328   [Review] Leonard, Anne. *Canadian Materials* (Toronto ON) 7, No. 1 (Winter 1979): 18. Review of *Protective Footwear*

H329   [Review/Essay] Brown, Alan. "Beyond the Crenel—A View of Bowering." *Brick* (Ilderton ON), No. 6 (Spring 1979): 36–39. Review of *A Short Sad Book*, *Poem and Other Baseballs*, *Concentric Circles*, and *The Catch*

H330   [Review] Davies, Gwendolyn. *The Fiddlehead* (Fredericton NB), No. 121 (Spring 1979): 134–136. Review of *Concentric Circles*, *A Short Sad Book*, and *Protective Footwear*

H331   [Essay/Context] Davey, Frank. "The Explorer in Western Canadian Literature." *Studies in Canadian Literature* (Fredericton NB) 4, No. 2 (Summer 1979): 91–100. Also in *Surviving the Paraphrase*; see H448. [Note: includes comments on *George, Vancouver*]

H332   [Review] Surette, Leon. "Mostly Middle." *Canadian Literature* (Vancouver BC), No. 82 (Autumn 1979): 84–86. Excerpted in *Contemporary Literary Criticism*. Volume 15. Detroit: Gale Research Company, 1980. P. 84. Review of *A Short Sad Book*

H333   [Review] Colombo, John Robert. "Polemics and Lyrics." *The Globe and Mail*, 15 September 1979. Review of *Another Mouth* [and *Droppings from Heaven*, by Irving Layton]

H334   [Review] Norris, Ken. "Clearly Minor." *The Gazette* (Montreal PQ), 15 September 1979. Review of *Another Mouth*

H335   [Review/Short] Abley, Mark. "Poetry That Fell from the Sky." *Maclean's* (Toronto ON) 93, No. 41 (8 October 1979): 54–58. Review of *Another Mouth* [and four other books]

H336 [Review] Adachi, Ken. "It's Jocks 11, Writers 1 in Bland Book." *The Star* (Toronto ON), 17 November 1979. Review of *Great Canadian Sports Stories*, edited by GB [and *The Hockey Sweater and Other Stories*, by Roch Carrier]

H337 [Review] Harrison, Claire. "Bowering's Perspective Clear." *The Ottawa Journal* (Ottawa ON), 24 November 1979. Review of *Another Mouth*

H338 [Review] Faustmann, John. "Simply Good and So-So Aren't Great." *The Sun* Supplement (Vancouver BC), 30 November 1979. Review of *Great Canadian Sports Stories*, edited by GB [and *Great Canadian Adventure Stories*, edited by Muriel Whitaker]

H339 [Review] Pearson, Ian. *Quill & Quire* (Toronto ON) 45, No. 14 (December 1979): 28. Review of *Another Mouth*

H340 [Review/Short] Quaife, Darlene. "Canadian Poetry Round-up." *The Herald* (Calgary AB), 22 December 1979. Review of *Another Mouth* [and four other books, including *The Sad Phoenician*, by Robert Kroetsch]

H341 [Review/Short] Allison, Garry. *The Lethbridge Herald* (Lethbridge AB), 29 December 1979. Review of *Great Canadian Sports Stories*, edited by GB

H342 [Essay/Context] Henighan, Tom. "Shamans, Tribes and the Sorcerer's Apprentices: Notes on the Discovery of the Primitive in Modern Poetry." *The Dalhousie Review* (Halifax NS) 59, No. 4 (Winter 1979/80): 605–620. [Note: includes comments on GB's "Hamatsa" and "Windigo"]

H343 [Review] Coles, Don. "Deeper Origins." *The Canadian Forum* (Toronto ON) 59, No. 695 (December 1979/January 1980): 37. Review of *Another Mouth*

1980

H344 [Essay] Blaser, Robin. "George Bowering's Plain Song." *Particular Accidents*. By GB. Vancouver: Talonbooks, 1980. Pp. 9–28. [See A36]

H345 [Review] Fagan, Cary. *Canadian Book Review Annual 1979*. Ed. Dean Tudor, Nancy Tudor, and Kathy Vanderlinden. Toronto: PMA Books, 1980. Pp. 168–169. Review of *Great Canadian Sports Stories*, edited by GB

H346 [Review] Larsen, Michael J. *Canadian Book Review Annual 1979*. Ed. Dean Tudor, Nancy Tudor, and Kathy Vanderlinden. Toronto: PMA Books, 1980. Pp. 134–135. Review of *Another Mouth*

H347 [Review] Dickie, Barry. "Lonely Walks and Short Stops." *Books in Canada* (Toronto ON) 9, No. 1 (January 1980): 13–14. Review of *Great Canadian Sports Stories*, edited by GB [and *79: Best Canadian Stories*, edited by Clark Blaise and John Metcalf]

H348   [Review] Ruebsaat, Norbert. "Poet Flirts with Form Too Much." *The Sun* (Vancouver BC), 18 January 1980. Review of *Another Mouth*

H349   [Review/Short] Pietersz, Carlyle. *The Colombo Sun* (Colombo, Sri Lanka), 16 February 1980. Review of *15 Canadian Poets Plus 5*, edited by Gary Geddes

H350   [Essay] Quigley, Ellen. "*Tish*: Bowering's Infield Position." *Studies in Canadian Literature* (Fredericton NB) 5, No. 1 (Spring 1980): 23–46.

H351   [Review] Boone, Mike. "Twelve Solid Victories in the Sport of Fiction." *The Gazette* (Montreal PQ), 15 March 1980. Review of *Great Canadian Sports Stories*, edited by GB

H352   [Review/Short] Moritz, A. F. *The Windsor Star* (Windsor ON), 12 April 1980. Review of *Another Mouth* [and *Rag Doll's Shadow*, by Myron Turner]

H353   [Review] Scobie, Stephen. "The Ears Have It." *Books in Canada* (Toronto ON) 9, No. 5 (May 1980): 12, 14–15. Review of *Another Mouth* [and *East of Myloona*, by Andrew Suknaski]

H354   [Review] Billings, Robert. *Quarry* (Kingston ON) 29, No. 3 (Summer 1980): 75–79. Review of *Another Mouth* [and *Anniversaries*, by Don Coles]

H355   [Review] Ploude, Roger. "The Purity of the Act—And Some Not So Pure." *The Fiddlehead* (Fredericton NB), No. 126 (Summer 1980): 136–139. Review of *Great Canadian Sports Stories*, edited by GB

H356   [Review] Rae, Patricia. "Creative Estrangement." *The Whig-Standard* Supplement (Kingston ON), 7 June 1980. Review of *Another Mouth*

H357   [Review/Short] *Kirkus Reviews* (New York NY) 48, No. 17 (1 September 1980): 1173. Review of *Burning Water*

H358   [Review] French, William. "Bowering Novel Entertains, History Takes the Hindmost." *The Globe and Mail*, 4 September 1980. Review of *Burning Water*

H359   [Review] Gervais, Marty. "Wiebe and Bowering Pry Open Past, Pour Out Novels." *The Windsor Star* (Windsor ON), 13 September 1980. Review of *Burning Water* [and *The Mad Trapper*, by Rudy Wiebe]

H360   [Review] Hancock, Geoff. "Vancouver's Founder Gets a Drubbing." *The Star* (Toronto ON), 13 September 1980. Review of *Burning Water*

H361   [Review] Barclay, Pat. "A Biography But Who's the Subject?" *The Times-Colonist* (Victoria BC), 27 September 1980. Review of *Burning Water*

H362   [Review/Short] *Publisher's Weekly* (New York NY) 218, No. 14 (3 October 1980): 57. Review of *Burning Water*

H363   [Review] Simpson, Leo. "An Elegant, Funny Story of Mission to the North." *The Spectator* (Hamilton ON), 11 October 1980. Review of *Burning Water*

H364   [Review] Faustmann, John. "Why Is This Author Smiling?" *The Sun* Supplement (Vancouver BC), 24 October 1980. Review of *Burning Water*

H365   [Essay] Oppenheimer, Joel. "A Likely Story." *The Village Voice* (New York NY) 25, No. 44 (29 October–4 November 1980): 40. [Note: a prose piece with GB as the central figure]

H366   [Review] Scott, Chris. "A Bum Rap for Poor George Vancouver." *Books in Canada* (Toronto ON) 9, No. 9 (November 1980): 9. Review of *Burning Water*

H367   [Review] Obee, David. *The Lethbridge Herald* (Lethbridge AB), 22 November 1980. Review of *Burning Water*

H368   [Review] Silvester, Reg. "Communication Lacking in Self-Centred Novel." *The Edmonton Journal* (Edmonton AB), 29 November 1980. Review of *Burning Water*

H369   [Review] Hamilton, Seymour. *Books Now* (Halifax NS) 3, No. 26 (1 December 1980): n. p. Review of *Fiction of Contemporary Canada*, edited by GB

H370   [Review] McLintock, Peter. "Grab-bag of Books." *The Winnipeg Free Press* (Winnipeg MB), 6 December 1980. Review of *Burning Water* [and other books]

H371   [Review] Rankin, William A. "Post-Modern Web of Words." *The Edmonton Journal* (Edmonton AB), 20 December 1980. Review of *Fiction of Contemporary Canada*, edited by GB

H372   [Essay/Context] Francis, Wynne. "Beyond Language, Literature, and Nationalism." *English Studies in Canada* (Fredericton NB) 6, No. 4 (Winter 1980): 475–492. Review/Essay on *Out-Posts*, by Caroline Bayard and Jack David [Note: comments on the GB interview; see C113]

H373   [Review] Whiteman, Bruce. "Love the World and Stay Inside It." *Essays on Canadian Writing* (Toronto ON), No. 20 (Winter 1980/81): 220–223. Review of *Another Mouth*

H374   [Review] Whiteman, Neil. "He Would Have Been a Hell of a Poet." *Contemporary Verse II* (Winnipeg MB) 5, No. 2 (Winter 1980/81): 19–20. Review of *Letters from Geeksville*, edited by GB [Note: a special issue on BC writing, edited by Colin Browne]

1981

H375   [Bibliography; Biographic sketch] Henry, Jon Paul. "Bowering, George" —"Bowering, George." *A Select Bibliography and A Biographical Dictionary of B. C. Poets 1970–80*. Burnaby BC: SFU, 1981. Pp. 8–9, 37–38.

[Note: biographic sketch on p. 37 says GB was born in 1934 in West Summerland BC]

H376   [Bibliography] Walker (Nichols), Miriam, Rosemary Griebel, and Madeleine Kierans. "George Bowering." *The Coast Is Only a Line: A Selected Bibliography.* [SFU: Burnaby BC], 1981. Pp. 9–17. [Note: includes poets studied in "Contemporary Poetry in B. C.," a Summer School Program of two courses offered by guest teachers Warren Tallman and Eli Mandel]

H377   [Essay] Moss, John. "Bowering, George." *A Reader's Guide to the Canadian Novel.* Toronto: McClelland and Stewart, 1981. Pp. 19–24. Revised second edition, 1987. Pp. 28–35. [Note: on *Mirror on the Floor, A Short Sad Book,* and *Burning Water*; revised in second edition]

H378   [Essay/Context] Kroetsch, Robert. "For Play and Entrance: The Contemporary Canadian Long Poem." *Dandelion* 8, No. 1 (1981): 61–85. Also in *Robert Kroetsch: Essays*; see H464. [Note: mentions GB in relation to a number of Canadian long poems]

H379   [Review] Newman, Cliff. "Canadian Poet Is Inaccurate and Irrelevant." *Canadian Yachting* (Toronto ON), January 1981: 71–72. Review of *Burning Water*

H380   [Review] Hancock, Geoff. *The Windsor Star* (Windsor ON), 10 January 1981. A longer version was published as "Canadian Fiction Collection Antiquated" in *The Star* (Toronto ON), 7 February 1981. Review of *Fiction of Contemporary Canada*, edited by GB

H381   [Review/Short] Kuiper, Elske. *Quill & Quire* (Toronto ON) 47, No. 1 (January 1981): 24. Review of *Burning Water*

H382   [Essay] Rodgers, Kathleen. "Bowering: Why Copy World?" *Nelson Daily News* (Nelson BC), 13 January 1981.

H383   [Review] Duffy, Dennis. *The Globe and Mail*, 24 January 1981. Review of *Fiction of Contemporary Canada*, edited by GB

H384   [Review] Heward, Burt. "Experimental Prose Collection Designed for Serious Readers." *The Citizen* (Ottawa ON), 24 January 1981. Review of *Fiction of Contemporary Canada*, edited by GB

H385   [Review/Short] Aubert, Rosemary. "109 Poets." *The Tamarack Review* (Toronto ON), Nos. 81 & 82 (Winter 1981): 94–99. Review of *Another Mouth* [and six other books of poetry, including *In England Now That Spring*, by Steve McCaffery and bp Nichol]

H386   [Review] Barbour, Doug. "Canadian Poetry Chronicle: IX, Part 2." *West Coast Review* (Burnaby BC) 15, No. 3 (Winter 1981): 43–49. Review of *Another Mouth* [and other books of poetry]

H387   [Review] Watts, Charles. *Periodics* (Vancouver BC), Nos. 7 & 8 (Winter 1981): 193. Review of *Burning Water*

H388   [Letter] McFadden, David. "To the Editor." *Nelson Daily News* (Nelson BC), 28 January 1981. [Note: one of a series of such letters in January and

February debating the merits of GB after his visit to David Thompson University Centre in Nelson BC]

H389   [Review] Geiger, Roy. "Whimsical Approach Smug, Irksome." *The London Free Press* (London ON), 14 February 1981. Review of *Burning Water*

H390   [Essay/Context] Linguanti, Elsa. "Allo-fanie: i poeti canadesi della West Coast." *Letterature D'America* (Rome, Italy) 2, No. 7 (Spring 1981): 123–153. [Note: in Italian; discusses West Coast poetry with excerpts from GB's "Circus Maximus," *Baseball*, and *Allophanes*]

H391   [Review] Quigley, Ellen. "A(n)nót(át)ing Nothing." *The Fiddlehead* (Fredericton NB), No. 129 (Spring 1981): 111–122. Review of *Another Mouth* [and *A Book of Numbers*, by Paul Dutton; *Intimate Distortions*, by Steve McCaffery; *Shore Lines*, by Douglas Barbour]

H392   [Review] Chambers, Thomas. *Canadian Churchman* (Toronto ON) 107, No. 3 (March 1981): 20–21. Review of *Burning Water*

H393   [Review] Harrison, Jeanne. "Avant-Garde CanLit." *The Whig-Standard* Supplement (Kingston ON), 7 March 1981. Review of *Fiction of Contemporary Canada*, edited by GB

H394   [Review] Gervais, Marty. "Coming of Age in B. C." *The Windsor Star* (Windsor ON), 21 March 1981. Review of *Particular Accidents* [and the five other titles in Talonbooks' series of Selected Poems, including Fred Wah's *Loki Is Buried at Smoky Creek*, edited by GB]

H395   [Review/Short] Twigg, Alan. "They Built a Monument." *The Province* Supplement (Vancouver BC), 22 March 1981. Review of *Particular Accidents* [and eight other Talonbooks publications]

H396   [Review] McDougall, Arthur. "Bowering's Work Belittled in Poetry Reading." *The Lethbridge Herald* (Lethbridge AB), 27 March 1981. Review of a reading in Lethbridge

H397   [Essay] Peterson, Leslie. "B. C. Writer Again Wins Top Award." *The Sun* (Vancouver BC), 24 April 1981. [Note: on GB winning the Governor General's Fiction Award in 1980 for *Burning Water*]

H398   [Essay] Twigg, Alan. "Contest Ignores Canada's Finest Novelists." *The Province* Supplement (Vancouver BC), 26 April 1981. [Note: on the Governor General's Fiction Award for *Burning Water*; also on the same page, a brief news item, "B. C.'s Bowering Takes Top Prize"]

H399   [Essay] "Bowering Wins National Award." *SFU Week* (Burnaby BC), 7 May 1981: 1.

H400   [Review] Serafin, Bruce. "Poet Allows Writing to Lead Her Around by the Nose." *The Sun* Supplement (Vancouver BC), 8 May 1981. Review of *Particular Accidents* [and *Net Work*, by Daphne Marlatt; *The Arches*, by Frank Davey]

313

H401   [Review/Essay] Lamb, W. Kaye. "History As She Wasn't." *The Sun*
       (Vancouver BC), 29 May 1981. Review of *Burning Water*
H402   [Review] Craig, Terrence. "Fronting for Post-Modernism." *WQ*
       [Writer's Quarterly] (Toronto ON) 3, Nos. 2 & 3 ([Spring/Summer]
       1981): 32. Review of *Fiction of Contemporary Canada*, edited by GB
H403   [Essay/Context] Bentley, D. M. R. "A Stretching Landscape: Notes on
       Some Formalistic Continuities in the Poetry of the Hinterland." *Con-
       temporary Verse II* (Winnipeg MB) 5, No. 3 (Summer 1981): 6–18. [Note:
       quotes and comments on GB's "A Sudden Measure"]
H404   [Review] Giltrow, Janet. "Fast-Forward Man." *Canadian Literature*
       (Vancouver BC), No. 89 (Summer 1981): 118–120. Review of *Burning
       Water*
H405   [Review] Neilsen, Lorri. "Short Stories Show Canadian Writing's Image
       Has Changed." *The Herald* (Calgary AB), 11 July 1981. Review of
       Fiction of Contemporary Canada, edited by GB
H406   [Review] McGoogan, Kenneth. "Looking at 'Anti-Realism' in Canadian
       Fiction." *The Herald* (Calgary AB), 8 November 1980. Review of *Burn-
       ing Water* [Note: includes interview remarks by GB made during a visit
       to Calgary to promote *Burning Water*]
H407   [Review/Interview] Mennell, Ken. "George Bowering Answers His
       Critics." *Comment* (Burnaby BC), Farewell edition (Summer/Fall 1981):
       10–11. Review of *Burning Water* [Note: includes, alongside the review,
       an excerpt from *Burning Water*; see D781]
H408   [Review] McWhirter, George. "School Books for a School of Poetry."
       Interface (Edmonton AB) 4, No. 8 (September 1981): 48–49. Review of
       Particular Accidents, and Fred Wah's *Loki Is Buried at Smoky Creek*,
       edited by GB [and the four other Talonbooks' Selected Poems] [Note:
       GB responds in February 1982 issue; see D793]
H409   [Review/Essay] Kamboureli, Smaro. "*Burning Water*: Two Stories/One
       Novel: Narrative As Exploration." *Island* (Lantzville BC), No. 10 (Fall
       1981): 89–94.
H410   [Review/Short] Dempster, Barry. *Poetry Canada Review* (Toronto ON)
       3, No. 1 (Fall 1981): 3. Review of *Particular Accidents*
H411   [Review] Billings, Robert. *The University of Windsor Review* (Windsor
       ON) 16, No. 1 (Fall/Winter 1981): 111–116. Review of *Particular Acci-
       dents* [and *The Visible Man*, by Robert Priest; *Easy Over*, by Judith
       Fitzgerald]
H412   [Review] McCarthy, Dermot. *The University of Windsor Review* (Wind-
       sor ON) 16, No. 1 (Fall/Winter 1981): 104–109. Review of Fred Wah's
       Loki Is Buried at Smoky Creek, edited by GB [and *The Arches*, by Frank
       Davey]

H413   [Review] Norris, Ken. "Six Poets in Search of an Audience." *The Gazette* (Montreal PQ), 5 September 1981. Review of *Particular Accidents*, and Fred Wah's *Loki Is Buried at Smoky Creek*, edited by GB [and the four other Talonbooks' Selected Poems]

H414   [Review] Twigg, Alan. "Local Poetry's Supergroup." *The Georgia Straight* (Vancouver BC) 15, No. 723 (16–23 October 1981): 16. Review of *Particular Accidents*, and Fred Wah's *Loki Is Buried at Smoky Creek*, edited by GB [and the four other Talonbooks' Selected Poems]

H415   [Review] Eggertson, Eric. "Bowering Never Again to Write 'Normal' Book." *The Ubyssey* (Vancouver BC), 4 December 1981: 19. Review of *Burning Water*

1982

H416   [Essay/Context] van Herk, Aritha. "Mapping As Metaphor." *Zeitschrift der Gesellschaft fur Kanade-Studien* (Germany) 2, No. 1 (1982): 75–86. [Note: includes comments on *Burning Water*]

H417   [Essay] Watson, Sheila. "Preface." *West Window*. Toronto: General Publishing, 1982. Pp. 7–9. [See A37]

H418   [Review] Cosier, Tony. *Canadian Materials* (Toronto ON) 10, No. 3 (1982): 178. Review of *West Window*

H419   [Review/Short] Edwards, Jane. *Canadian Book Review Annual 1980*. Ed. Dean Tudor, Nancy Tudor, and Betsy Struthers. Toronto: Simon and Pierre, 1982. Pp. 131–132. Review of *Particular Accidents* [and *The Arches*, by Frank Davey; *Net Work*, by Daphne Marlatt]

H420   [Review/Short] Lucas, Alfred. *Canadian Book Review Annual 1980*. Ed. Dean Tudor, Nancy Tudor, and Betsy Struthers. Toronto: Simon and Pierre, 1982. P. 106. Review of *Burning Water*

H421   [Review] Brennan, Anthony S. *The Fiddlehead* (Fredericton NB), No. 131 (January 1982): 85–87. Review of *Burning Water*

H422   [Review/Essay] Stewart, Frank. "Wonderfully Conscious Poetry." *Brick* (Ilderton ON), No. 14 (Winter 1982): 26–29. Review of *Particular Accidents*

H423   [Review] Thorne, Sarah. *Quarry* (Kingston ON) 31, No. 1 (Winter 1982): 91–95. Review of *Particular Accidents*

H424   [Review/Short] McBeth, Ruby. *BCSLA Reviews* (Vernon BC) 7, No. 3 (February 1982): 7–8. Review of *Particular Accidents*

H425   [Review/Context] Paul, Sherman. "Serial Poems from Canada." *North Dakota Quarterly* (Grand Forks ND) 50, No. 2 (Spring 1982): 108–118. Review of *The Long Poem Anthology*, edited by Michael Ondaatje; see C128 [Note: includes comments on *Allophanes*]

H426   [Review] Barbour, Douglas. *Event* (Surrey BC) 11, No. 1 ([Spring] 1982):
        161–164. Review of *Particular Accidents*, and Fred Wah's *Loki Is Buried
        at Smoky Creek*, edited by GB [and the four other Talonbooks' Selected
        Poems]

H427   [Review] Woolley, Bryan. "Anti-realism in the Canadian West." *The
        Dallas Times Herald* (Dallas TX), 14 March 1982. Review of *A Short Sad
        Book* and *Burning Water*

H428   [Review/Short] Nynych, Stephanie J. "Poems to Appeal to All the
        Senses." *The Star* (Toronto ON), 15 May 1982. Review of *West Window*
        [and three other books]

H429   [Review] Lapierre, René. "Appelez-moi George." *Le Devoir* (Montreal
        PQ), 22 May 1982. Review of *En eaux troubles* [*Burning Water*; see A35
        and G13]

H430   [Review/Short] Hoy, Helen. "Letters in Canada 1981: Fiction." *Univer-
        sity of Toronto Quarterly* (Toronto ON) 51, No. 4 (Summer 1982):
        318–334. Review of *Burning Water* [and other books of fiction for 1981]

H431   [Review] Chantraine, Pol. *Livre d'Ici* (Montreal, Que) 7, No. 37 (16 June
        1982). Review of *En eaux troubles* [*Burning Water*; see A35 and G13]

H432   [Review] Gervais, Marty. "Bowering Has a Way with Words." *The
        Windsor Star* (Windsor ON), 17 July 1982. Review of *A Way with Words*

H433   [Review/Short] Barbour, Douglas. "Seeking the Particulars." *The Star*
        (Toronto ON), 21 August 1982. Review of *West Window* [and *The
        Shunning*, by Patrick Friesen; *The Life of Ryley*, by Monty Reid]

H434   [Review/Short] Twigg, Alan. *The Province* Supplement (Vancouver BC),
        22 August 1982. Review of *A Way with Words*

H435   [Review] Nowlan, Michael O. *The Daily Gleaner* (Fredericton NB), 10
        September 1982. Review of *A Way with Words*

H436   [Review] Serafin, Bruce. "Bowering's Away with Words." *The Peak*
        (Burnaby BC), 23 September 1982: 11. Review of *A Way with Words*

H437   [Review] Peirce, Jon. "The Poet As Traveller." *The Canadian Forum*
        (Toronto ON) 62, No. 722 (October 1982): 27–29. Review of *West
        Window* [and three other books]

H438   [Review] Bemrose, John. *The Globe and Mail*, 2 October 1982. Review of
        A Way with Words and *West Window*

H439   [Review] Serafin, Bruce. "Three-Ply Language." *The Sun* (Vancouver
        BC), 8 October 1982. Review of *West Window*

H440   [Review/Short] Kempling, Chris. *Canadian Materials* (Toronto ON) 10,
        No. 4 (November 1982): 250. Review of *A Way with Words*

H441   [Review] Mathews, Robin. "In Search of a Canadian Poetic." *The Cana-
        dian Forum* (Toronto ON) 62, No. 723 (November 1982): 31–32. Review
        of *A Way with Words*

H442   [Review/Short] Helwig, David. "Urgently Needed: A True Anthology of Women Poets." *The Star* (Toronto ON), 20 November 1982. Review of *Smoking Mirror* [and three other books]

H443   [Review/Short] Matyas, Cathy. *Quill & Quire* (Toronto ON) 48, No. 12 (December 1982): 23. Review of *A Way with Words*

H444   [Review] Oughton, John. "Lives of the Poets." *Books in Canada* (Toronto ON) 11, No. 10 (December 1982): 20–21. Review of *West Window*

1983

H445   [Bio-critical sketch] "George Bowering." *An Anthology of Canadian Literature in English*. Volume II. Ed. Donna Bennett and Russell Brown. Toronto: Oxford University Press, 1983. Pp. 374–375.

H446   [Essay/Context] Davey, Frank. *The Language of the Contemporary Canadian Long Poem*. Lantzville BC: Island Writing Series, 1983. Also in *Surviving the Paraphrase*, pp. 183–193; see H448. [Note: pamphlet of the paper for "The Coast Is Only a Line" Conference, SFU, 25 July 1981; available on tape, Special Collections, SFU]

H447   [Essay/Context] Moss, John. "Invisible in the House of Mirrors." *Canada House Lecture Series*, No. 21 (Ottawa: Department of External Affairs, 1983). [Note: discusses Canadian poetry and several poems by GB, Daphne Marlatt, and Robert Kroetsch]

H448   [Essays/Context] Davey, Frank. "The Explorer in Western Canadian Literature"—"The Language of the Canadian Long Poem." *Surviving the Paraphrase: Eleven Essays on Canadian Literature*. Winnipeg: Turnstone Press, 1983. Pp. 137–149, 183–193. "The Explorer in Western Canadian Literature" is also in *Studies in Canadian Literature*; see H331; see also H446

H449   [Essay] Cooley, Dennis. "Bowering, George." *Oxford Companion to Canadian Literature*. Ed. William Toye. Toronto: Oxford University Press, 1983. Pp. 79–80.

H450   [Essay/Context] Geddes, Gary. "British Columbia, Writing in." *Oxford Companion to Canadian Literature*. Ed. William Toye. Toronto: Oxford University Press, 1983. Pp. 83–86.

H451   [Essay/Context] Bennett, Donna. "Criticism in English." *Oxford Companion to Canadian Literature*. Ed. William Toye. Toronto: Oxford University Press, 1983. Pp. 149–166. [Note: includes a brief comment on GB's *A Way with Words* and *The Mask in Place*]

H452   [Essay/Context] Francis, Wynne. "Literary Magazines in English." *Oxford Companion to Canadian Literature*. Ed. William Toye. Toronto: Oxford University Press, 1983. Pp. 455–461.

H453   [Essay/Context] Meyer, Bruce. "Literary Magazines in English: The Seventies." *Oxford Companion to Canadian Literature*. Ed. William Toye. Toronto: Oxford University Press, 1983. Pp. 461–463. [Note: mentions GB's *Imago* and gives dates 1965–73; should be 1964–74]

H454   [Essay/Context] Gadpaille, Michelle. "Novels in English 1960–1982: Other Talents, Other Works." *Oxford Companion to Canadian Literature*. Ed. William Toye. Toronto: Oxford University Press, 1983. Pp. 587–594. [Note: mentions GB's *A Short Sad Book* and *Burning Water* in a section on "Experimental Fiction"]

H455   [Essay/Context] Hošek, Chaviva. "Poetry in English: 1950 to 1982." *Oxford Companion to Canadian Literature*. Ed. William Toye. Toronto: Oxford University Press, 1983. Pp. 660–669. [Note: GB's poetry is briefly profiled]

H456   [Essay/Context] Davey, Frank. "*Tish.*" *Oxford Companion to Canadian Literature*. Ed. William Toye. Toronto: Oxford University Press, 1983. Pp. 790–791.

H457   [Review] Girard, Louise H. *Canadian Book Review Annual 1982*. Ed. Dean Tudor and Ann Tudor. Toronto: Simon and Pierre, 1983. P. 162. Review of *West Window*

H458   [Review] Goldie, Terry. *Canadian Book Review Annual 1982*. Ed. Dean Tudor and Ann Tudor. Toronto: Simon and Pierre, 1983. Pp. 225–226. Review of *A Way with Words*

H459   [Bibliography; Biographic sketch] Ripley, Gordon and Anne V. Mercer. "Bowering, George." *Who's Who in Canadian Literature 1983–1984*. Toronto: Reference Press, 1983. P. 41. [Note: says GB was born in Okanagan Falls BC on 1 December 1936]

H460   [Bibliography; Bio-critical sketch] "Bowering, George 1935–" *Contemporary Authors: New Revision Series*. Vol. 10. Detroit: Gale Research Company, 1983. Pp. 64–65. [Note: says GB was born in Keremeos BC]

H461   [Review] Kroetsch, Robert. *Books in Canada* (Toronto ON) 12, No. 1 (January 1983): 31–32. Review of *Smoking Mirror* [and seven other books from Longspoon Press]

H462   [Review] Conklin, Jamie. "More Fuel to Feed a Literary Feud." *The Winnipeg Free Press* (Winnipeg MB), 8 January 1983. Review of *A Way with Words*

H463   [Review/Short] Morley, Patricia. "Essays on Poet's Craft Indicate Vitality of Intellectual Traditions." *The Citizen* (Ottawa ON), 19 February 1983. Review of *A Way with Words* [and *The Insecurity of Art*, edited by Ken Norris and Peter Van Toorn]

H464 [Essay/Context] Kroetsch, Robert. "For Play and Entrance: The Contemporary Canadian Long Poem." *Robert Kroetsch: Essays.* Ed. Frank Davey and bp Nichol. *Open Letter* (Toronto ON) Fifth Series, No. 4 (Spring 1983): 91–110. Also in *Dandelion*; see H378

H465 [Poem] Harris, John. "The Raspberry." *Writing* (Nelson BC), No. 6 (Spring 1983): 29. [Note: a parody of "The Raspberries" from *Autobiology*]

H466 [Review] Jackel, David. "Particulars." *Canadian Literature* (Vancouver BC), No. 96 (Spring 1983): 151–153. Review of *Fiction of Contemporary Canada*, edited by GB [and *Manitoba Stories*, edited by Joan Parr; *Sundogs: Stories from Saskatchewan*, edited by Robert Kroetsch]

H467 [Review] Peirce, Jon. "Bowering's CanLit Stars." *The Whig-Standard Supplement* (Kingston ON), 26 March 1983. Review of *A Way with Words*

H468 [Review] French, William. "Bowering Maintains a Playful Attitude on Subject of Death." *The Globe and Mail,* 28 April 1983. Review of *A Place to Die*

H469 [Review/Short] Williamson, David. "Short Stories Excel." *The Winnipeg Free Press* (Winnipeg MB), 30 April 1983. Review of *A Place to Die* [and *Dark Secrets*, by Veronica Ross]

H470 [Review] Templeton, Wayne. "Disrupted Syntax and Puns Aplenty." *The Sun* (Vancouver BC), 6 May 1983. Review of *A Place to Die*

H471 [Review/Short] Boire, Gary. *Canadian Literature* (Vancouver BC), No. 97 (Summer 1983): 166–168. Review of *Particular Accidents* and Fred Wah's *Loki Is Buried at Smoky Creek*, edited by GB [and three other Talonbooks' Selected Poems, including *As Elected*, by bp Nichol]

H472 [Review] Hancock, Geoff. "Exploration of Our Bizarre World That Is Always Engaging, Offbeat." *The Star* (Toronto ON), 14 May 1983. Review of *A Place to Die*

H473 [Review] Brown, Alan. "1982: A Baker's Dozen." *Quarry* (Kingston ON) 32, No. 3 (Summer 1983): 79–88. Review of *Smoking Mirror* [and other books in 1982]

H474 [Review/Short] Djwa, Sandra and R. B. Hatch. "Letters in Canada 1982: Poetry." *University of Toronto Quarterly* (Toronto ON) 52, No. 4 (Summer 1983): 343–358. Review of *West Window* [and other books of poetry in 1982]

H475 [Review] Marshall, Tom. *University of Toronto Quarterly* (Toronto ON) 52, No. 4 (Summer 1983): 501–503. Review of *A Way with Words*

H476 [Review] Collins, Anne. *Books in Canada* (Toronto ON) 12, No. 6 (June/July 1983): 26–28. Review of *Burning Water* [and other books]

H477 [Review] Garebian, Keith. *Books in Canada* (Toronto ON) 12, No. 6 (June/July 1983): 28–30. Review of *A Way with Words* [and other books]

H478   [Review] Sutherland, Cheryl. "Short Story Writers Show Intriguing Variations of Form." *The Star-Phoenix* Supplement (Saskatoon SK), 18 June 1983. Review of *A Place to Die* [and *Dark Secrets*, by Veronica Ross]

"A Return: For George Bowering," by George Johnston; see H484

H479   [Review] Morley, Patricia. "Ah, Bowering's Sexy, Violent Mystery of Life." *The Citizen* (Ottawa ON), 2 July 1983. Review of *A Place to Die*

H480   [Review] Whiteman, Bruce. "Un Ballo in Maschera." *Prairie Fire* (Winnipeg MB), Nos. 4 & 5 (July/August 1983): 54–57. Review of *The Mask in Place*

H481   [Review] Hancock, Geoff. "A Look at Innovative Fiction." *The Star* (Toronto ON), 17 July 1983. Review of *The Mask in Place*

H482   [Review/Short] Black, Barbara. "Alienation Unifying Theme in Short Stories." *The Gazette* (Montreal PQ), 13 August 1983. Review of *A Place to Die* [and three other books]

H483   [Review] Yearsley, Meredith. "Wit, Wordplay and the Future of Canadian Fiction." *The Sun* (Vancouver BC), 20 August 1983. Review of *The Mask in Place*

H484   [Poem] Johnston, George. "A Return: For George Bowering." *Brick* (Ilderton ON), No. 19 (Fall 1983): 3. [Note: an acrostic poem—"Nice poem you Wrote About Me GeorGe"—in response to GB's acrostic poem for George Johnston in "Irritable Reaching"; see A39 and A47]

H485   [Review/Essay] Brown, Russell. "Words and Places: Bowering as Critic." *Brick* (Ilderton ON), No. 19 (Fall 1983): 7–10. Review of *A Way with Words*, *The Mask in Place*, and *A Place to Die*

H486   [Review] Orange, John. "The Scratch, Not the Itch." *Canadian Literature* (Vancouver BC), No. 98 (Autumn 1983): 104–106. Review of *A Way with Words* and *West Window*

H487   [Review/Short] Homel, David. *Quill & Quire* (Toronto ON) 49, No. 9 (September 1983): 72. Review of *A Place to Die*

H488   [Review/Short] Kinczyk, Boh. *Canadian Materials* (Toronto ON) 11, No. 5 (September 1983): 199. Review of *A Place to Die*

H489   [Review/Short] Martindale, Sheila. "Pure Literary Acumen." *The London Free Press* (London ON), 16 September 1983. Review of *A Place to Die* [and *Dark Secrets*, by Veronica Ross]

H490   [Review] Greenwood, John. "Mysteries and Puzzles." *The Whig-Stand-ard* Supplement (Kingston ON), 17 September 1983. Review of *A Place to Die*

H491   [Review] Williamson, David. "An Example of Esoteric Claptrap." *The Winnipeg Free Press* (Winnipeg MB), 24 September 1983. Review of *The Mask in Place*

H492   [Review/Short] Garebian, Keith. *Quill & Quire* (Toronto ON) 49, No. 10 (October 1983): 30–31. Review of *The Mask in Place*

H493   [Review] Fitzgerald, Judith. "The Poet As Astute Critic." *The Globe and Mail*, 8 October 1983. Review of *The Mask in Place*

1984

H494   [Essay/Context] Norris, Ken. *The Little Magazine in Canada 1925–80: Its Role in the Development of Modernism and Post-Modernism in Canadian Poetry*. Toronto: ECW Press, 1984. [Note: originally a disser-tation for McGill University, 1980]

H495   [Poem] Ondaatje, Michael. "Rock Bottom" [excerpt: "the 'George' poem"]. *Secular Love*. Toronto: The Coach House Press, 1984. P. 80.

H496   [Review] Keith, W. J. *Canadian Book Review Annual 1983*. Ed. Dean Tudor and Ann Tudor. Toronto: Simon and Pierre, 1984. P. 194. Review of *Smoking Mirror*

H497   [Review/Essay] Knight, Alan R. "The Dilemma of the Public Critic; Or, Does George Bowering Have *A Way with Words*?" *Studies in Canadian Literature* (Fredericton NB) 9, No. 1 ([January] 1984): 5–19.

H498   [Review] Collomb-Boureau, Colette. *Afram Newsletter* (Paris, France), No. 18 (January 1984): 59–60. Review of *Smoking Mirror* [in French, along with other Longspoon Press books] [Note: Publication du Centre d'Etudes Afro-Américaines et des Nouvelles Littératures en Anglais du l'université de la Sorbonne Nouvelle]

H499   [Review] Seim, Jeanette. "Not Finding Out." *The Canadian Forum* (Toronto ON) 63, No. 736 (February 1984): 33–34. Review of *A Place to Die*

H500   [Review/Short] Twigg, Alan. "Two Angles on the Short Story." *The Province* Supplement (Vancouver BC), 4 March 1984. Review of *A Place To Die* [and *Chameleon & Other Stories*, by Bill Schermbrucker]

H501   [Review] Butling, Pauline. "A Mixture of Strengths." *Books in Canada* (Toronto ON) 13, No. 4 (April 1984): 26–27. Review of *The Mask in Place*

H502   [Essay] Kröller, Eva-Marie. "Postmodernism, Colony, Nation: The Mel-villean Texts of Bowering and Beaulieu." *Revue de l'Université d'Ottawa/University of Ottawa Quarterly* (Ottawa ON) 54, No. 2 (April/ June 1984): 53–61. [Note: discusses GB's *Burning Water* and Victor-Lévy Beaulieu's *Monsieur Melville*]

H503   [Review] Engel, Marian. "Shapely Lyrics on Death." *The Globe and Mail*, 7 April 1984. Review of *Kerrisdale Elegies*

H504   [Review] Flack, Brian L. "Lost in the Maze." *Books in Canada* (Toronto ON) 13, No. 5 (May 1984): 26–27. Review of *A Place to Die*

H505   [Review/Short] Hoy, Helen. "Letters in Canada 1983: Fiction." *University of Toronto Quarterly* (Toronto ON) 53, No. 4 (Summer 1984): 320–333. Review of *A Place to Die* [and other books of fiction in 1983] [Note: "August" on cover; "Summer" on title-page]

H506   [Review] Djwa, Sandra and Ronald B. Hatch. "Letters in Canada 1983: Poetry." *University of Toronto Quarterly* (Toronto ON) 53, No. 4 (Summer 1984): 342–359. Review of *Kerrisdale Elegies* [and other books of poetry in 1983] [Note: "August" on cover; "Summer" on title-page]

H507   [Review] Jacobson, Dale. *North Dakota Quarterly* (Grand Forks ND) 52, No. 3 (Summer 1984): 307–308. Review of *Smoking Mirror* [and *Gramsci x 3*, by Wilfred Watson]

H508   [Review] Tapping, Craig. "Free Words." *Canadian Literature* (Vancouver BC), No. 101 (Summer 1984): 158–161. Review of *Smoking Mirror* [and three other books]

H509   [Review/Essay] Whalen, Terry. "George Bowering's Way with Words: His Writing about Writing." *The Fiddlehead* (Fredericton NB), No. 140 (Summer 1984): 101–111. Review of *A Way with Words*, *West Window*, and *Smoking Mirror* [and *Capitalistic Affection!*, by Frank Davey]

H510   [Review] Persky, Stan. "Four Westcoast Poets." *The Reader* (Vancouver BC) 3, No. 2 (June 1984): 7–10. Review of *Kerrisdale Elegies* [and *Opening Day*, by George Stanley; *Syntax*, by Robin Blaser; *Seagull on Yonge Street*, by bill bissett]

H511   [Review] Harding-Russell, R. F. Gillian. "Beauty Is the First Prod of Fear." *NeWest Review* (Saskatoon SK) 9, No. 10 (June 1984): 6. Review of *Kerrisdale Elegies*

H512   [Review/Short] Scobie, Stephen. *The Malahat Review* (Victoria BC), No. 68 (June 1984): 146–147. Review of *Kerrisdale Elegies*

H513   [Review] Galt, George. "Mud and Metaphor." *Books in Canada* (Toronto ON) 13, No. 6 (June/July 1984): 19–21. Review of *Kerrisdale Elegies* [and *Woman in the Dust*, by Patrick Lane]

H514   [Review] Mandel, Charles. "Poets Recapture Youth in Versified Memoirs." *The Edmonton Journal* (Edmonton AB), 15 July 1984. Review of *Kerrisdale Elegies* [and *Morning and It's Summer*, by Al Purdy]

H515   [Review] Hatch, Ronald. "Kerrisdale Elegies: A Feast of Familiar Scenes." *The Sun* (Vancouver BC), 18 August 1984. Review of *Kerrisdale Elegies*

H516   [Review] Billings, Robert. "Battle Lines." *Canadian Literature* (Vancouver BC), No. 102 (Autumn 1984): 109–111. Review of *The Mask in Place* [and *Robert Kroetsch: Essays*, by Robert Kroetsch; *The Canadian Novel: Modern Times*, edited by John Moss]

H517   [Review] Brennan, Anthony. *The Fiddlehead* (Fredericton NB), No. 141 (Autumn 1984): 90–93. Review of *A Place to Die* [and *Displaced Persons*, by Fred Bonnie; *Dark Secrets*, by Veronica Ross]

H518   [Review/Short] Beardsley, Doug. *The Times-Colonist* (Victoria BC), 1 September 1984. Review of *Kerrisdale Elegies* [and other books]

H519   [Essay] Berry, Reginald. "George Bowering: Line Drives from Both Sides." *Span*, No. 19 (October 1984): 2–7. [Note: journal is subtitled "Newsletter of the South Pacific Association for Commonwealth Literature and Language Studies"]

H520   [Excerpt from an essay] "*Portraits d'Ecrivains*/Writers' Portraits: George Bowering." *Associazione Italiana Di Studi Canades* (Messina, Italy), No. 5 (December 1984): 5–7. [Note: a brief biographic sketch followed by an excerpt from *A Reader's Guide to the Canadian Novel*, by John Moss, the section on *Burning Water*; see H377]

H521   [Review] Dempster, Barry. *Poetry Canada Review* (Toronto ON) 6, No. 2 (Winter 1984/85): 3. Review of *A Way with Words*

H522   [Review] O'Brien, Peter. *Rubicon* (Montreal PQ), No. 4 (Winter 1984/85): 231. Review of *Kerrisdale Elegies*

1985

H523   [Bibliography] Platnick, Phyllis. "Bowering, George." *Canadian Poetry: Index to Criticisms (1970–1979)*. [Ottawa]: Canadian Library Association, 1985. Pp. 36–39. [Note: a bibliography of work on GB]

H524   [Essay] Barbour, Douglas. "Bowering, George." *The Canadian Encyclopedia*. Volume 1. Ed. James H. March. Edmonton: Hurtig Publishers, 1985. P. 212. Revised edition, 1988. P. 262.

H525   [Essay] Harding-Russell, R. F. Gillian. "Open Forms of Mythopoeia in Three Post-Modern Canadian Poets: Gwendolyn MacEwen, George Bowering, Michael Ondaatje." PhD Dissertation, University of Saskatchewan, 1985.

H526   [Essay] Kamboureli, Smaro. "A Window onto George Bowering's Fiction of Unrest." *The Canadian Novel, Volume IV: Present Tense: A Critical Anthology*. Ed. John Moss. Toronto: NC Press, 1985. Pp. 205–231.

H527   [Essay/Context] Keith, W. J. "Chapter 6: Plain Talk about Past and Present." *Canadian Literature in English.* London/New York: Longman, 1985. Pp. 96–117. [Note: comments briefly on GB and *Tish*]

H528   [Essay] Moss, John. "Himmler's Got the King: An Essay on *Badlands* and *Burning Water.*" *The Canadian Novel, Volume IV: Present Tense: A Critical Anthology.* Ed. John Moss. Toronto: NC Press, 1985. Pp. 249–264. Also in *Re-Visions of Canadian Literature,* edited by Shirley Chew. Papers presented at a Seminar in Canadian Literature held at the University of Leeds, April 1984. University of Leeds, 1985. Pp. 89–102.

> 18 four questions for George Bowering
>
> *Michelin Green Guide:* "The University [of Bologna], founded in 11C, had 10,000 students in 13C. At that time the professors were often women and a solemn chronicler reports that one of them, Novella d'Andrea, was so beautiful in face and body that she had to give her lectures from behind a curtain to avoid distracting her pupils."
>
> You who wrote the *Kerrisdale Elegies,* tell me:
>
> Does the body teach us nothing?
> What is it that we seek to learn instead of beauty?
> What do they mean, "distracting her pupils"?
>
> I too once lectured in Bologna.
> It was February, the room was cold,
> I was more than adequately dressed.
> No one put up a curtain.
>
> What would happen if, just as you slid into home plate,
> the pitcher threw the catcher an orange?

"Four Questions for George Bowering," by Robert Kroetsch; see H531

H529   [Essay/Context] Pache, Walter. " 'The Fiction Makes Us Real': Aspects of Postmodernism in Canada." *Gaining Ground: European Critics on Canadian Literature.* Ed. Robert Kroetsch and Reingard M. Nischik. Edmonton: NeWest Press, 1985. Pp. 64–78. [Note: comments on Robert Kroetsch's *The Studhorse Man* and *Gone Indian* and GB's *Burning Water*]

H530   [Essay] Watson, Sheila. "About Seventy-one Poems for People." *Seventy-one Poems for People.* By GB. Red Deer AB: Red Deer College Press, 1985. P. 123. [See A45]

H531   [Poem] Kroetsch, Robert. "Four Questions for George Bowering." *Advice to My Friends.* Don Mills ON: Stoddart, 1985. P. 26.

H532   [Review] Bregman, Alvan. *Canadian Book Review Annual 1984.* Ed. Dean Tudor and Ann Tudor. Toronto: Simon and Pierre, 1985. P. 297. Review of *The Mask in Place*

H533   [Review] Steele, Charles R. *Canadian Book Review Annual 1984.* Ed. Dean Tudor and Ann Tudor. Toronto: Simon and Pierre, 1985. P. 216. Review of *Kerrisdale Elegies*

H534   [Essay] [Mennell, Ken]. "George Bowering." *Simon Fraser University.* Burnaby, SFU: 1985. P. 18. [Note: a profile with comments by GB]

H535   [Essay/Context] Miki, Roy. "The Lang Poem: The Cosmology of the Long Poem in Contemporary Canadian Poetry." *Open Letter* (Toronto ON) Sixth Series, Nos. 2 & 3 (Summer/Fall 1985): 71–84. [Note: GB is briefly mentioned in the context of other poets]

H536 [Letter] Ubriaco, Rita. "Bowering's Inferno." *Books in Canada* (Toronto ON) 14, No. 5 (June/July 1985): 42. [Note: a brief response to "Between the Lines"; see D845]

H537 [Essay/Context] "Auteurs Naar Amsterdam." *Parool* (Amsterdam, The Netherlands), 19 June 1985. [Note: news article on Canadian artists and writers in Amsterdam during the Holland Festival, GB among them]

H538 [Review/Essay] Easingwood, Peter. "Aspects of the Canadian Literary Tradition." *Bulletin of Canadian Studies* (Edinburgh, Scotland) 9, No. 2 (Autumn 1985): 192–197. Review of *The Mask in Place* [and *Canadian Literature in English*, by W. J. Keith; *Surviving the Paraphrase*, by Frank Davey]

H539 [Review] Noyes, Steve. "Bowering, Collector of West Coast Voices." *The Sun* (Vancouver BC), 28 September 1985. Review of *Craft Slices*

H540 [Review] Monkman, Leslie. "One Man's Literary Piano." *The Whig-Standard* Supplement (Kingston ON), 12 October 1985. Review of *Craft Slices*

H541 [Review] Fitzgerald, Judith. "A Slice of Literary Pie." *The Windsor Star* (Windsor ON), 19 October 1985. Review of *Craft Slices*

H542 [Review] Jirgens, Karl. *Books in Canada* (Toronto ON) 14, No. 8 (November 1985): 23. Review of *Craft Slices*

H543 [Review] Sileika, Antanas. "Tough and Slushy Words on Writing." *The Globe and Mail*, 9 November 1985. Review of *Craft Slices*

H544 [Review/Short] Scobie, Stephen. *The Malahat Review* (Victoria BC), No. 73 (December 1985): 127. Review of *Craft Slices* [Note: cover is dated January 1986; the error is acknowledged in the March 1986 issue]

1986

H545 [Bibliography; Essay] Quartermain, Peter and Meredith. "George Bowering." *Dictionary of Literary Biography: Canadian Writers Since 1960: First Series.* Volume 53. Detroit: Gale Research Company, 1986. Pp. 84–92.

H546 [Essay] Pache, Walter. "Narrative Models on the Canadian Short Story." *Encounters and Explorations: Canadian Writers and European Critics.* Ed. Franz K. Stanzel and Waldemar Zacharasiewicz. Würzburg, Germany: Königshausen and Neumann, 1986. Pp. 82–93. [Note: includes a discussion of *Fiction of Contemporary Canada*, edited by GB]

H547 [Essay/Context] Davey, Frank. "Die *Tish*-Bewegung" ["The *Tish* Movement," trans. Michael Mundhenk]. *Die Horen* (Hanover, Germany) 31, No. 1; issue No. 141 (1986): 135–141. A German translation of the "Introduction" to *The Writing Life*; see H231. [Note: a special issue

devoted to Canadian writing, art, politics, and culture, edited and translated by Michael Mundhenk]

H548   [Essay/Context] Buitenhuis, Peter. "Canada's America, Or Lost in the
Funhouse." *Southern Exposure.* Ed. David H. Flaherty and William R.
McKercher. Toronto: McGraw-Hill Ryerson, 1986. Pp. 134–151. [Note:
comments on GB's *Kerrisdale Elegies*]

H549   [Essay] McCaffery, Steve. "Under the Blowpipe: George Bowering's
Allophanes." *North of Intention: Critical Writings 1973–1986.* New York/
Toronto: Roof Books/Nightwood Editions, 1986. Pp. 131–142. Also in
Line; see H559

H550   [Essay] Twigg, Alan. "Lions Gate." *Vancouver and Its Writers.* Vancouver: Harbour Publishing, 1986. Pp. 133–134. [Note: on GB and his first
novel *Mirror on the Floor*]

H551   [Review] Blackburn, William. *Canadian Book Review Annual 1985.* Ed.
Dean Tudor and Ann Tudor. Toronto: Simon and Pierre, 1986. P. 229.
Review of *Craft Slices*

H552   [Review] Cook, John. "Blah, Blah, Blah." *Writers' Quarterly* (Toronto
ON) 8, No. 2 (1986): 24. Review of *Seventy-one Poems for People* [and
Rootless Tree, by John V. Hicks]

H553   [Review/Essay] Neuman, Shirley. *Journal of Canadian Poetry* (Ottawa
ON), No. 1 (1986): 12–20. Review of *Kerrisdale Elegies*

H554   [Review] Stieg, Elizabeth. *Canadian Book Review Annual 1985.* Ed.
Dean Tudor and Ann Tudor. Toronto: Simon and Pierre, 1986. P. 168.
Review of *The Contemporary Canadian Poem Anthology*, second edi-
tion, edited by GB

H555   [Interview; Bibliography] Davey, Frank. "The Work of George Bowering," interview by Sandra Martin. *The Academy on Canadian Literature.*
Ed. Loralee Case. Toronto: The Ontario Educational Communications
Authority, 1986. Pp. 61–65. [Note: this publication is the program to
accompany a video on GB; see E83]

H556   [Review] McKinnon, Barry. *BCLA* [B. C. Library Association] *Reporter*
(Vancouver BC) 30, No. 1 (January 1986): 17–18. Review of *Craft Slices*

H557   [Review] McNeill, Allan. *Canadian Studies Bulletin* (Toronto ON),
(February/March 1986): 6–8. Review of *Seventy-one Poems for People*

H558   [Review] Davidson, Arnold E. *The American Review of Canadian Studies* (Burlington VT) 16, No. 1 (Spring 1986): 98–99. Review of *The Mask
in Place*

H559   [Essay] McCaffery, Steve. "Under the Blowpipe: George Bowering's
Allophanes." *Line* (Burnaby BC), Nos. 7 & 8 (Spring/Fall 1986): 184–193.
Also in *North of Intention*; see H549

H560   [Essay] Adams, James. "B. C. Poet Shuttles from High Art to Pop." *The
Edmonton Journal* (Edmonton AB), 1 March 1986. [Note: on GB while

he was in Edmonton to read and to promote *Seventy-one Poems for People*]

H561 [Review] Scobie, Stephen. *The Malahat Review* (Victoria BC), No. 74 (March 1986): 125–127. Review of *Seventy-one Poems for People* [and *The Louis Riel Organ and Piano Company*, by Frank Davey; *Waiting for Saskatchewan*, by Fred Wah]

H562 [Essay] Gregg, Andrew. "Authors Join Students for Writing Seminars." *The Whitehorse Star* (Whitehorse, Yukon), 16 April 1986. [Note: a news article on the forthcoming visit to Whitehorse by writers GB, Paulette Jiles, and Charles Lillard; see also the report on their workshops, "Workshop Opens Doors," *The Whitehorse Star*, 18 April 1986]

H563 [Review] Eggertson, Eric. "Writing Can Be Fun, Too." *The Yukon News* (Whitehorse, Yukon), 18 April 1986. Review of a reading and workshop by GB, with Paulette Jiles and Charles Lillard; see H562

H564 [Review] Wheeler, Robert E. *Canadian Materials* (Toronto ON) 14, No. 3 (May 1986): 129. Review of *Craft Slices*

H565 [Review] Leahy, David. *Queen's Quarterly* (Kingston ON) 93, No. 2 (Summer 1986): 412–414. Review of *Craft Slices* and *Seventy-one Poems for People* [and *Feeling the Worlds*, by Dorothy Livesay]

H566 [Review] Brown, Doug. *Books in Canada* (Toronto ON) 15, No. 5 (June/July 1986): 26. Review of *Seventy-one Poems for People*

H567 [Review/Short] Holland, Carroll. "Craft Slices Essays Introduce Poets." *The Citizen* (Ottawa ON), 26 July 1986. Review of *Craft Slices*

H568 [Review/Essay] Dragland, Stan. "The Bees of the Invisible." *Brick* (Ilderton ON), No. 28 (Fall 1986): 14–25. Review of *Kerrisdale Elegies*

H569 [Essay] Berry, Reginald. "A Deckchair of Words: Post-colonialism, Post-modernism, and the Novel of Self-projection in Canada and New Zealand." *Landfall* (Christchurch, New Zealand) 40, No. 3; issue No. 159 (September 1986): 310–323. [Note: the essay focuses on GB's *Burning Water* and C. K. Stead's *All Visitors Ashore*]

1987

H570 [Essay] Kamboureli, Smaro. "Ungrammaticality of Genre: The Contemporary Canadian Long Poem." PhD Dissertation, University of Manitoba, 1987. [Note: two sections in Chapter 5, "Signing the Text" and "Stealing the Text," discuss GB's *Kerrisdale Elegies*; a revised version was published in *Canadian Literature*; see H606]

H571 [Essay] Lobb, Edward. "Imagining History: The Romantic Background of George Bowering's *Burning Water*." *Studies in Canadian Literature* (Fredericton NB) 12, No. 1 (1987): 112–128.

H572   [Essay/Context] Precosky, Don. "Of Poets and Hackers: Notes on Canadian Post-Modern Poets." *Studies in Canadian Literature* (Fredericton NB) 12, No. 1 (1987): 146–155.

H573   [Review] Berry, Reginald. "Miscellaneous Remains." *CRNLE Reviews Journal* (South Australia), No. 1 (1987): 53–56. Review of *Craft Slices* [and *The Blue Notebook: Reports on Canadian Culture*, by Doug Fetherling] [Notes: special Canadian issue; CRNLE stands for Centre for Research in the New Literature in English]

H574   [Review] Edwards, Brian. *Mattoid* (Victoria, Australia), No. 29 (1987): 108–111. Review of *Caprice*

H575   [Essay/Context] Barbour, Douglas. "Extended Forms: One Book & Then Another: The Canadian Long Poem." *Australian-Canadian Studies* 5, No. 2 (1987): 81–89. [Note: GB is mentioned but the essay focuses on bp Nichol's writing]

H576   [Review] Vasius, A. *Canadian Book Review Annual 1986*. Ed. Leslie McGrath and Katherine McGrath. Toronto: Simon and Pierre, 1987. Pp. 88–89. Review of *Delayed Mercy*

H577   [Review] Precosky, Don. *BCLA* [B. C. Library Association] *Reporter* (Vancouver BC) 31, No. 1 (January 1987): 26. Review of *Seventy-one Poems for People*

H578   [Essay] Precosky, Don. "Method in Bowering's *Allophanes*." *Canadian Poetry* (London ON), No. 20 (Spring/Summer 1987): 61–66.

H579   [Review] Roberts, Paul. "Bowering's Western: Woolly Post-Modernist Chic." *Quill & Quire* (Toronto ON) 53, No. 5 (May 1987): 19. Review of *Caprice*

H580   [Review] Ferguson, Trevor. "Zane Grey Heroine Turns Western Novel Upside Down." *The Gazette* (Montreal PQ), 9 May 1987. Review of *Caprice*

H581   [Review/Short] Smart, Carolyn. *The Whig-Standard* Supplement (Kingston ON), 9 May 1987. Review of *Delayed Mercy*

H582   [Review/Short] Walker, Morley. "At Least It's Easy to Read." *The Winnipeg Free Press* (Winnipeg MB), 16 May 1987. Review of *Caprice*

H583   [Review] Helwig, Maggie. "Bowering's Capricious Western." *The Star* (Toronto ON), 17 May 1987. Review of *Caprice*

H584   [Review] McGoogan, Kenneth. "Smart-Aleck of Can-Lit Scores Again." *The Sunday Herald* (Calgary AB), 17 May 1987. Review of *Caprice*

H585   [Review] Garvie, Maureen. "The Old West, Made New." *The Whig-Standard* Supplement (Kingston ON), 23 May 1987. Review of *Caprice*

H586   [Review] Loran, Tom. "Bowering's Unique Approach Lifts Story Out of Ordinary." *The Star-Phoenix* Supplement (Saskatoon SK), 23 May 1987. Review of *Caprice*

H587   [Review] Mandel, Charles. "Horsing Around." *The Globe and Mail*, 23 May 1987. Review of *Caprice*

H588   [Review] Scanlan, Larry. "Note Book." *The Whig-Standard* Supplement (Kingston ON), 23 May 1987. Review of *Caprice*

H589   [Review] Starkins, Ed. "Witty, Gripping Novel from Poet Bowering." *The Sun* (Vancouver BC), 23 May 1987. Review of *Caprice*

H590   [Review] Twigg, Alan. "Bowering's Best." *The Province* (Vancouver BC), 24 May 1987. Review of *Caprice*

H591   [Essay] Wilson, Peter. "Writer of Anti-Western Says He's at Home in the Bunkhouse." *The Sun* (Vancouver BC), 26 May 1987. [Note: a news article on *Caprice* with comments by GB]

H592   [Review] Manning, Jeane. "Bowering Book Characters Gallop Through Old Fairview Mining Town." *The Oliver Chronicle* (Oliver BC), 27 May 1987. Review of *Caprice*

H593   [Essay] Kröller, Eva-Marie. "Trieste and George Bowering's *Burning Water*: A Note." *Open Letter* (Toronto ON) Sixth Series, No. 8 (Summer 1987): 44–54.

H594   [Review] McGoogan, Kenneth. "As for Me and My Horse." *Books in Canada* (Toronto ON) 16, No. 6 (June/July 1987): 15–16. Review of *Caprice*

H595   [Review] di Michele, Mary. *Books in Canada* (Toronto ON) 16, No. 6 (June/July 1987): 23–24. Review of *Delayed Mercy*

H596   [Essay] McMorrow, Maureen. "Bowering's Stand Is No Caprice." *The Vancouver Courier* (Vancouver BC), 10 June 1987. [Note: a profile with comments by GB]

H597   [Review] Heward, Burt. "B. C.'s Wild West Loses to Artifice." *The Citizen* (Ottawa ON), 13 June 1987. Review of *Caprice*

H598   [Review] Bemrose, John. "Angel with a Lariat." *Maclean's* (Toronto ON), 29 June 1987: 49–50. Review of *Caprice*

H599   [Review/Short] McMorrow, Maureen. "No Ordinary Western." *Easy Living* (Vancouver BC) 9, No. 7 (29 June–26 July 1987): 20. Review of *Caprice*

H600   [Review/Short] Smith, Patricia. "Three Poets Dare to Reject Labelling." *The Star* (Toronto ON), 4 July 1987. Review of *Delayed Mercy* [and *Islands*, by Ken Norris; *The Collected Poems of George Whalley*, by George Whalley]

H601   [Review] Sutherland, Fraser. "Literary Tricks and the Larger Concerns." *The Globe and Mail*, 8 August 1987. Review of *Delayed Mercy* [and *Afterworlds*, by Gwendolyn MacEwen]

H602   [Essay] L. R. [Laurie Ricou] "Triptych." *Canadian Literature* (Vancouver BC), Nos. 113 & 114 (Summer/Fall 1987): 4–10. [Note: an editorial divided into three parts; in his part, Ricou quotes and discusses GB's "The Swing"]

H603   [Essay] McCallum, Larry. "Libraries Hosting George Bowering Readings." *The Whistler Question* (Whistler BC), 17 September 1987. [Note: introduction to GB for his forthcoming reading at Whistler BC]

H604   [Essay] Twigg, Alan. "For Batter Or Verse." *Books in Canada* (Toronto ON) 16, No. 8 (November 1987): 7–8, 10. [Note: a profile of GB based on an interview; cover photo of GB with caption, "Keeping Score on George Bowering"]

H605   [Review] Precosky, Don. *BCLA* [B. C. Library Association] *Reporter* (Vancouver BC) 31, No. 6 (November 1987): 31. Review of *Delayed Mercy*

H606   [Essay] Kamboureli, Smaro. "Stealing the Text: George Bowering's *Kerrisdale Elegies* and Dennis Cooley's *Bloody Jack*." *Canadian Literature* (Vancouver BC), No. 115 (Winter 1987): 9–23.

H607   [Review] Peterman, Michael. "Resident & Alien." *Canadian Literature* (Vancouver BC), No. 115 (Winter 1987): 144–146. Review of *Sheila Watson and* The Double Hook, edited by GB [and *Women Writing in America*, by Blanche H. Gelfant]

1988

H608   [Essay/Context] Hutcheon, Linda. *The Canadian Postmodern: A Study of Contemporary English-Canadian Fiction*. Toronto: Oxford University Press, 1988. [Note: includes various comments on GB's *Burning Water*]

H609   [Poem] Cooley, Dennis. "Georgian Chant." *Dedications*. Saskatoon: Thistledown Press, 1988. Pp. 33–35.

H610   [Review] Goldie, Terry. *Journal of Canadian Poetry* (Ottawa ON), No. 3 (1988): 11–15. Review of *Delayed Mercy*

H611   [Poem] n. b. pickle's kitchen help. "Poem Written for George (1)." *Nexus* (Burnaby BC) 2, No. 4 (February 1988): 40.

H612   [Essay/Context] Kroetsch, Robert. "The Veil of Knowing: Narrating Canadian." Keynote Paper for *The Study and Teaching of Contemporary Canadian Literature*. Tri-University English Departments Conference. University of Victoria, Victoria BC, 19 March 1988. Published in *The Lovely Treachery of Words: Essays Selected and New*, by Robert Kroetsch. Toronto: Oxford University Press, forthcoming 1989. [Note: the essay focuses on Howard O'Hagan's *Tay John* but discusses GB in the opening section]

H613 [Review] Ricou, Laurie. "Constable Blur—Kamloops Detachment." *Event* (New Westminster BC) 17, No. 1 (Spring 1988): 99–102. Review of *Caprice*

H614 [Review/Short] S. P. [Sylvester Pollet] *Sagetrieb* (Orono ME) 7, No. 1 (Spring 1988): 204–205. Review of *Delayed Mercy*

H615 [Essay] Dragland, Stan. "Wise and Musical Instruction: George Bowering's *Caprice.*" *West Coast Review* (Burnaby BC) 23, No. 1 (Spring 1988): 74–87.

H616 [Essay] Whalen, Terry. "Discourse and Method: Narrative Strategy in George Bowering's *West Window.*" *Canadian Poetry* (London ON), No. 22 (Spring/Summer 1988): 32–39.

H617 [Bibliography] Drumbolis, Nicholas. *George Bowering Condensed.* Toronto: Letters Bookstore, June 1988.

H618 [Acrostic] Trainer, Mary. "Acrostic #4." *Simon Fraser Alumni Journal* (Burnaby BC) 6, No. 1 (Summer 1988): 23. [Note: uses an excerpt from "Elegy One," in *Kerrisdale Elegies*; see D884]

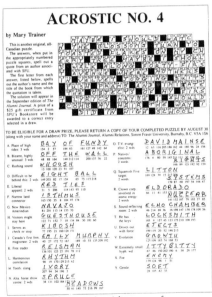

Double acrostic with excerpt from
Kerrisdale Elegies; see H618

Index

Titles of books, pamphlets, and plays by GB are set in italics. Other titles appear within quotation marks; each of these is followed by its genre abbreviation in brackets. These abbreviations are used:

[E]	Essay	[Pl]	Play
[Ed]	Edited by	[Pr]	Prose
[I]	Interview	[R]	Review
[Ib]	Interview by	[S]	Story
[L]	Letter	[St]	Statement
[N]	Novel	[T]	Translation by
[O]	Other	[To]	Translation of
[P]	Poem	[Tk]	Talk
		[UM]	Unpublished Manuscript

Excerpts from works are identified by the letter *E* preceding the genre abbreviation. An excerpt from a poem, for example, is shown as [EP].

Periodicals and books to which Bowering has contributed are set in italics. Also listed here are names of individuals, publishing companies, and universities with which Bowering has been directly associated. For items in section H (Works on George Bowering), names of authors and publications, but not titles of works, are indexed.

Each item is indexed by entry number rather than page number. Material preceding the bibliography proper has not been indexed.

Many of Bowering's works have appeared in a number of publications, and on occasion there have been differences in the punctuation or even the spelling of the title as published. In these cases, the title is transcribed as published for the bibliographic entry, but only one form of the title has been chosen for the index.

Bioy Casares, Adolfo, A35
"Birds in the Tiergarten" [P], D861
Birney, Earle, A5, A19, A21, A44, C7,
   C74, C113, D553, D604, D647,
   D651, E19, E21, E37, F2, F3
"Birney's Advent" [E], A44, D553
"Birney's Rage" [E], A44, C74, D651
"Birney Steps into the Dada
   Borderblur" [R], D553
bissett, bill, A19, A36, A40, B12, C24,
   C36, C45, C46, C54, C93, C113,
   D625, F2, H160, H510
Bitterroot, D172
Black, Barbara, H482
Blackburn, Paul, A25, B1
Blackburn, William, H551
"Black Eyed Girl" [P], D642
Blackfish, D551, D607, H164
Blackhead, Erich (pseud. of GB), D566,
   D568, D570
Black Moss, D448, D450, D527, D557,
   D600, D697
Black Moss Press, A25, A30, C92,
   H231, H284
Black Mountain, A2, A32, D565, D729
"Black Mountain College" [E], D565
"Black Mountain Influence, The" [EN],
   D729
Black Mountain Review, B1
Black Night Window [R], D428; [ER],
   C135
Blais, Marie-Claire, H62
Blaise, Clark, B4, B8, H347
Blake, William, A2, A4
Blaser, Robin, A19, A24, A36, A37, B1,
   B6, B12, D240, D621, E38, E55,
   H344, H510
"Blaser & Levertov" [R], D240
blewointmentpress, C24, C36, C45,
   C46, C54, C93
*blewointmentpress end uv th world
   speshul, th*, C93
blewointmentpress occupation issew,

C24
blewointmentpress oil slick speshul, C36
blewointmentpress poverty issue, C45
*blewointmentpress what isint tantrik
   speshul, th*, C54
Blind Man's Holiday [R], D162
"Blood Poem, The" [P], D46
"Blood Red Fuck, The" [P], A7, D214
Blown Figures [R], D669; [ER], C95
"Blue, The" [P], A7, C49, C119, D221,
   E10
blue grass, D78
Blue Pig: Sleeping Sickness, D573
"Blue Shirt, The" [P], A4, C6, D320
"Boat, The" [P], A9, A15, C6, D222,
   D258
"Body, The" [P], A17, A36, E35
Boire, Gary, H471
Boland, Viga, H268
Boldface Technologies, A49
Bolt, Robert, D297
"Bomb Run" [P], D663
Bone, Windy, A48
"Bones Along Her Body" [P], A39,
   A47, C199
"Bone Thoughts" [R], D34
Bone Thoughts [R], D34
Bonnanno, Giovanni, C184
Bonnie, Fred, H517
*Book Cellar's Choice: A Small
   Anthology of Poems*, C37
Book of Dreams [R], D83
Book of Occasional, A [R], D603
Book of Process, A, C64
Books in Canada, D745, D749, D758,
   D766, D769, D783, D792, D802,
   D803, D818, D821, D831, D836,
   D845, D865, D875, E74, H157,
   H158, H161, H171, H211, H241,
   H290, H295, H314, H347, H353,
   H366, H444, H461, H476, H477,
   H501, H504, H513, H536, H542,
   H566, H594, H595, H604

H464, H509, H538, H547, H555, H561

Davey, Linda (McCartney), A32, A43, D689

"David" [P], A3; [To], G1

David, Jack, A29, A36, B2, C113, C114, C144, C150, C151, C202, D77, H284, H289, H372

"David Bromige" [P], A19, D625

"David Iron" [Ed], B2, D741

"David McFadden" [P], A19, D609, D618, E47

Davidson, Arnold E., H558

Davies, Gwendolyn, H297, H330

Davies, Richard, C140, C169

Davinci, D674

Davis, Chuck, E70

Davis, Earle, D471

Davis, Wayne, A44

Dawson, David, A1, A12, B2, C10, C83, D281, H29

Dawson, Fielding, A25, B1, B6, D565, D655

"Day Before the Chinese A-Bomb, The" [P], A3, A25, A36

"Day in May, A" [P], D239

Daymond, Douglas, C112, C180

"DC7B" [T], A45

D-Day and After [R], D111

"Dead Duck, A" [P], D317

"Deadman Falls" [E], E75

"Dead Poets of Vancouver, The" [P], A45

"Dead Sailors, The" [EN], D737, D738, D739, D748, D757, D762, *see also* *Burning Water*

"Dear AS" [L], D607

"Dear John" [L], C103

"Dear Path, The" [P], A17, A36, D597

"Dear Person" [P], A7

"Dear Tishers—" [L], D204

"Deathmaker at San Quentin, The" [P], A45

de Barros, Paul, D714, D748

de Beck, Brian, B2

"Declaration, A" [P], C200, D383, D388, D430, D439

Dedications, H609

"Déjenme Entrar Déjenme Salir" ["Let Me In Let Me Out"] [To], G6

de la Pena, Jose Ma., G2

De la Roche, Mazo, A29

Delayed Mercy and Other Poems, A39, A47, D842, D857, E79, H576, H581, H595, H600, H601, H605, H610, H614

"Delicate Deer" [P], A9, D377

"Delivering Fiction" [E], A44, C33, D580

Dell Publishing Company, C81

"Delsing" [UM], A23, D21, D55, D575, F1, F2

"Delsing and Me" [E], A44, C33, D580

Delta, C66

Delta, D49, D120, D344

Demels, M., H273

Dempster, Barry, H294, H410, H521

Denham, Paul, H165

"Denise Levertov" [E], D572; [EE], C136; [P], A19, D605

Dennison, Shane, H275

Dent (J. M.) & Sons, C32

"Dentro del Tulipan" ["Inside the Tulip"] [To], G1

"Deputy Sheriff, The" [S], D339

"Derelicts in the Metro Station" [P], A28

"Der Rasenmäher" ["The Lawnmower"] [To], G17

Desbarats, Peter, C25, G7

Descant, C153, D663, D703, D790, D869, D887

Descant Editions, C153

"Descent, The" [P], A3, A15, A36, E7, E19

"MacEwen's Music" [E], A44, C134, D188

McFadden, David, A19, A20, A21, A33, A38, A40, A44, B1, B2, B4, B11, B12, C14, C91, C128, C129, C196, D10, D114, D359, D381, D406, D483, D535, D542, D565, D608, D618, D683, D748, D767, E27, E47, F1, F2, F3, H96, H117, H140, H185, H239, H285, H388

"McFadden Shopping Bag, The" [P], A40, D483

"McFadding" [E], A44, D683

MacFarlane, Susan, A44

McGill Daily, The, D533, H116

McGoogan, Kenneth, H406, H584, H594

McGovern, Robert, C21

McGrath, Katherine, H576

McGrath, Leslie, H576

McGraw-Hill Ryerson, B13, C87, C100, C130, H548

McInnes, John, C62

MacIntosh, Keitha K., B1, C77

McKay, Don, H277

Mckay, Roberto, A45, D753

McKeen, David, D507

McKellar, Iain, H291

MacKendrick, Louis K., H233

McKercher, William R., H548

McKim, David, H295, H314

McKinnon, Barry, B1, B7, B12, C83, C91, D126, D647, D885, E44, E62, F2, H255, H556

MacKinnon, Kenneth A., C143

Macklem, Michael, A19, A23, A38, A42, A44, B8

Maclean's, D604, D623, H168, H172, H335, H598

MacLennan, Hugh, A29

McLeod, Dan, D128, D149

McLintock, Peter, H370

McManus, Michael, E83

Macmillan, A4, C57, C78, C91, C98, C167, H210

McMorrow, Maureen, H596, H599

McNamara, Eugene, H295

McNeill, Allan, H557

McPherson, Hugo, A13

McPherson, Jay, A47

McRobbie, Kenneth, D104

McWhirter, George, D793, H203, H209, H211, H212, H408

Magazine, D169, D385, D407, D425, D461, D549

"Mais le rien perce" [P], A33, B6, D658

"Make It New (Night Thoughts)" [P], D261

Maker, D718

"Making" [P], D214

"Making a Virtue of Necessity" [P], A21, D498

Making of Modern Poetry in Canada, The: Essential Articles on Contemporary Canadian Poetry in English, C10, H7, H44

Malahat Review, The, D386, D708, D735, D861, H196, H512, H544, H561

Malanga, Gerard, B1

"Malediction for Madam Nhu" [P], A45

"Malign Headless Dancers" [T], D672

Malone, Moses, B8

Malus, Michael, D162

Mamashee, D726

"Mandatory Spring Poem" [P], A28, D694

Mandel, Ann, B2, C71

Mandel, Charles, H514, H587

Mandel, Eli, A37, A44, C49, D98, D447, D759, D806, D848, H376

"Mandel's Shift" [E], A44, D447

Man For All Seasons, A [R], D297

Manhattan Review, D353

Manimals [R], D511

Merian, G18
"Mesa de Cocina" ["The Kitchen Table"] [To], G1
"Meta Morphosis" [P], A2, D154, D280, E4
"Metaphor 1" [P], A1, D81
"Metaphor 2" [P], A1, D88
"Metaphor 3" [P], D142
"Meta Physic in Things, A" [P], A2; [EP], A25
"Metaphysic in Time: The Poetry of Lionel Kearns" [E], A38, C142
"Metathesis" [P], A2, D146
Metcalf, John, C33, C61, C183, D852, H145, H347
"Mexican Dog" [P], A11, D250, D252
"Mexico" [P], A11
"Mexico City Face" [P], A11, A15, D214
"Mexico, D. F." [P], A11
"Mexico Quake" [P], A11
"Mexico Walk" [P], A11, D240
Meyer, Bruce, H453
"Michael McClure" [P], A19
Michaux, Henri, B6
Michelangelo, B2
"Middle-Aged Poet Dumpt at Last into the Iambic, The" [P], A33, D724
"Midnight Lunch" [P], A21, D636
Miki, Roy, C204, D843, D850, E55, E56, G14, H535
"Militia Man" [T], A45, D465
Militz, Helga, G17
Miller, Arthur, D288
Miller, Fred, D647
Miller, Henry, D61
Miller, Peter, A2
Mills, C. Wright, D40
Mills, John, E57
Milot, René, A48
Milton, John, A21
"Milton Acorn" [P], A45, D285
"Milton Acorn (1923-1986)" [E], D867

Minden, Robert, D673
Mingus, Charles, D626
Minnesota Review, The, D305, D415, H66
"Minnesota Twins, The" [S], D652
Mirror on the Floor, A5, C33, D238, F1, H48, H49, H50, H51, H52, H53, H54, H55, H56, H58, H59, H60, H62, H63, H64, H66, H67, H69, H71, H73, H377, H550
Mirrors: Recent Canadian Verse, C76
"Mirrors Show" [P], A39, A47, D811
Miss Chatelaine, D576, D592
Mistral, Gabriela, D150, D382
Mitchell, Beverley Joan, H138
Mitchell, Ken, C96
"M. M." [P], A2, D115
"Moaning of the Cow" [T], D283
Modern Canadian Stories, C7, H46
Modern Canadian Verse: In English and French, C11
Modern English-Canadian Poetry, H283
"Modernism Could Not Last Forever" [E], A41, C180, D760
"Modernist Lives" [R], D817
Modern Romanian Poetry, C101
"Moisture" [P], D530
Molière, D312
"Mollusc" [P], A47
"Mom, Baseball and Beaver Pie" [R], D833
"Moment: Cars" [P], A1, A2, D85
"Moment of Truth" [P], D280, E4
"Moment: 2 a. m." [P], D77
"Moment: White" [P], D69, D147, D165
Monday Morning, H147
Mondragón, Sergio, A3, A11, B1, C5, D182, D283, D405, F3, G1
"Money" [P], D350
"Money Is Least Important" [I], D736
Monk, Lorraine, C56, C148, G12
Monkman, Leslie, C112, C180, H540

Z